CONTRACT LAW IN AMERICA

A SOCIAL AND ECONOMIC CASE STUDY

by
LAWRENCE M. FRIEDMAN

Classics of Law & Society Series

Quid Pro Books
New Orleans, Louisiana

Copyright © 2011 by Lawrence M. Friedman. All rights reserved. No material in this book may be reproduced, copied or retransmitted in any manner without the written consent of the current publisher. Foreword copyright © 2011 by Stewart Macaulay.

Originally published by the University of Wisconsin Press, Madison and Milwaukee, Wisconsin. Copyright © 1965 by the Regents of the University of Wisconsin. Library of Congress Catalog Card Number 65-13504.

Published in 2011 by Quid Pro Books.

ISBN: 1610279794 (pbk)
ISBN-13: 9781610279796 (pbk)
ISBN-13: 9781610279772 (Kindle)
ISBN-13: 9781610279789 (ePub)

QUID PRO, LLC

5860 Citrus Blvd., Suite D-101

New Orleans, Louisiana 70123

www.quidprobooks.com

Publisher's Cataloging-in-Publication

Friedman, Lawrence M.

　　Contract law in America: a social and economic case study / Lawrence M. Friedman.

　　　　p. cm.

　　Includes note references, appendix, and index.

　　Series: *Classics of Law & Society.*

1. Legal history—United States. 2. Law—United States—contract law. 3. Law—United States—commercial law. 4. Law—United States—Wisconsin. I. Title. II. Series.

KFW2550 .F7 2011

To Leah

Contents

Foreword, 2011, by Stewart Macaulay i

Preface, 2011, by the author ix

Preface, 1964 xi

Introduction . . . {3} 1

I   Toward a Working Definition of Contract . . . {15} 11

II   Contract Law in the Wisconsin Supreme Court:
     An Analysis of Fact-Situations . . . {27} 21

III   Contract Law in the Courts:
      A Legal Analysis . . . {82} 65

IV   Contract Law and the Legislature . . . {140} 111

V   Contract Law in the Courts: What the Study Shows . . . {184} 147

Appendix: Tables III and IV . . . {219, 220} 175

Notes . . . {221} 177

Index . . . {273} 217

About the Author 225

Page numbers to the right in this table reference the pagination used in this edition. Those numbers are shown at the top of the page. Page numbers above in {brackets} refer to the pagination used in the original edition of this book. Those numbers are found embedded into the text of this edition by use of {brackets}, for purposes of continuity and citation.

FOREWORD | 2011
Dodos, Unicorns and Sleeping Rattlesnakes

There are many reasons to read a book that was published over 45 years ago. We could want to smile at the quaint assumptions of those working in the pre-computer age. We might want to feel some satisfaction that we have solved the problems raised by the book. We might wonder whether we could understand positions taken today if we traced their origins back to those who worked in the field at an earlier time. However, the best reason to read an older book is that it raises important problems that have not been solved yet. It is even better if the book offers important insights relevant to a solution.

Lawrence Friedman's first book, *Contract Law in America*, still challenges those who research, write and teach in the field of contracts. His findings and arguments still call for a serious response today. He looked at the contracts cases coming before the Supreme Court of Wisconsin at three periods: (1) the organization of the Wisconsin Territory to the Civil War (1836-1861); (2) the Progressive era in the first two decades of the twentieth century (1905-1915); and (3) a time ten years after World War II (1955-1958). He asked what kinds of contract cases came before the court, and how did it decide them? Once Friedman established this, he looked at scholars restating, writing and teaching contract law. The conventional ideal is a contract law that is abstract and formal. This kind of law should be highly predictable. However, some professors see the actual American contract law, in Duncan Kennedy's phrase, as a hard core of pure doctrine surrounded by a soft periphery of justice-seeking "exceptions." Nevertheless, peripheries tend to expand and push aside cores.[1] We always must watch out for the difference between what courts say and what they do.

Friedman found that the Supreme Court of Wisconsin did not confront the major economic issues of the state in its contracts decisions. People did not bring those issues before the court very often. Most cases were settled before or during litigation. Cost barriers increased, and more and more business involved long-term continuing relations which have their own norms and sanctions for failing to do what was promised. Moreover, during the periods that Friedman studied the court's contract decisions, the subject matter of pure contract was taken away by other bodies of law. For example, the areas of insurance, employment and trade regulation all removed disputes from the domain of pure common law contract. However, few legal

---

[1] See Duncan Kennedy, "Form and Substance in Private Law Adjudication," 89 *Harv. L. Rev.* 1685, 1737 (1976).

scholars noticed this. As a result, instead of hard, abstract and formal contract law, the court used malleable concepts such as waiver and estoppel, and substantial performance, and it limited damages to the difference in value of what was delivered and what was promised. It sought what it saw as just results on the facts of the particular case before it.[2]

Friedman asked what this means for contract research and teaching. He answered in a manner designed to offend many contracts scholars in 1965 and perhaps today as well. First, he said, "[T]he subject matter had long since flown away. Instructor and student were grappling with trivia."[3] Second, he put the situation in his own metaphor: "Carried into modern times by treatise writers and the Restatements, the common-law approach to law in the schools and in legal literature at its worst could be compared to a zoology course which confined the study to dodos and unicorns, to beasts rare or long dead and beasts that never lived."[4]

In a recent review of this book,[5] I sought to add a qualification to Friedman's position. Much contracts scholarship is focused on dodos and unicorns. However, contract law itself could at times better be described as a sleeping rattlesnake that only looks dead. In appropriate (or sometimes inappropriate) situations, lawyers and courts could wake it up and it could bite the unsuspecting. My example was the way corporate lawyers undercut consumer and employee protection laws by hiding an incomprehensible arbitration clause in fine print that few consumers or employees would find and understand before the deal was closed. Then the lawyers assigned the arbitration to a kangaroo court in Patagonia. Some courts enforced these pretend contracts. Others found them unconscionable. I know, I know . . . not all consumer and employee arbitration has to be a joke, and *some* arbitration providers may be better for consumers and employees than courts. Maybe even the terrible arbitrators serve to cut costs, and maybe these savings are passed on to the total group of consumers and employees. In this way, perhaps those who are treated badly are sacrificing for the rest of us who get lower prices. The sleeping rattlesnake woke up and bit those who are suffering for the rest of us.

Friedman did see a role for courts applying what could be called contract law. Contract was the law of leftovers. He wrote:

---

[2] See Ronen Shamir, "Formal and Substantive Rationality in American Law: A Weberian Perspective," 2 *Social & Legal Studies* 45 (1993). Shamir argues that American law reflects cycles of seeking abstract formality and then substantive justice. When we experience enough of the negative sides of each, we tend to jump to the other in a predictable pattern.

[3] Friedman, *Contract Law in America*, at xi {page viii in original edition}.

[4] *Id.* at 19 {page 25 in original edition}.

[5] See Stewart Macaulay, "The Death of Contract: Dodos and Unicorns or Sleeping Rattlesnakes?," in Robert W. Gordon and Morton J. Horwitz, eds., *Law, Society, and History: Themes in the Legal Sociology and Legal History of Lawrence M. Friedman* (Cambridge Univ. Pr. 2011), at 193. The present Foreword is adapted and expanded from my chapter in the Gordon and Horwitz book.

So long as social change remained possible, so long as new kinds of business, new products, new techniques kept emerging, the court retained a small but vital role. Between the time when new business practices evolve and the time when the kinks have been smoothed out of forms and documents relating to the emerging practice, some agency of law must be ready to solve unforeseen problems. When continuing relations break down, or in cases of novel business problems or fluid business hierarchical arrangements, the court performed this role.[6]

How have contract scholars responded? Friedman's book was widely reviewed, and it was quoted and praised in Grant Gilmore's *The Death of Contract*.[7] Gilmore's 1974 book provoked much writing that defended the "old time religion, it was good enough for grandpa, and it's good enough for me." For example, Professor Stanley Henderson wrote:

> That each beginning law course carries a designated title confirms the existence of an established body of learning, organized and subdivided into fields. In presenting one of these fields to students we are space-bound by received classifications; there is a language to be learned and a culture to be passed on.[8]

Professor Robert Childres taught (at that time) at New York University Law School. He challenged Friedman's method. He objected to generalizing from the experience of "one provincial state."[9] I am reminded of Saul Steinberg's *A View of the World from Ninth Avenue*, a classic cover from *The New Yorker*.[10] I don't think that Childres fairly could argue that a study of New York appellate opinions would come to a different result from Friedman's findings without doing the hard work of gathering and analyzing the cases.

---

[6] *Contract Law in America*, at 160-61 {page 201 in original edition}.

[7] As Jean Braucher said: "Gilmore quoted a long passage from Friedman, part of which referred to Friedman's central point about the marginalization of contract law, but Gilmore did not engage with this point. Rather, Gilmore gave loving attention to the beautiful trees (the reasoning of cases in his account of the rise and fall of classical contract doctrine), while Friedman kept his eye on the big picture, seeing that much of the forest had been chopped down." Braucher, "The Afterlife of Contract," 90 *N.W.U. L. Rev.* 49, 76-77 (1995).

Robert Gordon observed that Gilmore was a case-law realist while Friedman was a behavioral realist. A case lawyer, Gordon asserted, sees the study of deciding appeals as the "master process whose study reveals the rest, as the microscopic study of a beetle was believed in the 18th century to unlock the pattern of the mind of God." Behavioral realists "refuse to limit their universe of investigation to cases.... Behaviorists ... ask not only what social functions are performed by courts but also who else in society, official agencies or private parties, performs those other functions. Once the focus of study is thus shifted, they assert, the work of courts is seen to shrink to near insignificance." Gordon, Book Review, 1974 *Wis. L. Rev.* 1216, 1222-23.

[8] Stanley D. Henderson, Book Review, 124 *U. Pa. L. Rev.* 1468, 1475 (1975).

[9] Robert Childres, Book Review, 18 *J. Legal Education* 478, 484 (1966).

[10] *The New Yorker*, March 29, 1976. This cover shows a bird's-eye view of the city from Ninth Avenue looking westward, with perspectives becoming ever more condensed, and leading to Asia. Most of the middle of the United States simply does not exist in the drawing. Of course, it doesn't exist for many or most of the natives of New York who look west from Ninth Avenue.

Indeed, I can think of three classic New York Court of Appeals opinions that have appeared in many casebooks. *Mitchill v. Lath*[11] is the well-known ice house case. Ms. Mitchill argued that the sellers of property had promised to tear down what she saw as an ugly ice house that spoiled her view. However, this promise did not make it into the written real estate purchase contract. The Court of Appeals (the state's highest court) drew on formal abstract principles to deny her claim. She was not allowed to offer evidence of the alleged oral promise.

In *Jacobs & Young v. Kent*,[12] a wealthy lawyer was unhappy with the way a general contractor had built the lawyer's expensive house. The owner looked for an out. He found that while the written contract called for cast iron pipe throughout the building manufactured by the Reading Pipe Company, the contractor had substituted another brand of pipe. There was evidence that the quality of the two brands of pipe was the same. Judge Benjamin Cardozo, writing for the court, found that the contractor had substantially performed, and so it was entitled to recover the contract price less the owner's damages. However, Cardozo then calculated the owner's damages as the difference in value between a house with Reading pipe and one with the brand actually installed. There was no difference, and so there was no damage.

In *Allegheny College v. National Chautauqua County Bank*,[13] a donor made a promise to make a contribution to a college. Judge Cardozo construed the facts to find a return promise to use the funds for a memorial fund. As a result, the promise was supported by consideration.

Notice that none of the three New York cases involved transactions of great significance to the economy. Two of the three fit Friedman's assertion that when this was true, a "court is more apt to turn to the particular situation before it, and to seek an adjustment which accords with current notions of fairness in the particular situation, untroubled by considerations of grand generality."[14] Of course, these are only three cases, but they suggest that the pattern that Friedman had found in Wisconsin might not be limited to that odd provincial state.

Perhaps more telling today than these examples is Professor Robert Scott's study of appellate opinions applying Article 2 of the Uniform Commercial Code, particularly those sections calling for contracts to be interpreted according to the norm of commercial reasonableness.[15] Scott looked at a much later period than was covered by Friedman's work. Scott found, in

---

[11] 247 N.Y. 377, 160 N.E. 646 (1928).

[12] 230 N.Y. 239, 129 N.E. 889 (1921).

[13] 246 N.Y. 369, 159 N.E. 173 (1927).

[14] *Contract Law in America*, at 155 {page 194 in original edition}.

[15] Robert E. Scott, "The Uniformity Norm in Commercial Law: A Comparative Analysis of Common Law and Code Methodologies," in Jody S. Kraus & Steven D. Walt, eds., *The Jurisprudential Foundations of Corporate and Commercial Law* (2000), at 149, 168 n.68.

Friedman's terms, that the courts have not sought to create or apply abstract formal norms. Scott complains: "[C]ourts have consistently interpreted these statutory instructions not as inductive directions to incorporate commercial norms and prototypes, but rather as invitations to make deductive speculations according to 'Code policy' or other noncontextual criteria."[16] Scott is unhappy with what the courts have done; Friedman is not. However, Scott's work supports Friedman's factual findings if not his normative judgment.

Friedman's charge that traditional contracts scholarship and teaching involve "grappling with trivia" remains. Are we writing and teaching in a fashion that "could be compared to a zoology course which confined its study to dodos and unicorns, to beasts rare or long dead and beasts that never lived"?[17] First, we need some idea of what our courts do and what intellectual tools they use. Second, we need some picture of what is going on in the world of people drafting contracts and struggling to resolve disputes. Here we must ask whether the approaches taken by appellate courts matter much and how. We can expect that the answers might differ as we look to contracts issues in different kinds of cases. Industrial purchasing might be very different from contracts involving borrowing large sums of money or contracts to take over a large corporation. Standard form contracts and consumers may be still another world.

Is the goal of contract law to adjudicate disputes accurately or is it to coerce settlements and compromises? Again, we can ask what function it is playing and has played in the past. We can ask whether what it has done or is doing are good things. David Campbell says provocatively: "Far from it being the function of the law of contract to (so far as possible) prevent breach, the function of the law is to make breach possible although on terms which the law regulates."[18] In all but the exceptional situation, he notes, the aggrieved party will be limited to the difference between the contract price and the market price as damages. This duty to mitigate means that the cost of buying a substitute or the loss on a resale of the goods must be great enough to make a lawsuit a good risk to assume. If the damages are really large and would tempt even a contingent fee lawyer, we then run into *Hadley v. Baxendale*. Really big damages can be challenged as unforeseeable and not a risk assumed in the bargain. When a plaintiff can jump the *Hadley* hurdle, then she must get past the proof-of-damages-with-reasonable-certainty barrier. Moreover, sellers routinely disclaim consequential damages in standard form contracts. Add to this the practice of "the settling judge" who twists arms to get cases settled and off his or her docket. How should all this play

---

[16] Robert E. Scott, "The Case for Formalism in Relational Contracts," 94 *N.W.U. L. Rev.* 847, 868 (2000).

[17] *Contract Law in America*, at 19 {page 25 in original edition}.

[18] David Campbell, "The Relational Constitution of Remedy: Co-operation as the Implicit Second Principle of Remedies for Breach of Contract," 11 *Tex. Wesleyan L. Rev.* 455, 456 (2005). See also Stewart Macaulay, "Renegotiations and Settlements: Dr. Pangloss's Notes on the Margins of David Campbell's Papers," 29 *Cardozo L. Rev.* 261 (2007).

into scholarship and teaching?

Or we can point to some of the work of Claire Hill.[19] She finds that lawyer-drafted contracts often are unnecessarily long and complicated. They frequently have ambiguities that allow for multiple interpretations. Sometimes parties decide to leave matters uncertain. This way, each side has an argument in any potential litigation. Had they tried to negotiate the matter, they might have been forced to accept a clear rejection of their position. Moreover, some terms are hard for anyone to define precisely, and parties may read them differently. It is far easier to use terms such as "material," "reasonable," and "best efforts" than to try to give such matters a precise definition. Hill argues that uncertainty in drafting increases the costs of litigation, and this creates a bond against precipitous recourse to the courts. Each side knows that if it starts a lawsuit, the other will be able to impose significant costs. "What the murky contract does is lower the costs for the party sued to countersue."[20] What should we do with the tactics of negotiation and contract drafting? Do we get better settlements if the parties must speculate about what courts are going to do with such a case? Does it matter whether courts use formal abstract rules or attempt to find the just result with qualitative standards? Or is it enough that in many cases difficulties in proving the facts create a large degree of uncertainty whether a plaintiff might win?

What should contract teaching and scholarship be about if we are to avoid dodos and unicorns? How do we deal with sleeping rattlesnakes and contract law as duct tape, serving to patch up problems in a messy fashion that is hardly elegant? Good questions and questions just as alive as when Friedman wrote *Contract Law in America*.

In addition to struggling with alive problems, reading *Contract Law in America* will allow readers to experience the writing of Lawrence Friedman. He marches to his own tune. He went to the University of Chicago Law School but was not converted to an unquestioning faith in law and economics. He was a student and a young professor when Karl Llewellyn's codification of legal realism in Article 2 of the Uniform Commercial Code was all the rage, but he was skeptical of what difference passage of the Code might make. Neutral principles and legal process didn't do much better. Friedman asked where did these definitions of the roles of judges, legislators and presidents

---

[19] See Claire A. Hill, "Bargaining in the Shadow of the Lawsuit: A Social Norms Theory of Incomplete Contracts," 34 *Del. J. Corp. L.* 191 (2009).

[20] *Id.* at 208, 213. Hill also notes: "Whether a dispute arises depends largely on whether one or both parties become unhappy in the relationship, which often turns on the world changing in the way the parties didn't expressly anticipate, and in a manner that they didn't and couldn't have comprehensively and satisfactorily provided for before the fact. More effort thrown at drafting within any reasonable range is not likely to ameliorate the problem commensurately with the added cost." *Id.* at 217. See also Claire A. Hill, "A Comment on Language and Norms in Complex Business Contracting," 77 *Chi.-Kent L. Rev.* 29, 55 (2001) ("The shadow of the law is ever present, but quite pale. For most contracting parties, the law's specter is one of many reasons to do what they promised to do, and often, not the most important reason.").

come from? Empirically, the roles that they actually had played throughout history were very different. Critical legal studies also failed to capture his total allegiance. He wanted some evidence that people were misled by the rules of law or that these rules affected their world view and behavior. Instead, Friedman combines scholarship that takes him into dusty archives with insight into the broader effect of both public culture and legal culture. I am continually and pleasantly surprised when I read Friedman.

Moreover, he is fun to read. Long ago, Lawrence and I taught a constitutional law class together. Often when I read Supreme Court opinions, I don't know whether to laugh or cry. But it is more fun to laugh and so I try to do that. Nonetheless, I found that my role in that class was to play straight man and help set up Lawrence's funny, if not outrageous, comments. I love his reaction to those law professors who criticized Chief Justice Earl Warren's opinion in *Brown v. Board of Education*. They assumed that had the opinion been written better by their standards, it would have had a bigger impact. Friedman responded: "But anybody who feels that a more tightly crafted and better reasoned opinion in *Brown* would have had a bigger (or even different) impact on life in rural Mississippi (or Washington, D.C., for that matter) than what Warren actually wrote, can't be living on this planet."[21] If you keep in mind Friedman's sense of humor well mixed with his anger at stupidity that hurts people, you can understand him better. And just in case all this praise makes any reader question my objectivity about the work of a good friend and coauthor, I'll raise an objection: Lawrence uses too many semicolons.

STEWART MACAULAY
Malcolm Pitman Sharp Professor and
Theodore W. Brazeau Professor,
School of Law
University of Wisconsin

Madison, Wisconsin
August, 2011

---

[21] Lawrence M. Friedman, "Brown in Context," in Austin Sarat, ed., *Race, Law, and Culture: Reflections on Brown v. Board of Education* (1997), at 52, 60.

PREFACE | 2011

More than 45 years have passed since this book, my first, was published; and it was a strange feeling to pick it up and read it, once more, after all these years.

Does it stand up, now that so much water has gone under the bridge? I suppose that's not really for me to say. To be honest, I think it does stand up; but of course the author is not to be trusted.

What I can say, somewhat more objectively, is that this work has not been superseded by a flood of later, more rigorous, and more detailed studies. Let me say a word about the background. I wrote this book at the University of Wisconsin, where I was a young professor in the law school. The law school in those days was a remarkable institution. It definitely marched to its own drummer. The dominant figure at the school was Willard Hurst.

And it was Hurst who encouraged me to do this study; and the study, in turn, owes a lot to his influence. It was one of a series of studies of Wisconsin's legal history for which Hurst acted more or less as a godfather.

It is not much of an exaggeration to say that Hurst invented American legal history. Invented: at least as a serious discipline, and as a branch of general social and economic history. For Hurst, law could not be understood outside of its social context. What I tried to do here was to take the decisions of the Wisconsin Supreme Court, in three separate periods, and look at them from this standpoint. It does not sound like rocket science; but nobody much had done this kind of thing before.

A lot has happened since 1965. A lot of books have been written. A lot of serious studies have been carried out. Legal history is a flourishing field. But surprisingly few studies that I know of have looked at high court decisions, in state courts—or federal courts, for that matter—from the angle of vision that this book exemplifies. And, again, with a few honorable exceptions, the teaching of contracts as an academic subject has not found it useful or important to take this kind of work into account. Economic analysis: yes, to an extent. But history, culture, and the like; social context: very little indeed.

Of course, I am delighted to see this book in print again. Maybe a contract teacher or two will find it profitable to leaf through the pages. I hope my colleagues in legal history will take a look at it, and perhaps find something useful in its pages. If I had it to do over, I would try to simplify the prose and make the text more concrete, more vivid, more readable. Still, I have moved on, I hope; and on the whole I am satisfied with this, my first-born literary child.

I want to thank Alan Childress, who is responsible for the brash idea of bringing this book back to life; and Stewart Macaulay—for my money, the finest contracts scholar working in the academy today—for honoring me with a foreword. And I thank in advance that small band or readers—not, I hope, too terribly small—who will thumb through the pages. I hope they find what they are looking for.

LAWRENCE M. FRIEDMAN
Marion Rice Kirkwood Professor of Law,
School of Law
Stanford University

Stanford, California
September, 2011

PREFACE | 1964

The research on the subject of this study was largely accomplished during successive summers spent in Madison, Wisconsin, financed by a grant from the Rockefeller Foundation, administered through the University of Wisconsin Law School. Some of the work on the final draft was hammered out during a year's leave from teaching duties financed by a grant from the Ford Foundation Law and Policy Program at the University of Wisconsin Law School.

This work is one of a series of monographs undertaken at the University of Wisconsin Law School by members of the faculty and visiting scholars, in the general field of American legal history, but with emphasis on Wisconsin materials and with a pronounced bias toward examining the relationship between legal development and economic, political, and social forces at work in the community as a whole. The latter bias (one hopes) hardly needs defending. The emphasis on Wisconsin poses the danger of falling into parochialism or triviality, but bears the promise of increasing knowledge of the legal and social order through attacking primary sources intensively and thoroughly. On the whole, the experiment must be pronounced a success, since the researcher who (as I did) begins his work not as the pioneer but in the middle of the series finds his task lightened and enlightened by the cumulative efforts of those who preceded him. Moreover, what legal history in this country has sorely needed is precisely this: the cumulation of sustained and persistent work on a limited body of data. Probably nothing has so crippled historical study of American law as the traumatic effect of some fifty jurisdictions.

Nothing, that is, unless it is the devastating obsoleteness of legal education, which (except for some meager palliatives in upper-class seminars) tends to develop notions and habits of thought inimical to the study of law either as a branch of human behavior or as a chapter in the book of human ideas. Legal education, in general, seeks to teach students "how to think and act like lawyers" and turns its back on imparting "mere facts." "Mere facts" (if this means rote learning) should of course not be the prime goal of education; but overemphasis on skills training has severe drawbacks of its own. It substitutes manipulation of data for understanding of data. In general, the law schools fail to teach the legal system as a whole, let alone the legal system as part of society; they teach disjointed fragments of a fragment.

This study was not begun as an attempt to debunk legal education or, in particular, the value of spending a good share of the first year of legal education on the classical contours of the law of contracts. But as the study proceeded, I became more and more convinced that the traditional coursework in contracts was outmoded. The subject-matter had long since flown away. Instructor and student were grappling with trivia. The fixed traditions of legal education permit this situation to continue. The conventional discipline is defended as "fundamental"; it grounds students in basic skills and basic legal habits of thought. The typical contracts course never questions the relationship of law to the functioning of our economic system. The materials of study are appellate cases classified by concepts and wrenched out of their social context. They do not pose large issues and are inappropriate for studying such issues. The world of legal education seems strangely unaware of how minor the subject matter of this "fundamental discipline" has become. And yet, in view of the small, residual function of the law of contracts, and the small, residual role of appellate courts in creating principles, institutions, and techniques for governing our economic life, is there any vital reason for the inordinate attention still paid to the classical law of contracts in the law schools? I would argue that there is not. The typical current course might be justified as an excursion into history; but it is not so taught. It might be justified on practical grounds—as a course on fundamental business law and dispute settlement in business. It is not so taught, and cannot be so taught, so long as appellate cases form the bulk of the teaching materials. The traditional course can only be justified as a mental exercise, as a way of inducting the young into the world of the law. But if so, why not inculcate legal reasoning through the study of living, vital institutions, viewed in the full richness of their social and economic meaning?

These are my personal convictions. They are not unrelated to the data of this study. Nonetheless, they involve a mental leap for the reader which (if he is not a law teacher) he may not be interested in making, or (if he is a law teacher) he may be philosophically uninclined to make. This is not a study of legal education, but of the legal system in its social context. It will, I hope, be persuasive in demonstrating certain connections between legal and social institutions. The idea that law is a product of its environment and responds to social and economic forces is certainly commonplace enough. But precise demonstrations of the manner in which law makes this response, and the degree of influence of particular social facts on the law, have not been commonplace. And such demonstrations have been particularly rare for common law (non-statutory) fields, of which contract law is one. This gap in research justifies this undertaking. The reader may judge whether the results in turn justify the effort.

In writing this book, I have run up an enormous intellectual debt to Professor Willard Hurst of the University of Wisconsin Law School. He has been the leading spirit behind the development of the program of research of which this book is one product. His own writings have provided a wealth of ideas and approaches to the field of legal history, particularly American legal history. In addition, he reviewed my work at every stage, spending countless hours discussing it with me, and subjecting the drafts to page after page of searching and invaluable criticism. It is no exaggeration to say that this book would not have been possible without his help.

Many others were of service to me, and I would like to express my gratitude. My colleague Stewart Macaulay made many useful suggestions, drawing on his large and precise knowledge of contract theory and current business practice. Professor Addison Mueller of the University of California at Los Angeles, and Professor Harold Havighurst of Northwestern University read the final draft and made valuable comments. Professor Malcolm Sharp of the University of Chicago read and commented on the manuscript at an earlier stage of its development. I also owe much to the faculties and staffs of the two law schools with which I was connected during the years this project was underway, St. Louis University Law School, and the Law School of the University of Wisconsin, where I presently teach. During the early stages of my work, Eileen Searls, Law Librarian of St. Louis University, went out of her way to be of service. The tortuous course of writing this book demanded the time and effort of many typists, secretaries, and administrative staff-members at the University of Wisconsin. I cannot name them all, but Ann Wallace and Sherry Bate deserve particular mention. Mrs. Ruth Wright helped me greatly with the tedious job of checking the accuracy of my citations. Finally, my wife Leah aided me immeasurably in my work, by serving as sounding-board, guinea pig, proof-reader, and all-purpose helper.

LAWRENCE M. FRIEDMAN

Madison, Wisconsin
Summer, 1964

Contract Law in America

INTRODUCTION

THE study which follows deals with legal materials in the mass—cases, legislation, reports of the Attorney General of Wisconsin, other records of the proceedings of legal agencies. In particular, the study analyzes more than 500 contract cases, decided over a period of more than a century by the Wisconsin Supreme Court. It is easy to forget that each of these cases embodies the skeletal remains of a unique human situation: even at its most matter-of-fact and businesslike, the legal system rests on human raw material, both for its personnel and for the work which flows through its agencies. Indeed, one of the major points which this study will make is how the body of contract law—a body of law which presents, on the surface, an almost marmoreal imperviousness to the particular—changed under the attrition of a constant stream of concrete events moving in a definite direction. Before we plunge into the wilderness of theory and induction, it would be well to set out three such cases, drawn from each of the periods which form the major blocks of research effort. These are not random cases, but cases rich in implication. They are presented as a prelude to what follows.

Brown v. Peck (1853).[1] Rosaline Peck was the first white woman to settle in the area of Madison, Wisconsin. She and her husband built an inn, to feed and house the workmen who were building the new state capitol. In 1845, Rosaline's husband deserted her; he went to Oregon, leaving her in possession of a tract of land in Sauk County, which she occupied without title. The "times were very hard when this land, together with others, came into market." For lack of money, Mrs. Peck was unable to perfect her squatter's title by buying the land from the {*page 3 ends; page 4 follows*} federal government. In May, 1847, the land was sold to Chauncey Brown, who paid for the land through the register of the land office at Mineral Point.

On November 23, 1847, Brown was "in bed in the tavern house of one Marcus Warren, in Prairie du Sac, Sauk county." After he retired for the night, "one or two men came into the house and inquired if Mr. Brown was there." Later, "five, six, or eight, or ten more strangers" came into the barroom. "They talked pretty loud." After a while, they brought Brown downstairs with "nothing on but his shirt." Warren talked the men into letting Brown dress. After he dressed, the men brought him down again, with "as many as five or six" holding his arms and legs. They threatened to throw him in the river, but "compromised by rolling him in the mud ... he was rolled in the mud and snow two or three times." Then he was taken to Fife's Tavern in Prairie du Sac; Cyrus Leland, the notary public, was called in, and came with a deed already prepared. Brown was "wet, muddy, cold and shivering"; he "spoke with difficulty." Brown signed the deed conveying the property to Mrs. Peck. The price was $100, which somebody threw down on the table.

Brown "did not count the money or touch it at all."

In 1849, Rosaline conveyed the premises to Abraham Wood; Wood executed a mortgage in her favor, "to secure the payment of seven hundred dollars, according to the condition of five promissory notes." The deed and mortgage were recorded.

In 1850, Brown filed a bill in equity, in the Circuit Court of Sauk County, to set aside the two deeds and the mortgage. He won the case. Mrs. Peck and Wood appealed to the Wisconsin Supreme Court. But here, too, Mrs. Peck met with disappointment. As she later put it, sarcastically, "our beautiful Court of Equity at Madison ... mulcted me." Judge Abram Smith, speaking for the court, found it "perfectly apparent" that the conveyance by Brown to Mrs. Peck had lacked that "free assent" which is "essential to a valid contract.... The free, voluntary meeting and mingling, or acquiescence of minds." A court could not enforce such a contract, made under duress; to do so would be "to withdraw the protection of the court from those unable to protect themselves, and prostitute its sacred functions to the purposes of lawless violence and outrage."

This was the essential point; collateral issues were brushed aside by the court, which was determined that this should be "the last instance of the kind, which may ever come to our notice" (words spoken about {5} the inglorious role of the notary). Wood stood in no better position than Mrs. Peck; he was no "actual *bona fide* purchaser without notice." Clearly, he knew the story of the deed; he "lived in the neighborhood," where the incident was "a subject generally known, talked about and understood." Nor was Brown barred from suit by "his delay in asserting his rights." If "the feeling of indignation towards him was so rife and so general in that neighborhood," he may well have acted "wisely" in "delaying a resort to legal means."

Judge Smith did, however, set aside one paragraph of his opinion to castigate Brown. The court, said Judge Smith, had no intent to "justify or palliate" Brown's actions. The "dictates of humanity" should have prompted him to leave the squatter's land alone and "seek other fields for speculation or profitable investment." But the law does not punish all "departures from a high standard of moral conduct"; some "departures" must "find their desert before that social tribunal erected by public sentiment." If she read that paragraph (which is doubtful), Mrs. Peck derived small comfort. The land was the point; and that was Brown's.

Pratt v. Darling (1905).[2] At the turn of the century the village of Manawa, Wisconsin, situated in Waupaca County, northwest of the Lake Winnebago region, had a population of about 1,000. E. L. Darling ran a general store in Manawa; so did the Schuelke brothers (Adolph and William). Five other general stores and two druggists were located in the village. On March 31, 1903, a salesman named C. W. Killen paid Darling a call. Killen was the Wisconsin salesman for Walter Pratt & Co., a partnership, of Iowa and Chicago, "Manufacturing Chemists and Perfumers." Though Darling dealt in "Dry Goods,

Hats, Caps, Boots, Shoes, Groceries, Provisions and Lumberman's Supplies" he did not stock many toilet articles. Killen had come to remedy that situation. On the day in question, in Darling's own words:

> I was standing in front of the store, between 7 and 8 o'clock in the morning. Mr. Killen came along the street and introduced himself, told me what he had; and I told him I didn't think I cared to have anything to do with a line of that kind if it was to be placed in more than one place in a town.

Killen was more than willing to promise Darling exclusive rights. (Mr. Fritz, the clerk, "heard part of the talk" from the store.) Killen went back to his hotel, got his sample case and "showed up the stuff he had." {6} Darling still wanted assurances that nobody else in town would get the line. Killen told him, "Bless your soul, I don't want to sell it to anybody else if I can place it in this store." Darling's sales resistance was overcome. On the same day (March 31) he signed an order for a bill of goods, including Farina Cologne, Roger's Hair Grower, Invisible Toilet Powder (white), Invisible Toilet Powder (flesh), Pratt's Dentifrice, Cherry Lip Pomade, many kinds of Handkerchief Extract (including Parisian Rose), and White Rose, Jasmine, Crab Apple Blossom and Crushed Violet perfumes. It all amounted to $133.38; Darling agreed to maintain the stock through re-order; Pratt offered "free" one Atomizer, a show case, a "Sample Sterling Silver Thimble," advertising material, and a "perpetual" promotion plan. The standard order form said nothing at all about exclusive rights in Manawa, but it did declare that: "Separate verbal or written agreements with salesmen are not binding upon Walter Pratt & Co. All conditions of sale must be shown in this order. Positively no goods on commission or open account. This order not subject to countermand." On April 2 (or thereabouts), the goods were shipped by rail. They arrived in Manawa on April 14; James Fowzer, resident agent of the Green Bay & Western Railroad Company, took possession. But the goods were never claimed by E. L. Darling. On April 6, Darling had written the company countermanding his order; he had discovered that Killen had visited Schuelke Bros. on March 30, 1903, one day before Darling signed his own order, and that Schuelke Bros had bought the identical bill of goods—the same Farina Cologne, the same invisible toilet powders, the same Crab Apple Blossom Perfume. Darling had other complaints against Pratt, but this was the main one: his exclusive rights were a myth. Walter Pratt's answer was firm; the order said nothing about exclusive rights; in fact it specifically said that the contract was complete as written. Furthermore, the line was "a staple line of goods"; there was "no reason why you should not be able to handle this line successfully," despite any competition in Manawa.

Darling, however, was adamant; he neither collected nor paid for the goods, and Walter Pratt brought him to court. At the trial, Killen did not testify, although he still worked as a salesman for Pratt. Darling won the case, and Pratt appealed to the Wisconsin Supreme Court. The court seemed to have little trouble with the decision, which it handed down in the January term, 1905. Winslow, J., for the court, crisply affirmed the lower court decision. Killen had made a {7} "fraudulent representation"; the testimony on this point was "absolutely undisputed." It was also "very certain" that Darling would never have bought the goods except for false promises made by Killen. The only difficulty was the parol evidence rule,* specifically reinforced by the terms of the written order. But Killen had already made his sale to Schuelke Bros.; his promise of exclusive rights was not "a mere promise" (which the rule might conceivably bar) but a false "statement as to an existing fact." Testimony on this point was excluded neither by the contract nor the rule; the court therefore had a right to hear and act on its information. Judgment was affirmed; Walter Pratt & Co. remained unpaid; and perfumes, hair lotions, and toilet articles, to the wholesale value of $133.38, remained where they were, piled up in the back room of the depot at Manawa, Wisconsin.

Kelley v. Ellis (1956).[3] Harlan W. Kelley, a blind and legless lawyer of Baraboo, Wisconsin, maintained an active professional career in law and politics despite his grave physical handicaps. He was elected District Attorney in 1951, but lost out in the primary in 1954. His term of office was due to expire on January 1, 1955. Before then, therefore, he had to make plans to return to private practice.

Baraboo is the county seat of Sauk County. In the 1950's, the town had a population somewhat in excess of 6,000. Kelley was anxious to find a place where, if possible, he could "combine living quarters with office space"; he needed to be "near the courthouse ... and the banks." Convenience of location was unusually important, because of Kelley's physical handicaps. One day, Kelley's wife, Louise, noticed an advertisement in the paper for what seemed a possible place; Willott Warren, a local real estate broker, was managing the sale. One night, when the Kelley's "were eating dinner at Uphoff's," they "happened to bump into Mr. Warren." The property was discussed. Louise, Kelley's father, and a contractor named Malone later went out to examine the premises. It seemed to be just what the Kelleys needed. {8}

The house was owned by Mrs. Helena Ellis, a widow nearly 80 years old. She was anxious to be out of the house before winter, and listed it with Warren, suggesting a sale price of $11,500. The Kelley's first offer was $8,000; on November 12, 1954, they raised their bid to $9,000; and the parties executed a contract at that price. The documents were in standard form. Kelley paid $500 in earnest money, and executed an offer form; Mrs. Ellis accepted it in writing. The offer did specify, however: "Possession to be agreed upon [by] buyer and seller."

---

* The core of the rule is this: when negotiations have resulted in a written agreement, which seems to cover the whole subject-matter of the bargaining, the court will treat that agreement as embodying the whole agreement of the parties; and it will not pay attention to evidence, oral or written, of what went on in the prior period of bargaining, if that evidence contradicts the written agreement. (Some writers would say that, in order for the rule to operate, the court must find that the writing was "intended" to cover the whole subject matter of the bargaining.)

Baraboo is a small town, and the sale of Mrs. Ellis's house was mildly newsworthy. The next day the following appeared in the local paper:

DISTRICT ATTORNEY HAS PURCHASED HOME AND OFFICE

Mrs. F. P. Ellis has sold her home and office space located at 123 Fifth Avenue, Baraboo, to District Attorney Harlan W. Kelley, who, after January 1st will practice law at this location. Mr. Kelley plans extensive remodeling to provide both offices and home on the ground floor, which will be advantageous to both himself and his clients. Both parties in the transaction were represented by Willott Warren, Realtor.

Warren was probably himself the source of this item. Most of the citizens of Baraboo no doubt read this piece of news with indifference; but it had a totally unforeseen effect at 123 Fifth Avenue. Mrs. Ellis reacted strangely and strongly; she lost faith in the way Warren had represented her interests. She may have felt that Kelley, with his grandiose plans for remodeling, had gotten a marvelous bargain at her expense. She called Warren on November 13, told him she was backing out, and that "she had been taken advantage of as to price." She hired an attorney, who wrote a letter to Kelley saying that "This matter was misrepresented and Mrs. Ellis is not going to do anything further in the matter." Kelley refused to bow out. He went to court and sought specific performance of the contract to sell. Mrs. Ellis counterclaimed for fraud and misrepresentation. At the trial, Kelley was absolved by the court of any fraud or misrepresentation; specific performance was decreed; on August 16, 1955, Mrs. Ellis appealed.

Before the Supreme Court, discussion mainly turned on the unfortunate phrase "Possession to be agreed upon." Mrs. Ellis's counsel insisted that there was "no meeting of the minds of the parties on an essential element of the contract, and, therefore, equity could not decree specific performance." The court was not impressed. Currie, J., pointed out that "where a contract of sale of land is silent as to time of {9} change of possession, the law will imply a reasonable time." The contract in *Kelley v. Ellis* was not entirely silent on the time of possession (since it included the ambiguous phrase), but it spoke in a whisper, and the court thought the rule of a "reasonable time" ought to be applied. There was some evidence, said the court, that both parties had a reasonable time limit in mind. Mrs. Ellis wished to avoid ordering coal for the winter, and preferred to auction off her furniture while the weather was still warm. The Kelleys needed possession by January 1, 1955. The court said: "It is thus apparent that both seller and purchaser did not have in mind any date for change of possession extending beyond a reasonable time. Furthermore, when Mrs. Ellis repudiated the contract ... she did so on other grounds than that there had been no meeting of the minds as to the time for yielding possession." This amounted to saying that Mrs. Ellis's reliance on the "meeting of the minds" was a lawyer's afterthought. Was this the critical point? One cannot tell. But the court affirmed; specific performance was decreed. The house on Fifth Avenue, in Baraboo, was transferred irrevocably to Harlan Kelley, by command of the Wisconsin Supreme Court.

This study rests on these men, women, and events: on people like Rosaline Peck, Chauncey Brown, Walter Pratt and E. L. Darling, Harlan Kelley and Mrs. Ellis, the immediate actors; and on a large subordinate cast—the notary public, the eager salesman, the Baraboo broker, and others. Nor must one forget the role of the judges in these little dramas. The cases end up as statistics; in formal legal scholarship, each one is filed away in the law's elaborate indexing system as an abstract proposition, establishing or confirming some precept of the law of contracts. Yet each case was firmly rooted in its time and place: a tract of pioneer farmland, a village store in the days of Theodore Roosevelt, a house on courthouse square. In addition, each case as it takes its place in the printed records of the law of Wisconsin speaks, in however muffled a voice, to the judges who apply the law, to the lawyers who act on and under that law, and to the clients who seek their advice. These are basic raw materials, out of which the law of contracts is made.

This study undertakes to examine the relations between the law of contract and the general life of society (particularly economic life) in one state (Wisconsin) over the course of a century, beginning with the {10} period of intensive settlement prior to the Civil War and ending with the 1950's. The law of contracts has been much studied, examined, dissected, and analyzed in legal literature, but usually simply to achieve a pattern of formal concepts rationally classified so as to serve the needs of lawyers and judges who use contract concepts as tools of analysis, draftsmanship, and decision. The dominant purpose of contract scholarship has been taxonomy, despite an occasional glance at broader social, economic, and psychological implications of the concepts of the law of contract. This study asks, however, what more can be learned about contract behavior and contract law (and about the common law in the United States in general) by taking an approach less formal and static. From the standpoint of the historian or social scientist, one trouble with formal legal scholarship is that it tends to exhaust its energy with presenting the body of law (which is the end product of social and legal development) as if it were a timeless catalog of existing rules, without differentiating the contents in terms of their age, importance, and utility. An exposition of "current" contract law will typically tell nothing of the economic importance or unimportance of particular precepts; whether they are adhered to in practice or not; whether they pertain to living issues or to rare or peripheral situations. Yet contract law is essentially a series of rules inductively arrived at through generalizing appellate court cases; these cases typically arise out of bargains in the marketplace or behavior which can be analogized to marketplace behavior; economic and social forces must, therefore, have played a major, probably decisive, role in determining the character and content of contract law. Since the economic system of the United States gives freedom of contract (on which contract law depends) more legal scope than do preindustrial and socialistic economic systems, the causal connection between the social background and the law of contract can be taken as axiomatic. It is also axiomatic that law changes along with its society, although the relative rates of change and the modes of interaction between legal and other social institutions have never been adequately researched.

In this study, we seek to examine contract behavior and contract law with greater emphasis on (a) the development of values and processes through the accretion of experience and custom (that is, "doctrine" considered as a product of time or history); and (b) the functions which contract behavior and contract law more or less fulfill in the {11} service of larger institutions of society (the legal order itself, the market, political, and social processes).

Legal scholarship has been much enriched, particularly in recent years, by adopting a historical, sociological, or economic approach in case-studies of the legal development of particular fields of law. Most of such studies, however, have chosen to explore statutory fields of law—railroad law or corporation law are two major examples. Case-studies of common-law fields have been much rarer. This study deliberately chooses a field—contract—which is basically judge-made. Study of such a field sacrifices the advantages of dealing with data which have major economic or political importance in themselves; no contract case is likely to be a great case which gives rise to public controversy and debate. On the other hand, the study gains the advantage of dealing with a field whose importance lies, if anywhere, in the aggregate of many mine-run cases and instances and which therefore may tell more about the legal and economic substratum of our society than a story written in blood or headlines.

This study explores contract law and contract behavior as revealed in the opinions of the Wisconsin Supreme Court and the work of some other agencies of Wisconsin government, especially the Wisconsin legislature. Our focus on Wisconsin is taken to obtain the benefits of a close, sharp view of the concrete reality of events. The choice of Wisconsin does not imply that the law of contract was a body of law which Wisconsin originated. Indeed, Wisconsin lawmakers did not greatly influence the general course of contract law. What we study is a general body of law whose formal contours were derived from other sources, modified and applied in the context of a particular social setting. We study Wisconsin contract law as a dialect, as it were, of the parent speech; like all dialects, it may shed valuable light on the parent speech as well as on the characteristics of its own native speakers.

The decisions of the Wisconsin Supreme Court on contract questions form the basic material of the study. These cases have been drawn from three periods. Period I covers the time between the organization of Wisconsin Territory (1836) and the outbreak of the Civil War (1861); the study embraces all reported contract decisions during this span of years. This period is significant in that it marks the beginning of Wisconsin's functioning legal system; it also coincides with the "frontier" period in the state, a period which had just about ended at the time of {12} the Civil War. For Period II, 1905-1915, the cases were drawn from the years 1905-1907, and 1913. This period is equidistant in time between Periods I and III; more important, it provides a sample of legal materials drawn from the age of the Progressives in Wisconsin. This was a time in which the consequences of a maturing economic system and the effects of the post-Civil War industrialization and urbanization of the state had been strongly felt, and had called forth a set of major legal and social responses which reached a kind of climax during the days of the La Follette Progressives. For Period III (the decade of the 1950's), the cases were drawn from the years 1955-1958. The major characteristics of this period, on the threshold of the present, will be known to most readers: the post-World War II economic boom, the growth of the metropolitan areas, the cold war, the continuance of the big government of wartime and depression, and an ever increasing unification of the country through mass communications and transport. In Periods II and III, the volume of decisions of the Court was heavier than in Period I, and reporting was more complete. For these two periods, it was necessary to use a sample (large but limited) in order to examine the materials with the necessary intensity.

Within each period the cases were analyzed and tabulated according to their underlying fact-situations and their use of legal doctrines. The total number of tabulated cases comes to 553. Intensive use was made of the briefs and records of the cases as well. Unfortunately, for Period I most of these have been lost; for Periods II and III the records were full and invaluable. Within each period some examination was also made of non-contract cases, which shed incidental light on major topics and helped place the contract cases in perspective, i.e., in relation to the general flow of appellate court business.

The second major source material for the study was the output of the Wisconsin legislature. For Period I the entire legislative output up to 1861 was surveyed, for Period II the sessions of 1905 through 1915, for Period III the sessions of 1955 and 1957. Selective use was also made of bills which did not pass and of whatever legislative history was available. The newspapers were an important source for Period I. For Periods II (especially) and III the opinions of the Attorney General of Wisconsin were quite useful. Manuscripts, treatises, government documents, and secondary sources of all sorts were used as much as possible where they seemed to be needed. The work of the lower courts offers a potentially {13} rich, though unwieldy, source, but one which was on the whole inaccessible because of the costs of exploring it. The study, therefore, can promise accuracy and rigor of measurement only insofar as it relates to the high court and the legislature.

Wisconsin: the Background.[4] Wisconsin was the last state east of the Mississippi to be admitted to the union. The Wisconsin Territory was created in 1836 when Michigan became a state and what was left of Michigan Territory was reorganized. The boundaries of the Territory then included, in addition to the present state of Wisconsin, what is now Iowa, Minnesota, and portions of the Dakotas. Until the 1820's, this area had been occupied sparsely by

Indians and fur-traders. Lead mining, in the southwest corner of the state, brought in several thousand miners in the 1820's. Land offices were opened in Green Bay and Mineral Point in 1834. In 1836 the population was about 11,000; by 1840 it had grown to almost 31,000. In the next decade a flood of settlers poured into the southeast and central parts of the state and along the Michigan shoreline, increasing the population by more than 800 per cent, to 305,391. In 1860 the population was 775,881. Since then the population has risen steadily, by increments of approximately 300,000 per decade, though naturally the percentage of increase has been declining. Between 1950 and 1960, however, more than one-half million people were added to the population of the state. According to the 1960 census, the state population was 3,952,765, a little less than double the 1900 population (2,069,042).

After the fur-trading and lead-mining days, the state settled into a typical agricultural pattern. The major cash crop before the Civil War was wheat. In northern Wisconsin the lumber industry grew spectacularly, but by the turn of the century had largely passed into history. Since the late nineteenth century Wisconsin has been famous as "America's dairyland." But the urban-industrial aspects of the state's economy have been constantly increasing in importance. In 1850 about 90 per cent of the population was classified as "rural." In 1900, 38.2 per cent was urban, in 1960, 63.8 per cent. The definition of "urban" and "rural" has not remained constant since the first censuses, but in any event the trend is unmistakable. In 1960 more than one out of every four residents of Wisconsin lived in Milwaukee County. The population in farm and timber counties was static and declining; in the urban areas, the growth was phenomenal. Basically, the state had only one great metropolitan area—Milwaukee, but other urban areas (e.g., Madison) were also growing rapidly while the population of Ashland County, in the far north, was about two-thirds what it had been in 1920. The shift from rural to urban population paralleled a shift in the major occupations of Wisconsin's residents. The farm population constantly declined as the industrial-commercial population rose. Where men trapped fur-bearing animals and later farmed, now factories, stores, and offices pre-empted land and energy. Parallel with the increases in population, and the rural-urban population shift, went changes in economic organization: trails and plank roads were replaced by a railroad net and modern highways; marketing methods went through successive stages of increasing complexity, rationality, and economic interdependence. The precise flow of social events, the precise economic and demographic base that developed over the course of the century was unique to Wisconsin; but the waves of change were (in general) of national or at least regional significance. It was always a fact, for Wisconsin as for every other American state, that the boundaries of state jurisdiction were political barriers only, not economic or social. {page 15 follows, to begin the next chapter}

I
TOWARD A WORKING DEFINITION OF CONTRACT

OF COURSE, to study contract we need a definition of that term. Preferably, a definition of contract should be more than conventional, that is, it should describe at any given time some real phenomena, some genuine subject matter, in addition to marking the boundaries of a formal concept of classification. The usual textbook definitions[1] are not particularly helpful. They are typically of marvelous vagueness. Furthermore, many text writers feel a need to frame a definition which can cover not only actual agreements (deliberately arranged transactions) but also a wider range of relationships between parties which the law has treated as contractual by fiction or analogy. Also, the law of contract changes subtly as it moves through space and time, even within the time span treated in this study.

If our aim is to understand the relations of law to the patterns and processes of the general life of the community, then our definition of "contract" should properly begin with the kinds of behavior which create needs which the law of contract seeks to serve in the period and the society under study. This behavior is, in the ordinary situation, and in the ordinary use of language, the effort to achieve and carry out voluntary agreements. A contract in the popular sense of the word is an agreement between two or more parties, usually for the exchange of what the parties consider equivalents. Not all agreements are enforceable through the use of legal process, and a good deal of the content of the Anglo-American law of contract is concerned with deciding which agreements are enforceable and why. One man's promise to pay $10,000 to another man for an assassination is an agreement which cannot be enforced in our society; this agreement is said to be "against public policy" or "illegal." Both the assassin and his employer are guilty {16} of a crime, of course, but it does not necessarily follow that the assassin must be deprived of his chance to collect money for successfully carrying out the murder. In some states, a person responsible for the death of another may inherit his victim's estate or collect his insurance.[2] Members of a free people are said to be, in general, free to make whatever agreements they want to; and the law promises to enforce these agreements, if asked to. The concept of "illegality" means that there are exceptions to this general rule. It therefore narrows (admittedly to a minor degree, since the common-law concept of "illegality" had and has small scope) the universe of possible enforceable contracts in Anglo-American law.

Let us look at another kind of agreement, an agreement between two corporations, both in the business of making soaps and detergents, both large and successful. The two corporations agree to merge, after many years of economic warfare. Corporation lawyers draw up long documents, which certainly comply in every formal respect with the lawyer's law of "contract." Is the agreement to merge valid, that is, enforceable? Certainly there is a "contract" here, in the sense that the parties have intended to make a formally valid agreement, but the "contract" may violate the Sherman Act or some of the other statutes and rules of law which make up the field called anti-trust law. This agreement to merge does not offend the law of contracts; it may offend some other body of law, which has enough shape and vigor of its own to have a name, a roomful of literature, and (in this case at least) a body of government officials charged with applying, administering, and enforcing it.

The assassin's contract and the soap companies' contract have certain similarities. Some consideration external to the formal aspects of the contract steps in and prevents enforcement. Conventionally, the assassin case might be called a "contracts" case, while the soap case would be recognized by lawyers as an "anti-trust" case and not a "contracts" case at all. This difference in classification comes about for a number of reasons. Judges invented the first limitation; in contrast, though a rudimentary concept of restraint of trade existed at common law, anti-trust law is largely statutory. More important (though connected with this difference in official source) is the fact that anti-trust law is institutionalized: it is a body of policy of enough complexity to be separately studied, it has great impact on business and legal behavior, and it is administered by specialists of its own. Still, in both {17} instances, the outcome of a weighing of policy is that the agreements are denied enforcement.

A third case might be put which differs in one respect from these two. Let us assume a fairly elaborate employment contract—say a contract between a university and a professor of chemistry—which specifies the annual salary, grants tenure to the professor, provides for automatic renewal unless timely notice is given, specifies that any inventions or discoveries of the professor belong to the university, and also forbids membership in any teacher's union. Presumably most disputes arising under the contract would be subject to the law of contract; but the no-union clause is not valid, at least in Wisconsin, under Wisconsin Statutes §103.46(1). Here the contract as a whole is valid, or at least its validity will be tested by the general law of contract. But a specific provision of "labor law" has subtracted one particular provision from the universe of allowable clauses in the contract. There are also some mandatory consequences which flow from the fact of the contract; they cannot be bargained away and are never even expressed. For example, the employer will withhold for income tax purposes some of the gross salary, paying the money withheld to the federal government. In other words, if we start (perhaps naively) with the idea that the law of contracts is coextensive with the universe of enforceable agreements and all allowable terms of all possible agreements, then any positive rule of law or statute which subtracts from or adds to the universe of allowable terms or agreements narrows or expands the potential area of the law of contracts. The law of contract, then, is residuary; it applies to those agreements that are not subject, in whole or in part, to special legal treatment, by virtue of some special statute or legal rule (the tax law, the statute on union membership clauses, the anti-trust law).

It may be worthwhile to approach the matter from another angle. Quite clearly, Anglo-American law now pays more attention to contract than medieval English law ever did. The rise of contract to legal prominence is fairly recent. Blackstone's classic exposition of the common law was written shortly before the American Revolution; in it, only a few short sections concern contract, while the special doctrines of real-property law fill almost the whole of one of the four books of the *Commentaries* and color much of the rest. The second edition of Viner's *Abridgment*, published in the late eighteenth century, gives 47 pages of text to the subject "Contract and Agreement," out of a work of {18} many volumes.[3] The nineteenth century was very different. Even in the lawyer's narrow sense, the law of contract swelled into one of the main branches of legal learning.[4] There were no important treatises on the law of contracts published until the nineteenth century; the appearance then of such works was a sure sign that the lawyers saw bread-and-butter importance to the field. When Christopher Columbus Langdell, in the 1870's, undertook to reform legal education and to establish the case method of instruction, he began the career of the law school case-book with a volume on contracts.[5] In mid-twentieth century the subject remains an immutable pillar of the first-year curriculum of every law school.

This success was (at first) no accident. Contract law was not, in the nineteenth century, a set of new doctrines to deal with changing technology (like railroad law), or with new kinds of behavior. It was rather an old set of doctrines which grew by meeting and partially destroying its rivals. The subject matter of contract expanded remarkably. Many Wisconsin cases where the court at least talked "contract" were cases about land—the sale of land, the financing of land, the exploitation of land. In these cases land was treated as a commodity traded on the open market. Even for Period I, and much more so for later periods, we shall have to qualify the statement that land was treated as a commodity. But the Wisconsin land contract cases were certainly quite different from the classic English land cases, which filled the crabbed pages of the medieval year books and the Renaissance reports. The difference was more than one of style. Older land law was characterized by rules leaving little room for voluntary arrangements. Thus, in the descent of lands, when a landowner died, his property descended according to a set statutory scheme. The classic common law recognized primogeniture: it gave the land to the decedent's oldest son, who inherited by virtue of his status as oldest son. Volition, intention, had nothing to do with the matter. Naturally, medieval land law was no chance development; a society organized in the manner of medieval England required a system of law which, compared to nineteenth-century law, was more rigid, less concerned with volition, more formal, technical, procedural, status-conscious. Contracts in nineteenth-century Wisconsin were instruments for manipulating external reality through private volition in a market economy. Changes in the structure of land law favoring private contract were the sort of change which has been characterized (using concepts developed {19} by Sir Henry Maine)[6] as the movement in law from status to contract. These terms, whatever their general applicability, certainly described a real trend in the common law.

When we say, then, that in the nineteenth century land might form the subject of contract, we mean that it could be bought and sold free of legal restraints. Contract is intimately connected with the domain of private property. The Mississippi River may not lawfully be owned by a private person: its use may not be the subject of contract; no one may buy it or sell it. A life estate in labor cannot be bought or sold, at least since the abolition of slavery. There are many lesser examples of restraints on contractual dealings; these may not amount to the removal of the subject matter of the restraint entirely from the domain of property and hence of contract; they are partial only. Thus, during and after the Second World War, the United States has sold certain bonds (the "E" bond series, for example) which may not be transferred. In other words, the government has refused to recognize as valid certain contracts whose potential subject matter was the "E" Bond. When the law so acts, with reference to a thing or a right, it removes the thing or right to that extent from the domain of the law of contract.

Modern law has endless examples of the phenomenon of which the "E" Bond is one instance. Statutes without number displace general contract law for particular subjects or particular classes of persons. A minimum legal wage of $1.00 an hour means that by law the usual doctrines of contract are replaced in one respect by a rule specially applicable to a particular matter (labor). Rules about the contracts of minors displace the general law of contract with regard to the specific class of contractors who are under twenty-one. Children, like the feebleminded, are said not to have "capacity" to form a contract. This is in part simply a common-sense limitation on contract generality. A newborn baby, to be sure, is mentally and physically incapable of contracting. But the law's refusal to hold a high-school junior to his contract has a different basis. The "freedom of contract" of this seventeen-year-old has been impaired, for some reason of public policy. Everybody admits that a line must somewhere be drawn—like the line which decides at what age minors may vote, drive a car, or get married. Other lines drawn around the freedom of contract of particular classes of people (for their benefit or detriment) have been and still are more controversial. A great number of exemptions from abstract contract law have been enacted into law because of an assumed need to protect {20} the weak against the strong, the farmer against the railroad, the laborer against the employer, the borrower against the lender, and so on. When these arguments prevail, new rules are born, and to that extent contract is displaced.

Basically, then, the "pure" law of contract is an area of what we can call abstract relationships. "Pure" contract doctrine is blind to details of subject matter and person. It does not ask who buys and who sells, and what is bought and sold. In the law of contract it does not matter whether the subject of the contract is a goat, a horse, a carload of lumber, a stock certificate, or a shoe. As soon as it matters—e.g., if the sale is of heroin, or of votes for governor, or of an "E" Bond, or labor for twenty-five cents an hour—we are in one sense no longer talking pure contract. In the law of contract, it does not matter if either party is a woman, a man, an Armenian-American, a corporation, the government, or a church. Again, as soon as it does matter—if one party is a minor, or if the transaction is one in which a small auto company sells out to General Motors, or if a seller of legal services happens to be a corporation instead of a partnership or individual—we are no longer talking pure contract. When the relationship of parties to land is treated as creating distinctive legal issues, simply because land is involved, this is land law or property law, but not contract. In contract cases land is treated as a commodity on the market, the same as every other commodity, and the rules are supposed to be the same as the rules for horses and cows. If a court says that an insurance contract is "just another contract," or that contracts between the state of Wisconsin and a citizen follow the same rules as any other contracts, the judges are making the same kind of point, are asserting the same abstraction. Contract law is abstraction—what is left in the law relating to agreements when all particularities of person and subject-matter are removed.

This abstraction is not what people think of when they criticize the law as being too abstract, implying that the law is hyper-technical or unrealistic. (Though often it is.) The abstraction of classical contract law is not unrealistic; it is a deliberate renunciation of the particular, a deliberate relinquishment of the temptation to restrict untrammeled individual autonomy or the completely free market in the name of social policy. The law of contract is, therefore, roughly coextensive with the free market. Liberal nineteenth-century economics fits in neatly with the law of contracts so viewed. It, too, had the abstracting {21} habit. In both theoretical models—that of the law of contracts and that of liberal economics—parties could be treated as individual economic units which, in theory, enjoyed complete mobility and freedom of decision. All goods could be treated as substitutable, one for the other, in money terms. All claims ("choses in actions") were assignable. All rights could be valued in monetary (economic) terms.

In fact, there was never any point at which the law of contract corresponded exactly with such an economic theory. But in a rough way, the rise and fall of the law of contract paralleled the rise and fall of liberal economics as a working philosophy. Mention of a few of the doctrines of the law of contract shows how closely the two ideological systems fit together. The classical doctrine of consideration* rejected the notion that any price fixed freely

---

* "Consideration" is often said to be one of the prerequisites of a legally enforceable contract. The concept in the law of contracts is complex, ubiquitous, and tricky. The core idea, as it came to be understood in the nineteenth century, is that a contract to be enforced ought to be an exchange, that is, a two-sided arrangement, with something contributed by

by two parties might be condemned in law as unfair (inadequate); only the market, as evidenced by what a willing seller paid a willing buyer, measured value. The law of contract damages took into account only generalized types of economic damage, ignoring any personal element (for example, embarrassment or humiliation resulting from breach of contract). Recoverable damages for breach of contract to deliver goods were computed on the basis of the difference between contract price and market price at the moment of breach. This formula assumed a frictionless and perfect market, operating instantaneously and universally. Conversely, the law of contract would not enforce contracts for which no market price was conceivable (for example, a contract so vague or one-sided that it had no ascertainable value) or purely personal agreements (such as a promise to attend a social function). The correspondence between law and economic theory was never exact. Contract law was not a book written by Adam Smith. Nobody purposely sat down to turn contract {22} law into an applied branch of liberal economics. But a free market developed, and grew; the law of contract was the legal reflection of that market and naturally took on its characteristics. Contract was abstract; the free market was abstract; and the two institutions directed behavior along similar channels.

From the standpoint of this study, the rough equation of the free market and the law of contracts has value. For one thing, it furnishes a workable criterion for measuring and defining what cases and activities should be treated as part of the law of contract. Among the cases decided by the Wisconsin Supreme Court, we can select all those which talk contract law in conventional terms, and in addition, those in which the fundamental issue confronting the court was to determine the borderline of the application of contract law; where abstraction ends and particularity begins. The mapping of this boundary can be quite difficult, but it is the heart of this study. A war-time statute decreeing price-controls is the most brutal, obvious sort of limitation on pure contract law. The slow drip, drip of case-law wearing away the stony abstraction of the law relating to insurance contracts, through waiver or estoppel,* was a different process, but still a clearly visible one. The manner

---

both sides. In the ordinary contract, it is easy to find "consideration"; thus, when two parties agree to sell a piece of land for $1,000, the conveyance of the land is "consideration" for the promise to pay $1,000, and the $1,000 is "consideration" for the promise to convey the land. A promise to make a pure gift, however, "lacks consideration," because it is said that the donor gets nothing in return. The classic doctrine, that the law will not look into the adequacy of consideration, means that in the example above given a court will enforce the contract to convey the land and will refuse to consider whether $1,000 is or is not a "fair" or "adequate" price.

* Both "waiver" and "estoppel" are common—and very amorphous—legal concepts. The term "waiver" plays a part (according to Professor Patterson) in "probably one-third to one-half of the lawsuits between insured and insurer involving the validity or enforceability of the contract." The core meaning in insurance law is "any conduct of the insurer or its agents that is legally sufficient to dispense with a requirement imposed on the insured

in which the whole law of contract, as applied by the Wisconsin Supreme Court, gradually and subtly changed direction is still a third kind of change. To detect this last sort of movement, there is no escape from the tedious job of reading, counting, and arranging hundreds of cases.

The working definition of contract developed here helps explain two {23} peculiarities of this field of law: (a) why, in a century of fantastic legal and economic change, the "rules" of a body of law intimately concerned with the operation of the economy remained relatively static; (b) why contract law persisted as a "common law" (judge-made) field, despite the tremendous encroachments of the executive and legislature into almost every other area of public policy.

(a) Since the law of contract concerns and provides legal support for the residue of economic behavior left unregulated (the free market), it naturally spends much of its energy asking: what range and type of transactions fall within the sphere of contract? The law of contract spends less energy, then, in defining value judgments and doctrines to superimpose upon those transactions it finds to be truly contractual, that is, governed by the market rather than by regulatory rules of law. Therefore, the law of contract is basically negative, passive and untechnical. The old English land law (for example) used a special, highly technical legal jargon; the law of contract has a much less colorful terminology. With few exceptions, the vocabulary of contract employs common English words—"offer," "acceptance," "performance," "condition"—which never wander too far from their general colloquial sense. Litigated contract cases usually turn on their facts, or present difficulties to the court because they go close to the brink of the area of abstract relationships. Contracting parties may usually by agreement displace the rules of the textbooks; the rules are stop-gaps to govern questions on which the parties did not speak. The basic rule of contract law is that contracts are presumptively valid and enforceable according to their terms. Major exceptions to this "rule" are indeed changes in the effective content and reach of the law of contract, but they do not look in form like changes in the law of contract; they look like labor law, insurance law, social security or public utility regulation. Contract law expanded and narrowed its applicability to human affairs primarily through a process of inclusion and exclusion. The

---

by the terms of the contract." Suppose a policy requires proof of loss within 30 days of the occurrence of the loss. The insured asks for permission to file proofs a week later than this deadline. If the insurer agrees, it may have "waived" its right to insist on prompt filing. In this case, the company might also be said to be "estopped" from insisting on prompt filing. "Estoppel" means a "legally irretrievable" utterance, irretrievable (usually) because it has been relied on to the detriment of the person relying. In the instance given, for example, the insured may have relied on the extension of time, and failed to file within 30 days. It would be unfair to allow the company to change its mind. (Edwin W. Patterson, *Essentials of Insurance Law* [New York, 1935], 418-21.)

These concepts have played a particularly important role in the development of insurance law. For their general use see below, pp. 122-24.

rules themselves changed less than the areas covered by them. No substantive revolution in nineteenth-century contract law could compare to contemporary changes in the law affecting inheritance, women's rights, procedure, tort, and government regulation of business. By definition, no revolution could take place because contract law acted as a residual category, its content determined mainly by what law did in other respects affecting economic behavior. Instead, types of transactions marched in and out of the area of contract. In the early {24} part of the nineteenth century, the law of contract grew fat with the spoils of other fields. Land became more and more a marketable commodity; leases, claims, rights, and intangible interests became subject to bargain and sale; in the north, free labor replaced slave and bound labor; the Revolutionary flirtation with price control was abandoned. The most dramatic changes touching the significance of contract law in modern life also came about, not through internal developments in contract law, but through developments in public policy which systematically robbed contract of its subject-matter. Some of the best known of these developments have been mentioned—labor law, antitrust law, insurance law, business regulation, and social welfare legislation. The growth of these specialized bodies of public policy removed from "contract" (in the sense of abstract relationships) transactions and situations formerly governed by it:

> The driving force which brought together fragments from every section of the law to make a uniform law of contract was thus the same as the force which eventually excluded certain other departments of law which might logically have been included in the field of contracts.... Feudal relations, domestic relations (such as master and servant), trust relations, have been converted at the magic touch of business into contractual relations. At the same time certain other relations, notably those between the State and its citizens, between public utilities and their patrons, and between employer and employee are being gradually, but definitely withdrawn from the control of the pure contractual principle of assent.[z]

(b) Because of its residual character, contract law resisted the tendency to be codified and included in the swelling volume of legislative-executive activity which marked legal growth after 1850. "Resist" is, in fact, the wrong word. Since contract law is basically negative and abstract, legislation mostly defines and limits it; there is no need to change the internal structure of contract doctrine. Regulation is largely statutory; the law of unregulated economic transactions (contract) does not require specific, detailed statutory expression. Actually, however, an astonishing quantity of statute law concerns the working significance of contract law. Even in early Wisconsin—where, aside from the Statute of Frauds and a few other instances of less effect, it would be very hard to find any "contract" statutes—a mass of legislation limited or promoted free contract. Homestead-exemption laws are a classic example of such a limitation: just as a minor is protected against some of his contract creditors, so the exemption laws immunized the homestead from seizure for debts. The statute limited the involuntary {25} alienability of homesteads; it removed the homestead, as homestead, from the general, abstract realm of contract. Period I could supply many more examples; the general growth of statutory regulation caused such instances to multiply many times over in later periods. The legislature had therefore little need to bother with internal, substantive details of contract law. Contract as a field of law is relatively amorphous. The goals of economic legislation were (and are) achieved more readily by fragmenting or augmenting general contract law.

Again, it was commonly accepted that proper division of labor between court and legislature gave contracts to the court. Legal theory assigned to the court the exclusive power of declaring "law" in the sense of basic, universal, underlying principles. The legislature, on the other hand, dealt with expedient, temporary, local or specialized variations (except insofar as legislation treated public utilities, franchises, banks, and the currency—institutions rather than principles). Legislative change in the fundamentals of the common law was thus "in derogation" of what was regarded as the main body of law; judge-made law was the norm, statutes the exceptions. This, at any rate, was the conventional view, particularly as it developed in the late nineteenth century. Measured by early nineteenth-century practice, the theory had, of course, a core of truth, though without the emotional and mystical overtones imparted to it by some later legal scholars. Oddly enough—though not accidentally, as we shall see—at the very point where theory began to become most patently obsolete, the "reforms" of Langdell turned outworn theory into the foundation-stone of legal "science."[8] Carried into modern times by treatise writers and the Restatements,* the common-law approach to law in the schools and in legal literature at its worst could be compared to a zoology course which confined its study to dodos and unicorns, to beasts rare or long dead and beasts that never lived. {26}

The relationship between contract law and the free market, as described here, brings us face to face with a central problem of the history of the law of contract. The problem is to map with as much precision as possible the changes which have occurred in the area covered by the law of contract and then to explain why these changes have taken place. The two branches of the problem are in close connection. As far as the contract docket of the Wisconsin Supreme Court is concerned, much of the change in the court's mode of handling its cases can be explained by the kinds of cases which came before it; the pattern of cases in turn is influenced by changes in society, and changes in the court's role in society. Society and the law constantly inter-

---

* The Restatements of the Law were drafted under the auspices of the American Law Institute, founded in 1923. The Institute engaged leading legal scholars to "restate" the law, divided into conceptual categories (Contracts, Torts, and Conflict of Laws were the first three areas selected). The Restatements took the form of a logically ordered and consecutively numbered series of abstract propositions of law, each proposition followed by one or more explanatory "comments." The propositions were designed to clarify and simplify existing law—to generalize the doctrines espoused by the best and most numerous jurisdictions—not to reform the law. In a number of instances, however, the Restatements did innovate. There has been a great deal of controversy among legal scholars concerning the legitimacy and feasibility of attempting to "restate" the law.

act; one obvious effect of the interaction, on the law, is a constant shifting and realigning of the power and importance of the various institutions which singly and collectively make the law. But because contract law in the classical sense is court law, the rise and fall of contract law is also the story of the shifting role of the Wisconsin Supreme Court in expounding that law.

In the study that follows, Chapter II will present an analysis of Wisconsin contract cases classified according to their underlying fact-situations. Chapter III will discuss the same cases classified according to doctrine. Chapter IV treats the role of the other major legal institution studied, the legislature; and Chapter V sums up the findings. {page 27 follows}

II
CONTRACT LAW IN THE WISCONSIN SUPREME COURT: AN ANALYSIS OF FACT-SITUATIONS

A CLASSIFIED inventory of fact-situations (Table III in Appendix) forms the basis of the detailed discussion in this chapter of contract law in the court. Since the Wisconsin Supreme Court is a functioning institution, its role cannot be understood without examining the raw material upon which it worked. In the following catalog and discussion we will summarize the relative quantity of types of contract litigation during the three periods, note how appellate litigation offers evidence of the course of economic history, and note the way in which particular main lines of public policy appear in the handling of the different types of cases (notably the relative emphasis upon abstraction, as against treatment which abandons abstraction to seek results more consonant with the court's view of individual or social justice). So far as the outcomes of the cases show this, we will note the effects on the case-law of judicial techniques and procedures, as compared with results reached through the legislative process. We will also attempt to measure very roughly what elements—loyalty to the legal tradition, economic or political ideology, the search for individual equity, or the pressure of public opinion—seem to have been most decisive in molding particular results of particular cases. These same general lines of inquiry will be followed in Chapter III, where we will deal with the same cases classified according to "doctrine." The emphasis shifts somewhat, as the material dictates: the chapter on doctrine will reveal more about outcomes; the chapter on facts will provide more details of the everyday processes of social and economic history.

Table III shows the basic classification of the 553 cases of the sample according to their general fact-situations. The 206 cases of Period I, 227 cases of Period II, and 120 cases of Period III have been divided into 12 general categories, 11 of them common to the three periods, the {28} twelfth (Testamentary Claims) used for Period III only. The discussion which follows takes up these categories one by one for further analysis.[1]

Land Transactions. This was an important category in all three periods. In Period I, 54 cases tabulated (26 per cent) were so classified; in Period II, 46 cases (20 per cent); in Period III, 22 cases (18 per cent). The land cases were most dominant in Period I; this dominance of land extends, in fact, throughout the tabulation: the sales cases concern agricultural commodities, and the debt cases usually involve notes secured by landed security. Considering the nature of Wisconsin's economy in Period I, the prominence of contract issues concerning land, agricultural commodities, and landed security is quite natural.

Land appears in the case-tabulations for Period I as a marketable commodity. This characteristic follows from the very fact that these can be called contract cases at all. The fundamental distinction in law between real and personal property still had great significance in Period I, as indeed it did in Period III, a century later. The distinction was not, however, so deep and tenacious as it had been in the older common law. It was a marked characteristic of English medieval law that the main concern of the common-law courts was the settling of disputes relating to real property. The special treatment accorded to real property interests in England served, first, the interests of the feudal system, and, later, the political and economic power of the landed gentry. At no point did the English legal system treat land as a pure commodity, freely transferable on the open market, though slow and steady movement toward freedom in conveying and handling real property interests occurred from the Middle Ages onward. Despite considerable progress in this direction, the common and statutory law of real property which formed the immediate background of the law of real property in the United States was an elaborate and delicately balanced system of intricate rules which most clearly served social interests other than those of a rapid and mobile land market. In the United States in the mid-nineteenth century, and particularly in a frontier state such as Wisconsin, the feudal, aristocratic incidents of the land law had no relevance. This was plain to everyone. A Wisconsin judge said in 1849:

> The tendency of modern legislation and of modern judicial decisions ... is obviously towards a relaxation of the ancient strictness in relation to the {29} alienation of real estate.... [P]rinciples ... originating in the policy of the feudal ages, are, in many instances, entirely inapplicable in a country like ours, and particularly in the new states and territories, where there is such a vast public domain, where the spirit of emigration is so rife, and where the genius of our institutions, as well as an enlightened public policy, favors the removal of all unnecessary restraints upon the alienation of land.[2]

This statement did recognize, however, that frontier Wisconsin shared with old England a special legal concern for land, though this concern was of a different sort. In Wisconsin, land was the chief form of wealth, sometimes almost the only form. But although a wealthy eighteenth-century London merchant might buy a country estate with manor house, park, and farms for prestige and comfort, the wealthy New York merchant who bought western wilderness land bought it for speculation, not for status and pleasure. For settlers, western land was an object of speculation and utility. The abstraction of the land cases was therefore not mere theory; it reflected a fact of life. The primacy of land in Wisconsin law arose not because land was not treated with more respect than a mere commodity, but to the contrary, because land was the chief commodity available.

The frontier attitude toward land was proclaimed by Wisconsin's Constitution: "All lands within the state are ... allodial, and feudal tenures are prohibited.... [R]estraints upon alienation ... are ... void."[3] The prohibition of feudal tenures was not necessary to the solution of any current Wisconsin social problem. The prohibition was borrowed from New York, which did face social unrest centered in the Hudson Valley, where the survival of non-allodial tenures led to violent upheaval.[4] But while Wisconsin had no particular need for the constitutional ban on feudal tenures, the ban fit in well with the state's legal attitude toward land. Abstraction was the basic trait of the court's land cases. One symptom was the consistent equation of deeds with contracts, in word and act. In *Welch v. Sackett*,[5] Chief Justice Dixon explained that "every deed or conveyance ... is a contract.... Like every other contract, there must be a meeting of the minds of the contracting parties." In another case, discussing the admitted difference between the rule of law applicable to warranties in deeds, and that applicable to warranties in sales of personal property, Dixon said:[6]

> The rule that there are no implied covenants on a deed ... grows out of the character of the instrument, and is not founded upon the nature of the {30} property transferred. The purchaser of land ... takes care to have inserted in the instrument ... the necessary covenants... The price often depends as much upon the nature of the title and the form of the conveyance, as the intrinsic value of the land itself, and where there are no covenants, it is presumed that the title is at the risk of the grantee, and that there was a corresponding deduction in price.

In other words, deeds and contracts of sale differed objectively, in the customary business practice which had grown up around them. There was no magic in the subject-matter; legal differences were reflections of objective, market phenomena. This approach—pragmatic, economic—runs through all of the land cases of Period I.

The land cases of Period I naturally concerned themselves with the problems of getting land and settling it, with the dynamics of the process by which raw land was acquired, traded, and developed. A fairly accurate picture of the methods of settling Wisconsin might be constructed from the facts of the tabulated cases alone. The cases point up the extent to which land was treated as a commodity. Many land deals were handled by land-agents who acted on behalf of Eastern investors. Some of the men whose names are famous in early Wisconsin history began their western careers as resident agents for Eastern investors—Moses Strong, for example, and Cyrus Woodman, who represented Senator Hubbard of New Hampshire.[7] Local residents encouraged such investment, since many of the pioneers were as much financial go-betweens and speculators as they were settlers and farmers. In 1856 Increase Lapham of Milwaukee wrote to a Swiss correspondent, recommending investment in Wisconsin real estate. "I shall be happy," Lapham wrote, "to take charge (for a small commission) of any funds you or your monied friends may wish to invest here."[8] Some enterprising easterners came in person with money to finance settlers. The legal system (the abstract law of contract and such parts of the land law which were apposite) provided a framework for structuring dealings in land; the legal system also provided a corps of professionals (the lawyers) whose training and ambitions suited them to render important service to the functioning of the land market.

Lawyers were prominent in the ranks of the land-agents. George Gale, a Vermont lawyer who settled in Trempealeau County in 1851,

> ... operated a general office for the entering of land, paying taxes on it, and acting in a legal capacity.... Second, he acted as a kind of real estate broker. Men would come to him to buy tracts for residential or farming purposes. {31}
>
> Often these prospective purchasers did not have enough funds.... Gale acted as a one-man mortgage company.... He obtained amounts of money from various sources to apply to land sales and then acted as a collection or serving agent on the lands.... A number of small contributors living in the East sent Gale small amounts and relied almost wholly on his judgment.[9]

Lawyers like Gale performed an invaluable function on the frontier, even when their professional education was hardly better than that of the mythical Simon Suggs, Jr., Esq., the boot-strap lawyer of the "flush times" of Alabama and Mississippi, graphically described by Joseph G. Baldwin. Many of them, however, were young men on the make, who came from the East with a sound stock of Blackstone, a good education and a lot of ambition. Some cases betray the sad effects of do-it-yourself draftsmanship; others show how the lawyers tended, in time, to introduce whatever measure of sophistication was necessary.[10]

The land of the land cases was usually rural land; very often it was wild and as yet untamed by the plow. Such land was frequently bought by non-residents, sometimes sight-unseen, either as an investment or as a possible future homestead. The cases often complain of misrepresentations by residents against absentee owners, either to induce the stranger to buy too dear or to sell too cheap. In one such case, Edward G. Casey, of Massachusetts, had been induced to sell; he complained that John C. Bellangee of Milwaukee falsely told him that Casey's lands were "very low and wet," far from the city, and quite useless, since Bellangee owned all the surrounding land except for the interest of certain Canadians and "some women in England."[11]

Though the treatment of land as a marketable commodity constituted a dominant note of the case-law of Period I, the attitude of the population toward the market and toward the land market in particular was never one of complete ideological commitment to a philosophy of individualism or laissez faire. Rather, the community owed general allegiance to such goals as prosperity and economic growth, ends which the free market was believed to serve. Particularly before 1850, many Wisconsin "settlers" were in fact squatters who lived on public lands not yet released for sale by the federal government. In *Pratt v. Ayer* (1851), Hubbell, J., discussing the validity of a transaction entered into by a settler on government lands, remarked that "possession was of value, in the estimation of the settlers.... Sales and transfers of such ... 'claims,' were frequently made, and for large sums actually paid. They were, then, worth money, because they would bring it; and {32} it is too late in the day to say that the occupant was a mere trespasser....

Such alleged trespassers have peopled and fertilized the great west, until the wilderness was made to bud and blossom as the rose."[12] Beneath the rhetoric are two cardinal points. First, the market normally tests the legality of a bargain; if an interest has a market, is worth money, it can presumptively form the subject of a contract. But this rule of policy rested on the faith that the free market fostered economic growth—made the wilderness flower. Free contract was seen not as an end in itself, but as a method of releasing economic energy. Neither the case-law nor the operations of the legal system in general fit neatly into any framework of ideology. Hubbell spoke of the government's "tardy" action in releasing the lands for sale. Wisconsin, though as yet thinly populated and lacking its later economic complexities, existed in no legal state of nature. The free market in land presupposed certain governmental actions: accurate survey of lands, public or private sales, a system of distribution and recording. History bears abundant evidence of the demands made upon the legal system which went beyond actions simply lending structural support to the free market. The Constitution of 1848, for example, admonished the legislature to pass "wholesome" debtor exemption laws,[13] an admonition that was promptly and vigorously followed. These laws (their detailed examination belongs to another chapter) were not consistent with the pure abstraction of contract: they discriminated in favor of debtors and against creditors, and the debtors in question were the farmer-settlers who wielded major political and social power in the community. Public opinion distinguished between "labor" and "capital"—between the settlers who turned their land into productive acreage and the hated "speculators" who created no wealth but kept lands off the market waiting for a rise in prices. The distinction was not economic, but rooted in popular attitudes. This pattern of attitudes, rather than any consistent economic theory, explains why contract law was allowed to widen or narrow its scope of coverage of transactions. On the other hand, after the panic of 1857 had adversely affected land values, depression, and not oppression, was probably at the root of dissatisfaction with some land deals in ensuing years.

The court's attitude toward land is well illustrated by an interesting group of cases dealing with "school land certificates." These documents were issued, under a statute of 1849, to those who bought the state's school lands on credit. The certificate holder was entitled to a patent when the state had been paid in full. The certificates described the {33} land and were expressly made assignable. The certificate provided vivid evidence of the fact that public wealth, no less than private wealth, consisted mainly of land. In a system which by and large treated land abstractly, land certificates made land market operations simpler and quicker. The nineteenth century created many kinds of land paper—certificates for military land bounties, and the scrip issued under the 1862 federal land-grant act are other examples. Yet the prices, terms, and conditions of these nineteenth-century documents were never purely abstract; public programs which such documents reflected were too much concerned with specific policy objectives—getting people on the land, favoring the small settler (or trying to), rewarding veterans, and attaining other goals not necessarily consistent with pure abstraction. The Wisconsin court, handling the legal problems of the school land certificates, pursued a course designed to take into account both abstraction and social policy. For example, the court ruled that the certificates were "contracts" and not negotiable instruments. Thus the certificates were freely transferable, but lacked the special consequences of the law merchant (a body of doctrine originally applicable only to merchants and now simply part of the corpus of commercial law), which would strip a defrauded transferor of his legal defenses against holders in due course.[14] By "custom" the certificates were often assigned in blank and circulated like bearer paper. But the court refused to give effect to this custom; this usage was "clearly not a compliance with the statute." The court also held that the certificates were not "personal property" but symbols of interests in land;[15] as a result, a pledgor of the certificates had an equity of redemption.*

The judicial attitude toward land cases was therefore strongly colored by considerations of public policy as the court conceived them. It follows, then, that the court's allegiance toward elements of continuity in the legal tradition—precedent, for example—was tempered by the court's sense of a higher allegiance in critical cases to more immediate policy goals. While the court at all times worked within the framework of the existing legal system, it examined that system with a critical eye. Certain lease cases show how the court was willing to bend the legal {34} tradition in favor of local custom as well as local policy (these cases also incidentally paint a vivid picture of the way Wisconsin's towns were built up). The "custom" in Milwaukee, "of many years' standing in that city," was "to allow lessees of naked or vacant lots, upon what are commonly called *ground leases*, to erect buildings ... and to remove such buildings ... at or before the expiration of their leases."[16] This custom was not confined to Milwaukee: a lease of a barn and lot in Janesville gave the lessee "the privilege of putting any building or shed on the lot" and removing it "at the expiration of the lease." In another case, the members of the "Palmyra Brass Band" subscribed money to build "a hall or house for the purpose of meeting to practice music," on land leased from member Higgins. The majority of the band had the right "to remove the building off from the land at any time." The hall when built, said the court, was "undoubtedly a chattel," and Higgins had no standing to protest its removal. A "custom" which could make buildings into chattels vividly illustrates the dynamic attitude toward land use in a new, growing state (not to mention the casualness of its architecture); the court's recognition of this custom turned the inherited law of fixtures on its head.[17]

The land cases of Period II are smaller in number, and a world away in

---

* The phrase "equity of redemption" here refers to the right of a property-owner, whose interest has been foreclosed by a mortgage creditor, to redeem his land by paying the amount for which the land was sold at the foreclosure sale, plus interest, within a given period of time. See Rev. Stats. Wis. 1849, ch. 121, § 11.

tone from those of Period I, with its rapid market and its sense of urgency. Some land cases in Period II are strongly reminiscent of a group in Period I—cases between land dealers, or land dealer and speculative investor with the investor complaining of fraud or misdescription of the land.[18] Most of these atavistic cases concerned "cutover" lands of northern Wisconsin. There, after the passing of the great age of lumbering, tracts of land stripped of timber were placed on the market for new uses. Holders of northern land were naturally anxious to "develop" the region. The north was attempting to duplicate the successful transition that had occurred 60 years before in south and central Wisconsin when timber land was cleared for agriculture. In the hope of bringing new blood and new people to revive the economy of the north, private and public promoters sought to attract farmers. James A. Frear, Chairman of the State Board of Immigration, at the U.S. Land and Irrigation Exposition at Chicago on "Wisconsin Day," November 18, 1911, promised a "warm welcome" for sturdy farmers who might settle the cut-over lands; while growing "profitable crops," their land values would skyrocket, bringing an "unearned increment" that would "more than double the interest rate" normally paid by banks; and all the while the farmers would earn a good living from {35} their farms.[19] Frear's speech was cast in terms which matched the hope and the rhetoric of emigrant propaganda of the 1850's. The marketing of the northern lands differed from the land-marketing techniques of the rest of the state in Period II. The corporate land company was not a major factor in the real estate business except in the north, where land could still be treated as an undifferentiated commodity and traded in volume in Period II. In 1911, the J. L. Gates Land Company, founded by the colorful "Stump-Land Gates," owned 150,000 acres of land, mostly in the north. Gates could and did trade in land as a marketable commodity, his stock-in-trade.[20]

But in most of the land cases of Period II, land was not treated abstractly. Land was now rather treated as representing differentiated space value, as distinctive location to which, in the course of time, unique use properties had accrued, sharply setting off one parcel from another in character and value. These properties were not merely the inherent physical advantages of one tract of farm land over another, but also those properties which accumulate with the historical development of an economy—position, good will, going-concern value, sentiment, tradition, and beauty. For commercial real estate in the cities the land cases of the two periods differ only in scope and degree. In the twentieth-century city, land use was more complicated than in the past, or in small towns; the big cities supported amusement parks, opera houses, and specialty shops as well as general stores, saloons, and hotels. In the cities, the going-concern value of real property had assumed great significance. As an economy matures, property accumulates certain intangible values; land-owners are naturally anxious to preserve them. In Period II the psychology of business reflected great awareness of the values of achieved business position. Greater importance than before was attached to business "good will," location and a fixed clientele; this attitude was reflected in the wide use in employment contracts and in sales and leases of commercial property of the covenant not to compete. This covenant is a legal barrier against the destruction of "good will."[21]

Most of the tabulated land cases of Period II concern agricultural land. But the cases did not concern "farm land" as much as "farms." The "farm" is not a factory for crops, but a home, a homestead, a person's "estate." Long before 1861 much of south and central Wisconsin had begun to undergo the change from farm land to farm. Homestead legislation reflected deep feelings of land-owners for their social situation. By 1905, two generations rooted in specific plots of land had {36} powerfully supplemented these emotional and social meanings of land legislation and land law.

The single most frequent fact-situation underlying the land cases of Period II was the "support contract"—a conveyance, usually of a farm, in exchange for a promise to support the former owner.[22] Almost all of these transfers took place within the immediate family circle and from the older to the younger generation—e.g., from father to son. In many cases, the family was of German descent. It seems pretty clear that immigrants from Central Europe brought the traditional form of the support contract with them to Wisconsin. This in itself is striking. Foreign legal practice rarely survived passage over the Atlantic. But the support contract was a legal institution only in a narrow sense; more accurately, it was a custom which contract law, basically permissive, recognized and enforced. (Other foreign customs, such as the *padrone* labor system among Italian immigrants of the 1890's, could not be readily assimilated into American law.) The support contract survived in Wisconsin and reached its legal climax in the 1900's. Reported cases were at their peak in Period II; field studies of the actual use of these contracts confirm the fact that these contracts were never so popular before or after. Yet the Germans had been flocking into Wisconsin since at least 1848.[23]

The support contract permitted the head of a family to retire from active farming, with enough income (in cash and kind) to live on, while he used the farm itself as security. The farm secured performance of the contract not through any formal institutional set of doctrines (such as clustered about the mortgage), but because the court would allow rescission for breach of contract. The contract also kept the family farm in the family; and it let the children stay on the farm as owners, without waiting for their parents to die. In theory, both sides benefited. The sons got independence and their own farm; the old folks enjoyed a dignified and comfortable retirement.

The use of the support contract implied a definite social and economic pattern: a stable family unit, rooted to a particular plot of land. In the pioneer days, the sons of the farmers—or even the farmers themselves—were apt to pull up stakes and follow the agricultural frontier. Probably most farms did not produce enough to support more than one adult family. And the population of the state was composed of relatively young men and young women. By the turn of the century, however, many Wisconsin farms had been "in the family" for two {37} generations. Problems of continuity and succession had become more important. Sons were no longer so likely to leave home for the new west. The drift to the west was replaced, though not completely, by the drift to the cities. But an old farmer could not usually afford to retire to town or city. In later times, when the old folks were more likely to go to the city, the support contract lost much of its importance.[24] Beyond a doubt, most such contracts were carried out without trouble. But the contracts and deeds were often home-made and artlessly written. Trouble lurked in traditional phrases. Some agreements set out far too much detail, inviting quarrels over trifles. For example, in one such contract (which ended in the courts), the grantee agreed to pay "yearly to plaintiff twenty bushels of wheat, three hundred pounds of dressed pork, fifty pounds of beef, fifteen bushels of potatoes, feed and pasture for one cow, twelve chickens and feed for same, twelve cords of four foot hardwood, $20 in cash"; the grantor could also "have the main room and bedroom in the stone house on the premises," "medical treatment" during illness, and in general, "good care." The excessive detail was bad enough, although the realities of farming made it easier to pay in chickens than in cash. "Good care" was, however, much harder to measure than chickens. Some contracts invited controversy by setting even vaguer standards of performance; in one example, the grantees promised to be "good and kind" to the grantor. Case after case in the tabulation showed the same pathology: bad blood, a little quarrel getting bigger, then accusations of bad faith and the collapse of the whole arrangement. As far as the evidence of the Supreme Court cases goes, the old folks were almost invariably the plaintiffs, bitterly complaining about their children and demanding rescission of the entire arrangement. In the language of Timlin, J., "unfortunate family controversies [are] almost inevitable when exacting and irritable old age contracts with selfish youth for those attentions which are ordinarily the gift of filial love rather than the obligations of contract." Another case the court called a "tale of insult, abuse, crimination, and personal violence upon both sides which is not pleasant to contemplate."[25]

Timlin's characterization of these situations is worth stressing, since it points to a fact of the deepest significance for the law of contract. These were "contract" cases, but they had almost nothing to do with the market. By stretching a point, one might make a market case out of *Gall v. Gall*,[26] where the plaintiff and her witnesses said that "some of {38} the pork was too hard ... to eat.... The beef was not so very bad. The wheat was pretty bad, it was fit for chicken feed." Possibly these failures of quality of performance could be measured objectively. But what of *Mash v. Bloom*,[27] where defendants failed to keep the plaintiff company and "entertain her in her loneliness"? And even in *Gall v. Gall*, Kerwin, J., had to scold the defendant for bad conduct: "though bound by contract, if by no other tie, to care for and minister to the wants of his aged mother, [he] did not speak to her when he met her on the road ... and spoke in the most cruel and inhuman manner of her in public..." Obviously, whatever technical language the court might speak in these cases, the abstraction of the market did not fit the relationships. The judges' comments show that they were aware what these cases were really about. Yet, most of these cases were brought *as* contract cases, and the results were embodied in decisions that talked this language.[28]

The support contract cases are only one clear example of "contract" law in a non-contract setting. Others of the land cases are almost as personal and emotional. In one sale of land, the seller was suspected of murder; he sold his land and fled to Canada. In another case, a bachelor was accused of "undue intimacy" with a married woman; he sold his land to insulate it from the lawsuit he feared would arise out of his misconduct. In another case, the court set aside a land transaction in which (in the words of the court) an "enfeebled old lady of weak mentality" fell "into the hands of the Philistines" and was "overreached by designing and unscrupulous persons."[29] Reduced to essentials, this was a case where the court reacted to what it felt to be gross inequality of bargaining power and intelligence; the disposition of the matter sounded a relatively new note in the case-law. Indeed, just as the dominant note of the land cases of Period I was the abstraction of the land market, with some policy counter-currents, so the main theme of the land cases in Period II was the overshadowing of the businesslike dispute in the Supreme Court's contract docket by problems of a more personal nature, cast in contract form. The cases of Period II did not, and could not, address themselves to major economic and business problems of the community. They stood out from the printed pages in all their unique particularity. What gave these cases their interest is not the architectural scope of the judges' opinions (as was true of some cases in Period I), but the humanity of the fact-situation.[30]

Again, the land cases of Period III formed a quite distinctive group. The support contract cases had vanished. Investment land reappeared {39} as a significant element in appellate litigation; this land was not, however, the cut-over lands of the north, but subdivision land on the outskirts of the cities. After the end of World War II, thousands of families left the cities for new homes in suburbs and subdivisions. War veterans led the way, under government assistance analogous in many ways to nineteenth-century public encouragement of western settlement.

Considering the social importance of the suburban real estate boom, its impact on the case-law of contract was not great. Still, some contemporary economic and social developments of comparable importance had no impact at all on patterns of appellate litigation. Like land transfer in general, the development of the urban fringes had some tendency to spawn lawsuits. A new form of business, or a heightened form of an old business, can expect the legally unexpected; even the best legal advice cannot completely compensate for imperfect experience and tradition. The real estate development business was risky and speculative; people buy homes only a few times at most in their lives, and homebuyers never form a "clientele." Compared to the labor market, the real estate market was more or less unregulated. Nonetheless, in the twentieth century, government's reach and impact were pervasive. Statute and ordinance were full of new risks for land dealers. The business was subjected to unpredictable political decisions. In some of the tabulated cases, consummation of a land deal depended not only on the parties, but on some arm of the government. Annexation, platting, sewer services, zoning ordinances—each of these types of official action affected at least one case in the tabulation.[31] Then, too, except for a few big city examples, land development was in the hands of small businesses, corporate or not. For those who tried to cash in on the housing boom, financing could be a major problem; but on the other hand, it took less to buy a tract of land and put up ranch houses than it did to run a steel mill, and shoe-string operators went in (and out) of the field. The market was volatile and (hopefully) profitable. In one case, a tract on the edge of Milwaukee was contracted for in November, 1952, at a price of $8,250; it was sold to a third party about three years later for $15,000.[32]

The tabulated land cases of Period III, by and large, conform to a pattern in which the subdivision cases fit well. A striking element of the cases is the extent to which they reflect the presence of marginal transactions, novel businesses, and amateur businessmen. It can hardly be accident that certain types of business appear in the tabulation out of proportion to their economic importance. In Period III three cases {40} (two of them factually connected) concern the problems of the drive-in movie.[33] The "resort" business also made its mark on the tabulation. A "resort," in Wisconsin, could consist of a group of ancient cottages on a small lake; the capital investment needed to run this kind of resort was comparatively small, and far too many inexperienced people imagined themselves in the role of resort proprietors. The Beiler family, who bought a resort called "Sandy Shore," in northern Wisconsin, presented a depressing picture of the "contract" litigant. Mr. Beiler had never finished high school. He and his wife and eight children were unfamiliar with the area in which they invested their meager savings. According to their story, they were told that the resort would yield $900 a year; in fact, gross income for 1952 had been $334, net income, $77. Beiler's business methods were rudimentary. He testified: "I did not ask for their tax returns or income ledgers.... All of [the] ... representations were oral."[34]

A marginal business is, nonetheless, a business. The sale of a house is not entirely a business transaction, though it takes place in the market. Cases of house sales were well represented in the tabulation of Period III. Nonbusiness, personal elements, as they affected the operations of the real estate market, give these cases their interest and cogency. *Kelley v. Ellis*, the case of the house on the square in Baraboo,[35] illustrates the admixture of personal, unique problems with considerations of the structure of the real estate market. Legal and business institutions developed which sought to maintain the rationality of the market for homes in the face of the fact that so many non-economic factors may enter into decisions to buy or sell. To take an example which is represented in the tabulation, in Period III most contracts for the sale of homes were made "subject to financing."[36] The phrase was not meant to give the buyer (or seller) an unrestricted option to back out, but the non-business buyer would not be held to his contract unless he could get a loan. Conceivably, trade might have developed a practice requiring the buyer to arrange for a loan before signing his contract. But lenders did not look only to the buyer's credit-rating; they looked to the value of the property as security. It would slow the market for houses to require, in effect, a "closing" prior to the contract. Consequently, individual deals usually proceeded in two stages: a "contract" stage, then—after financing was arranged and the title searched—a "closing" stage. The contract must bind, but not too tightly. The system was determined by the character of the private housing {41} market, its velocity and broadness of base, the wide availability of credit and the rush of large numbers of buyers into the market. The lender's decision to finance or not was a critical factor in contracts for the sale of homes—almost a condition precedent to closing, in fact as in law. In sales between amateurs the lender applied professional skill, presumably impartial and scientific. Refusal to lend often meant that, in the lender's opinion, the price was too high to support the loan. Lenders, brokers, and appraisers developed a gossipy, intimate knowledge of neighborhoods; they knew who owned what houses, what prices were paid for houses, what kinds of houses were easy or hard to sell, what people looked for in a house and what they avoided. Lenders, brokers, and appraisers brought this inside information to the party they represented, carrying about price know-how and market insight for the amateurs, like so many walking ticker-tapes. Thereby they kept prices in balance, within a normal range of fluctuation. They helped in this way to preserve for the free market system the traffic in private homes, even though all parties were usually amateurs; they rationalized the market and helped to exclude the purely personal, irrational, and sentimental elements of a business which stood constantly in danger of losing its rationality; where irrationality crept in, as in *Kelley v. Ellis*, the professionals were hardly to blame.[37]

Labor and Service Contracts. This large category here includes all labor, service, manufacturing, and professional contracts. In the three periods this class has ranked either first or second in size to land transactions. In Period I, 31 cases (15 per cent) were so classified; in Period II, 61 cases (24 per cent); and in Period III, 34 cases (28 per cent). The size of the category is hardly surprising. All but a tiny fraction of adult males pursue some occupation, and typically they either enter their occupation by contract or hire themselves out by individual contracts. But only a narrow range of occupations is represented by the cases. A few occupations appear in appellate litigation in marked disproportion to the whole; in Periods II and III, for example, cases involving real estate brokers were especially prominent. On the other hand, in no period did the manufacturer play any important role as a litigant.

To a certain extent, the labor and service cases of Period I give a truer picture of the contemporary economy than the cases of this class in later periods, as the economic order grew more complex. The labor {42} and service contracts of Period I reflect the necessities of a frontier economy—house-building, farming—and the activities of the older professions (law and medicine) and of the agents who handled land sales and marketing.[38] These cases, therefore, also document the primacy of land for the economy of the 1850's. They are actions for work done to, on, or concerning land. There are no cases yet for cultural services (e.g., portrait painting) or, at the other end of the spectrum, any cases dealing with factory labor; the labor here is by and large rural. And the cases do not reflect the work of teachers and ministers.

The labor and service cases, then, even in Period I, do not give an accurate or complete picture of the economy. It seemed accidental that farm labor appeared in the tabulation at all. The farm laborer either did not sue or sued only in the lowest courts. When an action to collect a wage of $6.25 for threshing wheat found its way to the Supreme Court, the judges were genuinely surprised. The claim, they said, was "so trifling in amount, as that nothing but the sacred rights of labor would justify the prosecution of it";[39] they criticized the defendant for his misplaced zeal in defending the action. The only employment contract case of any importance involved a high-salary, long-term contract to manage a saw-mill.[40] Nor, apparently, did employers sue their workers for breach of contract except in rare instances. The "sacred rights of labor," by necessity, were protected in the main by legislation. The legislature passed mechanics' and artisans' lien laws,* a "boat and vessel" act giving a lien to maritime laborers and suppliers, log-lien legislation for the toilers of the forest, and, in the 1850's, a specific statute to help railroad construction workers collect their wages. Except for the mechanics' lien laws, the Supreme Court saw little of these acts.[41]

The mechanics' lien was not simply a protective labor device. The statute, a native American invention, was of course pro-labor, in the sense of favoring those who contributed to what people most readily recognized as real wealth. On the surface, the mechanics' lien seems to favor the laborer over the landowner, the worker over the farmer. It would have been odd, however, for a state like Wisconsin, dominated by the interests of small land-owners, to pass a law inimical to the {43} interests of farmers. In fact, judging by the evidence of Wisconsin's mechanics' lien cases, the thrust of the statute was somewhat different. The average farmer did his own labor: only the wealthy farmer, the businessman, the mill operator or the substantial city-dweller hired craftsmen. The reported lien cases usually involved fairly substantial amounts of money; the plaintiffs were skilled workers or materialmen (i.e., suppliers). In one case, a millwright, John L. Uline, filed his petition for a lien in the amount of $482.25, for labor on a "double saw mill"; in another case, the plaintiffs claimed an unpaid balance of $305 for labor and materials "in the erection of an iron fence on certain lots of the defendant, in the city of Milwaukee, on which the defendant's dwelling house was situated."[42] For the time, these were not small claims. One further and

---

* A mechanics' lien is, in general, the statute-given right of a workman or supplier of materials to hold the property on which he worked or for which he supplied materials as security for his wage or supply claim. An artisans' lien is a similar device for artisans with respect to the property upon which the artisan practiced his craft.

significant point about the mechanics' lien is easily overlooked. By the act of giving real security to the worker, the statute gave a line of credit to the landowner; hopefully, building and improvements would thereby be fostered. The mechanics' lien was a promotional device, no less than the land grants.

Period I had a relatively high number of construction contract cases. Construction methods in Period I were usually crude, by later standards. Only a few trained architects worked in Wisconsin; and only elaborate buildings (hotels, substantial homes) were built from architects' plans.[43] Construction contracts typically embody one-time relationships and are more subject to litigation than other types of contracts. Even in a "frontier" economy, vagaries of weather, materials, and taste posed legal hazards to smooth dealing under a construction contract. Many construction cases centered on fact-disputes over the quality of performance. The "frontier" aspect of the economy and the shortage of hard money were visible in contract terms calling for payment in kind in some construction cases. Thus, in one case part payment was to be made by transfer of "clear title" to a lot and assignment of an "account and demand against L. E. Lane of Fulton, Wisconsin, at twenty per cent discount"; in another, $400 due was to be paid for in "2 one-horse democrat wagons, with half springs under the body and seat, set upon iron legs" valued at $55 each, the balance in other wagons; in another case, payment was to be made in lumber; payment terms in still another called for delivery of "full paid shares of the capital stock" of the La Crosse and Milwaukee Railroad.[44] Where payment was stipulated in such unstandardized units, the parties added one more hazardous variable to the contract. {44}

Though industry was as yet little developed in Wisconsin in Period I, cases on manufacture or installation of machinery played more of a role in the tabulation than in subsequent periods. The relatively primitive condition of manufacture helps explain this fact. Manufacture in the sense of large-scale production of standardized goods hardly existed in Wisconsin. The line (if there was a line) between the millwright and the "manufacturer" of machinery was slim indeed. Like farmers, artisans and "manufacturers" were representatives of "labor"; the manufacturer was not yet a "capitalist." Insofar as the making and installation of machinery was custom-tailored to the needs of particular buyers, the problems raised in lawsuits were fact-problems of quality and taste, somewhat similar to the questions arising under construction contracts. Water wheels, a lumber slide, fulling-mill irons, threshing machines, a boat's boilers and steam engines[45]—these products, which were the subject matter of the period's "manufacturing" cases, were less like modern factory products than like handicrafts; even the threshing machines were made to order.

The professional man made an occasional appearance in the cases of Period I—a doctor once, a farrier once; the lawyers a little more often. The "land agents" were the most litigious of the occupational specialists.[46] The agents dealt in lands for their own account; for investors, they viewed, selected, and entered lands, bought, sold, and placed land warrants, and bought and sold land on commission. Many of them were lawyers, like Stephen O. Paine of Platteville, "counsellor and attorney at law and solicitor in chancery, Justice of the Peace and General Land Agent"; but many were not, for example, Dr. B. B. Cary of Racine, who advertised his "Land Agency" in the local newspapers.[47] The lawyers were an educated class, relatively speaking, and skilled in the legal forms needed for trading in land. Much of their legal business was collection work; since people had more land than money, lawyers' fees and collections were often paid in land. Banking was crude and untrustworthy; the land agents acted, necessarily, as general financial go-betweens. This class, then—mobile, ill-defined, unorganized—corresponded to the real estate brokers and the commissioned salesmen who in later times replaced them as contributors to the court's contract docket.

The labor and service cases of Period II constitute the single largest group of cases in the period. As Table I shows, however, the distribution of these cases among the various occupations followed by {45} the residents of Wisconsin does not reflect the relative economic importance of these occupations. In Wisconsin's rich, varied and maturing economy of great agricultural productivity (not to mention the important industrial complex centered in Milwaukee), the appellate contract cases have little or nothing to say about the major industries and occupations of the population.

TABLE I

Labor and Service Cases of Period II

Brokerage	18
Building and construction	15
Personal service (home and farm)	8
Lumbering	5
Insurance services	5
Manual labor	2
Professional and artistic	2
Miscellaneous	6
TOTAL	61

Simple wage claim cases continued to be very rare; the sporadic examples—an action to recover $39 for "work and labor"; a dispute over farm labor worth $32.39—were mysteries of triviality.[48] The farm laborer was a low paid, marginal member of his society; he was unaware of his legal rights or uninclined to enforce them. The judicial system was not so structured as to facilitate efficient collection of farm labor wage claims. Even on the trial court level, actions by laborers (and against them for breach of contract) were apparently uncommon.[49] The industrial worker was even less inclined to use the courts. Although the state, through legislative-administrative action, intervened in the labor market (for example, by establishing public employment agencies in some cities),[50] the labor market never developed the contract-enforcement machinery which the commercial market developed (e.g., judgment notes, repossession, garnishment), devices which paid off because they could be used in volume. Even for commercial claims, the cost of going to law favored the larger business with many credit customers, just as the chain store later had the advantages of volume over the corner grocery. No similar collection machinery, legal or extra-legal, was yet devised to handle wage claims, either for or against the worker.

One type of labor service claim was, however, frequent enough—claims {46} for services essentially personal, performed within the family.[51] Some of these opinions talked about "implied" contracts; in all of them the economic grievance was real enough, but the talk about contract was metaphorical only. The son who works hard for his father, expecting a legacy, has a claim which he thinks of as legitimate, just as much as a cold-blooded bargain in the business world. An abstract system of contract law can tolerate a certain number of these fringe cases; legal theory has long recognized their existence and attempted to account for them. But if such cases arose in volume, they inevitably infected and warped standard contract law; perceptive judges could not help noticing how little general contract theory fit their facts.

The most striking aspect of the labor and service cases of Period II was the ubiquitousness of the real estate brokers. In eighteen cases brokers brought suit to collect their commissions. The use of real estate brokers was common in Period II. Of the thousands of sales through brokers every year, only a handful were litigated; even fewer were appealed. Nonetheless, compared with other occupations, the brokers took up far more than their fair share of the court's time.

The basic reason can be found partly in the nature of the business, partly in consideration of the type of brokers who litigated. The brokerage business was relatively disorganized. Entry into this business specialty was free to all. Professional organizations had not assumed control and the state did not yet license brokers. The nature of the business, indeed, was not conducive to internal control. The potential customers were a fluid, constantly shifting group. Buying and selling were usually non-recurring acts; the stabilizing effect of a "course of dealing" was lacking. The business required little specialized knowledge, despite what the "professionals" said. Any layman could fill in printed forms for ordinary deeds and learn how to handle a land transfer with a little experience. Then, too, Wisconsin (and America in general) had a long tradition of part-timers dabbling in real estate.

The land marketing and brokerage business was rich and colorful. At one end of the scale the large land companies of the north were highly organized and rationalized. The Tomahawk Land Company, which flourished after 1910, selected settlers, financed them, even rented them stump clearing machines. J. L. Gates sold land through agents who received $1 an acre for their pains.[52] In the cities and small towns, there were dealers who operated regular brokerage businesses over the years, as well as part-time dealers, some of whom sold a lot or two and {47} then quit. In the palmy days of land speculation, the farmer was lightly attached to the soil; land to him was (relatively speaking) emotionally colorless; every man was a potential land dealer. Perhaps the great number of fly-by-night brokers was an inheritance from this by-gone age. At any rate, real estate was an attractive side-line, not only for complete amateurs, but also for insurance men, lawyers, and stockbrokers. Thus we meet in one case with William J. Willis of Fond du Lac, who began by plastering and calcimining houses and ended by selling them.[53] It is easy to see why brokers were harder to "organize" than doctors and lawyers.

Of these various types of brokers, our eighteen cases concern, primarily, only one: the part-time or marginal operator. These were litigants like one Zitske, who devoted "full time" to real estate. But his contract was oral; he had no office and no records. He lived "just outside ... New London in Outagamie County.... I travel on foot, sometimes with a team, and sometimes on the cars."[54] The cases show great variations in the commissions charged, a situation which hints at that most dreaded of occupational diseases, price-cutting. Commissions seemed to range from 2 per cent to 5 per cent; the magnitude of the sale made a difference. In some cases the seller fixed a minimum sale price and the broker took everything he could get over that price, or split the excess fifty-fifty with the owner.[55] Undoubtedly, the part-time and marginal brokers had the most price flexibility; a man like Zitske had no overhead to worry about. Many of the part-timers were probably out only to earn fast, occasional dollars. But in a disorganized market the "regulars" had not much chance to maintain their own rates. A broker of Green Bay testified frankly, if ungrammatically: "We have not at all times regular ironclad rules which governs us all in our actions. It depends on the people I am dealing with, and the amount of property, etc."[56] Undoubtedly, another problem faced by the brokers was widespread public misunderstanding of the schedules of rates (indeed, of the nature of the brokerage commission altogether). The occasional buyer and seller of a house might view the broker's commission as an unjust exaction, a large price paid for a trifling amount of work. Nor did the public readily accept the broker's claim—more or less agreed to by the courts—that the commission was earned if he brought a buyer to the seller, even if the broker did not actively negotiate, or if the seller backed out of the deal. These problems were most critical for the marginal operators, whose business methods were the {48} loosest. Such a broker was not a member of a real estate "board," thus not sympathetic to the "gentlemen's agreements" of the trade; he haggled about rates and service, undercut the regulars, competed with them for available business, and brought the whole corps of brokers into disrepute through "unprofessional" conduct.[57]

Insurance agents were a similar group; they too figured in the cases of Period II. Selling insurance was another frequent side-line business; in addition, the agent occupied an ambiguous position, now representing the company, now the customer.[58] As a salesman, the agent might be compared to the itinerant perfume merchant in *Pratt v. Darling*;[59] as a kind of middle-man entrepreneur, to the real estate brokers; as a member of a loosely organized business hierarchy, to the franchised dealers who played a prominent role in the tabulation in Period III. In the fluidity and unstandardized nature of his relationships, the insurance agent reinforces the general impression of the kind of person for whose disputed affairs the court was the appropriate forum.

Construction cases continued to be frequent in Period II. Here, too, continuing relationships between customer and builder were uncommon. Satisfactory performance was difficult to measure; often at issue were questions of taste, beauty, and quality which were largely imponderable. This was most obviously true, for example, in a contract to paint or decorate a private home, of which the tabulation contains two instances.[60] But the problem existed even in situations turning on more impersonal performance. The architect's certificate, in common use in Period II, represented an attempt to find a rational and objective measure of performance in building contracts; the certificate symbolized the increasing organization and rationality of construction. Big construction companies no doubt behaved like big business in general. Advances in technology and technique forced out of business the amateur builders; the part-time home builder, unlike the part-time broker, could hardly compete with the mechanized, financially powerful builders of tall buildings and sturdy mansions. Construction was in the hands of those who could mass a team of skilled and equipped workers, pay them, and finance the materials and lumber needed. Consequently, although "building contracts" were a constant source of litigation, large-scale industrial and residential construction in the hands of established builders was underrepresented in the cases. The marginal builders, the obscure, upwardly mobile, imperfectly rationalized businessmen appeared in the cases instead. Period II's brokers, {49} insurance agents, and "builders" were brothers under the skin and had similar competitive problems.[61]

In sum, the labor and service cases of Period II strongly suggest the following hypotheses: (a) contract litigation, particularly on the appellate level, was not used as a mode of dispute-settlement either by big business or by the worker (farm and industrial); (b) appellate litigation was attractive to members of some service occupations who were marginal, pursued badly rationalized business methods, and whose occupations had failed to achieve tight internal control over methods of doing business and occupational standards; (c) in addition, contract appellate litigation was called into play to solve some basically personal and family disputes which used the language of abstract contract law metaphorically.[62]

In the main, the labor and service contracts litigated in Period III reinforce the impressions of Period II. Most occupations were totally unrepresented. The use of contract appellate litigation for non-business claims was represented by three claims against estates—basically ethical claims—of which two were brought by members of the family of the deceased. In the third, and most colorful, a penitent garage owner wrote out a death-bed check, payable to an auto mechanic he had underpaid for years. The decedent directed that the check be delivered after his death. Unfortunately, law and banking practice prevented payment, leaving the mechanic no choice but to hire a lawyer and search for appealing precedents.[63]

TABLE II

Labor and Service Cases of Period III

Commissioned or managerial employees	8
Brokerage	8
Building and construction	5
Personal service (testamentary claims)	3
Organized labor	3
Insurance	2
Professional services	2
Miscellaneous	3
TOTAL	34

Interestingly enough, the brokers' cases continued to come before the court. Unlike the brokers of Period II, the new crop of broker-plaintiffs were regularly licensed brokers, members of an active {50} professional group, with established businesses and fairly standardized business practices. Regulation, licensing, and tighter internal control had driven away the marginal brokers; but the inherent problems of customer relations were not so easy to cure. In one 1958 case the broker claimed commissions on repeated renewals of a lease first executed in 1937.[64] Probably the client was thoroughly disgusted with these "unearned" commissions. In other cases, it is clear that to a certain extent the brokers had brought their troubles onto their own heads. In five of these cases the customer's defense was based on a special section of the Statute of Frauds, passed in 1917, and applying only to real estate brokers. The "reputable" brokers themselves had hatched the statute, as a weapon against the marginal and part-time brokers who so plagued them.[65] Forty years later, through a cruel irony, the licensed brokers themselves felt the major bite of the statute.[66] In some broker cases enterprising brokers experimented with novel business schemes in such a way that their experience and customary business practices failed them.[67]

The most interesting and, except for the brokers, most numerous class of labor and service cases of Period III was that in which commissioned employees (chiefly salesmen) or employees with managerial responsibility were parties. A commission method of compensation can be troublesome; it is more complicated to administer than a straight salary; it cannot be standardized; moreover, it is used by highly competitive, struggling young businesses. In addition, the salesman meets the public face to face; his success sometimes depends upon building up a clientele primarily loyal to him, not to the company; success vests in him the power to hurt his company if he leaves to go out on his own. In *Fullerton Lumber Co. v. Torborg*,[68] Torborg managed a retail lumber yard in a small town for a Minnesota company. He violated a covenant not to compete and opened his own yard. Fullerton's business then declined by about two-thirds.

In *Georgiades v. Glickman*,[69] Georgiades signed a three-year contract to manage an outdoor theater near the city of Janesville. He was entitled to a salary plus a share of the theater's earnings. The contract was long and elaborate, and came out of the offices of a prominent Chicago law firm. Still, for all its care, it had a fatal flaw. The concept of earnings was not defined well enough to avoid the dispute which later arose. High depreciation on the books cut down the company's paper "income," and eliminated Georgiades' bonus. One of the partners {51} in the business, defending the company's depreciation policy, testified: "When we built our theater, there had been no drive-in theater ever built in any city in this Northern part of the country, not in excess of 100,000.... We were actually the pioneers." This was a new form of venture. The problems of draftsmanship and prediction were such that no law firm, no matter how skilled, could have foreseen all the details. Only experience would close up the gaps. The general problem (the drafting of clauses relating to the definition of net income) was predictable and in fact predicted, since the contract covered the situation as best it could. The specific problem, in relation to the specific (novel) form of business was not adequately covered.

A slightly different twist appeared in *Nelsen v. Farmers' Mutual Auto Insurance Co.*[70] Nelsen was "district supervisor" for an insurance company from 1937 until 1953. The company finally fired him for selling competing lines of insurance. The original agreement was oral. The company was small, but struggling to build itself up at the time. It gave Nelsen a good deal of power and discretion. This was a matter of business necessity:

> It was a small company and a company which is assessable, ... we had to go to appoint agents, ... to go out on their own expense ... and work, get up an organization. It took them years ... before they could make a living....
>
> I told this to all district men ... here is a great opportunity...; sure it will take some of your money and a lot of your time, but you will have something here after you get it built up for yourself. I told them they'd own their business. They would own the sales force....

Here the original agreement was free and informal—not because of bad draftsmanship, but because the business was young and the risks on both sides were great. Lack of standardization followed from the fluidity of the business situation. When the company succeeded, it sought to rationalize its business methods, and to reduce the power of the district supervisors; these men ruled virtually independent fiefdoms, and the time came to put them in their place. At this point the contracts were reduced to writing, standardized, and the demands on men like Nelsen made more precise. But Nelsen clung to his old privileges until the final rupture.

The relationships in *Nelsen* were necessarily fluid; their fluidity predisposed the matter to solution in court, not out of court. Yet this same fluidity meant that the court could not invoke the standards of a regularized, abstract market; nor could the court bring to bear on the {52} problem any specific legal experience, since by the nature of the relationships, specific precedent or doctrine was not available.

Sales. This category contains 30 cases (14.5 per cent) in Period I, 32 cases (14 per cent) in Period II, 12 cases (10 per cent) in Period III. To differentiate stages in economic dealings, "sale" has been defined here to include only sales at retail or for use, including casual sales between non-merchants, certain sales of crops by individual farmers, and private sales of corporate stock (but not issues of stock by corporations). Sales for resale have been classified as mercantile and are discussed in a later section.

Even as so defined, the figures for cases falling within this category must be used with special caution, because the tabulation does not include sale cases which turn on concepts of the law of sales proper. As is well known, the commercial law fields have their own particular history and terminology. It is true, that all sales cases are, in the broad sense, contract cases. But the common law has consistently differentiated between the concepts of sales law and the concepts of contract law. Within any given sales transaction, it is possible to divide roughly the "sales" element from the purely contractual element. Very generally, the distinction has been along these lines: contract law consists of those general principles of an abstract nature which apply to all contracts; sales law has embodied a set of other principles, not necessarily inconsistent with contract principles, but with stricter attention to a standard body of mercantile practice. The law of sales, in the technical sense, was never part of the law of contract; and by the time of Wisconsin's territorial organization, was in rapid process of becoming even more "special." The law of sales underwent a highly interesting development, becoming a curious amalgamation of common law and law-merchant elements, patched together to serve nineteenth-century needs. Since this study is designed to cast light on the social purpose of the law of contracts, care was taken to separate from the tabulation those cases turning on problems peculiar to sales law as a separate discipline (for example, the passage of title),[71] although the sales cases were taken into account in studying the ideology of contracts.

The sales cases of Period I concerned two chief types of transaction: the sale of agricultural products and domestic animals; and the sale of machines (chiefly agricultural machines). {53}

The sale of agricultural machines was just beginning to assume importance at about the time Wisconsin became a state. The first case, on the sale of an "eight-horse power threshing machine, and separator attached," was decided in 1853.[72] Agricultural machines were expensive; and they had to be sold on credit or not at all. The twentieth-century conditional sales contract was unknown. Chattel mortgages were well developed and governed by a Wisconsin statute; but although merchants may have used this device to raise money on stocks of goods, and although farmers were familiar with crop mortgages, agricultural machines were not sold through this financing device.[73] The McCormick reaper and its competitors were marketed by agents who worked their own "territories" in the state. Prospective buyers were asked to execute a standard form contract. In 1850 and for a few years afterwards, the form called for a cash down payment, the balance payable in December of the year of sale—that is, after the farmer had had a chance to sell his crop. The buyer was supposed to sign a note for the balance, but only if, after a trial, the reaper performed as warranted, and only "when called upon." The agents were apparently allowed considerable freedom to arrange the amount of the down payment. These terms were quite favorable to the farmer-buyer; reapers were new to the market, and the agents had to overcome the sales resistance of the farmers. As the reaper became more widely accepted, the terms of the standard contracts stiffened. Soon the contract required the note to be executed "after the commencement of the harvest." By 1856 the note had to be executed at the same time as the contract. The contracts spoke of a promise by the company to "manufacture" a reaper. In fact, these became not contracts to manufacture to order, but to sell a machine produced in quantity.[74]

Very few, however, of the tabulation's sale cases concerned manufactured goods—the sale of varnish by a varnish maker to a carriage maker, the sale of a pump for lead mining and the sale of a wagon are almost the only examples.[75] The most characteristic cases were closely tied to the land and its production—domestic animals (horses, sheep, and oxen) and crops, particularly wheat, which was the great cash crop of Wisconsin during most of the period.[76] Most of the cases involved simple transactions. Warranty problems were predominant.

By the time of Period II, the law of sales had become even more clearly separated from the law of contract. The adoption in Wisconsin of the Uniform Sales Act, in 1911,[77] symbolized the divorce of the two {54} fields. Yet the development of sales law paralleled, in many ways, the development of contract law. Both achieved their greatest formal perfection in the middle and late nineteenth century; both began immediately to dissolve into ambiguity and confusion. The process was at once heightened and retarded for sales law by its statutory form. Tremendous diversity in the economy, swift advances in financing and marketing techniques, and the rise of a mass consumer market threatened the law of sales with irrelevance at the very moment it was being stated in grammatical purity. The "law-merchant" as reflected in formal sales law was engulfed by the crowds of consumers and overwhelmed by the rationality of big business. In its own way, the life course of the law of sales mirrored dilemmas which plagued the law of contracts in the late nineteenth and early twentieth centuries.

With all due allowances for the separation of "sales" from "contract," the tabulated cases of Period II still represent a most peculiar collection. No more than the land and labor cases do the sales cases reveal the normal retail processes of the day. Many of the cases, in fact, reveal nothing more than common high-pressure schemes of the day, as practiced on farmers or in the country towns. At least seven of the cases grew out of the same general fact-situation: a promotional device for the sale of breeding stallions. Winslow, J., described the process in this way:

> A stallion of alleged high breeding and great value is proposed to be sold in shares to a number of neighboring farmers for the philanthropic purpose of raising the standard of draft-horse stock in the vicinity and incidentally of making money for the owners. An agent spends weeks or months going from house to house ... painting in glowing terms the benefits which must result from the venture, generally seeking to obtain subscriptions to so-called shares of stock in the enterprise, or signatures to notes for such shares, or both, upon condition that a certain required number of shares are subscribed for. The agent has many talks ... in the field ... at the village store or saloon. At these talks there is always more or less puffing of the horse, and word-painting of the probable profits.... Finally the requisite number of subscriptions or signatures is obtained and a meeting of the subscribers is held where the deal is consummated, the money and notes turned over and the printed pedigree delivered, and a more or less formal association of the subscribers perfected. When ... the notes are presented for payment it is frequently found that the roseate pictures painted by the agent have not been fully realized....[78]

In some of the cases the farmers were on the offensive, demanding cancellation of their notes and rescission of their contracts. Other cases {55} were brought by the holders of the notes, trying to collect—and piously insisting that they held as holders in due course without notice. The court thus sometimes had its choice of two fields of law to apply—the special doctrines of negotiable instruments or the law of contracts.

Possibly most of the stallion sales were perfectly legitimate; there is no way of telling from the reports. The cases were bunched together in the years 1906 and 1907. They went in no clear-cut direction. The farmers lost most but not all of the cases. Apparently, the court had no very strong feelings on the matter and was willing to let the technical merits of each case control; the documentation of the stallion sales was well enough drafted to withstand most legal attacks.

Even less reputable than the stallion scheme were certain endless chain plans and doubtful patent-right sales practiced at about the same time. One promoter, the Twentieth Century Company of Tomah, Wisconsin, appealed to "Thinking Men," "bright, active, intelligent gentlemen" who wanted to make "surprising amounts in a few days without much effort." The thinking man who responded bought the "exclusive right and privilege of reselling [the] Pole and Thill Coupling, Patent No. 718, 893 with double spring improvement, in the County of Gates and State of Wisconsin, to residents only of, and for use in, said Gates County, for a term of 17 years." More important, the thinking man obtained the right to sell to subpurchasers exclusive rights to work other counties, turning over half the proceeds to the company, and keeping half for himself. Apparently, the subpurchasers also had the right to sell counties to their own customers. Since there are only so many counties in the United States, the scheme could not go on forever. Participation cost the thinking man $500. The trial court saw nothing wrong with the plan; the Supreme Court, however, was convinced the plan was no "legitimate business enterprise" but a scheme to defraud "a greater or less crowd of dupes."[79]

Stallion and patent-sale cases made up almost one-third of the sales cases of Period II. The rest of the cases were scattered. Small retail sales were not represented in the tabulation. The age of the installment plan had not yet arrived, although some luxury consumer goods (e.g., pianos) were sold on time.[80] Farm machine cases were less prominent than in Period I. Sales were no longer made by itinerant "agents"; dealers had taken root, and had show-rooms where buyers could come to look over the merchandise. There are a few cases of casual sales of horses; but regular dealers and brokers had taken over a good deal of {56} this business, too."[81] The development of institutional forms of trade made the court's role in regulating the sale of goods more and more random and unimportant.

Few cases dealt with sales of raw materials to processors or manufacturers, or of manufactured goods to industrial users.[82] Most of the cases were really disputes over the quality of the product. Most of the defendants were foreign corporations, and the legal defense was that these companies were doing business in Wisconsin without a license. These, then, were cases in which a legal technicality encouraged some buyers to believe that they could successfully resist paying for goods they did not want or were dissatisfied with.

Period II offers some examples of controversy over the sale of corporate stock. The stock was stock of small, local corporations, or highly speculative mining stocks. The investors were men and women with little understanding of the securities market. For example, the buyer in one case was a widow who operated a hotel; the stock was sold to her after being talked up by her insurance agent.[83] The salesmen were part-time or marginal stockbrokers—men of a type familiar from analysis of the other contract cases. In *Davidor v. Bradford*,[84] the stock was sold by the "solicitor" for a mining company, who approached the buyer with a "deal" for joint purchase of a block of these risky shares. The regular, orderly, and tightly organized stock exchanges did not appear in the case-materials, and in only one case was the sale made through a high-grade stockbrokerage house, Catlin & Powell Company of New York. Even in this case, the "buyer" was not buying for his own account, but acted as a middle-man for "another party" who later backed out. The subject of the sale was capital stock of the Arizona Copper Mountain Mining Company of Phoenix, Arizona—doubtless unlisted and unsung—at 35 cents a share; and the foreign corporation defense gave the lucky buyer a chance to avoid payment, which he pursued to the limit.[85]

The twelve sales cases of Period III fall into two main groups. Some were not purely sales of goods, but added a "service" element to the bargain, for example, the sale of Perma-loy siding with a white enamel outer surface, to be installed on a private home; or the sale and installation of air-conditioning equipment.[86] In most of the cases the subject matter of the sale was a relatively expensive consumer product, particularly one suited for leisure-time activities. Commercial cases were {57} scanty. The goods sold included cars, home improvements, a refrigerator and a pleasure boat.[87] Usually, whatever legal issues were posed by the record and opinion, dissatisfaction with the goods sold touched off the dispute. The cases often had to discuss some technical question of warranty law; but "contract" notions came into play, either to avoid some specific provision of the Uniform Sales Act or to sidestep or enforce some specific clause in the governing instrument, for example, a clause cutting off parol promises or an exculpatory clause.[88] These, then, were cases in which private parties invoked contract law, not in its traditional (abstract) character, but to legitimize claims based on the particular (in substance personal) equities of the situation—not in support, but in derogation of standardized business methods and the abstraction of the market.

One or two cases of sales of farm animals also appeared in Period III. In *Ebenreiter v. Freeman*,[89] a cow and two heifers were auctioned. The animals were suffering from brucellosis; Wisconsin by law prohibited sales of such animals without a "report of complete negative brucellosis test." In another case, a statute prohibiting the sale of adulterated animal feed rose up to haunt a company which sold mink food to a mink rancher.[90] In still another case (the sale of a used car), the "speedometer" law, which struck at the common trade practice of tampering with the mileage of used cars, encouraged the buyer to resist paying for his used Nash.[91] These cases resembled the pure "contract" cases, except that statute rather than contract principles gave the defaulting party his chance to avoid the bargain.

The sale cases of Period III further document the fact that appellate contract litigation was avoided by major business enterprises. In only one of the twelve cases could any party possibly be called a big business.[92] No automobile dealership is big business; in one case, indeed, the dealer was in fact a subdealer of a Fond du Lac agency and the Lincoln auto sold was the man's "only Lincoln deal" of 1952.[93] Although incidental mention of financing methods occurred, the cases basically reflected random incidence of issues and concerned not finance but quality of product—that element of a sale hardest to standardize. The consumer sales were of products which people buy only occasionally (automobiles, refrigerators) and which take a deep bite out of their disposable funds. The money at stake encouraged stubbornness, while the moderating hand of course-of-dealing was absent. {58}

Mercantile Contracts. This was in all periods a small category: in Period I, 12 cases (6 per cent); in Period II, 15 cases (7 per cent); in Period III, four cases (3.3 per cent). Since mercantile contracts are the lifeblood of commerce, the poor showing of this category argues against any view that the court played an important role in the economy through the application of contract law. Period I at least had the excuse that the state's economy was at an early period of development. Wisconsin's commercial life, compared to that of the eastern seaboard, was rudimentary. But even from the start, this inland state depended on lake and river traffic; the merchants, like the lawyers, arrived at most two steps behind the earliest pioneers.

Before the blessings of a functioning railroad net reached Wisconsin, merchants frequently went East to buy their stocks of goods in person. The eastern houses who sold to them ran considerable credit risks. The Wisconsin buyer, if he could, might go East armed with a primitive letter of credit. Some of the more desperate eastern creditors were not above the use of strong-arm methods to collect delinquent accounts; in one case, a local merchant, Fay, in debt to a Buffalo merchant, was handcuffed and threatened (under color of an indictment in New York state) until he came to terms. The court hinted that this was no isolated incident.[94] Bulk goods, not requiring personal selection, could be ordered by mail and telegraph from eastern suppliers. Protracted litigation followed an ill-fated order of 350 barrels of salt, sent by boat from Buffalo to Milwaukee, which were lost in a lake storm while on board the *Juniatta Patton*. The buyer, Higby, owned warehouses and piers in Milwaukee; at a time when trade was so dependent on water routes, the connection between warehousing and wholesaling was very close. In the interior of the state, itinerant peddlers served the needs of the farmers. Though these peddlers excited some harsh legislation, they left no trace on the case-law of the period.[95]

Lake commerce was mostly "through" commerce, from eastern lake ports. But some coastal trade existed; we read about "a certain vessel called the Dolphin, used in navigating the waters of lake Michigan, and in the business of carrying lumber on said lake," which transported three cargoes of lumber from Manitowoc to Racine.[96] And a federal case mentioned a cargo shipped at Two Rivers, to be delivered at Milwaukee.[97] The court tended to treat lake commerce cases contractually, avoiding the technical specialities of admiralty law, in line with the court's general preference for the abstraction of contract. {59} Admiralty questions were often siphoned off into the federal courts, though until *The Genessee Chief* (1851),[98] the full sweep of the admiralty jurisdiction was not clear.

Between 1861 and the beginning of Period II, mercantile law became more and more subject to the special field of commercial law (sales, negotiable instruments) while the federal courts handled major admiralty problems. Even more important, large urban merchandisers and their suppliers did not readily use the courts to enforce contracts. Except for one isolated instance,[99] the big department stores of Milwaukee did not appear in the tabulation in Period II. Business in that period liked to keep disputes "in the family," formally or informally. For example, the Wisconsin Retail Lumber Dealers' Association had, in 1906, an unwritten "code" which provided guides to adjust differences between "the members of the wholesale and retail associations."[100] Rather than involving large scale trade, the mercantile cases of Period II were of the type of *Pratt v. Darling*. We hear of small storekeepers buying drugs, dry goods, perfumes, and toilet articles from drummers and traveling salesmen who represented small, high-pressure houses.[101]

The trouble in cases like *Pratt v. Darling* arose from a vexing triangle. The seller was anxious to reduce business risks and promote efficiency through standard forms. The small merchant was jealous of his little competitive bailiwick. The aggressive salesman was anxious to make sales. These aims conflicted with each other. The goods sold were unusually susceptible to fluctuating tastes and fashions. Perhaps it was important for the companies to establish a tough reputation, and to maintain legal independence of their salesmen's rash promises. To be sure, a few cases exhibited more standard mercantile problems—of quality of performance and product.[102] But these, as we noticed, had their own hazards. In two cases—one out of the Green Bay fur trade, another between rag dealers—the court struggled with the mysteries of private business usages.[103] Even in these instances, difficulties can be traced directly to imperfect standardization in the trades concerned.

Carson v. Milwaukee Produce Company (1907)[104] stood apart from the other cases. The company dealt in bean futures through a member of the Detroit Board of Trade. A short sale proved to be a disaster, since, unhappily, the price of beans went up; thereupon, the Milwaukee company became a sudden convert to the idea that trading in futures was immoral. Hostility to "speculators" was an old and deep {60} strain in American law and life; outcries against "monopoly" and the "cornering" of markets had been heard for years. But earlier in the nineteenth century the vice of "cornering" of markets was that (as people imagined) it choked off economic growth. From the Civil War on (e.g., "Black Friday"), the public fear took on a somewhat different cast. Manipulation of a closed economic system distorted the pricing mechanism, and fostered unequal division of the national wealth. The farmers may well have felt that to tamper with commodity prices was to slash at their jugular. Futures speculation was, in legal language, "gambling," hence against public policy. But this characterization was only a metaphor. Speculation was not viewed as personal immorality on the order of cards, dice, and betting on horse races, but as a crime against the economy. The public failed to understand the uses of a free commodity market. The commodity market reacted to public attack in predictable ways, tightening its internal organization and revamping its business forms. In *Carson*, for example, the broker's confirmation form read: "we solicit and will receive no business except with the understanding that the actual delivery of the property bought and sold is in all cases contemplated and understood." This declaration of intent did not save the contract; the court held the transaction invalid.[105] Probably Carson sued in the hope that Wisconsin would let him enforce his contract since no Wisconsin statute expressly prohibited futures speculation at the time.

Of the four cases of Period III, it is sufficient to mention only one example, a contract to grow sweet corn for a vegetable company.[106] The agreement was verbal. The farmer dealt with a man named Gatzke, who worked for two companies. Both companies were controlled by the same management, but Gatzke at the time of the contract was not sure which of the two he would "operate under." The extreme looseness of the business arrangement and Gatzke's autonomy were familiar elements of contract litigation in Period III. As far as the usual run of mercantile arrangements was concerned, Period III's tabulation was silent.

Insurance. The distribution of insurance cases among the three periods was somewhat erratic. In Period I there were only 8 cases, less than 4 per cent of the tabulation; in Period II, however, there were 15 cases (7 per cent); in Period III, 9 cases (7.5 per cent).

The relative scarcity of insurance cases in Period I is easily understandable. Except for fire and marine insurance, insurance was not {61} widely used in pre-Civil War Wisconsin. A capital-scarce economy was hardly a fertile field for insurance. Insurance made much more of a mark on the caselaw of the eastern seaboard states. Even marine insurance, historically of the greatest significance, played all in all a minor role in Wisconsin law. Of course, lake cargoes were often insured; in *Ranney v. Higby*,[107] for example, the shipper of salt bought insurance from an agent of the Utica Insurance Company in Buffalo. But the policies were written in the East, by and large; and if litigated at all were litigated there or in the federal courts.

Almost all the insurance cases of Period I dealt with fire insurance. In early Wisconsin, however, even fire insurance was not in universal use in the business community. L. J. Higby carried no insurance on his piers at Milwaukee; when fire destroyed them in 1852 he stood the loss himself.[108] The marketing of insurance had to take into account the critical shortage of money. Instead of paying a cash premium, the buyer often executed a premium note on which assessments were made as needed.[109] Life insurance was not widely held in Period I; few men could afford it. In 1856 the International Life Assurance Society of London and New York advertised in the newspapers the virtues of life insurance for clergymen, for "men engaged in Mercantile or Manufacturing pursuits," and for farmers with mortgaged farms. Only the last-named class was at all numerous in the state, and few of its members had the resources to take advantage of life insurance. Only one case in the tabulation concerned life insurance.[110]

The cases showed the court's basic bias in favor of abstraction; the "same rule of construction," said the court, "applies to policies of insurance as to all other contracts."[111] Still, insurance companies represented "capital" and they were mostly foreign corporations. Even Period I showed signs that the court assessed the value-choices at stake in such a way as to warrant a tendency to decide cases against the insurance company. This process eventually resulted in the creation of a special "field" of judge-made insurance law, even apart from the large legislative superstructure of insurance regulation.

By Period II, insurance had become a subject of much greater importance to the public; and the law of insurance had moved far from the abstraction of contract. The legislature spent a tremendous amount of energy on the insurance business. In the 1905 session alone the legislature passed 25 acts or amendments of acts relating to the insurance business, some minor, some major. At the 1907 session, 75 bills concerning insurance were introduced in the legislature.[112] As a result {62} of legislation, a separate and voluminous body of "insurance law" was built up; consequently, the law of insurance and the law of contract came to stand to each other in a relationship something like that of the relationship of the law of sales and the law of contract. All insurance cases imply an underlying contract; but they are theoretically divisible into "insurance" elements, and "contract" elements. It becomes, then, necessary to delete from the tabulation all "pure" insurance cases, just as all "pure" sales cases were deleted, and as "pure" labor cases might subsequently be handled.

Despite the tremendous growth of insurance legislation, in one corner of insurance law the court played an important part: claim adjustment (in the broadest sense). Through concepts like waiver and estoppel the court made notoriously hard the way of the transgressing company. In so doing, the judges stretched the language of contracts and policies, but arguably this aided the market rather than harming it. Clarence Morris has praised the courts for changing insurance "from a service safely bought only by sophisticated businessmen to a commodity bought with confidence by untrained consumers," from a "custom-made document" to a "brand-name staple."[113] This means in effect that the court attempted to rationalize and standardize the insurance contract for the consumer, who could not do this for himself. But it must be pointed out that what is rational for one party may be wildly irrational for the other. The more the courts standardized for the public, the more unpredictable the law of insurance claims became for the company.

Of course, the overwhelming majority of insurance claims were paid or settled quickly. However, it is not profitable for an insurance company to pay the life insurance claim of the beneficiary of any particular policy, and (except for very large accounts) only rarely is it profitable to pay a fire or casualty claim merely to keep the customer happy. The customer, on the other hand, could choose from many competing companies. He, too, would never compromise a claim just to keep his company smiling. Insurance claims, therefore, contain many seeds of litigation; the interests of insurer and insured conflict. This conflict could not be totally eliminated by rationalizing the internal structure of the industry. Insurance policies were contracts of adhesion (that is, pre-packaged deals); by their draftsmanship the companies could go a long way to devise contracts favorable to themselves. But the public asserted its interests with increasing force. Incessant statutory tinkering {63} with the internal affairs, marketing practices, and finances of the companies was followed by legislation forbidding certain terms in policies and demanding others. The climax of this movement, symbolically at least, was the Wisconsin Standard Fire Insurance Policy of 1895, a statute designating a policy form mandatory on the insurer. Cases arising under the Standard Policy construed not a freely bargained contract, or even a contract of adhesion, but a statute.[114]

The legal struggle between customer and company took place primarily in the legislative forum. But though the court's role was peripheral, it had some impact. For example, the court's tendency to stretch a point in favor of the little man's claim against the reluctant insurance company must have attracted some marginal claimants into court, to gamble on the sympathy of a jury and the favor of a benign judge. The Wisconsin Supreme Court, in its insurance opinions, vacillated between abstraction and a more particularistic approach. Some cases repeated ancient texts—insurance contracts are "the same as others," said the court; questions arising under them must be decided by the "elementary principles" of contract law.[115] This was the language of abstraction. In another case, however, Dodge, J., bitterly criticized an insurance company for its "reckless interposition of defenses" to a claim— defenses which had "no foundation even, apparently, in the imagination of the defendant." Such behavior was "not creditable to a corporation organized to supply indemnity to those unfortunate enough to lose their property."[116] This was language which recognized a public interest in the conduct of the companies which could not be left to the impersonal forces of the market for solution. Indeed, it would have been strange had the court adhered to abstraction in all its purity for a class of cases so heavily freighted with legislative attention. All agreed, however, that the companies had legitimate interests to assert. The insurance business needed standardization and predictability of risk and loss. Understandably, the companies resisted claims which stretched their credulity; they treated with skepticism contentions that insurance agents had made oral contracts to insure;[117] they insisted on strict adherence to their own formalities. Cases perceived by the company as arising under dubious claims were frequent in Period II.

In many respects, the insurance cases strike notes familiar from review of other cases in Period II. The vexing triangle of *Pratt v. Darling* finds its echo in cases where the legal difficulties arose because a middle-man (the insurance agent) attempted to maximize his sales {64} through dispensing with forms or formalities essential to the rational conduct of his principal's business. The overrepresentation of small and marginal business is reflected also in the insurance cases. Fraternals and small mutual insurance companies produced more than their fair share of cases. With smaller resources than their big brothers, these companies may have had cruder claim-adjustment machinery. Some litigation arose under sickness and benefit certificate contracts.[118] Here the danger of fraudulent claims was particularly great.

The insurance cases of Period III were quite different from those of Period II. The Wisconsin Supreme Court spent much of its time in Period III on personal injury cases brought by the victims of car and truck accidents. Often these cases were really battles between insurance companies; and once in a while a case took on a contract coloration.[119] Nonetheless, these insurance cases were only random byproducts of the personal injury problem. The highway accident had replaced the industrial accident as the bread-and-butter business of the courts; judicial systems everywhere were clogged with them. Of the hundreds of thousands of auto insurance claims every year, only a trivial number went to court; even less were appealed. Even so, the judicial system had a substantial role to play in accident compensation, and tort liability undoubtedly influenced rates and methods of claim adjustment. Insurance companies were tempted to defend certain kinds of suit, to keep costs in line, to discourage unyielding claimants, to present a tough image to shady suitors, to fight dangerous changes in tort doctrine. Plaintiffs were encouraged by big verdicts; contingent fees financed the poor plaintiff; the common belief that insurance companies were the "real parties in interest" may have influenced the behavior of juries; and it was possible to sue a poor man so long as a rich insurance company stood behind him. In any event, the insurance "contract" as such had little to do with the large number of auto insurance cases in court.

The other insurance cases of Period III, though highly scattered, tended to concern novel uses or kinds of insurance—e.g., "monthly reporting insurance," designed to provide constant coverage for a fluctuating stock-in-trade, group insurance and "key man" insurance.[120] In general, the fact that the category of insurance shrank in importance in Period III, while the insurance business continued to expand in importance, was evidence of the decline of the functional vitality of contract law. {65}

Business Ventures. This category contains those cases in which parties contract, not to provide a service or sell goods, but to promote a business venture, manage it, or finance it. In Period I, there were 11 cases (5 per cent); in Period II, 16 cases (7 per cent); in Period III, 10 cases (8 per cent).

Probably only in Period I, however, can the cases be said to reflect with any range the leading problems of business venture. Business promotion was an important element of economic growth. As such, it was a central topic of debate in Period I. People talked and argued and fought about corporations with the vigor of later debates about slavery, anarchism, and prohibition. A great share of the legislative output was devoted to corporations—chartering them, amending their charters, even regulating them a little. Insofar as the corporation represented an efficient vehicle for gathering and controlling capital for development ventures, it commanded wide respect during periods of expansion and optimism. The railroads came to Wisconsin as corporations, promising access to farm markets, population increases, rising land values, and general prosperity. Freedom of access through private contract to the use of the most efficient organizational form for the structuring of business, seemed perfectly consonant with the goals of the majority of the population.[121] To form a corporation required a special charter (or, in some cases, compliance with a general incorporation statute). The prevalence of an attitude of abstraction toward business organization implied, however, that charter and corporation act ought to become purely ministerial, that is, that the benefits of corporate form ought to be available to anyone who complied with simple, standard, abstract statutory requirements. On the other hand, when depressions and panics occurred, it was easy to blame corporations—the wild-cat banks, the corrupt and robbing railroads—for most of the state's economic grief; the never muted cries of "monopoly" and "soulless corporations" grew louder, coupled with demands that freedom of access to corporate form be limited sharply.

The cases of Period I on business venture, like the land cases, illustrate the dominance of abstraction (the free market). The land cases also provide abundant evidence that abstraction was means, not end; and that widely accepted ends of social policy were more highly valued than strict adherence to the ideal of abstraction. The business venture cases were, however, heavily freighted by the ideal of abstraction, because they faced directly one of the most salient facts of economic {66} life in Period I: the shortage of capital in Wisconsin. Hopes for the future and men's promises based on that hope served as substitutes for current cash, which was simply unavailable. When the future seemed bright, promises could be mortgaged or discounted in the present. In the absence of a sufficient supply of current cash, development had to be financed from outside, and natural resources (chiefly land) and future prospects served as collateral. These facts influenced the structure of business organization. Ventures were begun on the strength of written promises, cast into legal forms which enabled them to be sold (discounted) for cash, either in the future or in some market where liquid capital was more plentiful. The abstraction of contract theory was a vital necessity for the state's economic growth, since only through free assignment and discount of claims, promises, rights, and shares could Wisconsin build a civilization in the wilderness.

The most primitive method of forming business ventures was through a sort of barter or promise in kind. Standing timber could be sold, to be paid for out of the proceeds of cut timber. In a lead mining case, the owners of the land and the owners of the mining right sold their interests, not for cash, but for a share in the lead to be mined.[122] More sophisticated was the subscription device. In 1852 the "citizens of the town of Elkhorn," to secure "the benefits and advantages that would accrue" from the "erection in said town of a steam flouring mill," subscribed to pay various amounts of money to the builders of the mill, if the mill were completed according to certain specifications (e.g., "The building to be of sufficient size and dimensions for three runs of stone, and to be made of brick of good merchantable quality") and by a definite date.[123] A much more elaborate and socially significant example of the same phenomenon was the farm mortgage system of railroad finance, which flourished (if that is the word) in the 1850's. The farmer subscribed for railroad stock. He paid no cash, but executed instead a promissory note secured by a mortgage on his land. The interest due on the mortgage (generally 8 per cent) was to be paid out of dividends, optimistically scheduled at 10 per cent; the balance of the "dividends" would help pay off the principal. No money changed hands between railroad and farmer; but the promises were cast in a legal form capable of being discounted in the East or wherever cash was available. The railroad promoters promptly discounted notes and mortgages in the money market. The farm mortgage system collapsed when faulty railroad administration and economic depression {67} impaired the solvency of the railroads and threw the note-holders back on the farm mortgages which secured their obligations. In *Clark v. Farrington* (1860)[124] the court was asked to hold the whole program illegal on the grounds that the railroads had exceeded their legal power in promoting the system. Paine, J., refused to do so. Railroads were "enterprises impossible to private, unassociated capital," he said, and pointed out that, "no railroad was ever built in the country without disposing of more or less stock in payment for labor, materials, or land."

In *Clark*, the court met the issue directly, saw the choices and chose. The court well understood the business background and decided accordingly, although the court preferred to express its decision in terms of formal concepts—a shrewd move, since the collapse of the farm-mortgage system raised delicate political issues. In a period when insurance policies were issued against premium notes, when mines were worked on shares, when the notes of private banks provided what circulating money existed, and when promissory notes were the standard medium of payment, stock subscriptions made by a relatively sizeable number of investors of no independent means could hardly have been anything else but an exchange of liability for promise, not cash. And when the court held consistently that subscriptions for stock were "contracts," and therefore could be freely assigned,[125] the judges were making more than the usual point about abstraction; they were demonstrating that abstraction was not theory for the West, but its chief hope of ultimate wealth.

The 1907 case of *Smith v. Burns Boiler & Manufacturing Company*[126] bore a superficial resemblance to the subscription cases of Period I. The Business Men's Association of De Pere, Wisconsin, raised money by subscription to induce the Burns Boiler Company of Green Bay "to establish a factory at De Pere for the manufacture of their boiler." The significant difference between this and the subscription cases of Period I lay in the fact that De Pere was competing with Green Bay, its sister city, for the economic benefits of the boiler factory. Even in the rush to develop the cut-over lands, Period II was not primarily concerned with populating a wilderness, but rather with saving for productive use labor, business, and built-in values that existed *in situ* in areas threatened with ruin by economic change.

The scramble for competitive position is the key to the business venture cases of Period II. Three cases in this category sought {68} enforcement of an agreement (covenant) by a seller of a business, promising not to compete with the buyer after sale.[127] All three businesses were small—a livery business in the village of Bloomer, a laundry in Milwaukee, a drug store in Racine—but the small businessman's passion for stability, guaranteed market, and freedom from "unfair" competition outweighed his usual abhorrence of litigation and its costs. The offending druggist "has held and now holds the friendship, confidence and esteem of many ... physicians ... upon whose goodwill said business was and is largely dependent for patronage and success." The offending laundryman disrupted plaintiff's labor relations; he "hired my forelady," "took my engineer," forced plaintiff to raise his wages. These interests were, at least in the mind of the plaintiff, worthy of any exertion.

With trifling exceptions, the business venture cases of Period II dealt with businesses not much larger than these laundries and livery services; sometimes they involved complete amateurs. In one case a twenty-two-year-old bank teller bought a half interest in the Westfahl File Company, after he let slip to Westfahl's treasurer, who patronized the bank, how eager he was to escape from the dreary teller's cage. In another case a doctor invested in a sanitarium venture. In another a banker who doubled as a real estate speculator teamed up with a farmer to run a dairying business in cut-over lands.[128] In *Rust v. Fitzhugh*,[129] two business chums dabbled in land, lumber, and logging, "individual deals ... carried on as individuals"; they never kept any books, but "did business in a very loose way." After one "partner" died, the survivor could not even remember the particular deal which was the subject of litigation. In still another case, the buyer of a creamery was told (falsely) that the creamery had 128 satisfied customers, and that the nearest competitor was 7 miles away. The buyer's investigation of the business he was buying was rudimentary. He testified: "I did not ask him to show me a book. He took a book and opened it and laid it on the table and said I could look ... if I wanted to see about what he was doing [at] the present time I should go up and look at the spindle on the wall, there was return slips of butter shipped."[130] Such cases showed the grief of the amateur foolishly venturing into a specialized, organized world, or two amateurs stumbling against each other. These "business venture" cases did not, however, conform to the theoretical contract model: a bargain between coequal units. If coequal, the units were coequal only in ineptitude; if unequal, we hear {69} complaints of unfair advantage taken of the weaker party, or of fraud, as in the sale cases of Period II. Large-scale business and finance, elaborately structured, its documents carefully drafted by skilled lawyers, its relationships careful and delicate, was absent from the tabulation.[131]

Loose business relationships characterized the cases of Period III. The line between a semi-independent employee and a partner in a business venture can be quite indistinct. The cases come close, in general economic background and tone, to those concerning commissioned salesmen. Three of the period's ten cases derived from patent-licensing arrangements—the archetype of a new venture.[132] In general, the business ventures of the tabulation were small: a buy-sell stock agreement in a closed corporation dealing in auto parts; a limited partnership in a bowling alley and tavern; an unlikely partnership between a grocer and a doctor to run a retail grocery business.[133] For the first time, too, the problems of the franchised dealer erupted into the case-law. In the important case of *Kuhl Motor Co. v. Ford Motor Co.*,[134] an auto dealer in Milwaukee sought to prevent Ford from cancelling his franchise. In another case, a gas station operator tried to break his contract.[135] These cases were in one sense exceptions to the dictum that major business interests stayed out of the appellate contract docket; Ford Motor Company and Shell Oil Company, litigants in these cases, are big business indeed. But the cases in other respects fit the pattern of the cases of Period III. The auto dealer and the gas station operator were not employees of Ford and Shell, but their relationship to their principals had elements in common with the relationship of commissioned salesmen and managerial employees with their employers.

Credit, Finance, and Suretyship. This category—dealing with debts and loans, guaranty of credit, and suretyship—is one of the few which showed considerable change in its relative importance over the three periods. In Period I there were 31 cases (15 per cent); in Period II, only 14 cases (7 per cent); and in Period II, only eight cases (6.6 per cent).

We can explain the multitude of debt cases in Period I by the shortage of hard currency—that pervasive influence on the contract work of the period. The promissory note was the fundamental instrument of credit and of (provisional) settlement of accounts, i.e., the use of a promise to pay instead of a present transfer of cash. In the form of {70} bank notes, these instruments provided the community with its hand-to-hand currency, not always a sound currency, however. The basic credit instrument was the personal promissory note, secured if possible, and if possible strengthened by the endorsements of men of substance. Even the standard promissory note was too close to money for many people in the pioneer days of Wisconsin. The early cases mention many chattel notes—one was payable in "good merchantable pine boards," another in "fifty-one bushels of corn at Drury's barn," another in logs, another in "five thousand three hundred and seventy-five lbs. of lead."[136] As late as 1856 the *Fond du Lac Union* was willing to let its subscribers pay their arrears in wood; and in 1857 McCormick reaper agents in Illinois were accepting "good wheat at a fair price" in payment of notes due.[137]

The personal promissory note was constantly used in the 1850's where a check would serve in the 1950's. Notes circulated to a certain extent; and in some cases debts were discharged by paying with a third party's note.[138] Promissory notes were governed by that branch of the law merchant applicable to negotiable instruments. The average resident of Wisconsin was doubtless familiar with the rudiments of the law and practice relating to notes, just as his twentieth-century counterpart understands how to endorse a check and knows he must do so before transfer. The cases mention notes payable to order and to bearer, demand notes and time notes, and the usual forms of endorsement.[139] Aside from the use of chattel notes in the early years, no obvious local peculiarities emerged. A number of cases demonstrate that the warrant of attorney to confess judgment was in common use, particularly in business transactions of importance. The device promised speed and economy in claim collection, a valuable consideration then, as later. The cases only occasionally dealt with negotiable instruments other than notes—the certificate of deposit, the bill of exchange, the bank draft. The bill of exchange was pre-eminently commercial paper, in use for remittance between merchants; the general public did not use it with any frequency.[140]

Land was well nigh the universal collateral:[141] land alone gave value to vast numbers of the promissory notes in constant use. Thus, exemption and homestead laws and the various liens enforceable against realty (e.g., the mechanics' lien) immunized from debt collection (or subjected to special preferences in favor of "labor") a high proportion of the state's wealth. The abstraction of credit cases must {71} therefore be understood against this background; the security of transactions in the market was affected, not so much by judge-made doctrines derogating from abstraction as by legislative programs which imposed special limitations on debt collection and enforcement.

In the light of the currency shortage, the high peaks and low troughs of the business cycle, and the existence of legal obstacles imposed by statute, it was natural that interest rates on loans were very high. Laws regulating the maximum rate of interest (the usury laws) were a constant subject of legislative tinkering; and the defense of usury appeared in the cases of Period I with monotonous frequency. The defense, and its frequent invocation, demonstrate once more the limitations on abstraction even during Period I. A usury law is not to be reconciled with the ideal of free trade in money; but at most points in the history of Wisconsin during Period I there was substantial agreement that unlimited interest rates would do the public a disservice by forcing scarce capital into the loan market or by allowing necessitous settlers to assume burdens impossible to bear during lean years.[142]

Relatively few of Wisconsin's debt cases in Period I involved banks. Bank loans and discounting were of little moment to the average Wisconsin farmer. The Wisconsin banks did not make many consumption loans or farm loans. When they were not busy printing paper money, they lent their credit to businessmen; the cases mention loans to lumber merchants, to wheat merchants, even to the board of directors of a railroad.[143] Nor did institutionalized suretyship exist in Wisconsin during the period, as a practical matter. Private individuals performed functions later associated with banks and surety companies. Accommodation endorsements and guaranties for the payment of notes were executed as often as people could persuade others to "go surety" for them. In these cash-poor days, the more good names a note bore, the more effective an instrument it was in market dealings, although the law was in general a jealous guardian of the rights of the surety. Functions of debt collection and enforcement were largely in the hands of lawyers. Collection work was the single most important item of many lawyers' business; and this work consisted largely of collecting overdue promissory notes. Promissory notes were mobile instruments. A note sent west for collection, whether it was executed there or in the East, could be endorsed to a resident or to a collection lawyer. He could then sue on it in his own name and, if successful, pay himself from the proceeds. Thus, a workable process of debt collection {72} (comparable to later, more institutional processes through correspondent banks and clearing houses) existed in Period I, given the economic circumstances of the period; but the process depended for its success upon the receptivity of the courts and the support rendered by the legal system through validation of the process of free transfer and assignment of instruments of debt.

In the light of these facts, the marked falling off of credit and debt cases in Period II is perfectly understandable. Bonding was now institutional; the corporate surety, using actuarial techniques, had replaced individual sureties in court and public bonding. Though it retained many uses, the personal guarantee of the personal promissory note no longer occupied quite so central a role in the credit system. A sounder banking and finance system in the United States and the end of Wisconsin's days as an underdeveloped state meant that the ordinary processes of debt collection and finance were handled through formal and regular institutional channels, without the necessity of recourse to courts. What problems of banking and finance remained were treated by special laws; where these laws failed to solve all problems, dispute-solving mechanisms internal to the affected trades filled the gaps if at all possible. The usury cases disappeared, too. Small loan and usury problems remained a source of political controversy in Period II, but the loan shark made his impact on legislation rather than before the Wisconsin Supreme Court. The elaborate mechanism of appellate litigation was too heavy to process the general run of questions presented by the small-loan business and its customers. In the main, financial institutions functioned and adjusted difficulties through their own operations. Governed by special commercial statutes, they asked two things chiefly of the law: permission to exist, and the use of lower courts as cheap, quick, debt collection agencies. The remaining debt and credit cases of Periods II and III were quite random. Some debt cases, indeed, were intensely personal, e.g., in Period III Helene Dyer's claim against her father's estate for "money loaned to him in 1943 in the sum of $2,500." Other cases showed the perils of private citizens who lagged behind the more rationalized standards of financial institutions.[144]

Where professional bonding and corporate sureties figured in the cases, these cases had little to do with the classical law of contract. One case, for example, concerned a contract to supply the city of Milwaukee with sand and gravel. Performance was guaranteed by a New {73} York bonding company. A trucker who hauled and delivered for the prime contractor sued on the bond. To handle the case the court had to deal with a bond required by law, with intricately worded statutes, with the obscure jargon of the bond itself and the contract, the facts of the case, and with the special problems of a professional surety—all of which operated to squeeze into the tiniest corner the "principles" of suretyship law, let alone the law of contracts.[145]

58 | CONTRACT LAW IN AMERICA

Public and Governmental Contracts. This category contained, in Period I, 15 cases (7 per cent); in Period II, 12 (5 per cent); and in Period III, 6 (5 per cent). According to a prevalent view, Period I was a time when government, by common consent, did as little as possible and acted as rarely as possible. In truth, government was feeble. But it was inactive only if measured by twentieth-century standards; and its major activities—for instance, its manipulation of its landed resources—were undertaken in response to pressure from the general public. In any event, even a minimal government had to administer justice and provide for its own housekeeping. The cases in Period I touched on these roles of government, and on others too—the building of roads and harbors, even municipal licensing of a grocery.[146] In early Wisconsin public contracts were valuable prizes, eagerly sought after. Government printing jobs, in particular, were the object of much wire-pulling behind the scenes—for example, the contract to print the 1849 statutory revision, finally awarded to C. Latham Sholes, after considerable scrambling and hauling. Contracts to print lists of forfeited or delinquent public lands and similar public jobs were matters of life and death to the small, strident, marginal newspapers that grew (and died) like weeds in the little towns and villages of the state.[147]

The abstract ideal of contract law demanded that public contracts be treated the same as any other: "a contract is a contract, whether made between individuals or between states, or between a state and an individual."[148] But the court did not consistently follow this principle. The legislature, which hedged public contracts about with restrictions, knew from its own experience (and on at least one occasion out of its own guilt) that these contracts might sometimes be "freely bargained" in an all too literal sense. Abstraction theory, however, expressed an ideal that the state, like private parties, was bound to the consequences of its solemn contractual obligations, an ideal related to the unfolding of doctrine under the contracts clause of state and federal {74} constitutions. Yet doctrine was equally firm that state officials and municipalities had limited powers, and that transactions of government outside the scope of those powers (*ultra vires*), would not be enforced. Many cases, whatever their legal dress, were attacks on the scope of the power of government or the manner in which power was exercised.[149] The law of contract gave dissidents a technical tool of offense which sometimes served where constitutional law could not.

The size of this category in Period II does not do justice to the great expansion in the contractual activity of government. But just as business developed internal mechanisms for solving contractual disputes, so government contract questions were often handled within the government itself. The published opinions of the Attorney General's office burst with rulings on the validity and form of proposed public contracts, on conflicts of interest, and on the administration of statutes prescribing how government ought to behave as a contracting party. Attorney General's opinions did not, theoretically, oust the courts from jurisdiction. In practice, local officials abided by what the Attorney General's office said; and his advice on how government contracts were to be formed was rarely challenged. Government was frequently a litigant, but legislation and practice had gone very far to create special, autonomous bodies of law for governmental transactions. Within the great range of government contracts, many types were specifically regulated: cities might, for example, buy their waterworks, but only in accordance with fixed statutory procedures. "Free contract" was not the norm for governmental bodies. The courts, too, were less likely to treat state or local government as "just another" contracting party. By the early twentieth century, the state and its local agencies were more likely to be looked upon as "trustees" for the benefit of the public. The contract relationships of governmental bodies were subject to an overriding general principle: government must act for the benefit of the public and in accordance with expressed public policy. The Progressive era, in particular, was obsessed with the notion of purifying government and insuring that it be responsive to legitimate public demands. Government therefore turned upon itself and became in effect one of the regulated industries. Of course, some regulation, such as the requirement of competitive bidding for public contracts, was not new.[150] But the Progressives stepped up the attack on loose government. Ironically, conservatives too had long desired regulation of the regulators. Those who exalted as an inviolate right the freedom to run {75} any business without state interference usually denied to the state alone the right to behave as a businessman or entrepreneur. Restrictions on government spending power, on municipal financing of internal improvements, or on state and local debt found ready acceptance both from right and left. The left was disgusted when government seemed to degenerate into a "tool" of "vested interests." The right was alarmed at the "socialism" and "tyranny" inherent in government-backed enterprise—an attitude in striking contrast to the early nineteenth century, when businessmen clamored for state aid, when state governments were sometimes represented on the board of directors of railroads, or even occasionally tried their hand at running the road.[151] After the Civil War, the tide began to run heavily away from allowing government to enjoy "freedom of contract." However, at the end of the nineteenth century, popular pressure demanded that government be used as a counterweight to the "trusts," as a friend of the weak, as intermediary between the public and its mightiest members. But a city in 1900, in taking over a gas company, street railway, or waterworks, did not act as entrepreneur or resource developer; its role was not that of "owner" but of "trustee"; it was not a free contracting party but a Gulliver, so shackled by restrictions that at times special legislation was required to dispense with the harshness of general laws, or to ratify contracts imperfectly executed under the statutes. There are many illustrations in the statutes and cases. How, for example, could the city of Milwaukee pave its street with "a permanent bitulithic pavement having a concrete foundation," when that process was "fully covered and controlled by patents belonging to a corporation known as Warren Bros. Company?" Could the contract specifications call for "Warren's Brand Nos. 19 to 24 Bituminous Water Proof Cement or Bitulithic Cement," without conflicting with the legal requirement of letting all such contracts through competitive bidding? The city's solution was finally validated only after litigation reaching to the Wisconsin Supreme Court.[152] In the competitive bidding cases, as in other cases in Period II in which units of government were contracting parties, the court worked with statutes so complex and apparently inconsistent that it was hard pressed to unravel them.[153] Under such circumstances, the court had no room to make broad policy, but it did perform the vital function of making some order out of poorly integrated legislation.

The ambiguities of Period II (which carried over into Period III) were difficult to avoid. In the high days of *Dartmouth College*,[154] {76} even sovereign functions of government were treated as proprietary—the state was just another landowner, merchant, employer. As government's role was enlarged, the attitude became more prevalent that government should not contract away its rights, powers, and duties; the proprietary was overshadowed by the governmental. The process was never carried to its logical extreme, however. The courts were particularly cautious with regard to local government. Local government had limited powers; local governments varied greatly in quality and honesty. Local government was close to the people, sometimes too close; it had many powers, like zoning powers, which despite their limited reach could be issues of life and death to small businessmen. Armed with state statutes and a set of malleable doctrines of contract law, the court threaded a careful, varying (but not arbitrary) path, continuing to maintain some measure of surveillance over the contractual behavior of local government.

The cases of Period III concerned local government and used (though often inarticulately) the distinction between sovereignty and contract. In one case[155] the city of Wisconsin Rapids bought a parcel of land for a "public comfort station." But later the city used other property for this purpose and leased the original parcel to Donald G. Beyer, who ran a shoe shop and proposed doing shoe repair work as well. George Smith owned a nearby shoe repair shop; he attacked the city's action. Smith's argument (which failed) opposed letting the city deal abstractly as a proprietor with its land; he insisted that nonmarket considerations must be taken into account. In another case,[156] a school teacher was fired by his school district after a battle with the school board. The court, examining the evidence, did not find any good "cause" for the firing. Teachers, said the court, "are not public officers. They are employees." They could be fired only if "guilty of breach of ... contract" in a way which "at common law would justify an employer in discharging his servant." This sounds like classical abstract contract law; but the result of the decision was to force the board to act fairly, in effect to use "due process" within its household. The real issue was almost one of civil liberties; the use of contract language as a technique was incidental, if not accidental. In a few cases, attempts to void city contracts—a Green Bay water pipe contract; the city of Hudson's plans for a municipal hospital[157]—centered, for want of any better legal argument, on the formal defects of the contracts. The court's role was that of a kind of reviewing board, guaranteeing the {77} technical and procedural purity of local government's actions. This was an old and respectable role for the court, and one of undoubted utility. But it was not the role contemplated by abstract theory and classical contract law.

Public Utilities and Transport. This category includes only a few cases, four in Period I, five in Period II, and one in Period III. Transportation companies (railroads, for example) played a great role in the tabulation, even in Period I, but not as "carriers." The concept of the common carrier was inherited from English law, and the Wisconsin court very early indicated its willingness to extend the underlying concept by applying it to the American Express Company.[158] In terms of the law of contract, the common carrier (like the later public utility) differed from private parties in that it must contract on reasonable terms. *Shepard v. Milwaukee Gas and Light Company*,[159] which first came before the court in 1858, was a prophetic case. The company had the "exclusive right to manufacture and sell gas for the purpose of lighting the city of Milwaukee." Shepard, a merchant of East Water Street, applied for gas, but refused to sign an agreement promising to abide by the rules and regulations of the company. The company declined to furnish him gas, and Shepard brought an action for damages. In the court's view, some of the company's rules were unreasonable; the plaintiff was not required to comply with them. Ordinarily, of course, a party to a proposed contract cannot be bound unless he assents to the terms of the contract, "reasonable" or not. But a gas company, said the court, is not like a "trading or manufacturing" corporation, "whose productions may be transported from market to market." Gas "is local, and hence not commercial"; it is "not an article of trade." It was not like a "soap and candle factory, or a hat or carriage factory," and would not be comparable even if such a factory had "the privilege of laying pipes in the public streets." "The citizen could procure his soap, candles, and carriages elsewhere. These are all articles of trade, capable of transportation from place to place." The court did not (and probably could not) explain to anyone's satisfaction the mysterious distinction between "local" and "commercial." That gas is "not an article of trade," furthermore, is a surprising observation from the mouth of a court which did not hesitate to treat contractually the most evanescent and shadowy of land interests, so long as these interests had a market value. The decision tried manfully to distinguish between the {78} abstract subject matter of contract and the services of a franchised public utility. Goods of trade, in classic economic theory, were absolutely substitutable one for the other; the units of economic theory were frictionless and mobile. The economic model did not seem to the court to fit public utilities, which led the court to search (somewhat ineptly) for an appropriate rationale.

By Period II, the law of public utilities and carriers had grown into one of the most labyrinthine of the special fields. Even in Period I, the noise over railroads, how to get them built, how to tame them. what to do with them, was so strident it threatened at times to drown out talk over most other issues of public policy. Debate over the railroads went right on through the rest of the century, with battles over freight rates, rebates, land grants, finance, railroad commissions, railroad lobbies, free passes, and railroad accidents. Consequently, the law for railroads (and to a somewhat lesser extent the law for grain elevators, warehouses, telephone companies, waterworks, and gas and light companies), even more than the law applicable to government contracts, had become embodied in a maze of statutes, cases, and administrative law so thick that pure contract principles could hardly enter the door.

In *Shepard*, the utility, not the customer, invoked contract principles. In utility cases in Period II, it was the customer, not the utility, who did so. In one case[160] the plaintiff complained that the Great Northern Railway breached "its agreement to supply him with a poultry car at Cavalier, North Dakota, on November 7, 1910"; the car came four days late, and "plaintiff suffered loss on account of the death of part of the poultry, shrinkage in weight and expense incurred in the care and feeding of the remaining part." The plaintiff could win only by showing that because of special agreement or special circumstances "contract" not "carrier" law applied. This was a reversal of the usual flow of contract history, in which contract principles were displaced gradually by "special" rules. The plaintiff's tactical problem was caused by the limited damages allowed by the law and practice of common carriers. Carriers stipulated away as much liability as they legally could. In addition, as regulated businesses, they were under the protection as well as the control of government. Though they grumbled and resisted as law defined their rights and duties ever more precisely, regulated industries had already achieved what other businesses ardently desired: risk and cost standardization and predictable liability, limited {79} in amount. Pure "contract" damages had headed in the same direction in *Hadley v. Baxendale*.[161] But experience was already showing that courts might be led by sympathy and circumstance to enlarge allowable recoveries. Thus, "contract" principles remained available for use by the court in dealing with common carriers, but only as one of many alternatives, and only as a technique or a tool.

Arbitration and Settlement. This was an appreciable category in Period I (eight cases); only in that period did the cases seem to show much about the many ways in which disputes were settled out of court. Small claim settlement naturally tended to disappear from the court's docket over the years. In *Slocum v. Damon* (1845),[162] the parties entered into a formal arbitration agreement to settle "certain differences" over "an alleged injury committed by the said *Slocum* to a gray horse." The later court was much too busy and its processes too expensive for disputes over gray horses. In the earliest days, formal arbitration was apparently in common use in Wisconsin; in one case, Gear and Bracken agreed in 1839 "under seal" to submit their differences "to the arbitration and award of the committee of awards of the Galena Chamber of Commerce," to be decided "according to the rules and regulations of the aforesaid chamber of commerce."[163] Extra-judicial settlements of a less formal nature must have also been common.[164]

Toward arbitration in the strict sense of the word, the court maintained a careful but not hostile attitude. Disputes, like claims, could form the subject matter of a bargain and be treated abstractly. In theory, the role of the court was simply to enforce the bargains of the parties. Settlement agreements were therefore not supposed to form a special field of law; they were part of the general law of contract.[165] But even in Period I, the state had an arbitration statute on its books, and the subject of "arbitration" was in a sense one of the "special" fields of law.[166]

Common law and formal (statutory) arbitration did not appear in the tabulation of Periods II and III. These traditional methods were probably no longer used to settle matters like Slocum's damage to Damon's gray horse.[167] Commercial arbitration was another matter. Particular old forms of arbitration may have become obsolete, but the idea was as attractive to business as in the days of the Galena Chamber of Commerce. Commercial arbitration provisions were common in commercial contracts. During Period II and shortly afterwards, the {80} need for a proper legal climate for wider use of arbitration was much discussed in the literature. The business community had no taste for cumbersome court procedure and felt that courts lacked insight into business problems. Each trade tended to develop its own forms of arbitration, as binding and cohesive as the trade could make it. "Friendly" arbitration could preserve working relationships; business could go on while dispassionate colleagues settled matters in dispute. In 1918 a commentator listed 94 trade organizations in Chicago alone which had agreed to promote trade arbitration; these ranged from the Chicago Board of Trade to the Retail Hardware Dealers' Association.[168]

Commercial arbitration had hope of success because the potential parties had a certain community of interest. The future of labor arbitration was not so hopeful; here something more than a good legal "climate" would have to be devised to avoid bloody violence or the ceremonial, stylized conflict of strikes, lock-outs, and boycotts. Community of interest was also lacking in personal injury settlements, the only settlement cases to make any mark on the tabulation in Period II. The poor man faced the rich corporation, in apparently unequal battle. Both sides developed institutions of dubious ethics: for the plaintiff, the "ambulance chaser"; for the corporate defendants, the (sometimes) unscrupulous "claim adjuster." The court upheld some settlements in Period II where the facts strongly suggest that the injured worker was overreached.[169] But these cases can hardly be explained on the grounds that the court's devotion to abstraction led them to swallow their distaste for particular results of cases. One suspects that the court felt rather that damages (for example, loss of future earning power) should be spread more broadly, as they would if a system of workmen's compensation arose out of revulsion against the inequities of tort law and tort settlement law.

Testamentary Claims. This special category for Period III contains eight cases. These centered on "contractual" claims to a share of an estate, or on claims which (by alleged agreement) were to be paid out of an estate.[170] The testamentary claims of Period III resembled in some ways the earlier family claims for "services"—a type-situation which continued into an occasional case in Period III.[171] But the size of the category and the precise type-situation were fairly novel. The burst of testamentary claims in Period III reflected in part the increasing use of "contract" as a means to legitimize ethical claims; and it also reflected the general spread of affluence, which increased the number of valuable "estates." Other factors were the court's role as final reviewing board of probate problems; the fiduciary duty of executors and administrators (required to resist questionable claims); the perils of home-made wills and intestacy; the requirement that probate claims be funneled through court, subject to contest and control by the court itself as well as by heirs, legatees, and fiduciaries. In a few of these cases the "contract" talk is metaphorical only; for example, when the court posed the question whether a joint will constitutes a "contract" which creates enforceable rights in a beneficiary.[172] Some of the cases seemed (but only seemed) impersonal and businesslike. In the nature of things, market considerations could have little to do with a bargain for an estate; shares of an estate are postponed expectations, whose value is real enough, but grounded typically on psychological and sentimental factors. Since documentary evidence of the "promises" in these cases was usually absent or flimsy, the court inevitably based its decisions on its grasp of the pattern of the "facts" or the "evidence," which in turn meant not only a judgment about trustworthiness, but about the ethical value of the supposed claim in the context of the parties' relationships. In general, the testamentary cases of Period III underscore how little the working law of contract, as it appeared in the Wisconsin Supreme Court's appellate docket, had to do with the high market abstraction of classical contract theory.[173] {page 82 follows}

III
CONTRACT LAW IN THE COURTS: A LEGAL ANALYSIS

ALTHOUGH this study concerns the interaction of law and society, we must not forget that the law itself is a social institution; the conceptual and verbal habits of the legal community are themselves social facts, customs, phenomena. Much can be learned by watching to see how Wisconsin subtly modified the inherited doctrines of contract. This chapter analyzes the case-law tabulated according to legal concepts (see Table IV in Appendix). Since counsel may heap one legal argument on top of another, and since the court may use many legal concepts in deciding a case, some cases have been assigned to more than one heading. For this reason (and others), the quantitative tables in this chapter were not as useful or revealing in appraisal of uses of doctrine as the tabulation of fact-situations. Much of the following discussion must concern the court's general approach to legal questions as legal questions, more as a matter of feel and tone than of rigorous computation.[1]

The legal headings used are quite familiar to students of contract law. They have been arranged, in the following order, roughly paralleling the legal life cycle of an agreement: (1) Requirements for the formation of a contract: capacity, offer and acceptance, consideration, mutuality; (2) Formalities: the statute of frauds, the parol evidence rule; (3) The fairness of the bargain: fraud, duress, mistake, misrepresentation, and warranty; (4) Fact-finding and the construction of contracts; (5) Illegality and public policy; (6) Performance and breach: performance and conditions, the breached contract (including waiver and estoppel); (7) The contract as claim: damages, assignment, parties; (8) Enforcement: procedural aspects, specific performance; (9) Constitutional law and contracts. It should be emphasized that this study does not tabulate all cases which were "contract" in {83} origin; if a Supreme Court case turns only on a point of procedure, the case has been omitted from the count. It is assumed that the blight that turns disposition of a lawsuit from a point of substance to one of procedure is random and falls more or less equally on all types of litigation.

The Elements of a Contract. A valid contract, said the Wisconsin Supreme Court in 1854, must contain the following "elements": "1. Persons or parties able to contract. 2. A thing or subject concerning which the contract is to be made. 3. *A lawful consideration...* 4. Apt and proper words to express the agreement... 5. The assent of the contracting parties."[2] This was standard doctrine in 1854 and was still standard one hundred years later. Lawyers then took it as axiomatic that no contract was formed unless the parties had legal capacity, unless their "minds met" by means of offer and acceptance, and unless "consideration" supported the bargain.[3] Whatever their origins, these "elements" seemed fitting for an abstract system of contract which enforced autonomous market agreements. All of these "elements" have to do with "assent," the so-called "meeting of the minds." Even the troublesome concept of consideration is based on a simple idea—that contracts are two-sided bargains. But the ramifications of these simple root notions have always posed problems for the law.

Capacity. The basic rules of capacity were traditional. In Wisconsin, as in other jurisdictions, minors and persons of unsound mind could not in general be held to their agreements. The nineteenth-century treatise of Parsons put it this way: "As the essence of a contract is an assent or agreement of the minds of both parties, where such assent is impossible, from the want, immaturity, or incapacity of mind, there can be no perfect contract."[4] The rules of capacity always implied considerations of social policy. They protected weaker members of society from exploitation, from "improvident bargains, and the artifices of designing persons";[5] and they defined the role in the social system of various groups of people.

Rules limiting contractual capacity are thus limitations on the abstraction of the law of contract. Only special concerns of public policy justify them. The incapacity of the alien to hold or inherit land at common law expressed particular social values, inconsistent with abstraction but consistent with the fact that in feudal society land {84} tenure was connected with military obligation. The alien, as a potential enemy of the state, was not to be admitted to the community's power structure. In the United States there was no such compelling reason to place disabilities on aliens, and these disabilities rapidly decayed after independence. In Wisconsin the common law rules were deemed especially obnoxious. The Wisconsin Constitution (1848) specifically provided that: "No distinction shall ever be made by law between resident aliens and citizens, in reference to the possession, enjoyment or descent of property."[6] The key word here was "resident." Economic growth and rising land values depended on population growth. Nothing was more desirable than heavy immigration, whether from other states or from abroad hardly mattered. At the time Wisconsin adopted its constitution, Englishmen, Germans, and Scandinavians had already settled in some numbers in Wisconsin, and additional immigration was welcomed. A Joint Resolution in 1860 took note of the proposed federal homestead act and exhorted Congress to let the act cover aliens as well as American citizens. The "greatest blessing" the act could bring was "an increased emigration of European farmers, artizans and laborers, to occupy and cultivate our vast unoccupied domain."[7] Naturally, one could hardly expect these attitudes to be coupled with stringent property disabilities for aliens. The incapacity of married women at common law was an expression of the woman's subordination to her husband socially and economically; as the social role of the married women changed, her legal rights were gradually redefined (largely by legislation). The incapacity of the slave in the pre-Civil War South is an even more obvious example of the dependence of rules of capacity on social facts.[8]

The relaxed Wisconsin view of alien landholding may serve as a symbol for the historical development of contract doctrine in Wisconsin law. Law responded to social change. The manner in which the Wisconsin Supreme Court reacted to facts of society and judicial role was complex. Classical contract law posited the abstraction of the free market, tempered by subservience to such higher goals (e.g., in Period I, economic development) as thrust themselves upon judicial consciousness with greater force. The increasingly peripheral and non-business nature of the court's docket, however, reinforced the ideological decline in the worth placed on abstraction. The case-law over the course of the years showed ever increasing manipulation of doctrine, in {85} the direction of seeking more particularistic solutions to the cases which came before the court.

Yet the traditional doctrines and concepts of the legal system, and social and political considerations of the distribution of power among various legal institutions always profoundly influenced the precise way in which socially induced changes in legal doctrine were manifested. For example, no great change in the rules of capacity resulted from the concern of the law in Period II with "inequality of bargaining power." The law preferred to develop doctrine for special fields (for example, insurance), which attacked the problem systematically, by type-situation, without distorting the apparent abstraction of contract law. In the case-law, the court preferred to leave the rules of capacity alone and to expand such concepts as fraud and mistake. In *Krueger v. Buel*,[9]

> the plaintiff, a woman of fifty-five years of age, had the appearance of and acted like a person of about seventy-five years, was infirm and childish, broken in health, weak-minded and easily susceptible to influence ... practically a helpless cripple and a mental wreck.... [S]he fell into the hands of persons who were able and willing to take advantage of her.... The case is one where ... an enfeebled old lady of weak mentality had fallen into the hands of the Philistines and had been overreached by designing and unscrupulous persons....

In this case, the court (perhaps deliberately) never once spoke the magic word "incompetent" as a basis for granting relief to the plaintiff from an oppressive transaction. The reason lay, perhaps, in the preciseness of rules of capacity. Minority, for example, is rigidly defined: the twenty-year-old is a minor; the twenty-one-year-old is not. Incompetence is not so precise a concept, but it has sharp and serious consequences (loss of power of testation, for example). The court preferred to work with more malleable concepts that could be fitted to the particular fact-situations before it. Moreover, law in the nineteenth century generally tended to reject creating large classes of legally incompetent persons—the slave and the married woman both cast off their legal shackles. The ideal of treating every person, to the extent possible, as an autonomous unit of economic action, militated against the creation of new classes of the incompetent, and encouraged the use of malleable concepts (such as fraud) which could be applied as needed to situations rather than to classes of people. {86}

The other limitation on the court's power over doctrine—the distribution of power among various legal institutions—was more serious. It is well illustrated by the complicated history of a cluster of doctrines closely related to doctrines of capacity: doctrines defining the powers of governmental bodies and of private corporations. Here the court had some elbow room in Period I. It exercised its power in characteristic manner. Thus the farm-mortgage system of marketing railroad stock was upheld by the court as an exercise of implied corporate powers, despite arguments based on *ultra vires*. To require cash payment for stock subscriptions would have been absurd, given the capital shortage in pre-Civil War Wisconsin; any such holding would have hobbled economic growth.[10] By Period II, the doctrine of *ultra vires* was moribund; whatever the wishes of the court, most private corporations had such broad charters that they could do anything businesslike they pleased. Specially regulated corporations (banks or insurance companies) might still, of course, confront or create issues of *ultra vires*. But under the "modern" rule, according to Marshall in 1907, an *ultra vires* corporate contract could not be "impeached by the corporation"; only the state had a remedy, "to punish the corporation for violating the law."[11] This view was related to a more general phenomenon of Period II, the shifting of emphasis from private enforcement of policy-charged remedies to public enforcement; but it left little real substance to the doctrine. For obvious reasons, the court still retained something of its former role in cases which attacked the acts of government itself as *ultra vires* (without using that phrase). Remedies against improper acts of government could not be left to government initiative without losing their effect. But here, too, the court could hardly do the job through the medium of contract law. One reason was that in Period II and even more so in Period III the tangle of statute law grew so thick that the court had no real freedom to maneuver in many type-situations.[12]

Offer, Acceptance, and "Assent." Offer and acceptance are commonsense ideas. Taken in their common-sense meaning, offer and acceptance were essentials of contract theory because, "there is no contract, unless the parties thereto assent."[13] Theory required parties who could be treated as economic units, free, autonomous, and able to calculate their own best interests. Along with the rest of the law of contract, the concepts of offer and acceptance also developed the bright polish of {87} high technicality. Most of the cases on these familiar concepts, in the familiar form in which law students know them, come from Period II. This is as expected. The rules were useful as rough guides in solving a persistent problem: the tension between amorphous reality and the business need for external, predictable standards of liability. The rules were helpful in deciding when shapeless give and take ("preliminary negotiations") had matured into a true agreement, definite enough to be enforced.[14] The so-called objective theory of contracts, developed by late nineteenth-century and early twentieth-century scholars, insisted that the law enforce only objective manifestations of agreement and rejected the notion that the essence of an enforceable contract was a subjective "meeting of the minds" of the parties.[15] This shift in legal theory was another way of expressing a preference for treating contracts in a standard (objective) manner, and eliminating the particularism that fit badly the basic abstraction of contract law. The parol evidence rule was another aspect of the same phenomenon.

In general, the law was much concerned in Period II with problems of reducing business risk and enhancing the predictable effect of transactions. These problems run through many of the cases; in some, the concepts of offer and acceptance came in for discussion, while other cases turned on consideration, parol evidence, mistake, and other doctrines.[16] It was a general characteristic of contract case-law in the Wisconsin Supreme Court in every period that the type-situations litigated were products peculiar to their time and place; the results were by and large also socially determined and peculiar to their age; but the doctrinal stuff of which opinions were woven was (superficially) much less mutable. In dealing with problems of documentation and business rationality, Period III was much more concerned with how the parties lived under an agreement than with the legal shape of the agreement itself.[17] But the use of the language of offer and acceptance in opinions, as of other legal concepts, gave little clues to the court's changing approach.

Mutuality and Definiteness. The concept of mutuality was central to the classical law of contracts. An agreement must be two-sided; otherwise it is not a bargain. More specifically, it is often said that there must be mutuality of obligation to a contract; both parties must be bound or neither is bound. In truth, courts use the word in a number of ways, quite difficult to define; "mutuality" indicates, in an exceedingly {88} vague way, a requirement of two-sidedness to a bargain, in an undefined manner above and beyond the requirement that the bargain be supported by consideration. But what that something extra is seems to vary from case to case.

The yearning of courts for "mutuality" has basically two aspects, one conformable to abstraction, and the other not. In colloquial usage, "one-sided" has two meanings: a bargain can be called one-sided because it is literally incomplete; or it can be called one-sided because it is grossly unfair to one of two parties. A refusal to enforce an incomplete contract fits in with market abstraction; such a contract can have no market. But the second type of one-sided contract, if recognized, opens up a whole line of non-market inquiry.

The same point may be made about the requirement of definiteness. Courts sometimes refused to enforce a purported contract on the grounds it was too "vague" or "indefinite." A court may deny enforcement to a contract it regards as excessively vague on grounds which are compatible with market theory: an agreement so lacking in specificity as to lack substantive value should not be enforced, since no one rationally buys or sells a mere guess. Or the court may refuse to enforce a vague, indefinite contract, believing enforcement to be unfair: enforcement would mean making up a contract for the parties, and imposing the result upon one party against his will.

It was not infrequent for parties to interpose the defense of indefiniteness or lack of mutuality to actions arising under contracts which omitted an important term (e.g., price, quantity, time of performance). The court was usually willing to fill in the imperfection, if business practice or the market provided a guide. Thus, in *Eastern Railway Co. of Minnesota v. Tuteur* (1906),[18] a contracting stevedore agreed to handle the railroad's freight; the railroad made no express agreement to provide any particular quantity of freight, or, indeed, any at all. But the amount of freight, said the court, was "fixed by the wants of an established business." The railroad had a terminal in Superior; it would certainly produce freight there, and in fact it had. On the other hand, in *Freeman v. Morris*,[19] testator agreed to "leave something" to a child in his will. No custom or business practice could possibly measure how much of a legacy would constitute "something." This contract therefore was too uncertain to be enforced.

This line of approach was market oriented. In Period III there were ten cases interposing the defenses in question; in seven of them the {89} court refused to allow the defense.[20] But the basic reason for the court's reluctance to uphold the defense in Period III was the court's insistence that a vague contract could be cured of its vices by the subsequent conduct and "practical" interpretation of the parties.[21] This approach often led to the same result as the market-oriented approach, but with a subtly different orientation. It is clear, too, that doctrine which would insist that agreements reveal their full meaning at the moment of execution would hardly fit twentieth-century business. Such a doctrine would be workable only for short-term agreements. Any rules of law which required that every contract be definite as to price could hardly suit long-term contracts. In long-term contracts, rigid, fully detailed documentation was excessively risky. Paradoxically, the more certain the contractual terms, the more uncertain the consequences. Taken at their word, the classic doctrines of mutuality and definiteness would render unenforceable whole classes of contract familiar to twentieth-century businessmen—e.g., out-put contracts, long-term buying and selling arrangements—which must leave the price term open. Recognition of this fact, and perhaps also the public's increasing sensitivity to the perils of inflation, explains why judges tended to relax the older views of mutuality and definiteness in later contract law. By the 1950's, most jurisdictions would freely enforce requirement and open-price contracts.[22]

But even though the decline of older notions of mutuality is explainable in terms of the special requirements of long-term and complex contracts, that is, of a maturing economic system, the idea of practical interpretation implies a definite rejection of values inherent in classical contract law. Classical contract law allowed any party to invoke his "rights" and make use of any legally available argument for whatever reason; likewise, classical contract law emphasized the parties' written texts rather than their subsequent behavior; in both regards, classical doctrine favored abstraction since the archetypical abstract subject matter of a contract was a faceless, impersonal unit of trade—like a dollar bill, or a stock certificate. "Practical interpretation," on the other hand, refers to individual, special, concrete behavior.

Consideration. This basically simple idea, which in the age of treatises degenerated into a logician's delight, was accepted without question by Wisconsin from the very beginning.[23] In the earliest period, to be sure, there were not many cases. The concept was taken for granted. Consideration {90} "limited the law's support to seriously intended undertakings" and "refused the law's aid to unconscionable coercion."[24] These two aims were not the same. The difference can be illustrated by the well-known doctrine that mere inadequacy of consideration is not grounds for upsetting a bargain: "when a thing is to be done ... be it never so small, this is a sufficient consideration."[25] Originally, this was a rule designed to validate a transaction through formality: either a seal or "consideration" of some sort, even nominal, was a formal requirement of an enforceable contract. In the nineteenth century the market abstraction of contract law reaffirmed the rule, not out of respect for the regularizing formality of consideration, but because values were to be fixed by the market, by private bargain, and not imposed by government, court, or law. Yet from the very beginning the court in fact did on occasion refuse to enforce a contract by arguing that the consideration was inadequate, even though the parties must have thought otherwise. In 1847 the court denied that there could be legal effect in the sale by a squatter of his naked land claim: "Half an acre of broken land in a prairie, uncultivated, without fence or house, cannot be an accommodation or benefit to a purchaser."[26] The point was, however, that the seller had not himself improved the land; as a squatter he had no legal claim, of course; he also lacked the customary and ethical claim of one who improved the land. The nineteenth-century emphasis on productivity, on increasing the community stock of wealth, made it possible to make the kind of distinction implicit in this case.

There were three basic uses of the concept of consideration: as technicality (form), as a symbol of a market transaction, and as an ethical limitation on enforcement of agreements—a three-fold use of a standard legal concept to which the discussion in this chapter affords many parallels. From the very beginning in Wisconsin, the three uses coexisted, but the use of consideration as an ethical limitation on enforcement of agreements grew somewhat more important as the hold of abstraction on the law of contracts weakened. In Period II, examples of the three uses can be easily documented. Thus, in *Rust v. Fitzhugh* (1907),[27] consideration of $1 was held enough to support the grant by one business associate to another of a quarter interest in a substantial timber land deal. The parties, said the court, were "accustomed to have important dealings with each other of a character explainable only upon the theory that each deemed himself thoroughly competent to protect his own interest." As a matter of fact, even the dollar bill never {91} passed hands. The case seems (but only seems) like a return to medieval formality, to the "peppercorn" theory of consideration. But, in effect, the case merely refused to disturb a working pattern of business relations on purely technical grounds. The court in another case rejected the notion that a party might avoid a contract by pointing out the disparity between the "true" value of a farm sold and the price paid by the buyer. To consider such an argument, said the court, "would be subversive of any considerable commercial activity." Yet in another case, the court allowed proof of inadequacy of consideration as evidence of "undue influence" upon a party. And in one of the stallion cases, the court flatly based its judgment of the validity of a contract on its opinion of what a horse was really "worth," completely ignoring, perhaps unconsciously, the classical rule of consideration.[28]

Formality. The older common law made much of the distinction between sealed and unsealed instruments, a typical insistence on form as a means of achieving order in relations. However, the seal had almost no practical importance in Wisconsin; as early as the territorial period, it had degenerated into a scroll or the letters "L.S." written or printed.[29] Corporations, public and private, had seals and used them; for individuals, the seal was unknown.

Over the course of the last two centuries, the common law has seemed to show a constant movement away from insistence upon formal regularity for its own sake. Contract law was a striking case; its emphasis upon upholding the autonomy of the parties embodied values which invited preference for substance over form. The tendencies away from formality of recent law can easily be overstated, however. The American common law has been zealous in discarding certain formalities—notably those which interfered with the conduct of business. In other respects, law has become more formal, not less. Certainly wills and deeds must still be formally executed; in the case of wills, formal requirements in the twentieth century were generally stiffer than a century earlier. What happened to the American deed form is that functional formality survived; ceremonial and obsolete formality was pruned away. Indeed ceremonial declined in our law. To foster economic growth, law must avoid excessive ceremonial. Forms which serve no function in rationalizing or ordering transactions frustrate the intent of the parties and add an unforeseen risk to economic transactions. The movement of traditional legal subjects out of their old {92} categories into the freer air of "contract" meant an emancipation from dysfunctional formality, an increase in rationalized abstraction. There was nothing new in the law's urge to strip itself clean of absolute ceremony, but the nineteenth century accelerated the pace. Procedural reform was a key part of the movement. Benthamism, frontier impatience with form, American pragmatism, these attitudes counted for something, but probably less than business necessity. The businessman had no use for ceremonial formalism as such. He valued substantive predictability. Economic decisions depended upon the ability to know, within limits, what was "the law." For the businessman—and in some sense, all farmers and settlers were "businessmen"—cases ought to turn on "the law," not upon the niceties of lawyers. Simplification of forms eliminated for the economic system a business risk difficult to gauge and take into account.

Yet "form" itself had a business function. Nothing could be more formal than a negotiable instrument; and its form was created not despite the wishes of the merchants, but because of them. The ideal of business abstraction favored the development of instruments and documents whose legal effectiveness depended upon their formal and abstract character; in order to have as perfect a market as possible, units of investment and bargain ought to be as fungible, that is, as standardized and uniform as possible. Land recording acts were another example of market-oriented formality.[30] The recording of land contracts and deeds helped maintain the security of transactions and helped smooth the work of the land market. Recording was also, of course, a mirror of the otherwise chaotic and unsettled character of land titles. The weakness of titles in the United States had many causes in various parts of the country: changes in sovereigns, e.g., from Spain or France to the United States in the Mississippi Valley, Texas, and Florida; overlapping and vague land grants; poor administration of public lands; squatters on land; and forgers of land documents. In an economy based on land values, weakness of land titles was a highly serious matter. From an economic standpoint, the weakness of titles meant that the prime commodity of trade was of uneven marketable quality. Weakness of titles might discourage emigration, hold down the market in land and perhaps depress prices. To the extent that a recording system imposed order upon a chaos of claims and interests, it performed a vital function.

The law tended to slough off only formality which was foreign to {93} popular business understanding. Recording, however, was well understood and highly acceptable. The common-sense notion that prior claims in time bore prior rights was part of the popular idea of justice; "staking a claim" was itself a kind of formality. People needed and wanted visible records of their claims to the land and wealth of the country. Mortgage records could be used to adjust conflicting interests; they also served as sources of market information, telling important facts about the value of particular assets.

Formality was also a way of enforcing public policy. This use—not in support of the market, but as a way of controlling it—grew tremendously over the years. Formality of the regulatory sort was mostly statutory; by the 1900's it was so extensive that it was taken for granted along with some of its tangible evidences, the certificates, licenses, forms, and cards which people carry in their wallets, and hang on their walls, and which record birth, marriage, and death. A regulated economy is and must be a formal economy. In market transactions, the boundary between contract and non-contract was often the boundary between form chosen freely by the parties and imposed form. The character of contract as the negation of state-imposed form helps explain indirectly why some kinds of case cropped up in the contract docket. For example, Period III has a number of "contract" cases which are really claims to a share of a decedent's estate. The usual evidence advanced to claim a share in an estate is by mention in a will; but a will is a formal document, which must be executed just so and not otherwise. Contracts can be informal, even oral, however; and this was one more reason why imperfectly formalized estate claims liked to masquerade as bargains or contracts. Notice, however, that these claims were usually not market transactions at all.

The most important example of (apparent) insistence upon formality within the standard lawyer's law of contract was the Statute of Frauds. The Statute was first passed in 1677, and has shown great powers of survival, particularly in the United States. Wisconsin adopted it from the start, in a somewhat atypical version borrowed from New York.[31] Adoption of the Statute probably did not represent sharply deliberated policy; the Statute was part of the general legal tradition, and it would have been daring to reject it. In essence, the Statute provided that certain kinds of contract could not be enforced unless in writing and signed by the person sought to be held to his bargain. Of the classes of cases covered by the original Statute, only {94} four are represented in the Wisconsin tabulation: land contracts; promises "not to be performed within one year"; promises to "answer for the debt, default, or miscarriage of another"; and contracts for the sale of goods "for the price of fifty dollars or more." The Statute, through most of its history, was treated by the courts in a most highhanded fashion. It engendered an amazing structure of rules and counter-rules, which often had little basis in the words of the Statute. In reality, the courts treated the Statute much the same as a common-law rule, instead of as a solemn enactment of the legislature; in part, the reason was that, as we have noted, the Statute (in Wisconsin at least) did not represent a distinctly deliberated enactment such as a tax law or a reapportionment act. The historic accumulation of sub-doctrines and exceptions to the rules of the Statute of Frauds meant that the Statute was (paradoxically) hardly a formality at all, at least in the sense that formality implies precision and regularity. It was simply a "doctrine," though one which related to the form of contracts of certain type. Consequently, the history of the Statute of Frauds stands outside the history of formality in the law of contracts; its closest relationships are with the history of such doctrines as consideration, which also evolved from formalistic beginnings.

The proliferation of rules and exceptions made the Statute a "frightful source of litigation," as the court remarked in 1855.[32] The phrase is exaggerated; but the Statute did supply the court with an inordinate share of its contract business. In Period I, 19 cases arose under the Statute—more than those touching any other point of contract law, with one exception. In Period II there were 17; and in Period III, 13. In the first two periods the court was unusually friendly to the Statute, reversing the historic trend. The court expressly disapproved of the "narrow and technical" way other courts had treated the law.[33] Barnes, J., in 1913, while admitting that the Statute "sometimes works hardships," declared it to be "the law as written by our lawmaking power"; it was "the duty of the courts to enforce it.... The good which it has accomplished far outweighs any wrong that has resulted from its operation."[34] The judges were as good as their word. For example, in Period II, of the seventeen cases on the Statute, two at most held that the Statute did not apply; one or two more were inconclusive; the rest applied the Statute in full vigor.[35] Period III, however, was different: the cases divided practically evenly, between application and rejection of the Statute. {95}

The changing fashions in the application of the rule were responses to changes in the particular facts of the cases and the type-situations to which the Statute was to be applied. In Period I, for example, most of the cases concerned the sale of interests in land, or alleged promises to answer for the "debt, default, or miscarriage of another." In the suretyship cases, the court was sympathetic to the surety, particularly to the gratuitous "accommodator," who had nothing tangible to gain and everything to lose for his kindness. In land transactions, vague, oral, hidden agreements endangered the orderly functioning of the land market; the Statute promoted abstraction. Period II continued the emphasis on land transactions and suretyship cases; the heavy use of the Statute in this period is not surprising, since cases arising under it were by their nature cases of imperfect business rationalization. In Period III, on the other hand, where no clear-cut attitude toward the Statute showed in the results of the cases, the suretyship cases were rare. Here, to a greater extent than in Period II, the court saw no clear policy issues except on a case-by-case basis. The court used or avoided the Statute as it suited the fulfillment of other (often ill-defined) values, that is, as a technical tool of judicial art rather than a specific expression of policy in and of itself.[36]

The Parol Evidence Rule. The parol evidence rule (see p. 7 *supra*) expresses the notion that a final, integrated document (if one exists) is the exclusive gauge of the legal meaning of that document or the contract it embodies. Like the doctrine of consideration, and the Statute of Frauds, the rule was received by Wisconsin as part of the general legal tradition. The "principle that a party to a written contract cannot vary or control it by a parol agreement, made before the written contract was entered into, or simultaneously with it, is too well settled to require the citation of any authorities," said the court in 1855, at a point when Wisconsin judges could hardly muster any native citations at all.[37]

There have been many attempts to explain or condone the parol evidence rule. The search for an integrated document can be explained as a search for the true intent of the parties. Some scholars, however, have seen in the rule the law's "distrust of the capacity of courts and juries to weigh human credibility."[38] This implies that variability of the findings of court and jury is the real vice of parol evidence, in other words, a failure of "objectivity," in the market sense. There is, therefore, {96} a relationship between the parol evidence rule and the "objective theory" of contracts. Both take as their model of a contract the abstract, impersonal agreement whose meaning is apparent to third persons, and which requires no subjective "interpretation."

In this, the parol evidence rule expressed a classic ideal; but in post-classical times, the rule exhibited, if not decay, then considerable imprecision of application. The parol evidence rule developed a magnificent set of exceptions which were as important as the rule itself. The rule was, after all, a rule of form, or at least, a rule which preferred formal, final expression to the informal or tentative. A legal system which puts any value at all on form, tempts people to adopt forms for their dealings which put those dealings in the best legal light. Frequently, two distinct "contracts" exist side by side, one written, one oral. The oral side agreement may be the "real" agreement, which has been hidden for one reason or another—sometimes because it is illegal. In Period I, no contract defense was more frequent than the defense of usury. One could hardly expect a usurious contract to admit its guilt on its face. Instead, notes and mortgages for more than the legal rate of interest sometimes hid usury behind discounts, inflated "commissions" or "exchange" charges, or bloated "solicitor's fees." Despite the philosophy of the parol evidence rule, the court consistently allowed the "real" transaction to be shown.[39] The parol evidence rule, in short, gave way before rules on fraud and illegality. *Downie v. White* (1860),[40] on the other hand, was a case in which the rule was applied. White subscribed for stock in the Milwaukee and Beloit Railroad Company. When called upon to pay for his stock, White told the following story: Reymert, who claimed to be an agent of the company, said he wanted White's name as a subscriber. White "refused to become a subscriber," but Reymert said he only wanted his name "as a matter of form." Since White was well known "in the towns through which the said railroad was to run," his signature would be useful to the company, but Reymert promised that White would "never be called upon to pay." The court made short work of this contention: "But we do not think the secret understanding which the defendant sets up ... constitutes any defense whatever. Such agreements are an obvious fraud upon the other subscribers; and the written subscriptions should be enforced without regard to them." Comparing this case with the usury cases, we can clearly see that the court applied a double standard—for good reason, of course. The parol evidence rule would be used to preserve {97} documentary integrity, and therefore help the orderly workings of the market; it would be ignored to protect the equality of position which the market assumed, or to enforce policy (e.g., anti-usury laws) which embodied clearly recognized exceptions to the market philosophy.

The parol evidence rule, and its satellite doctrines, was particularly important in Period II (16 cases). The rule was a weapon for the business firm against the customer's complaints of fraud, mistake, and misrepresentation. It was a natural instrument of standardization and rationality. The rule was particularly useful for maintaining the effect of form contracts used in business dealings. Form contracts guarded the company against customers, and also against salesmen who made rash promises to customers in their eagerness to sell. In *Pratt v. Darling*[41] and similar cases, the company did not content itself with the rule as an implication of law; the form contract specifically stated that "Separate verbal or written agreements with salesmen are not binding upon Walter Pratt & Co." The parol evidence rule, in its simplest form, fit in well with the abstraction of pure contract law. It demanded similar treatment of similar documents, excluding private, personal, and special features. The whole law of negotiable instruments was, in a sense, a flowering of the parol evidence rule. An endorsement is an endorsement, and it cannot readily be shown to be anything else, at least vis-à-vis a holder in due course. Relaxation of this rule would destroy or impair the marketability of commercial paper. On the other hand, when the parol evidence rule shuts off enforcement of the "real" agreement, it strikes at the concept of assent, which is basic to contract law. But since assent, abstractly speaking, ought to mean assent evidenced in objectively measurable terms, the parol evidence rule is more in keeping with classical contract law than not.

By Period II, the abstraction of contract law had been much weakened. Only 3 or 4 of the 16 cases actually applied the rule.[42] In *Pratt v. Darling*, for example, the salesman's statement was a "misrepresentation" and not a "promise," while the form contract disclaimed company liability only for "agreements" (promises). By a similar counter-rule, parol evidence was admissible to show failure to meet "conditions precedent" to a contract or—to strip away the jargon—that "the instrument never had vitality as a contract." Then, too, parol evidence was always admissible (as in the Period I usury cases) to show that a written contract masked an illegal scheme. Furthermore, the parol evidence rule would be refused if its application were "unjust" or in aid of fraud. {98} Again, the court might treat a series of documents as "cumulative"; if so, the last of the series was not necessarily the only document relevant to legal inquiry. And parties, of course, were free to "modify" written agreements as they saw fit; parol modification was as good as any.[43] The effect of all these counter-rules was to convert the parol evidence rule from an expression of policy to a technique.

The parol evidence rule complemented another doctrine, the "plain meaning" rule. No parol evidence would be allowed to refute the plain meaning of the words of a contract, to show that black is white or white is black. In *Berger v. Alan Realty Co.* (1956),[44] a grading and landscaping contractor fixed his prices at "work performed and materials furnished ... plus 10 per cent." The list of materials specified prices, e.g., "Top soil 6 yds. $14.00." Was 10 per cent to be added to these figures, or to the actual net cost to the contractor? Obviously, the percentage should be added to the former, said the court; the contract was plain and unambiguous. In the court's view, it was incredible that men of "training and experience" did not recognize that they had been billed all along for more than actual net cost. Consequently, both parties must have understood the meaning of the provision in the same way. Yet the court's attitude implies that the judges found the words "plain and unambiguous," not on their face, but only after looking at the facts of the case and assessing how the parties actually lived under their contract. Plainness became, then, a function of the situation, rather than of the naked text; this approach turned the "plain meaning" rule inside out. Of course, by doing so, the court remained consistent with its preference in Period III for "practical interpretation"—for what parties did, and how they acted, rather than what their documents or agreements said.

Fairness of the Bargain: Fraud, Duress, Mistake, Misrepresentation. In a market economy, price, performance, and all the terms of a contract are generally fixed by the parties themselves. Abstraction requires that the court pay no attention to the circumstances of the parties, or the nature of the subject matter. Hardship, supervening unfairness, a bad price—these should be generally ignored. "The duty of courts [is] simply to enforce contracts unexceptional on other grounds," said Mr. Justice Cole in 1859, "precisely as the parties have made them, instead of making new contracts for them to meet the emergencies of a particular case; or to avail some supposed inconvenience or hardship." {99} Chief Justice Dixon fully agreed. The agreements of the parties, "unless illegal, or contrary to public policy, are the law by which their rights are to be measured."[45] Of course, even in Period I, these sweeping statements were not to be taken too literally; Cole was careful to confine his statement to contracts "unexceptional on other grounds," and Dixon mentioned "illegality" and "public policy" as limitations on abstraction. In all periods, fraud and mistake were allowed as defenses to some kinds of contract actions. After all, contract was supposed to apply only to free bargains of free people. The assent of the parties had to be real, not forced.

That a fraudulent contract ought not to be enforced was a proposition with which no one could disagree. The law likes to frame its rules, whenever possible, as if they were homely truths; or even as statements of fact about the physical world. ("No res no trust" is a rule of this latter sort; or the maxim that "a man cannot grant or charge that which he hath not.")[46] But under cover of simple truths, the courts set standards of fair dealing; in extreme cases they sat in judgment on the wisdom of private contracts. Expansion of the concepts of fraud and mistake was one way in which the law of contract changed in fact, if not in theory. In this way much of what a later day regarded as the "harshness" of the classical law was mitigated; this "harshness" was nothing more than the prevailing abstraction of nineteenth-century contract law. Even in the high days of abstraction, fraud, duress, mistake, and misrepresentation were frequent defenses. In Period I no less than 23 cases discussed one or more of these ideas. Contract law in Wisconsin was never so abstract as the law of negotiable instruments. As early as the frontier days in Wisconsin, contract and the market were open to broad segments of the population, to persons who differed from each other in intellectual equipment, business judgment, and plain common sense. The high abstraction of (say) the law of negotiable instruments was shaped by a market in which professional merchants did business largely with each other. This was certainly never the case in Wisconsin.

In general, the way the court treated fraud and misrepresentation was influenced by the court's perception of the relative value of security of market transactions and the value of justice in the particular case. In *Mowry v. Hill* (1860),[47] the plaintiffs were trying to foreclose a mortgage, which secured a note given (in part) for the purchase of stock in the Watertown and Madison Railroad Company. Defendant {100} complained that the sale of stock had been induced by false statements "that the railroad company was then in a good and solvent condition, and that the capital stock thereof was then worth 100 cents on the dollar." In fact the stock was then worth only five cents on the dollar. The court saw no "fraud" whatsoever. "Representations as to value," said the court, "have not generally been held to constitute such a fraud as would avoid the contract, even though the value was greatly exaggerated." Nor did the statement that the railroad was "solvent" have any legal effect; it "might have been true, and still the stock have been worthless. The value of the stock of a company depends upon the value of its property over and above its debt."

In this case the court was insensitive, to say the least, to the notion that a seller must deal honestly with his buyer. The court upheld the "security of transactions"; but this does not really explain the decision. The key seems to lie in the court's idea of "value." "Value" can have a double meaning. It can refer to a (theoretical) inherent worth, based on actual input of resources, such as cash, raw materials, and labor. This is the investment "value" of a crop, or the rolling stock of a railroad. Another kind of "value" is speculative; it is the risk element, the potential capital gain that may accrue to an asset. Unliquidated claims, and insurance risks, have this kind of value. The distinction is analogous to the distinction which nineteenth-century public opinion drew between "capital" and "labor," between "speculation" and "development." These distinctions may be worthless, from the standpoint of economics, but they had popular force. There were those who labored and produced, and those who gambled and speculated. In *Mowry v. Hill*, the court defined the value of corporate stock in terms of corporate net assets, that is, in terms of the worth of the stock measured by the resources that had been committed to the enterprise. But the buyer here, the judge felt, had sought more speculative values; and thus the court was satisfied to leave the parties where it found them. The court judged fraud and misrepresentation cases, not primarily in moral terms, but in terms of the business meaning of the bargain—who had assumed what risk. In *Mann v. Stowell* (1851),[48] Stowell sued Mann "for the value of a wagon." Mann "gave evidence to prove that the wagon was paid for at the time of the purchase by delivering to the plaintiff the note of one Langley." To this Stowell replied that Langley was then in fact insolvent, although "represented by *Mann* to be solvent." This case is much like *Mowry v. Hill*; but the decision went the {101} other way. A dealer in wagons was not a speculator in personal promissory notes. Much the same approach was used by the court in handling cases of "mistake," only with a little more caution, since any losing contract is, in a sense, a mistake. A contract would be set aside or reformed for mistake only if the mistake was "material." Materiality, however, was measured by whether or not the mistake affected the price, that is, whether the mistake was related to measurement of value or risk.

Fraud and mistake were concepts frequently invoked in the cases of Period II. The two major problem areas of the cases—non-business agreements, and imperfectly rationalized business agreements—were natural breeding grounds for these defenses. Then, too, misinformation is the essence of the defenses of fraud and mistake; and as the economic system became more complicated, the value of free and accurate flow of market information became accordingly greater. Yet the court was increasingly faced with fact-situations in which market principles could give no guidance. The less the parties were or acted like economic men, the more subjective, necessarily, was the court's measure of such things as materiality of a misrepresentation. Thus, in *Brown v. Search* (1907),[49] a young girl, talked into taking a business course, complained of misrepresentations that some of her friends had also signed up for the course. "Association with her former classmates," said the court, was a matter of "substantial importance" to her. But how important? Nothing could measure it except the girl's own sayso—and the court's subjective reaction to her argument.

The court valued business rationality highly; it was not anxious to let people slip free of their solemn agreements for whimsical reasons. But the court was often implored to grant relief in hardship cases and for those who were weak and had been duped by the stronger and brighter. Sometimes the court stretched a point to favor the weaker of two parties; as we noted, the judges preferred to use malleable concepts such as fraud, mistake, and misrepresentation as legal vehicles for achieving particularistic results, rather than such firmer concepts as lack of contractual capacity.[50]

What the court did was follow tendencies, not rules. It did not reconcile cases; it decided them. How little the court of Period II cared for consistency can be seen if we take up, in chronological order, the cases in which a party advanced the argument that he had not read his contract, or did not know what was in it. Abstraction and business {102} rationality required that the court ignore any such argument. Sympathy sometimes pulled the other way. In *Loyd v. Phillips* (1905),[51] the parties had traded land in Outagamie County. Ada Phillips drew up the papers. She said "she had written the descriptions of her husband's land many times and was better able to draw the deed thereof correctly than any one else." The deed as drawn up had a covenant against incumbrances, but it excepted mortgage indebtedness. "Slight circumstances," said Mr. Justice Marshall, were enough to excuse Loyd's failure to look at the deed before signing it; his trust in Ada was a slight but sufficient circumstance. In *Kruse v. Koelzer* (1905),[52] the buyer of a tract of land found out that his lot was shorter on one side than he had imagined. The court said sternly that "Men ... cannot close their eyes to the means of knowledge equally accessible to themselves and those with whom they deal." In *Standard Manufacturing Co. v. Stallmann* (1906),[53] Adolph Stallmann, a small retailer, signed up for a bill of goods when the salesman told him that his brother Louis had said it was all right to do so. The Stallmanns, said the court, "had been induced by fraud to sign the contract under such false and fraudulent representations as were reasonably calculated to excuse them from reading it." In *Steffen v. Supreme Assembly of the Defenders* (1907),[54] a widow signed a settlement and written release of her claims under a benefit certificate. The court was adamant: law "does not allow a plea of mistake as to the contents of a written instrument which the signer has full opportunity to read but neglects to." In *Glassner v. Johnston* (1907),[55] another insurance case, Glassner tried to rescind an endowment policy. He was a retail dry-goods merchant, foreign born, "imperfectly familiar with the English language," who signed up for the policy without reading or understanding it. The "ordinary citizen," said the court, is not "chargeable" with the detailed actuarial knowledge one needs to decipher insurance jargon. Many of these cases could be matched in tone, if not in precise fact-situation, in Period III. Fraud and mistake fit in well with the court's bent in these years, too, since these ideas were convenient legal instruments for reaching a just result as the court saw justice, in terms of the distinctive dimensions of a given situation. Particular emphasis was placed on reliance and on a standard called the "right to rely"; these concepts had a direct bearing on the moral quality of the parties' acts, and their use and non-use by the court closely followed the court's perception of the equities of the case before it.[56]

{103} The history of the law of express and implied warranties provides many parallels with the history of fraud and mistake. A traditional rule implied a warranty of fitness for a particular purpose, with respect to manufactured goods ordered for that purpose; in sales of goods in specie, no such warranty was implied, and *caveat emptor* was the rule.[57] This was a distinction of risks based on the nature of the transaction. The same sort of warranty was implied for professionals who held themselves out as having particular skills; they warranted by implication that they could perform their ordinary professional tasks successfully. Thus, in Period I a cause of action was stated against a farrier who performed an "unskillful and improper castration of a colt, in consequence of which the animal died."[58] The implied warranty of title for chattels also rested on common understanding; nobody could fairly be supposed to be buying a claim or a speculation in a lot of "cabinet furniture."[59]

In fact, the maxim *caveat emptor*, which appealed to rugged individualists, was often evaded by the court even in Period I, chiefly by the use of implied warranties of one sort or another. The story is a long and complicated one, and in general belongs more to sales law than to contract. In the debates in California over whether the state should adopt civil or common law, much was made of the difference between *caveat emptor* and the civil law tendency to imply warranties in such a way as to hold the seller to a high ethical standard. The common law rule was praised as "protective of trade, and a free and rapid interchange of commodities"; it did not look upon man as "incapable of judging for himself."[60] Even in 1850, however, the Californians were laboring under an illusion as to what was being done in common law jurisdictions. A strict view of warranty law, to be sure, fit well with an abstract contract system; it tended toward clarity, certainty, and fungibility of goods. But the Wisconsin case of *Smith v. Justice* (1861)[61] subordinated these values to considerations of fairness. There, the seller of a horse said that the horse was "all right." The court made these words into an express warranty:

> a positive representation with respect to the quality of the thing sold, made by the vendor and relied on by the vendee at the time of the sale, amounts to a warranty.... Thus if the horse was purchased to use in harness, if the vendor said it was all right, and it was actually ungovernable in harness, though a good saddle-horse, that would be a breach of the warranty. The evidence here was that the plaintiff bought the horse to use in harness, and that this was known to the defendant. {104}

This ruling made the line between express and implied warranty very thin. *Smith v. Justice* had backing from some authority. But it was opposed to the classic statement of Chief Justice Gibson of Pennsylvania, in *McFarland v. Newman* (1839),[62] that "the naked averment of a fact is neither a warranty itself, nor evidence of it." For Gibson, the seller must have "consented to be bound for the truth of his representation." This statement—note the emphasis on "consent"—was sound classical contract law. It is not that Wisconsin rejected Gibson's doctrine altogether; but rather that, even in Period I, the cases in Wisconsin turned on the court's concepts of risk, value, and the particular business circumstances, rather than on the formal shape of the transaction.

A strict (Gibson) view of warranty was most appropriate to the purely mercantile situation—equal confronting equal. Ironically, then, the "special" (mercantile) law of warranty, if applied to all transactions, regardless of the trading character of the parties, was more stringent and harsh (from the consumer's standpoint) than the theoretically abstract and impersonal law of contract. Yet as consumers crowded into the market, the law of warranty itself began to lose its mercantile flavor and become more "equitable," though it did so somewhat more slowly than the law of contract, and its codification in uniform acts (the Sales Act, for example) put something of a brake on this process.

One particularly dramatic area of decay of warranty law deserves mention. Traditionally, only those who were in "privity of contract" with their seller could complain of breach of warranty. The contract set the limits of liability. Like the rule in *Hadley v. Baxendale* (1859),[63] and many nineteenth-century tort rules, this doctrine insulated manufacturers of machinery and food (and wholesale merchants) from risks which were remote, unpredictable, and difficult to insure against. Wider liability for tainted foods and poisons was the first important hole punched in the privity doctrine. Period II manifested great public concern with health and food standards; thus it was logical for the privity doctrine to give way here first. In *Haley v. Swift & Co.* (1913),[64] the Wisconsin court allowed the plaintiff, permanently injured after eating adulterated link-sausage, to jump the contractual chain past the small-town merchant to the manufacturer, a large and famous company. The manufacturer was liable to third persons if he sold articles "intended to ... affect human life," and which, if misprepared, would {105} be "immediately dangerous." This was an important step away from Gibson and *caveat emptor*.

Fact-Analysis and Construction (Interpretation) of Documents. In practically every contract case the court must necessarily analyze facts or "construe" a document (which is the analysis of a special kind of fact). In a great many cases the court does little else. These cases are not important, from the standpoint of classical contract theory, since they have little to say about doctrine and legal principles. Yet, paradoxically, cases involving a great deal of money, and complicated transactions, are peculiarly likely to turn on fact-analysis and construction (interpretation of the document). Again, in the flock of non-business cases which reached the court in Period II, there were many cases which were nothing but disputes over facts. Particularly was this true of the support contract cases. Quarrels over behavior began them and carried them through the courts. The traditional role of appellate courts in the judicial hierarchy deeply influences the fact-finding process in appellate courts. Since appellate courts depend upon and abide by the fact decisions of their subordinates, they have very narrow powers to control the framing of issues. Cases of constitutional law, where the court in Period II exercised policy-making power in the most obvious way, were also those cases where the "issue" was sharpest and could be least mistaken, and where the manner in which the "issue" was framed depended least upon disputes over behavior and the fact-finding powers of lower courts.

The basic rule of construction was a rule of objective judicial neutrality. The court had the duty to "give to the contract the construction which will bring it as near to the actual meaning of the parties as the words they saw fit to employ ... will permit."[65] This was a rule of abstraction. Yet, much of substantive contract law was in effect expressed in terms of rules of construction and fact-finding; given legal results followed only from the presence or absence of facts which had to be specifically found and weighed by the court. Decisions on warranty, on fraud, on "substantial performance," on the parol evidence rule—these were all, more or less, fact or construction decisions, expressed in terms of rules which actually had little content. Despite the supposed objectivity of construction and fact analysis, courts high and low often made and enforced policy by construing and fact-finding in such manner as to implement values the court wished to serve. Insurance {106} policies, for example, were "construed" against the insurer. But though this was construction for an ulterior purpose, it was still construction, not pure invention. Contracts were bent but not broken. In standardized business dealings, the court's perception of its own role suggested boundaries within which the draftsman could work on his forms. One scholar has described the trend of the Wisconsin insurance cases as "one long education of company lawyers," on how to draft better and tighter forms.[66] The tighter the language, the more the court was squeezed into a corner. At the extreme, the court had two hard alternatives: to label "illegal" (or against "public policy") some type of clause which the court disliked, or to swallow its distaste and enforce the clause. The court's vacillation and its inability (by virtue of traditional and functional limits on its law-making power) to suggest good forms instead of merely striking down bad ones, invited the legislature to take the initiative. In this indirect manner, the court paved the way for regulatory insurance statutes which cut down its own freedom of action along with that of the insurance companies.

Because no two construction cases were exactly alike, the court could, however, allow more play to muffled policy and the persuasiveness of the particular, without feeling the embarrassment of inconsistency. Many questions of construction of contracts were relatively colorless; some cases concerned documents badly drafted in nonrecurring manner; decisions of the court carried (or seemed to carry) few social consequences. Did the sale of "a complete sawmill" include a bull chain? Is cancer an "acute illness" under the terms of an insurance policy?[67] In the mass, questions such as these might prove important, fraught with policy considerations; but for the isolated case, the court often enjoyed the freedom given by issues of small consequence. Consequently, the court could do justice in the particular case, or achieve the more common-sense result, without worrying that the legal system as a system would suffer from possible error. Only when type-situations recurred could the court wake up to discover that it had created a "rule" of construction, e.g., that insurance contracts should be construed strictly against the insurance company. To say that a case presented "only" an issue of fact or construction meant, then, that the situation was too new or too unsystematized for experience and habit to have crystallized some standard way of handling it. This happened frequently in Period III, with its new business cases. In these, the court's role was administrative; since lower court fact-finding and {107} construction were entitled to respect, the court sat primarily as a reviewing agency, to see that the trial court did not step far over the bounds of propriety. This was a real power, and a useful one; but it was nonetheless both passive and limited. Moreover, during the peak years of (apparent) legal formalism, the courts were fond of developing rules of construction, similar to the "canons" which were used to reshape (and sometimes devastate) statutes. Strictly speaking, these rules were nothing but expressions of attitudes or empirical summaries of tendencies. But the rules satisfied the thirst for legal certainty, and helped to avoid the impression that decisions were random and capricious. Although some of the canons were (or purported to be) simply inductions based on the habits of those who write and speak English,[68] others expressed value preferences, e.g., the rule which demanded that in case of doubt a contract must be construed against the draftsman.[69] To the extent followed, this rule worked against those businesses who dealt with the general public (e.g., insurance companies) and who took the initiative in structuring their own transactions.

Performance and Breach (Including Conditions). This doctrinal category was large and important in all periods. Despite the century that separates Period I from Period III, changes in doctrine were not dramatic. But, as was typical of other aspects of the court's work, there were real changes in the way the court actually handled these cases, changes corresponding to shifts in the court's characteristic attitudes toward itself, the legal system, and the economy. Even such technical and treacherous doctrines as those turning on the concept of the "condition precedent"* were manipulated as artifacts of policy. In *Kellogg v. Nelson* (1856),[70] Kellogg, of Sauk County, sold to Nelson "one thousand bushels of Canada club wheat at sixty cents per bushel," to be delivered to Nelson & Company's warehouse. Nelson paid $200 down, the balance "on delivery of said wheat as it is hauled per load, said Nelson to furnish bags for hauling it." Only a small part {108} of the wheat was actually delivered. The Wisconsin Supreme Court, reversing for an error in instructions, held that Nelson had to show, as a condition precedent to recovery, that he had furnished the bags or stood ready to furnish them. The court cited cases—one on the dissolution of a mercer's business, another concerning a contract of apprenticeship, a third arising out of a shipping contract between a Spanish and a Havana merchant, a fourth concerned with building a turnpike[71]—but the precedents told the court only how it was supposed to analyze the situation before it; by no stretch of the imagination did they dictate the specific application of the rule to the dealings of Ephraim Kellogg and Ebenezer Nelson. More important to the result was the judges' opinion that the agreement to furnish bags constituted "part of the consideration" for the bargain. "We cannot doubt," said the court, "that this fact entered into the calculations of the parties when they made the contract, and influenced them when they fixed upon the price." This language seems to invite a subjective appraisal—like a search for the "intent" of the parties—but the approach taken was really abstract and objective. In effect the court made a judgment on a market basis: that sixty cents a bushel was the market price for wheat, but only if bags were furnished.

But the market basis of such an opinion depended on the judges' grasp

---

* When a court speaks of an action or fact as a "condition precedent" to recovery by a plaintiff, it means essentially that the plaintiff must show performance of the action or occurrence of the fact before he can complain of defendant's own nonperformance. Thus, if a contract calls for plaintiff to deliver goods on April 1, and defendant to pay on May 1, and the defendant is sued on the grounds that he has not paid on May 1, plaintiff's nondelivery on April 1 may well be used as a defense. A court allowing such a defense might term delivery on April 1 a "condition precedent" to plaintiff's recovery.

of market facts—the grain trade, in *Kellogg*. It follows that the court's skill in dealing with cases of condition precedent and subsequent diminished with the widening gap between the judges' grasp of business facts and the complexity of economic life. The court was on safest ground when its precedents were close to the point; but this happened only with regard to general business practice, and only when a steady flow of cases on one type-situation came to the court. So the court could enunciate and follow a rule that in installment land contracts, the right to collect the purchase price was absolute; tender of a deed was not a "condition precedent" to suit.[72] In any event, the utility of such a rule did not last long, because type-situations had the habit of disappearing after a brief life span. Abstraction and objectivity called for general rules, not the court's guesswork. But the small cases arose usually out of anomalous, imperfect, or non-business situations, while the big cases, though they arose in thoroughgoing business contexts, did not lend themselves to general rules. *Wisconsin Sulphite Fibre Company v. D. K. Jeffris Lumber Company* (1907)[73] was a major performance case; the contract called for the manufacture and sale of about {109} 5,000,000 feet of pine saw logs. The factual issues were so complicated that the action "was referred to a referee for trial." The Supreme Court's decision in this case, for all that the opinion talked about principles, had more the flavor of review of action by an administrative agency than of adjudication upon sharply isolated "issues" of law.

The characteristic performance case of Period II was the construction contract. The problem here was the lack of objective measurements for satisfactory performance. The business eventually defended itself from chaos by developing certain institutions, for example, the architect's certificate, that assessed quality as rationally and objectively as possible. This device worked quite well. It was not, however, foolproof. It depended, for one thing, on the impartiality and competence of the architect. He was the "agent" of the owner, not of the builder; if the owner prevented the architect from giving his certificate, or if the architect's refusal to certify was arbitrary, the builder could still recover. To let the matter depend on the "whim, or worse" of one party, was "too absurd for belief that parties' minds met thereon."[74] These were at root obvious and wholesome rules; but they were capable of general expansion. If the court smelled injustice, it was fairly easy to "find" arbitrary or collusive behavior.

"Whim," however, is but the pejorative equivalent of the word "satisfaction," which frequently appeared in building, repair, and construction contracts. For the court, "satisfaction" had to be measured objectively, not subjectively—that is, by the market. But in non-business cases, e.g., contracts to decorate a house, satisfaction was a matter of taste; no objective (market) standard was realistically possible, without the imposition of a ruthless abstraction on situations which abstraction did not fit very well.

One legal technique which helped the court in its dilemma was the doctrine of substantial performance, which operated to relieve from hardship builders whose work was almost, but not quite, perfect. Theoretically, in a free market, parties could agree on any specifications they wanted, and no party could be forced to accept work which did not precisely conform to specifications. But in a complex contract—for example, to build a large office building—perfect results were almost impossible. The rise of the doctrine of substantial performance followed, then, from the increasing richness and complexity of technology. If the builder had to sue for his pay, his recovery would be measured by the contract price, less the amount of harm caused by the {110} imperfections, valued objectively (by the market). Again, in non-business cases, no objective valuation was possible. How could a court decide whether painting a room white instead of off-white was "substantial" performance or not? Or decide how much the error should cost the painter? Yet in non-business cases the doctrine could free the contractor from absolute dependence on the customer's whim. Inevitably, the cases had to talk in moral terms; there was no other way to talk. It was unjust for a property owner to keep the benefit of performance without paying, even if the work was not perfect. However, "mere" retention of the work was not acceptance of it, said the court, thinking in one case of a coat of paint, in another of a heating plant embedded in the structure of a school.[75] The court was acutely aware of the land-owner's dilemma: either he had to take work he did not want or could not use; or he had to tear his building to pieces, or subject himself to substantial interference with its use in order to correct the error.

Thus, there were really two doctrines of substantial performance. One, for business cases, allowed recovery to be determined by the market value of performance or of the finished product. The other, for non-business cases, meant only that the court decided, by its own best judgment, whether a person's refusal to pay for an off-white living room was a whim or a dodge, or an honest allergy to off-white paint. But the distinction was not made explicit and it was difficult to apply.[76] And the legal situation was complicated by the availability of still another doctrine which permitted relief under some circumstances to a builder whose work was substantially but not entirely in accordance with his contract. This was *quantum meruit*, under which the calculus of recovery begins, not with the contract price, but with the "fair value" of the builder's performance. Thus the court had many options before it: it could award full recovery, if it found that in fact performance was without defect; it could award no recovery, on the ground that performance was not substantial enough or was willfully defective; it could award the contract price less owner's damages, through the use of the concept of substantial performance; or it could award the builder the "fair value" of his performance, less owner's damages, through the use of *quantum meruit*.

The general problem of the performance cases remained with the court in Period III. It was inherent in the nature of the court's contract docket. Market criteria fit non-market cases only awkwardly, while the {111} prevalence of cases with non-market considerations tended to shape doctrine along these lines, giving rise to judicial attitudes toward doctrine which affected even cases arising in market situations.[77]

Illegality and Public Policy as Defenses to Contract Actions. This is the largest single group of cases in the whole tabulation—36 in Period I, 33 in Period II, 14 in Period III. It includes those contract cases in which a significant assertion was made (usually by the defendant) that the contract sued upon was illegal or against public policy. The size of the category is not unexpected. Many of the cases lie on the frontier between contract and not-contract; they test the border between contract law and the "special" fields, and this constant redefinition of boundaries is an abiding task of the law of contract. Of course, if sweeping legislation created entire new fields of law, contract law in the classical sense no longer operated in the area covered by the statutes. The tabulated cases, then, concern less completely codified areas, or areas where "public policy" as defined by statute had not completely ousted the law of contract, but simply added a "defense" (e.g., that a foreign corporation might not sue in the state without a license to do business).

The big part played by this category in the tabulation is in striking contrast to the small part it played in contract literature and in the teaching of the law of contracts. Langdell's little *Summary* of contract law spent about one page on the consequences of illegal consideration. The sixth edition of Williston's case-book (1954) devoted 40 out of 1,211 pages to illegality.[78] After all, contract law was supposed to concern grand sweeping scientific principles. Illegality and specific public policy defenses were usually based on precise local statutes. Langdell's image of contract law abhorred the local and particular. Thus tradition-minded scholars felt justified in removing from study of the law of contracts one of its most vital parts.

Period I and Period II had in common a tendency which Period III did not share: a major portion of their cases had to do with a particular defense under this category. For Period I, this was the usury laws—23 out of the 36 cases were usury cases. Considering the great political impact of the usury laws of Period I, the shortage of fluid capital, the frustrating need for money to finance land acquisition and economic growth, this emphasis is not unexpected. This group of {112} cases almost completely disappeared in the later periods. In Period II, 10 cases invoked the foreign corporation defense. This defense vanished from the tabulation of Period III.[79]

A "disappearing" defense, however, may merely have disappeared from reported cases. Usury laws continued on the statute books, as did restrictions on the right of a foreign corporation to use the forum. Two phenomena have to be carefully distinguished: the public policy enunciated by the state's legislation, and the court's power to modify public policy and to create new policy. Most of the cases arose under specific statutes (e.g., the usury laws); some asserted general, common law concepts of public policy; and a few cases were of a mixed type. The cases of Period I were almost entirely statutory. Cases resting on judge-made definitions of policy were uncommon.[80] This must not be taken to mean a failure on the part of the court to take an active role in shaping legal policy. The court played such a role; but along lines which favored abstraction and generality, leaving to the legislature the major tasks of defining limits (such as usury laws) on the free market. The prevalence of usury cases reflects above all else the wide use of the court system in enforcing policy made in the legislative chamber.

In Period II, on the other hand, even though the court certainly had a less creative role in shaping substantive law than it had two generations before, there were nine cases of illegality in which judge-made concepts governed the decision. These judicial defenses were not invented by the Wisconsin court. Some were old defenses (e.g., restraint of trade) with a statutory blood relative (anti-trust laws) which reacted on each other. Others were old defenses given new meaning. A 1907 case[81] outlawed a futures contract on the Detroit produce market, labeling the transaction an illegal "gamble." The illegality of a gambling contract was centuries old, but the application to this situation was novel for Wisconsin. In general, the court's willingness at least to consider new headings of public policy on its own was a trait of some importance. By Period II the peak period of judicial activism in creating doctrines of common law had ended, though a new activism had replaced it, most notoriously in constitutional law. Judicial readiness to declare constitutional values (and in a small way the public policy cases) may have been partly inner compensation for the court's real loss of power over the economy. Another factor was the court's increased awareness of the economic and social interdependence of the community. It was becoming increasingly clear that the public had a {113} stake in what looked like purely private bargains. A 1907 case[82] which voided an endless chain scheme could well serve as a symbol of the times. Any plan which necessarily involved victimizing third persons, said the court, was immoral and unenforceable. The economy itself had become a kind of endless chain.

One common law concept, restraint of trade, found expression in each of the three periods, and makes for fruitful comparisons of judicial technique in the three periods. Period I's sole case was *Kellogg v. Larkin* (1851).[83] The contract was executed in 1849, between a group of mill-owners on the one hand, and a group of pier-owners and warehousemen on the other. The agreement was cold blooded and quite frank: the warehousemen agreed to give the millers "full, absolute and uninterrupted control of the Milwaukee wheat market, from the date hereof up to the first day of August A. D. 1850, so far as they shall be able." The parties constituted themselves an association (the "Produce Association") and the warehousemen agreed not to "purchase, store, or handle any wheat" except under direction of the millers. Maximum storage prices were also fixed. The case called the legality of this arrangement into question, and sent the deciding judge, Timothy O. Howe, off onto a long, rambling, but interesting opinion, in which he declined to declare the agreement illegal. In many ways the opinion is the epitome of the ideas and techniques of the court in Period I. Though the judge eruditely cited authority, and avowed his respect for the "spirit of the letter of the law, as it has been adjudicated for one hundred and forty years," he did not feel himself utterly bound by the legal tradition: "Now, in applying the rule to any given case, it is important that we attend to the reasons upon which it is founded. 'Who so knoweth not the reason of the law, knoweth not the law.'"

"Restraint of trade" was a concept of public policy; and public policy was primarily a matter for the legislature, "the fairest exponents of what public policy requires, as being most familiar with the habits and fashions of the day, and with the actual condition of commerce and trade." Legislative enactments "operate prospectively as a guide"; they do not "annul" contracts "already concluded in good faith." The judge's role, primarily, was to enforce private contracts, not to look out for the "public welfare." In characteristic Period I manner, Howe called to witness the fact that the state's resources were "imperfectly developed"; he suggested that the "better way to foster individual effort" was to allow absolute "freedom" to follow or abandon any calling. {114} Contracts in partial restraint of trade did not harm the public, and could not. The case of the Milwaukee wheat market demonstrated this—that trade was open to the fiercest competition in all the world. The agreement in question could not "depress the wheat market." Wheat "has a market everywhere, and a value in every market." Even if the contract had removed all competition, and the mill-owners thereby could lower the price they would bid for wheat, then either "that product would have been wholly driven from the market, or new competitions would have entered the field to purchase." The contract would thus have been self-defeating. But Howe did not defend free trade as an end in itself. He recognized the public interest in a free market, but in almost the same breath he adhered to a kind of roughhewn mercantilism. "If the argument needed any such beggarly support," said Howe, one might well ask whether the public interest was "promoted, rather than prejudiced" by an arrangement which preserved for Wisconsin some flour milling business which would otherwise have been siphoned off to "some eastern state." In any event, the maxim that "competition is the life of trade" is "in fact the shibboleth of mere gambling speculation." By "reducing prices below, or raising them above values (as the nature of the trade prompted), competition has done more to monopolize trade, or to secure exclusive advantages in it, than has been done by contract." Howe's logic was weak: the agreement in question could not be at the same time futile and beneficial. It was strange to argue that competition would automatically reduce the arrangement to toothless innocence, then later praise the arrangement as beneficial to the public. But Howe's illogic was the illogic of his times, a general preference for economic individualism severely qualified by current concepts of what was necessary to achieve economic growth.

There were five cases in Period II on restraint of trade. None of the cases was as important, economically speaking, as *Kellogg v. Larkin*. All except one were simply attempts to enforce covenants not to compete, ancillary to the sale of a small business. Three of the four decisions enforced the covenant as "reasonable." Abstraction won victories in these cases, since the court enforced contracts as written; perhaps also the court sympathized with legal devices (such as the covenants in issue) by which small business attempted to protect its narrow but precious competitive niche. In the fifth case,[84] two small telephone companies merged, in compliance with "the wishes of the {115} merchants and business men of the city of Cumberland." The contractual validity of the merger came under attack, on the grounds that it violated the state's anti-trust laws. The court felt that the contract was in truth beneficial to the public. It was also in "harmony with the policy of the state, embodied in the legislative regulations of public utilities." The "public welfare," said the court, was best served by "uniting existing facilities, under proper control and regulation, to meet the public convenience and necessity." In this case, the conflict between two types of statute—anti-monopoly and regulatory—gave the court an opening to apply a rule of reason, that is, to assert its own specific determination of public policy. That policy, however, was one which opposed the trusts, not because they destroyed competition, but because they were lawless and powerful. Since telephone companies were not lawless, but regulated, and since their power was subject to the control of the state, the rationale of anti-trust laws did not apply to the case.

The most interesting case of restraint of trade in Period III was *Fullerton Lumber Co. v. Torborg*.[85] Fullerton, a Minnesota corporation, had its main office in Minneapolis, but ran some retail lumber yards in Wisconsin towns. Albert E. Torborg managed the company's yard in Clintonville, Wisconsin. In 1946, he signed a contract in which he promised: "If I cease to be employed by the company for any reason I will not, for a period of ten years thereafter, work directly or indirectly ... handling lumber ... or fuel at retail in any ... town, or within a radius of 15 miles thereof, where I have served as manager for the company." In 1953 Torborg quit and opened his own yard at Clintonville, taking three other employees with him. Fullerton demanded an injunction.

The ten-year period was unreasonably long, in the court's opinion. This defect should have made the covenant void and unenforceable, as a restraint of trade. But the court was troubled by the facts of the case. Torborg had been a key employee; in a place like Clintonville, Fullerton's "good will" depended on the "efforts and personal assets" of Torborg. Business had tripled the first three years Torborg was on the job; in 1954, after he left, business fell off by two-thirds. The "evidence of irreparable damage" to Fullerton was "so strong" that the court undertook "a thorough reconsideration" of the Wisconsin rule "that a covenant imposing an unreasonable restraint is unenforceable in its entirety." As a result, the case was remanded, {116}

> for a determination by the trial court of the extent of time as to which the restrictive covenant with respect to defendant's operations in Clintonville is reasonable and necessary for plaintiff's protection, and for judgment enjoining defendant from a breach thereof. It appears to us that a minimum period of three years would be supported by the evidence.[86]

This new rule, deliberately framed by the court, was typical of the particularism of Period III. The rule could not be relied on by draftsmen and individuals; it would necessarily vary from case to case, depending on the particular situation. The court showed a willingness to rewrite the contract in question (as the dissent accused), but only in the light of the actual experience of the parties in living under the contract. And the court eschewed an all-or-nothing approach; it split the contract down the middle, using its sense of reasonableness as a guide.

The cases which arose under specific statutes serve as sharp reminders of the practical limitations on the judiciary in defining policy. The usury cases in Period I were decided under statutes which were amended or repealed so frequently that the court often construed a statute which no longer existed; the practical effect of the decisions was thus severely circumscribed. In the Period II cases which invoked the foreign corporation defense, the court had only a relatively narrow area of maneuver; it was squeezed between statutes, federal constitutional principle (the commerce clause), rules of the conflict of laws (including the concept of "comity"), as well as the court's own sense of its role in the legal system's distribution of power and function.[87] In Period III legislation was so pervasive and of such dense content that the court had little scope to use or invent policies on its own. The court admitted as much in *Putnam v. Deinhamer* (1955).[88] Here an insurance policy gave the company the unilateral right to cancel on written notice. The company claimed it mailed a cancellation notice. The insured insisted he never got it. Was the cancellation clause against public policy, in that it allowed the company to cancel by mailing a notice, "without requirement that the notice must be received by or known to the assured"? No, said the court. The legislature had "already modified the freedom of parties to contract in respect to liability insurance policies." The court would not go beyond these precise statutory limits; it would not add novel and disruptive burdens to a business so thoroughly regulated by existing law. In *Putnam*, unwarranted extension {117} of a regulatory code would have upset the existing administrative machinery, or would have called for more men or money than the state had then available, or would have foisted on an agency of government some sudden, unwelcome power.

The court's reticence in *Putnam* precludes one from endorsing completely the view of those critics of the American judiciary who insist that the courts must construe statutes more "liberally" than was the habit in the nineteenth century, and should even use statutory principles as analogical sources for the development of new common law.[89] Their point is well taken in regard to broadly phrased declarations of policy, but hardly applies to the minute, close grinding, and specific statutes with which the twentieth-century court increasingly has to deal. The difficulties of extending regulatory statutes to situations not precisely within their textual ambit are illustrated by two cases in Period III. In *Kuhl Motor Co. v. Ford Motor Co.* (1955),[90] the statute in question licensed automobile manufacturers to do business in Wisconsin and provided that the state might revoke the license of a manufacturer who unfairly canceled a dealer's franchise. Kuhl, a Ford dealer, sought an injunction to prevent unfair cancellation of his franchise. The letter of the statute said nothing about civil suits, but what of the spirit? Currie, speaking for a bare majority of the court, saw in the statute a "public policy" to "promote fair dealing," which would be enhanced by allowing civil suits. One year later *Chapman v. Zakzaska*[91] came up for decision. Zakzaska bought a used Nash from Chapman, a used car dealer; the price was $1,695 plus a trade-in. The Nash had traveled about 60,000 miles; but Chapman turned back the speedometer to 21,000. A statute provided that,

> No used motor vehicle shall be offered for sale ... unless the speedometer reading thereon shall be turned back to zero [or unless] ... readings thereon are indicated in writing ... and subsequently shown to purchasers.

Violation of the act was a misdemeanor. But could Zakzaska resist payment on the ground that the contract was void? No, said the court. "The statute does not purport to create a new civil violation.... [The] illegality in the instant case does not permeate the contract so as to furnish the reason for it." The contract was enforceable; but Chapman recovered only the actual value of the car at the time of its sale ($1,050), not the face amount of the note. As a result, Chapman did not profit {118} from his wrong-doing (though neither did he suffer for it); and Zakzaska did not get a free car. Both cases were decided by a divided court; *Kuhl* in particular gave the court uncommon difficulty. The cases appear inconsistent; but one can speak of inconsistency only on the assumption that it is possible to frame general principles to govern the question whether a criminal statute shall have civil consequences; or indeed the question whether statutes are to be analogically extended at all. In fact, the opinions prove mainly that by the 1950's power in the legal system was so distributed among non-judicial agencies that the intrusion of the judiciary would often amount to dislocation, not fulfillment, of the public policy and its structural basis.

The Contract as Claim: Assignment and the Identity of Parties. Abstraction demanded that the law allow contract rights of all sorts to be absolutely and freely assignable. The subject matter of contract could be treated as a colorless, economic integer; likewise the contract itself, as a claim, could be so treated. To reach this position of abstraction, the common law had to discard certain time-honored doctrines. Under theory prevailing until post-medieval times, "choses in action" (intangible claims) were not recognized as assignable. Equity led the way in allowing assignment of a chose in action.[92] The common law rule was still adhered to in Wisconsin in 1842,[93] but the existence of the equity rule meant that the inalienability of choses in action was a rule of procedure and form, not of substance. Even in this restricted sense, inalienability soon disappeared. New codes of procedure, whether borrowed directly from New York's famous Field Code, or developed independently, merged law and equity, and gave the "real party in interest" the right to sue in his own name. The new procedure reached Wisconsin in the middle 1850's.[94]

The new procedure, with its ideal of a businesslike attitude toward legal process, went hand in hand with contract abstraction, the new substance.

By and large, the Wisconsin court in Period I gave effect to the assignment by an owner of any claim, document, or right for which in fact a market existed. The transfer of claims was a business. Some men dealt in documentary claims (e.g., land warrants), just as brokers and factors in the twentieth century deal in accounts receivable. Assignment was more than a doctrine; it was a protean device, an institution, which took on innumerable uses. So, for example, attorneys took title by assignment to the claims of their Eastern creditor clients, partly to {119} avoid local prejudice against outsiders, partly to gain a free hand in collecting and to surmount the problems of distance and communication. Assignment then as later was also used as a financing device; railroads, as we noted, assigned stock subscriptions (evidenced by notes and mortgages) to raise ready cash. The courts, aware of the need of the roads for quick capital, upheld assignment in the language of abstraction: "A stock subscription is nothing but a contract,.... It would clearly be assignable as between individuals, and we can see no reason why it should not [be assignable], in the case of a corporation, acting in execution of the powers conferred by its charter."[95]

Assignability, however, like abstraction, was not an end but a means to an end. It had to give way before specific and countervailing policy considerations. The homestead exemption restricted involuntary alienation of socially preferred assets. Under certain acts of Congress, the rights to military bounty lands were expressly declared nontransferable. In *Ward v. Schooner Dolphin* (1845),[96] Ward and his partner, merchants of Milwaukee, furnished materials to repair the schooner, fitted it out with a set of sails, and also paid some of the hands who worked on repairing the boat. The merchants sued under the Wisconsin "boat and vessel act," which provided for a lien against vessels, but said nothing about the assignability of the lien. The court held that only the workers themselves might enforce the lien, not the merchants who claimed under their rights. The special statutory liens, after all, were themselves exceptions to the abstraction of contract law—special procedural preferences for the benefit of the "sacred rights of labor." The court did not favor the idea of extending such an exception to merchants (or worse, to speculators in claims). In *Maxwell v. Reed* (1859),[97] Maxwell, a tinsmith, executed a promissory note to Sidney Shepard, with a power of attorney to confess judgment on the note which recited: "I, said Maxwell, do hereby ... release, waive and forego all manner of benefit of exemption of property, real or personal, from levy and sale upon execution." Abstract theory did not prevent the court from striking down the waiver:

> to preserve the State the citizen must be protected; ... to live, he must have the means of living; to act and to be a citizen, he must be free to act and to have somewhat wherewith to act,.... If this be so (and who can doubt it, in view of our history?) can it be supposed that ... high State purposes, can be made dependent upon the contracting will or grasping genius of the individual debtor or creditor?

... However a man may sell {120} or mortgage, or give away the great privilege with which the constitution and law of the State may have invested him, the State will not allow its process to be used to undermine and destroy one of the great bulwarks of individual freedom and manly citizenship....

Assignment was often restricted for the benefit of a favored class; in this respect the law of assignment verged on the law of contractual capacity. Statutes in Period I, for example, limited the assignability of insurance policies in which married women had beneficial interests. These statutes survived into Period II.[98] Such restrictions affecting women slowly died; but the law developed other limitations on free assignability to accord with new notions of social policy, or with subtle changes in the climate of opinion. Even the alienability of land—the single most important example of the triumph of commercial mobility over feudalism—was limited, notably by homestead exemptions. The "spendthrift trust" doctrine, which came into its own in the late nineteenth century, borrowed its name from a category of incompetence; but the doctrine was in fact a way to seal the safety of a long-term dynastic trust. The doctrine allowed a trust settlor to insulate principal and income of his trust from the dangers of assignment (voluntary or not) by a beneficiary. It was an appropriate legal development for an insecure, conservation-minded age.[99]

Occasionally, the court or legislature made another kind of policy choice, between the sweeping negotiability of the law merchant and the simple assignability of the common law. During the farm mortgage crisis of the late 1850's and 1860's, the legislature tried to strip the quality of negotiability from the notes executed by farmers subscribing for railroad stock; thereby the statute sought to subject the holder in due course to the "equities"; local juries would certainly incline to find the "equities" favorable to farmers.[100] Also, in Wisconsin, state school land certificates (expressly made assignable by statute) were customarily transferred in blank, and treated as if negotiable. In a series of cases beginning in 1858, the court refused to recognize this practice as effective. The certificates were "contracts for the sale of real estate"; when used as collateral, they had to be enforced by foreclosure, and the land-owner retained his equity of redemption.[101] The cases were decided during a distressed period, and had the effect of helping a large class of settlers to stave off financial ruin. Historical patterns of doctrine served as alternatives, not determinants; the court chose from available models, but chose the model which most served the ends the court saw as desirable. {121}

In Period II, for the first time, third-party beneficiary doctrine played a prominent role in the tabulation. The doctrine gave to persons intended as beneficiaries of contracts made by others rights to enforce these contracts under certain circumstances. Practically speaking, the doctrine dated from *Lawrence v. Fox*, a New York case decided in 1859.[102] The rapid growth of the doctrine had some relationship to the concept of the real party in interest and was thus not inconsistent with the basic abstraction of contract law and the freedom of contractual arrangements. By the time of Period II, however, the doctrine had developed also a highly technical aspect; it was used metaphorically in a wide range of miscellaneous situations as a legal construct. *Whiting v. Hoglund* (1906)[103] was a particularly farfetched example. Whiting's intestate deeded a piece of land to Hoglund. The deed described the land as the "southwest one-quarter of section 17, town 35, range 1 east in Price county." This was a slip of the pen; the land actually lay in the northwest quarter. The deed was given back to the grantor to be corrected. The grantor executed a corrected deed, and gave it to the register of deeds of Price County for recording. After recording, the deed was returned by mail to the grantor. The grantor, unfortunately, died; and the question was whether the deed had been "delivered" to the grantee during his lifetime. The third-party beneficiary doctrine enabled the court to find a legally sufficient delivery. The register "impliedly" agreed to record the deed "for the grantee"—"an ordinary case of one for a consideration, at the request of another, agreeing to perform a service for a third person." Consequently, delivery to the register could be treated as delivery to the grantee. In Period III, most of the third-party beneficiary cases were of this nature. The doctrine, which began as a handmaiden of abstraction, ended up as a conceptual tool of the court, the uses of which were not necessarily related to abstraction at all. In a labor case, the doctrine allowed individual employees to sue (as "beneficiaries") on their union's contract with management. A sub-contractor might discover himself to be a "beneficiary" of his principal's bond. A surviving joint owner of a bank account might discover herself to be a "beneficiary" of her co-tenant's contract with the bank. A broker might rescue himself from the Statute of Frauds by discovering himself as a third-party beneficiary of the contract between buyer and seller (which included a written covenant to pay commissions).[104] These cases should not be dismissed as mere logic-chopping. One of the great ideas of Period II and beyond was that even private contracts were not isolated bargains between isolated {122} dealers, that they sent ripples of consequence in all directions through society. Third-party doctrine was some recognition of this fact. It gave a voice in the enforcement of the bargain to at least the nearest of the affected parties.[105]

The Contract as Claim: Estoppel, Waiver and Some Allied Concepts. It might offend a purist to talk in one breath of estoppel, waiver, ratification, election of remedies, laches, and accord and satisfaction. These were all different concepts, with different histories and uses. They had in common, however, that they all related to particular acts of particular parties, subsequent to the formation of a contract but affecting the contract rights of the actors. And they were all ideas that could be used to bend rules of higher generality. Though they themselves could be expressed in terms of rules, they constituted statements of reasons (derived from the facts of particular cases) why some more general rule should not be applied.

These concepts were not new, and Period I showed many examples. But they were most prominent in Period II, and quite prominent (though a little less so) in Period III. In Period II, about one-fifth of the cases at least talked about one or more of these ideas. It is easy to see why this was so. A concept like estoppel is in essence antithetical to pure contract abstraction. A party is "estopped" for reasons which are peculiar to his or his opponent's situation. Abstraction, however, abhors the special and the particular. In Period II, the court was fond of using these concepts to thwart the application of particular rules without the bother or embarrassment of making radical changes in formal doctrine. There would be no need to admit the indignity of past error, no need to go so far as to overrule prior cases, when waiver or estoppel could reach the right result without changing "the law." Not that the court used these concepts wholesale. Any such use was curbed by loyalty to the legal tradition, which prevented these concepts from running wild. Even more important, the court used the concepts to bend rules only when it felt the rules needed bending.

Waiver and estoppel were not used only on a case-by-case basis. If the court had a consistent bias of values in a given area of transactions, it sometimes applied one or more of these concepts consistently in handling such transactions. This warping and sliding process was characteristic of the way the common law developed. After a generation or two in which a court consistently found that not the general rule but {123} the "exception" applied to whatever case was at hand, the original general rule turned into a mummified corpse. Historically the insurance companies were on the losing end of such a process, which, by the use of "estoppel" and "waiver," created what amounted to a set of rules for construing insurance policies so as to aid the insured. This process of attrition took place frequently in the law; and in the twentieth century "legal realism" gave dead rules decent burial in many instances simply by pointing out that the old rules were no longer used even when legal literature still paid them lip service. This decline in legal dogmatism in Period III probably accounts for the fact that the use of such doctrines as waiver and estoppel was somewhat less frequent in Period III than in Period II.

By nature, the use of these doctrines was protean. They were primarily tools, not rules of binding generality. They were not only flexible in their application, they were even flexible in definition and formulation. Each doctrine had an express and an implied variety (that is, a real and unreal type) with various shades in between. Close analysis of the uses to which these doctrines were put shows that the doctrines were simply techniques used in furthering tendencies which could be documented through the analysis of use of other concepts. For example, in large-scale, complicated contracts, parties were bound to make mistakes; perfect performance was impossible. In some of these cases, the court used the concept of "waiver" of defects to excuse errors; this use of waiver was functionally equivalent to the doctrine of substantial performance in building contracts.[106] It also made a difference to the court who argued waiver or estoppel. "A county cannot waive the statutory requirements as to the filing of claims against a county," said the court in 1955;[107] but a nearly contemporary case "estopped" the city of Chippewa Falls from unfairly revoking a driveway permit.[108] On the basis of such cases, one might formulate a tentative rule that the doctrines of waiver and estoppel would not be used against an arm of local government if the effect was to diminish regularity in public contracts or to endanger the sanctity of public finance; contrariwise, the doctrines might be used against local government to prevent discrimination against individuals through the manipulation of lawmaking power. But in fact no such rule existed as such; the cases show only how the court used its conceptual tools to enhance the values it felt should be furthered through the system of appellate litigation.

Waiver could be a pure legal construct, but it could also rest on {124} actual intent. Thus the term was applied to express contractual provisions in which a party "agreed" to give up legal rights. Abstractly considered, a person has a perfect right, as part of a bargain, to give up (or sell) some privilege of his; yet the court in Period I refused to uphold a waiver of the homestead exemption. Nothing daunted, draftsmen devised form contracts in Period II which "waived" mechanics' liens;[109] and in *Ebenreiter v. Freeman* (1956),[110] the buyer of a "Holstein cow eartag M H-3446, Holstein heifer 2 yrs. eartag" signed a document which expressly waived "any and all claims of every nature whatsoever against the seller of the personal property herein described ... arising out of any ... warranties, representations, agreements, and promises." If the court disliked a waiver of this kind, it could sometimes construe it into harmlessness; but if the language of the contract was tight and explicit, the court had only two bitter choices: to give up the battle, or strike down the "waiver" as illegal. *Ebenreiter* ingeniously combined construction and policy. The heifers had been sold, without a statutory brucellosis certificate, under a conditional sales contract. The court ruled the conditional sales contract void, as a violation of the statute; therefore "the waiver provisions contained therein are of no effect." Resort to contractual waiver sometimes even generated political response—particularly as to contracts of adhesion (standardized transactions) and as to labor contracts. By 1911, twenty-one states forbade "contracting out" (waiver of accident claims) by employees as a condition of employment.[111] Abstraction had to yield to the legislature's conception of social control over inequality of bargaining power.

The Contract as Claim: Damages. The law of contract damages was of surprisingly late development. Damage questions were originally left more or less to the discretion of the jury. Although the common law recognized practically nothing but money damages, careful standards for measuring money damages were not defined by the courts until the period of a fully grown law of contracts. Medieval law was too engrossed in details of land law and procedure to perfect the subtle calculus of a mature law of damages. In the nineteenth century, an abstract, market-oriented law of contracts did demand a law of damages which would conform with the underlying economic theories of the body of law; and the modern law of contract damages developed on that basis. Damages were awarded according to fixed formulae, {125} which measured only those losses which the abstract law of contract allowed to be measured—generally without weight given to factors of loss peculiar to specific transactions or relationships. For example, damages for breach of a contract to deliver goods were the difference between the contract price and the market price at the time of breach.[112] This formula assumed a frictionless, universal market in the commodity traded; it assumed that identical units of the goods promised were immediately available at a market price. The rule was really appropriate only for merchants dealing in a commodity with a wide and objective market; it fit much less well bargains between casual buyers or sellers, and sales of goods without a ready market. But the law of contract damages assumed, as a general rule, the existence of an ideal market, even when no such market existed; it was up to the injured party to demonstrate to the contrary if he could. Damages inconsistent with the ideal market were usually excluded. Pain and suffering, disappointment, embarrassment or inconvenience in business—none of these was compensable. Breach of contract never gave rise to punitive damages, no matter what the circumstances. As a Pennsylvania court admitted in 1859, "violation of most contracts involves a breach of faith"; yet the law, in awarding damages, took no account of the breach of faith.[113] Motive and fault had no measurable legal consequences.

Hardly any rule of contract damages was more influential in the nineteenth century than that associated with the great English case of *Hadley v. Baxendale* (1854).[114] In *Hadley*, a mill stopped working when a crank shaft broke; a new shaft was sent for, but its delivery was delayed through the neglect of the defendants, "well-known carriers trading under the name of Pickford & Co." The mill had to be shut down for a few days, and this resulted in a loss of profits to the plaintiff. But the court refused to allow the recovery of these profits. The case limited recoverable damages to those which were the "natural consequences" of breach of contract. The rule spread rapidly throughout the common law world. Its success is not to be explained as slavish imitation; common law courts usually have imitated only what the prevailing values of their time have told them to imitate. Wisconsin's first case in point, *Brayton v. Chase* (1854),[115] can hardly be explained as an imitation of the English decision, which was handed down in the same year. In *Brayton*, the plaintiff, a farmer, ordered a "New York reaper" from Chase, to be delivered before the first of July. {126} The reaper was not delivered. Brayton claimed he had "large crops of winter and spring grain" that he could not handle without a "labor saving machine." But, the court said, Brayton might collect only damages which "resulted naturally and directly from the injury complained of." His crop losses "were too remote"; they resulted "rather from the peculiar situation of the plaintiff than from the breach of the contract."

The reference to the "peculiar situation of the plaintiff" does much to explain the rule of *Hadley v. Baxendale*. *Hadley* was a rule of abstraction. Actually, there was nothing "peculiar" about plaintiff's situation in *Bray-*

ton v. Chase; nor was loss of a crop really a "remote" consequence of a failure to deliver a machine to harvest the crop. Yet Brayton was apparently only allowed to recover the difference between the contract and the market price of the reaper (probably zero). The transaction, in short, was treated as if both parties were traders in reapers, as if the parties dealt abstractly with the goods, buying and selling them for profit. Had this assumption been correct, the standard damage formula would have come closer to compensating Brayton for his loss, if any. The rule (to which *Hadley v. Baxendale* gave classic expression) was perfectly abstract. No attention was paid in *Brayton v. Chase* either to the nature of the subject matter (a reaper) or to the roles of the parties (farmer and dealer). Only the deal itself, as an abstract mathematical occurrence, was considered, not its consequences.

Yet *Hadley* signified more than this. From the point of view of those in the position of the defendant in *Hadley*, the rule of the case was a risk-limiting rule, and therefore a way of standardizing costs and rationalizing enterprise. Like some of the nineteenth-century tort rules, it protected industry and commerce from ruinous losses; like abstraction in general, it won acceptance not simply because of its ideological appeal but also because it seemed to further a greater goal—economic growth and the encouragement of industry. The rule harbored yet another rationale. In *Hadley* the court pointed out that "in the great multitude of cases of millers sending off broken shafts to third persons by a carrier," no remote consequences would occur. For one thing, the mill might have had a spare shaft. The court thus implied that the optimal mill-owner would not allow himself to be caught without a spare. Avoidable consequences must be avoided by those with power to avoid them; it would distort the market system to allow an offender against this principle to cast his losses upon another party, since a market system required the penalties for bad planning of enterprise to {127} fall upon those who planned badly. Similarly, the law's insistence that those on the short end of a breach of contract must demonstrate the market price to establish their damages, was an insistence that enterprise continue to carry on, to hustle, and not rely on damages from the erring contract-partner.

Protectionist impulses and serene faith in the pure free market both passed slowly into history; as they did so, the rule in *Hadley* weakened. By Period II, the rule suffered from the pressures caused by popular resentment of "big business" and from a growing inclination to shift losses onto those thought better able to bear them. This inclination was the more difficult for a court to resist because of the increasing triviality of the contract docket. The disposition of specific cases seemed unlikely to produce broad policy ramifications; it was therefore easy to let the general rule slip, and let the more meritorious party win. Also, the greater scope of insurance may have subtly changed the notion of what risks were too much for business to stand. There were words in *Hadley* itself which a court could use as an instrument for undermining *Hadley*. In particular, the court could expand the concept of the "natural" consequence of breach or the foreseeability of loss. To ascribe to these words their later meaning as courts applied them would mean that *Hadley* had harbored seeds of its own destruction even as it was born. However, it was not *Hadley*, but the idea behind it, that allowed the changes to take place. The rule, like so many others, split into opposite tendencies—it became at the same time a formula for limiting and a formula for justifying consequential damages. In *Altschuler v. Atchison, Topeka & S. F.* (1913),[116] an action was brought against the railroad upon its contract "to transport the members of plaintiff's orchestra, their instruments and baggage from Denver, Colorado, to Milwaukee, Wisconsin." The railroad breached its contract "by failing to deliver the car containing the baggage and instruments to the Chicago, Milwaukee & St. Paul Railway Company at Chicago, in time to make connections with a certain train." Because of this delay, the orchestra was "unable to give a matinee performance at Milwaukee"; also, the "sale of tickets for the evening performance was diminished." The plaintiff recovered damages for the lost matinee, since the railroad "did know of the general character of the plaintiff's business, that he was traveling to give performances, and was booked to arrive in Milwaukee in the forenoon." The court thus brought the railroad within the foreseeability exception to *Hadley*'s risk-limiting rule. But no recovery was {128} allowed for the diminished ticket sales at the evening concert: these damages were too "remote" and "speculative." In another Period II case, the rule of *Hadley* was invoked to prevent recovery of potential profits in a small dairy business which never started operation. Yet a manufacturer of soda water, forced out of business after giving his customers undersized bottles, successfully sued the bottler. The loss of the business was a "natural and probable" result of the sale of bad bottles.[117] Past business experience provided a reasonable measure of lost profits. The distinction between the new business (the dairy) and a going concern (the soda-water maker), implicit in these two contrasting cases, fit neatly with the court's typical concern for settled, going-concern values.

It was still the general rule in Period II that contract relationships created their own little universe of costs, beyond which the recovery of damages was not allowed to go. For example, in construction cases, if a landowner prevented a contractor from finishing his job, the contractor might not recover more than the contract price, less the cost of finishing the job.[118] Businessmen believed in *Hadley*; construction contracts, with their provisions for an architect's certificate and liquidated damages, typified a general urge so to structure business conduct as to standardize costs and limit risks. This was exactly the aim of the *Hadley* rule; it was a means of limiting liability, like the resort to the corporate form of doing business. For that matter, the homestead exemption was of like significance. The major forms of limited liability and risk limitation through legal means can be traced back to times when the rugged individualist was supposedly the basic American personality type. Limitation of risk was looked on, not as a way of suffocating enterprise, but, on the contrary, as a catalyst.

Even in a weakened form, *Hadley* presented a rule of damages which attempted to serve economic ends. It had no application to the personal, non-business cases which became so common in Period II. An extreme case of this new type was *Hess v. Zimmer* (1913).[119] Miss Hess sued for breach of a "contract" by Zimmer to marry her. According to Miss Hess, Zimmer "seduced her under promise of marriage and at different times prior to June, 1911, he had sexual intercourse with her upon further promises that he would marry her." It proved difficult to get Zimmer to the altar; he had one excuse after another for delay; once, for example, "the weather was too stormy." In general he acted with "bad faith and deceit." The evidence showed that Zimmer owned {129} property worth $12,000. The jury awarded Miss Hess $2,000 in damages. The Supreme Court affirmed, since these damages were not "excessive." Exactly how the jury calculated these damages is hard to say, but the computations certainly had nothing to do with "contract" or the market value of performance.

There were only six damage cases in the sample of Period III. None concerned the rule of *Hadley*. This may be merely coincidence. Business certainly still cherished the idea; the form contract in *Milwaukee Cold Storage Co. v. York Corp.* (1958),[120] drawn up by York, disclaimed liability for "prospective profits, or special, indirect or consequential damages"—a standard clause of obvious usefulness. The six cases did, however, show something of a consistent pattern. Three of the six had to do with mitigation of damages. The classic rules, which were recognized in earlier periods, required an injured contractor to mitigate his damages; for example, a wrongfully discharged employee had a duty to seek another job.[121] The idea behind the rule was connected with the economic theories of damage law; the standard formula measured damages in terms of the difference between contract price and market, but in some kinds of cases (e.g., labor cases), the only way to measure the market was to go out and establish the market by trial and error. Mitigation rules helped to isolate the pure economic loss, which was the sole interest of the law of contract damages.

Interestingly, the court applied the general mitigation rule in none of the three cases in Period III. In one,[122] a district agent for an insurance company had been wrongfully discharged. The jury was told to find the value of the job as district agent, taking into account loss of future profits. The jury consulted its private oracles and came back with an award of $44,000. The court upheld the award, without allowing any offset for what the agent might have earned in some other job. The lost position was capitalized and treated as an "asset" of which the agent had been wrongfully deprived. In *Polley v. Boehck Equipment Co.* (1956),[123] plaintiff, who ran a sawmill at Tigerton, Wisconsin, bought a new Diesel engine from Boehck. However, Boehck delivered "an old used engine in a poor state of repair." After complaints, Boehck came out, tinkered with the engine, and replaced the fuel pump with a new $800 pump; the engine still did not work. Ultimately, Polley sued for damages. One question was whether the value of the new pump installed could be considered in mitigation. The court said no, choosing as the measure of damages in this type of sale case the "benefit-of-bargain" {130} theory rather than the "out-of-pocket" theory. Under the test adopted, damages were treated as the difference between the value of the property as it was when purchased and what the article would have been worth had it been as represented by the seller. Under the "out-of-pocket" theory, the price paid was compared to the actual value of the article sold. Usually, the two measures came out the same, but in *Polley* they did not: "Many new parts might have been added but that would not make a new machine out of a used machine." The benefit-of-bargain theory emphasized the seller's wrongful act—his misrepresentation—and fixed damages accordingly, adding a certain punitive element to the damages; the out-of-pocket theory purported only to restore the economic status quo. Too much should not be read into the words of a test of damages; but the cases did show an undeniable slant away from the kind of pure economic measures favored by the classical law of damages. Moreover, the cases showed a tendency to allow greater finality to the jury's findings of damages. And the jury after all was the voice of common opinion.

The Contract as Claim: Quantum Meruit, Implied Contract, and Specific Performance. Conventionally, there are said to be two types of implied contract—the contract implied in fact, and the contract implied in law. The latter is admittedly a legal fiction. But the line between implication in fact and in law is a thin one. In *Graves v. Smith* (1861),[124] plaintiffs shipped flour to defendants, warehousemen in Milwaukee. Defendants argued that the complaint was defective because it "did not aver that the defendants acted for hire"; consequently "it is to be assumed that they were to charge nothing, and that they were therefore liable only for gross negligence." To this the court responded that, "It is probably very seldom that express agreements are made with respect to the charges of such persons [warehousemen]. But when any one employs them in the usual course of their business, that imports a hiring, and that they are to be paid." The contract was elliptical; the payment term was nonetheless real though unexpressed. The implication of terms, therefore, was abstract and objective in one sense; it assimilated a contract to the general pattern of all similar contracts, and disregarded any possible private, subjective understanding. Yet it was not only objectivity, but fairness in the particular case which required that the warehouseman be paid. A legal tool of abstraction {131} also served quite easily as an instrument of equity. Thus, rules of implied contract showed the same double use as rules of offer and acceptance, consideration, performance—both in support of the abstraction of the market, and (increasingly) as means of doing justice in the particular case. The rules also served in the familiar third role, the metaphorical. The implied contract notion was frequently invoked, at least by counsel for claimants, in cases of supposed inter-family service contracts.[125] Implied contract (*quantum meruit*) supplemented, too, the doctrine of substantial performance in Period II. So long as imperfect work was not too imperfect or done in "bad faith" or "willfully," it laid the promissor under an ethical claim to pay for value received.[126] In such cases, implied contract was a moral substitute for pure contract theory, which struck the new generation as too hardhearted, and which also did not fit the growing complexities of the economic order.

Mention should be made of the extraordinary remedy of specific performance. This was a strictly limited form of relief; only rarely would it be granted to enforce promises to convey chattels or choses in action. But for contracts to convey land, the remedy was generally available; and indeed, was frequently used, especially in Period I, with its heavy concentration of land cases. Land was "assumed to have a peculiar value, so as to give an equity for a specific performance, without reference to its quality or quantity." Taken at face value, this rationale might seem to make specific performance an anachronism. If land was truly treated in Period I as an abstract commodity, the remedy was unnecessary. Dealers in land had no sentimental attachment to any particular plot. Although each tract of land is geographically unique, and although even vacant farmland or timberland varies in quality, the same is true of farm animals; each one is in a sense unique, and individual members of a species vary greatly in quality. Specific performance might seem, therefore, more suitable to an older phase of English law—class-conscious, interested in the feudal, ancestral, symbolic meanings of particular estates. But land had its special features in the United States, too. It was a North Carolina case, *Kitchen v. Herring* (1851),[127] which spoke of land's "peculiar" value. The defendant in that case had argued from abstraction that, " 'the land ... is chiefly valuable on account of the timber,' [thus] the case does not come within the principle, on which a specific performance is decreed." To this the court replied: {132}

> Our constitution gives to land pre-eminence over every other species of property; and our law ... gives to it the same preference. Land, whether rich or poor, cannot be taken to pay debts until the personal property is exhausted.... Land must be sold at the court house, must be conveyed by deeds duly registered, and other instances "too tedious to mention."

Among the other instances "too tedious to mention" the court could have named the homestead exemption; and it might have paid tribute to the practical fact that the farmer-settler held major political power in his hands. The uses of specific performance in Period I showed how important it was to deny abstraction to land and preserve this remedy. A lender who took title to lands in his own name, promising to convey after payment, could be forced to do so. To refuse the remedy would have endangered the possessory rights of many settlers.[128] The "sacred rights of labor" required protection for the occupant of the soil. In times of rising land values, the doctrine upheld the security of transactions, by protecting investors in their bargains. In origin, therefore, the doctrine was non-abstract; its preservation in the market-oriented body of contract law was, as *Kitchen v. Herring* shows, a deliberate stroke of judicial policy, a purposeful exception to the abstraction of classical American contract law.

Constitutional Law. There is so close a connection between contract law and constitutional law at several points that this study would be incomplete without some account taken of constitutional problems. The contracts clause was one of the most important constitutional clauses for Period I; in Period II, the due process clause (construed to include "freedom of contract") largely replaced it in importance. These constitutional uses of the term "contract" had a real connection with the grubby day-to-day work of the court in matters of private agreement, even though the connection was not strictly a doctrinal one.

The contracts clause of the federal constitution (and its state constitutional counterpart)[129] limited the power of the state to tamper with existing contracts and property rights. The clause itself was gnomic, even obscure. When the federal Constitution was framed, the clause attracted relatively little public attention; but before the Civil War, the clause had become perhaps the most prominent guaranty in the Constitution. Four landmark decisions in the history of the court's construction of the clause can be singled out. *Fletcher v. Peck* (1810)[130] extended the prohibition of the clause to executed "contracts" or deeds. {133}

The *Dartmouth College Case* (1819)[131] further extended the guaranty by applying it to a legislative grant of a corporate charter. *Ogden v. Saunders* (1827),[132] on the other hand, limited the clause to retroactive legislation, over Chief Justice Marshall's dissent. *Bronson v. Kinzie* (1843)[133] again extended the reach of the guaranty, to limit changes in existing procedures to enforce rights, when the court struck down an Illinois statute which extended a mortgagor's period of redemption, and forbade foreclosure sales at less than two-thirds of the appraised value of the property sold. These great cases paralleled developments in the law of private contract. *Fletcher v. Peck* and *Dartmouth College* radically expanded the concept of constitutionally protected contract. Charters, grants of land, even a legislative exemption from taxation[134]—all these were "contracts" beyond the power of the state legislature to impair. Public privileges and public contracts were treated as if they were bargains between state and individual; they were rendered abstract—in other words, brought within a market frame of values. The contracts clause was thought to serve a vital economic function. People could act on the assumption that the legal context of their transactions would not change radically between promise and enforcement; this assurance eliminated at least one hazardous economic variable. Pre-Civil War government did not have at its command large financial resources to expend in development. The contracts clause, like the protective tariff, performed certain functions of promotion and guaranty for business which government today might accomplish by using guaranteed loans or government-backed insurance. What the tariff did externally, the contracts clause, in a sense, did internally. In so doing, the contracts clause was also a weapon of conservatism, in the sense of tending to preserve existing distribution of power and property.

But in its most extreme form, the *Dartmouth College* idea did not and could not survive. The things to which it applied—land grants and corporate charters, for example—were of too broad public concern to be treated as of only private interest. A good deal of American history could be written in terms of the resistance to the *Dartmouth College* doctrine. Public opinion demanded protection for the "sacred rights of labor," that is, avoidance of concentration of political and economic power, and legislative flexibility to promote or preserve the economic interests of the farmer-settlers—protection which, particularly in times of crisis, could hardly be reconciled with the spirit of *Dartmouth College*. {134} Yet the counteracting legal response took on a contract coloration. If a corporate charter was a "contract," then the legislature might include as a term of the contract the reservation of a power to amend or repeal it; an amendment to the charter was then legally unobjectionable, since it had been "assented" to in advance. Wisconsin in its Constitution specifically reserved the right to alter or repeal charters.[135]

If the *Dartmouth College* doctrine can be equated roughly with the nineteenth-century movement toward the abstraction of the market, counter-currents of constitutional law underscore what we have frequently mentioned: that abstraction was viewed as means, not end. In *Charles River Bridge v. Warren Bridge* (1837)[136] Chief Justice Taney refused to imply that a bridge franchise granted by the state of Massachusetts was exclusive, and consequently impaired by a later, rival franchise. Grants which conferred special rights of use in common resources had to be strictly construed. This rule of construction was itself a breach in the wall of abstraction, in that it singled out a class of contractual relationships for special legal treatment. Taney explained that strict construction was necessary in the light of economic circumstances: the United States was "continually advancing in numbers and wealth"; if charters carried with them

> these implied contracts ... you will soon find the old turnpike corporations awakening from their sleep, and calling upon this court.... The millions of property which have been invested in railroads and canals, upon lines of travel which had been before occupied by turnpike corporations will be put in jeopardy. We shall be thrown back to the improvements of the last century.

Similarly, a statute abolishing imprisonment for debt did not violate the contracts clause. "Imprisonment," said Chief Justice Marshall, "is no part of the contract, and simply to release the prisoner does not impair its obligations."[137] A system of contract law which played down the moral element of debt and breach of contract, and which confined contract damages to a narrow economic range, had no taste for imprisonment for debt. Yet the abolition of imprisonment for debt had its humanitarian and popular side, and was related to the homestead exemption and the "sacred rights of labor." Free markets depended on free men. Free men depended on free markets.

These remarks on the significance of federal contracts clause cases apply equally well to developments in Wisconsin. Here, too, the judges vastly expanded the concept of constitutionally protected "contracts." {135} For example, in *Stephens v. Marshall* (1851),[138] the court held that a public statute when acted upon by a private person might constitute a "contract." The statute was the milldam law of 1840, which authorized "any person" to erect water mills and dams on non-navigable streams. Owners whose lands were flooded by the dammed-up water lost their right to common law damages; but the statute provided that the landowner might recover flowage damages from the dam builder in what amounted to a delegated proceeding in the nature of eminent domain. The act was repealed in 1850. After repeal, the question arose whether an injured landowner might now recover from the mill-owner, as for a common law trespass, for flowage by a dam first erected while the milldam act stood on the books, and promptly rebuilt after a flood had wrecked the original structure, but rebuilt also after repeal of the milldam statute. Judge Hubbell denied that the dam builder had, by the repeal, lost the right he had acquired by building the original dam under the sanction of the statute then existing:

> The intention of the legislature was, to favor the interests of mill owners and make investments in that species of property, desirable and safe.... The law, and the acts of the defendant in error, in pursuance of its provisions, constituted a contract between him and the plaintiff in error, and between the state and each of them. No act of either party could deprive the other of his vested rights under this contract; nor could the repeal of the law by the legislature, abrogate or impair its obligations.

Three years later, in *Pratt v. Brown* (1854),[139] *Stephens v. Marshall* was overruled. The milldam act was now construed as determining the prevailing public interest for such time as the legislature chose to maintain the statute. This conclusion, the court felt, was dictated by the fact that the legislature's sole authority to employ the power of eminent domain lay in its finding that this would serve a public purpose; if at any point the legislature decided that the justifying public purpose no longer existed, all rights previously held under such legislation must end. The repeal of the act was construed to mean that the legislature no longer found that private milldams constituted a use of resources in the public interest. Thus no vested, perpetual rights were created by the act. "As the law was repealable in its nature, the power of repeal remaining in the legislature, whoever availed himself of the privileges conferred by it took the same subject to such right of repeal. The risk was one of his own incurring." Notice that *Pratt v. Brown* talked contract in the same breath as it rejected invocation of the contracts {136} clause. Since the law was "repealable," anyone who acted under the statute assumed the risk of repeal as part of his bargain; repealability was a term in his "contract." The two conflicting cases both in fact spoke the language of contract. They testified to the power of the concept of contract, but they also showed how technique could be molded to accommodate different legal results.[140]

In *Bull v. Conroe* (1860),[141] Bull owned twenty-two acres near the city of Racine. In 1856, Racine annexed this land. In 1858, some of Bull's creditors levied execution on his land, for debts contracted before annexation. Bull demanded his right to a forty-acre agricultural homestead exemption, rather than the one-quarter acre exemption for land within a city. This right, he said, the city could not impair simply by annexing his land. Chief Justice Dixon described the exemption laws as "matters of legislative grace, and not vested rights growing out of grants from the State, or compacts between the State and individual debtors." The state, after all, "receives nothing, and debtors pay no price the consideration for which does not contribute to their own immediate and exclusive benefit." After laying this foundation (colored by contract language) Dixon turned to the policy issue:

> The respondent must be deemed to have ... gained in the increased value of the remaining portion [of his land] by reason of its nearness to a flourishing city.... [T]he opposite rule ... might be productive of wrongs.... For then the selfish and perverse debtor might see a large city grow up around him without laying out his grounds for the convenience of the public, and by still holding his forty acres in the most central and valuable portion, he might set at defiance both his creditors and the public.

Thus Dixon turned against Bull the fear, particularly widespread in the West, that "vested rights" too carefully protected would inhibit labor and prevent economic growth. The image of the "speculator," holding his land off from market, killing the great city, depressing land values, far outweighed for Dixon a technical and absolute reading of the contracts clause.

In Period II, the contracts clause was construed in a number of cases, but with fundamental difference in tone. In *Milwaukee Electric Railway & Light Co. v. Railroad Commission* (1913),[142] the argument was raised that Milwaukee ordinances fixing street railway rates (e.g., "not to exceed five cents for a single fare") were "contracts" which the state might not impair by undertaking to supersede them with its own rate regulation. The court was not persuaded. Chief Justice Winslow {137} wrote the majority opinion. Rate-fixing powers, he said, were "one of the attributes of sovereignty." In the past this "great power" was "seldom used"; life was simple then, "individual wants few, and individual resources generally sufficient to provide for them." The "ordinary citizen" drove his own horse, drank water from his own well, had no telephone, and "was dependent upon no public utility, either for the necessities or the luxuries of life." But no such life was possible in Winslow's day. "The progress of science and invention, combined with the tremendous growth of congested urban areas, has made the great mass of the people utterly dependent upon the great public utilities." Winslow's words reflected the revolution in opinion brought about by a widespread sense of dependence on institutions grown too powerful for easy or automatic control; and by the felt helplessness of the individual in the face of technological change and big business. Consequently, abstract doctrine was recast in favor of the authority of the state to intervene for the underdog. His opinion denied the proposition that the free market (here, the free market in state privileges) could and should hold full sway.

The "attributes of sovereignty" which in Period II were not to be given away were those of the so called "police power." "Due process" (including liberty of contract) defined the limits of the police power, that is, of sovereignty in its more directly regulatory aspects. The struggle of Period II was over the regulatory power of government, not over the rules under which the government dispensed public assets and privileges, or the extent to which abstraction was appropriate to governments as well as to men and businesses. By the time of Period II the scope of the court's constitutional veto power over economic legislation had markedly expanded, especially under the post-Civil War mandate of the due process and equal protection clauses of the Fourteenth Amendment. It had become commonplace for major economic statutes to run the constitutional gamut in a court test. The precise constitutional doctrine at issue varied with the case—from such a general standard as due process, to more specific, minor provisions of the state constitution.[143] The due process clause was the most important of all of these warrants for judicial intervention, and by virtue of its vagueness, was used with most telling effect.

In Period III the court used constitutional law less often, and less successfully, to limit the power of the legislature over the economy. The court's lesser role in constitutional pronouncement did not derive {138} from the same sources as its limited role in making new law to govern private relationships. Through codification and innovating enactment, the legislature had taken away much of the court's practical power to make law. But the old constitutional phrases stayed exactly as they were. So far as constitutional decisions were concerned, the change was not in the language of the law, but in the court's role in relation to constitutional values. The contracts clause and the due process clause were not repealed; but against the background of a generation of change in the relation between law and the economy, the court was now readier to defer to legislative judgments of public policy. Broader economic regulation by law was an accomplished and a pervasive fact. The court had no taste for blanket opposition; such opposition would, in fact, have been futile and self-defeating. Constitutional emphasis shifted to questions of "civil liberties." Here the power of the state confronted the political and social rights of the individual, more than his economic claims. These civil rights became more critical precisely because the state had succeeded in gathering to itself great economic power. The role of the independent judiciary as a bridle on the state's economic power had been worn away by public opinion and judicial self-restraint; the power to shape the legal system had been ground fine between the millstones of legislative and executive power and the businessman's distaste for litigation; the courts found some compensation in a relatively new role—as the forum for the little man's rights against great power aggregates. In *Graebner v. Industrial Commission* (1955),[144] the court upheld a piece of legislation, first passed during Period II, which allowed the Industrial Commission to deny a license to an employment agency if existing agencies, public and private, were "sufficient to supply the needs of employers and employees." The statute sought to restrict the area of competition, to say the least, and three judges dissented.

The majority talked mostly about whether or not the commission had "arbitrary" power; since they decided that it did not, they upheld the statute. For them, no area of economic life was closed to legislative regulation so long as the arm of government was required to act in accordance with some fair or measurable standard.[145]

Contract Doctrine in the Court: A Summary Conclusion. Under the complexities of detail, a few main strands can be isolated in dealing with the work of the court in handling doctrine. First, doctrine {139} changed less than the application of doctrine. Second, "rules" of contract law tended to develop into branches, verbally but not functionally reconcilable, which could be malleably applied to fit particular fact-situations. Third, one branch of each rule tended to fit the needs of the abstract approach to contract law; while another subserved particularistic ends. Fourth, the relative frequency of use of each branch was determined by the particular situation before the court; but changes in the nature of the court docket worked to present the court with more and more frequent instances in which the non-abstract use of a doctrine was the one which was more persuasive. Fifth, the cumulative effect of the changes in doctrine and application of doctrine resulted in appellate court decision-making in contract cases which was so far removed from the original abstraction of classical contract law that the abstract element could no longer be said to predominate.[146] {page 140 follows}

IV
CONTRACT LAW AND THE LEGISLATURE

BECAUSE contract law was basically abstract, that is, concerned with support of the unregulated free market, little of Wisconsin's legislative product directly governed the internal operation of the classical law of contracts. This remained as true in the 1950's as in the 1850's. The Wisconsin experience was typical. A few states (California, for example), more strongly touched by the nineteenth-century codification movement, enacted into statute many principles of their civil law, including the law of contract.[1] There was not much real difference between the code provisions of California and the Restatement of Contracts, which did little more than set out the common law as a set of abstract propositions purified of vagaries and localisms. Had the Wisconsin legislature enacted the headnotes of its contract cases, much the same results would have been achieved. At any rate, Wisconsin did not adopt a code, and the rules of offer, acceptance, performance, consideration and the rest remained where they were, in the breast of the court.

A few inherited, traditional statutes were part of the stock-in-trade of every common law jurisdiction. The Statute of Frauds[2] was the most important of these. Wisconsin's text was not typical, but its peculiarities were those of its New York source rather than anything indigenous. There were other traditional statutes which affected contracts, for example, the statute of limitations, and the fraudulent conveyance laws.[3] Other acts were traditional in the sense that every jurisdiction had one, but there was no received, standard text. The usury laws were of this kind. Usury laws were ancient limitations on the freedom of contract; usury was recognized (like the Statute of Frauds) as a traditional contract defense, though unlike the Statute of Frauds, controversy over statutory regulation of rates of interest raged throughout the century, {141} and at times sentiment for outright repeal of the laws was very strong. Similarly, prohibitions on enforcement of gambling contracts were common in the United States, but varied in their provisions from place to place. Another typical statute gave the effect of a seal to "any device" affixed "by way of seal"; this language appeared as early as the Territorial Statutes of 1839.[4]

Wisconsin participated all along in general legislation which codified the law merchant. In 1838 Wisconsin passed a limited partnership act, borrowed from New York.[5] New York was also the source of the early, sketchy legislation on negotiable instruments.[6] In the twentieth century, a commercial codification movement stronger than any nineteenth-century movement reached Wisconsin. The state adopted the negotiable instruments law, the Uniform Sales Act, and many other of the "uniform" statutes.[7] None of these had any special Wisconsin origins or were tailored to any specific Wisconsin needs. They represented what was felt to be an appropriate legal response to the economic unity of the country. Although these were "statutes," their national scope and their generality invites comparison with the common law doctrine presupposed by Langdell's contracts treatise and his innovations in legal education, and by the later Restatements of the law.

Immeasurably more numerous were statutes which affected contract law only indirectly, by removing areas of economic transactions from the realm of abstract contract law. In this sense, all economic regulatory law was concerned with contract. A complete discussion of "contract" legislation of this kind would embrace most of the statutes passed in Wisconsin. We will have to confine ourselves to those movements of legislation which seem particularly relevant to what was happening to the contract system, and to those instances in which concepts of the common law of contracts seemed to influence the state's legislative program in some significant way. As was true of the course of case law, statute law affecting the domain of contract showed considerable changes in theme and emphasis. Period I's great output of special charters[8] did not survive into the twentieth century; the concern with usury, debt collection, and debtors' exemptions of the 1850's was reflected in an output of statutes that did not recur in Period II and Period III. Period II saw a massive outpouring of statutes concerning labor, insurance, food and drug standards, and commodity dealings. The emphasis in Period III was placed much more heavily on marketing {142} and unfair competition. Both Periods II and III were busy with occupational licensing, but in somewhat different ways.

Period I: Debtors and Creditors. The dominant public policy theme of Period I was economic growth. Preoccupation with this objective profoundly influenced the work of the legislature; the single most important task of the lawmakers was to lay a foundation for the swift development of the state's economy. No matters more concerned the legislature than granting charters for the construction of internal improvements, encouraging settlement and immigration, and providing the legal framework for the development of local communities. Society was entrepreneur-oriented, but also egalitarian. Promotional tasks were undertaken for the benefit of the individual citizen, the farmer-settler primarily, not for some closed circle of financiers and industrialists. It is not usually true that most twentieth-century state legislators are professional politicians, in the sense of men whose livelihood depends on public office. It was even less true in Period I. Wisconsin's legislators then were generally young men on the make—lawyers, town-site boomers, financial middlemen, land speculators; they stood to gain financially as well as politically from the growth of the state's economy. They shared fully the common faith in the gains that all would reap from growth of the state's economy. They tended to reflect the ups and downs of community sentiment. Although they may have been in some sense business-minded men, they were not invariably tender to the claims of vested rights. Society was in turbulent growth, and under strong compulsion to make legal adjustments necessary for continued growth, even at some cost to "vested rights" at times.

From the first, the legislature acted with an eye toward balancing the fundamental free enterprise notions of the times with limitations on the market deemed politically necessary or necessary to the maintenance of the structural foundations of society (as they viewed it). The market was not an absolute. No man might sell himself into slavery. Imprisonment for debt was abolished.[9] The social system depended on autonomous small-holders; all men could aspire to be rich, but the economic system would not be allowed to make men completely destitute. Hence even the first (territorial) collection of statutes (1838-1839) included a list of property exempt from execution for debt: spinning wheels, the family Bible, a year's supply of fuel, household implements, clothing, bedding, "six knives and forks," and similar {143} chattels (up to $50 in value), the "tools and implements of any mechanic or miner necessary for his trade" (up to $100 in value), and farm equipment (up to the same amount).[10] In twentieth-century terms, this was not a list of major assets; but in its time it included the basic necessities of life (other than the land itself). One hundred dollars in farm equipment, and fifty dollars worth of chattels—these were certainly enough then to protect the average man in his basic possessions. The Wisconsin Constitution (1848) affirmed this policy by stating: "The privilege of the debtor to enjoy the necessary comforts of life, shall be recognized by wholesome laws, exempting a reasonable amount of property from seizure or sale for the payment of any debt or liability hereafter contracted."[11] In the same year, the first year of statehood, the legislature passed a homestead act; this law declared immune from seizure for a debt a "homestead" of not more than 40 acres "used for agricultural purposes," and the farmer's "dwelling house"; or a town or city lot, with its "dwelling house," of no more than a quarter acre.[12] The homestead exemption apparently originated in the Republic of Texas, probably as a "device for encouraging immigration."[13] It spread quickly to some of the southern states, and then northward. Wisconsin (probably in typical fashion)used it not only to encourage immigration, but as a form of debtor relief if, indeed, it is possible to separate these motives. In the same year (1848),[14] the legislature expanded the list of exempt chattels to include, for example, "all cooking utensils." The new legislature also raised the dollar limits of some categories; for example, the amount of exempt tools and implements of mechanics and miners was raised to $200. The merchant shared in the state's generosity; the statute exempted a "stock in trade" up to $200. An exemption for the "library and implements of any professional man, not exceeding two hundred dollars in value" gave some comfort to members of this class, particularly lawyers. Taken in conjunction with the homestead exemption, it would be no exaggeration to say that all the assets of 90 per cent of the population were immune from levy of execution to satisfy debts. Indeed, in 1848 the legislature seriously considered a proposal to repeal "all laws for the collection of debts."[15]

Thus in the highest days of the abstract law of contract, in the era of frontier individualism, the legal enforceability of market transactions in Wisconsin existed, or was allowed to exist, only with respect to surplus capital—which was scarce. The state of Wisconsin was a welfare state, promoting the general welfare in the way it deemed best: by immunizing {144} its citizens from the collection of certain of their debts. After all, the government was poor and weak; it could hardly support vast programs of relief. What it owned (besides its land) was the classic, irreducible stock in trade of a sovereignty—the monopoly of force; this it used, in a negative way, denying the availability of some key devices of legal process for the collection of debts owed by its residents except insofar as these residents were wealthy enough to enter into the area in which the market economy was allowed full scope. The principle of debtor relief was firmly established in law and over the years grew in a variety of small but significant ways.[16]

Yet throughout the period, there was one gap of great significance in the debtor's exemption statutes. The homestead exemption had to give way before the rights of a holder of a mortgage against the homestead property.[17] If the homestead exemption had applied against the mortgagee, too, then truly the bulk of the population would have been immune to legal process against their assets. Failure to include mortgage debts in the exemption statute was a matter of simple necessity. The settlers had enough trouble trying to get money to buy their farms as it was; without the security of the land itself, land financing would have been virtually impossible. A homestead exemption superior to a mortgage would also have added still another complication to the mysteries of land titles—an encumbrance on an encumbrance. As it was, the vulnerability of the "homestead" to mortgage foreclosure accentuated the natural tendency to secure debts whenever possible by real estate mortgage.

In a sense, the legislature's failure to extend the protection of the homestead laws to real estate mortgages was a negative, but critical, method of encouraging settlement and development of the state; it enabled the settler to use his land—the only capital resource which was not scarce—as collateral for financing the development of that land. The device was analogous to the twentieth-century use of tax abatement or tax forgiveness as a method of encouraging industrial development. The statutes of Period I are full of examples of the manipulation of contract remedies (broadly defined) as indirect means of encouraging development or favoring one form of economic activity over another. The proliferation of lien laws is a case in point. The "boat and vessel act," which first appeared in Wisconsin in 1838,[18] gave an action *in rem* to laborers and suppliers for their claims against vessels in local waters. The same policies lay behind the mechanics' lien laws and {145} related statutes. The mechanics' lien, a purely American invention, apparently began as a device to facilitate construction in the new capitol city of Washington, D.C.[19] It gradually expanded from a limited, temporary promotional act to a type of law of general application. The first Wisconsin territorial statute book contained an act "concerning the lien of mechanics and others for the cost of repairs and improvements on real estate."[20] The law applied in favor of specified craftsmen and suppliers of building materials. The smallholder, the farmer-settler, had little to fear from the lien; he "improved" his lands by his own efforts and those of his family, without much use of hired labor. The point of the law was its preference of the laborer and supplier over the financing creditor.[21] The legislature frequently amended the lien laws, in Period I, to make the lien broader or easier to enforce. A statute of 1858, for example, extended the act to wharfing and dredging work.[22] Lien laws in general were promotional devices to encourage men to put forth productive labor. In recognition of this underlying purpose, the mechanics' lien, for example, applied even against the homestead exemption, just as did the mortgage on land.[23]

The legislature's bold interference with the rights of creditors, following in the wake of the farm-mortgage crisis of the 1850's, basically took the form of tinkering with contract remedies. In 1858 an act gave foreclosure defendants "six months time to answer the bill or complaint filed," and provided that "the mortgaged premises shall be sold only upon six months notice given of the time and place of such sale."[24] Another act of the same year (applicable to "all suits" brought by "railroad or other companies or their assigns, to enforce the collection of any note or notes, or to foreclose mortgages") gave the maker of any farm mortgage notes the right to plead, even against holders in due course, that the note had been "obtained by fraud or false representation." All "fraudulent, false or untrue statements relating to the pecuniary circumstances" of the railroad, or its route or date of completion, were to "run with said note and mortgage."[25] This was an attack on the negotiability of the railroad's paper. An act of 1861, passed after the Wisconsin Supreme Court had voided this 1858 law, showed more ingenuity. The act was blandly entitled "An Act concerning proceedings in courts in certain cases"; but its wording left no doubt what "proceedings" and "cases" were meant. Section five of the act created this obstacle against holders of notes secured by farm mortgages: "if the defendants ... shall set up fraud ... or want of consideration, such {146} instrument shall be deemed *prima facie* ... held ... by the plaintiff... with full notice ... of all equities ... and the oath of the plaintiff shall not be deemed sufficient proof to remove such presumption." Section twenty of the act allowed either party to the suit four years to appeal, and provided that any appeal stayed all proceedings.[26]

The act of 1861 was the last of those farm-mortgage statutes which fell within the arbitrary limits of our Period I. It was not the last of the acts, however, nor the last word on the subject. The dialogue between court and legislature continued. The contracts clause prevented the state government from taking the simplest course, and canceling the mortgages. Since the United States Supreme Court conceded that a mere change in "remedies" did not impair the obligation of a contract,[27] legislation was invited to take the form of tinkering with contract enforcement procedures. Thus the combination of a constitutional concept and its judicial gloss influenced the form of legislative action. The state government could in addition have attempted direct relief for the suffering farmers. For example, subject to possible challenge to its constitutional authority, the state government could have undertaken to loan farmers tax-derived money. But, legal barriers aside, the state was too poor to do this. And payment would have drained off to the East capital that the state could hardly spare. Probably as a matter of practical policy, the state had little enough inclination to pay distant creditors. The whole farm-mortgage system was a promotional, development scheme to build up the state's railroad network. When it failed in its purpose, the average Wisconsin resident lost any benevolent interest he might have once had in eastern investors. Given the limited practical power (legal and economic) of state government, manipulation of contract remedies appeared the course of relief most promising of success.

Period I: Leviathan's Infancy. The poverty and weakness of the state government in Period I had a great impact on the course of public policy. Twentieth-century government depends on heavy taxes and a large, trained corps of government professionals. Frontier Wisconsin had neither. Its citizens were too poor to be taxed heavily, and without substantial taxes, the state could not maintain a large staff of employees. These facts were more important, perhaps, in explaining why government did not do as much as it might, than any theories about government's proper role in the economy. The state constitution put a {147} stringent limit on state debts; but this was not an expression of laissez faire as much as a reaction to the sad results of one particular kind of state intervention. There is little that government does in the twentieth century that does not have some analogy to what government wanted to do or tried to do, on a much smaller scale, in the nineteenth: relief for the poor, aid to dependent children, government enforcement of honest selling and purity of products, general promotion of the economy. But social policy was fragmentary in concept and local in implementation. Poor relief was administered at the lowest level of government, and as cheaply as possible. Though government was conceded the right and the duty to build roads, responsibility for roads was vested in town officials, who met to "assess the highway tax" on a yearly basis. Able-bodied men had the right to "appear and pay their highway taxes in labor"; they could be required to "furnish a spade shovel, axe or hoe," and if they were owners of a "team, plow, wagon, or cart," to furnish these, too.[28] Laws such as this bore eloquent testimony to the shortage of cash and the plenitude of muscle in early Wisconsin.

Private contract, too, could be used to further policy where more direct public action would be used in the twentieth century. It was cheaper to bind out indigent minors as apprentices than to support them with grants of money. The usury laws were another example of how contract served as a substitute for administrative action. Theoretically, usurers could have been controlled by a system of licensing loan companies and individual lenders, enforced by a staff of state inspectors. Any such system would have been expensive of men and money. But a law which shut the courtroom doors to the collection of usurious debts was ideally suited to the government of Period I: it was cheap, self-executing, and required no staff to enforce it (except for the courts, which were already there). Similarly, anti-gambling laws were fortified by making gambling debts uncollectible.[29] The court's refusal to enforce Sunday contracts, however sporadic, was probably the only living part of the blue laws, so far as the intervention of law was concerned. An act of 1850 "relating to the sale of intoxicating liquors"—a by-product of the strong contemporary temperance movement—provided that "No suit for retail liquor bills shall be entertained by any courts of this state," and that all "notes, accounts, or evidence of debt" for retail liquor bills were "void."[30] An act of 1853 "for the preservation of game" prohibited the sale of woodcocks, grouse, and prairie {148} hens out of season.[31] Yet surely the act was more interested in keeping people from killing the birds than in keeping the dead birds off the market. An act of 1854 "to prohibit the circulation of unauthorized Bank paper" declared "null and void" "all contracts" whose consideration consisted of forbidden paper, and "all payments made, in such unauthorized paper." The act followed an earlier version which had contained only criminal sanctions, and which had been "singularly ineffective."[32]

In a sense, too, permissive legislation acted as a device to support developmental activities. Legislation which freed corporations and municipalities from traditional contractual disabilities was a form of government aid. For example, an act of 1856 authorized railroads to use mortgage and trust deed financing; an act of the same year enabled "school districts to borrow money to build School Houses." Bounties for the killing of wolves enlisted private persons contractually to perform some public police functions. An act of 1861 authorized "the organization of societies for mutual protection against larcenies of live stock." The statute granted the societies power to choose "riders" who might "exercise all the powers of constables in the arrest and detention of criminals." Another act of 1861 authorized the banks of Milwaukee to "associate together for raising a joint fund to be placed in the hands of their common agent, for the redemption of their circulating notes in the city of Milwaukee or Madison, and also the circulating notes of other banks in such manner, and under such regulations, as may be agreed upon." The outbreak of the Civil War had precipitated a financial crisis; Wisconsin's banking and currency system was based on Southern bonds which turned into worthless paper when the war began. In the face of rioting and confusion, the Milwaukee bankers saved the state from disasters which the state government was apparently powerless to prevent. It is perhaps improper to speak of "delegation" of state power to private groups in this instance. A private group had assumed power in the first instance; the state merely ratified its initiative after the fact.[33]

The special corporate charter[34] can be viewed as a means of regulation of business through contract. It was more feasible, in theory at least, to regulate business which employed the corporate form by inserting desired terms into the state's "contract" with the company (the charter) than to inspect and regulate administratively the operations of the enterprise. Broad resort to chartered corporations and private {149} franchise to fulfill public needs was a confession of governmental weakness; railroad building, like road building, was recognized initially as a concern of the sovereign; but the sovereign lacked the resources to do the work itself, and therefore it delegated by contract a measure of sovereignty to those who gave promise of having the ability to raise the necessary funds. As charters and franchises multiplied, they tended to be carelessly drafted and to fall into routine patterns. In the heyday of charter and franchise, the state legislature of Wisconsin granted and amended so many of these that charter and franchise matters preempted an undue amount of the legislative output; and the legislature had to choose either to allot excessive time to such matters or to rubber stamp proposed charter and franchise acts. In any event, state "control" of the uses made of these legislative grants was virtually non-existent. When the state abandoned the special chartering of corporations in 1872, and when it increasingly turned over to public administrative bodies the job of supervising the exercise of public utility franchises, it recognized the waste and futility of controlling such matters through legislative "contract." So far as the general run of business corporations was concerned, after 1872 the state directly controlled their structure and processes only insofar as it set the terms of their organization through general incorporation statutes. Otherwise, discipline was left to what might be afforded through suits by dissident stockholders. Even in public utility franchises, the state was content to rely on somewhat tighter statutory grants, actions of local public prosecutors, or private lawsuits by disgruntled customers, until the end of the nineteenth century. Since local prosecutors and private litigants did not show significant energy, courage, or means to take effective and continuous action, as a practical matter no substantial control of the detailed conduct of these franchise holders existed until twentieth-century-style administrative regulation arrived on the scene.

The limitations of government, then, dictated the forms which regulation of business took, though they did not dictate areas of governmental concern. The hindsight of generations which are blessed (or cursed) with government rich in taxing power and staff may tend to confuse form with substance, that is, to ascribe unduly the spotty, local, and fragmentary nature of regulation in Period I to ideological self-restraint (though this was surely one factor). Within the limitations imposed by the facts of political and economic life, state government sought to achieve its ends through the use of forms of legislation {150} dictated by necessity. The most appropriate forms were those which were self-executing (eliminating the need for a bureaucracy which did not yet exist) and self-supporting (eliminating the need for heavy taxes in a time of cash scarcity). Thus an act passed in 1854 allowed those who found and made fast floating logs worth more than $10 to keep 10 per cent of the value of the logs.[35] This act generated its own support funds and also produced the activity to implement its policy. Disclosure laws were a more subtle variety of the same phenomenon. Under a general act of 1849 regulating ferries, it was the "duty of the clerk of the [county] board of supervisors, to furnish to every person to whom a license shall be granted to keep a ferry, a list of the rates of ferriage, which list the keeper of the ferry shall post up at the door of the ferry house, or some conspicuous place nearby."[36] The act of 1861 "to regulate the traffic in logs, timber and lumber on the Wisconsin, Black, Chippewa and St. Croix Rivers" provided for recording of log marks.[37] Marks and brands for "horses, cattle, sheep or hogs" had been recorded for years under another statute, which continued a practice recognized by the Massachusetts Bay colonists two centuries before, in 1646.[38]

All of these statutes embodied devices which had been in use elsewhere in the country, and some of these are still in use in the twentieth century. They gave the public necessary market information, helped trace ownership rights, and facilitated the orderly operation of the economy. Marking, posting, and branding laws made evasion of the law difficult, and made private enforcement easy.

The regulation of weights and measures was also the subject of several early Wisconsin laws. Early weights and measures statutes dealt with logs, "Lead Ore, Copper Ore, and other mineral substances," and "Flax seed, Timothy Seed and Potatoes," among other commodities.[39] To police weights and measures was easier than to police sales to prevent fraud. A similar, ancient device to help standardize dealings was the public market, which required all transactions of a particular type to be funneled into one time and place. The "market" in this sense survived in Wisconsin, but as a vestige without much vitality. The auctioneer's act of 1838 fined any licensed auctioneer who "shall sell any of his own goods, before sunrise or after sunset."[40] A Milwaukee ordinance of 1847 decreed that a "public stand" for the sale of "wood, hay, and other marketable articles" should be "established in the third ward."[41] Difficulties of communication across the majestic distances of {151} the frontier made a complete "public market" system impossible. Later, the complexity of the economy and the sheer numbers of those who bought and sold common commodities operated to the same effect.

It was ancient practice for courts to support themselves out of their fees. Whatever else could be said for the fee principle, it taxed users rather than the public and spared the government the cost of feeding a corps of civil servants. The elected "fish inspector" of the county of La Pointe, under an act of 1859, supported himself from inspection fees. A fence viewer was to be "paid by the person employing him, at the rate of one dollar a day"; a county surveyor might "demand," "for the first mile actually run with a compass and chain, three dollars," and a dollar for each subsequent mile.[42]

Of course, form and substance merge in regulatory legislation. Substantive regulation, where attempted, was ineffective if economic development outstripped the state's power to control it. The history of legislative rate-making illustrates this point. In later years, public review or superintendence of rate-making was sometimes condemned as if it were the worst form of socialism. If any substantial number of the hardy pioneers of Wisconsin thought so, they kept their opinions to themselves. The state consistently fixed the rate of toll for grist mills. At the time of the Revised Statutes of 1858, for "all grist mills in this state moved by water," the rate was declared to be "one-eighth part of all wheat, rye, or other grain, ground and bolted, or ground and not bolted, and no more."[43] The grist-mill rates were embodied in a general law. But it was more typical to specify rates for the "public utilities" of the day in special acts and charters, or by a combination of special and general act. The territorial charter of the "Beloit and Rock River Bridge Company" (a corporation) not only told the company its bridge should be "not less than eighteen feet wide," it also told the company what rate it could collect: "For any vehicle, drawn by one horse, twelve and a half cents," "for a single horse, six and a fourth cents," "for all animals in droves, if not less than fifty, three cents each," for more than 50, "two cents each"; hogs and sheep had their own lower rate, and the humble "foot passenger" went across the river free.[44] Franchises to individuals were equally explicit. Robert Wakeley, "his heirs, executors, administrators, and assigns," received, in 1852, a franchise to maintain a ferry across the Wisconsin River, in Portage County; his tolls were fixed by his franchise, e.g., "for cattle or horses in droves, five cents each"; Wakeley's pedestrians, unlike those on the {152} Beloit bridge, had to pay ten cents or swim.[45] Transport rate schedules could also be incorporated in general laws. Under the Revised Statutes of 1849, this was done for turnpike companies (e.g., "for every score of neat cattle, one cent a mile"); the same revision authorized county boards to license ferries, and to "order and direct the rates of ferriage."[46] The early railroad charters were sometimes drawn up as if railroads were simply new forms of the turnpike. The roads were conceived as metallic highways, freely usable by all toll-payers.[47] Soon, however, railroad charters recognized that the roads were common carriers, and the rate provisions in charters became more explicit. The Fox Lake Railroad Company, chartered in 1859, was authorized to charge "reasonable" rates, but such rates were not to exceed twenty-five cents per passenger, or one-half cent per bushel of wheat.[48] Some charters and some of the general laws boldly asserted policy that would have been subject to question later on. The general law on plankroad and turnpike companies, passed in 1848, specified that "in no case shall any such turnpike company charge or receive rates of toll which will enable it to divide more than 12% on its capital stock actually paid in cash."[49] On the other hand, the charter of the LaCrosse, Viroqua and Muscoda Railroad Company, granted in 1859, expressly reserved the state's right to alter tolls, but not "so that the profits of said company shall be less than 12 percent under the capital stock invested."[50]

Administrative follow-up of the terms upon which charters were granted was the weakest point of regulation in Period I. The state never had a Department of Bridges and Ferries or a Commissioner of Turnpikes, aided by a staff of clerks. Thus the rush for settlement and industrial and technological development for a time outstripped the practical power of the fledgling state. For its first generation, the state delegated a wide range of functions of public concern, and its attempt to combine delegation and regulation (including the rate-making power) failed; the delegation succeeded far better than the regulation. Consequently, it is easy to see why one of the most striking characteristics of Wisconsin's government in Period I was its tendency to behave like a wasting-asset corporation. Lacking money and staff, it pursued its ends by giving away what it did have—natural resources and governmental privileges. The state was rich in land, minerals, trees, water, and air. It was rich, too, in whatever powers and privileges were inherent in government. In a sense, land grants, special charters, and {153} franchises were all attempts by the state to achieve goals through the use of its natural and legal resources as bargaining units, rather than through futile attempts to govern beyond its means.

If one takes the Revised Statutes of 1858 as a rough summary of the legislative product (in the way of "general" laws) up to the eve of the Civil War, omissions were as striking as the actual contents. Most of the statute book was concerned with the bare fundamentals of government: the functioning and structure of state government, local government, elections, the court system and procedure, land law, and criminal law and process. Commodity marketing had received only a little legislative attention. Superficially, there was much resemblance between old English market-regulation and Wisconsin's legislation: both leaned heavily on weights, measures, and tolls. Some of the resemblance can be explained as institutional inheritance, by way of New England, New York, and the old Northwest. The first towns in what was later Ohio also had (in theory) auction houses, public markets, and weights and measures laws.[51] But the immediate background was more important than the institutional inheritance. The concern of the state with standards was important: since currency was in such short supply, standard weights and quality control of basic commodities took on added significance; particularly in early days, contractual payment in kind was frequent. A territorial act had authorized the governor to appoint inspectors of "shingles, wheat and rye flour, buck-wheat meal, pork, beef, fish, butter, lard, domestic spirits, and pot and pearl ashes."[52] A subtle shift in tone characterized a statute of 1856, punishing any "produce merchant, warehouseman, miller, or storage, forwarding or commission merchant" who used false weights or measures.[53] The inspection system had been abandoned, probably because it was impractical. The state decided that the "half bushel, and the parts thereof, shall be the standard measure for charcoal, fruits, and other commodities customarily sold by heaped measure";[54] but there was no statutory word about the quality of the charcoal and fruit. The territorial act cited was concerned with quality probably only because quality bore on the "merchantability" of potential export commodities. Regulation of sales for policy reasons was of the simplest variety, e.g., prohibition of the sale of intoxicating liquors to Indians.[55] In general, wage or salary labor was left untouched. The farmer, the laborer, and the manufacturer might do as they pleased; legislation was passed for their benefit, to create a climate favorable to their solvency and independence, {154} but restrictions were few and unimportant. Commercial middlemen, bankers, and insurance companies, on the other hand, were the object of much more legislative attention, not always friendly. But even here, the state concerned itself more and more with the form rather than the substance of business transactions, and not in a hostile sense, but with the aim of channeling economic potentialities into convenient and efficient frameworks.

Period II: Leviathan Unchained. The salient fact of Period II was that the two major weaknesses of government in Period I—poverty of men and money—no longer placed such drastic curbs on state government. Economic growth since the Civil War period meant that Wisconsin at the turn of the century was rich enough to tax and to spend and to hire, without bankrupting itself or its people. Just as in Period I it would be an error unduly to ascribe the limited scope of governmental regulation of economic life to adherence to laissez faire theory, so in Period II it would be an error to ascribe too much importance to the ideology which underlay the Progressivism of La Follette and his successors. It is true that Progressive emphasis on civil service, on the ideals of purity and impartiality in government, helped build a working bureaucracy for the state. Progressive tax reforms looked toward better ways of raising the money to pay for what the state wanted to do. But if one subtracts from the legislative output the net effect of specifically Progressive legislation, a substantial residue remains which owed little or nothing to La Follette, since similar legislation was passed in states quite impervious to Progressive influence.

Nor must one assume that state power was limited only by its staff and monetary resources. Federalism placed real curbs on state power. For example, control of transportation companies was less and less within the power of particular states, as such pioneer local lines as the tiny Muscoda and Viroqua Railroad Company were swallowed up in national and regional networks. Again, since more than 40 jurisdictions asserted sovereignty in their internal legal systems (though not in their economic systems), what might almost be called a free market for legal rules developed. A state could hardly impose burdensome regulations on various aspects of doing business unless other states set at least roughly comparable standards. But some states competed for business through attractive legal rules. Nevada's divorce laws debase and nullify the stricter divorce laws of other states. During the early {155} twentieth century, some of the smaller states fought for the role of state of incorporation. They offered as inducements permissive laws, lower taxes, or both. This was a kind of legal price-cutting for the purpose of doing a large volume of charter business. According to a 1908 report, whole businesses had grown up to handle the registration of corporations in New Jersey, Delaware, Arizona, South Dakota, Nevada, Washington, and Maine.[56] This competition made a mockery of strict domestic corporation laws. And corporation laws were only one example of many. It was a constant danger that repressive laws or heavy taxes would drive business out of a state or stunt the state's economic growth.[57]

The hidden effects of these less formal results of the federal system must have been great. Like constitutional doctrine, they affected not only what was done, which leaves a black and white record, but also what people dared or dared not do, which leaves no obvious record. The interdependence of legal communities, like the interdependence of communities and people in general, had a profound impact on the law. It also certainly encouraged, at least in the long run, the growing tendency to lean on Washington for sustenance. Everybody knows how the Interstate Commerce Commission sprang up like a phoenix out of the ashes of state regulation. There were many less dramatic examples of the same dependence on Washington.[58]

One other characteristic of the legislation of Period II must be mentioned at the outset. This was the sheer bulk of economic regulation. Each session of the Wisconsin legislature produced a mass of laws, regulating, controlling, forbidding, and defining economic and contractual behavior in ways that far outstripped the modest output of laws on these subjects in Period I. No other fact of legislation was quite so important. Leviathan was casting off its chains.[59]

Crime and Punishment. In form, most of the mass of economic regulatory law in Period II was also criminal law. Texts of economic legislation, long or short, almost always closed with a section imposing criminal sanctions—fine or imprisonment. Period II made criminal or imposed a penalty on such acts as selling insurance policies which did not conform to statutes, making supposed lemon extract from a "solution containing ... less than five percentum, by volume, of pure lemon oil in ethyl alcohol," catching Mississippi catfish "under 15 inches in length from tip to tip," and violating the usury laws.[60] Some of the new criminal statutes appended criminal sanctions to laws which also {156} made use of self-executing techniques, such as labeling, posting, and marking.[61] Most of them represented lack of faith in private enforcement of regulatory law, a growing realization that the judicial system functioning civilly could not cope with problems of a complex society. An act of 1913 which made it unlawful to sell cotton duck or canvas not marked with the "true and correct weight" of the material by ounces per yard,[62] rejected enforcement through the court system because any one transaction was too trivial to litigate. The buyer of a few yards of canvas would hardly file suit against his seller.

The use of criminal sanctions meant that people doubted the power of the free market to iron out problems through automatic economic process, and doubted also that the civil law of contracts would by itself suffice to enforce the statutes. Also, as to many commodity statutes (on quality and marketing), the private citizen did not have the skill to appraise whether statutory standards had been met. It took a lawyer or bureaucrat to know what the statutes said, a chemist or biologist to find out whether some technical, statutory standards had been violated. Sometimes (as in the case of some of the new insurance crimes), the state's invocation of criminal law rested on the implication that private enforcement could not achieve the goals of public policy because of inequality of bargaining power between customer and company. The great corporations, it was felt, could too easily delude, overbear, or wear out the simple citizen through litigation.

The new "criminal statutes" differed from traditional crimes in an important sense. Often they did not require proof that defendant intended the violation. In the context of this type of statute, criminality usually meant, not that statutory violations were necessarily branded as immoral (though this was often in fact the case), but that enforcement of some standard of business behavior was centralized and socialized. In the history of the regulatory process, three stages of enforcement are often met with: first civil enforcement, then criminal enforcement (that is, enforcement by the general law officers of the state), then administrative enforcement (enforcement by a specialized arm of the state). The second stage (criminal enforcement) involves a judgment that civil enforcement has proved inadequate; the remedy is socialized, placing the cost and the burden of prosecution on public law enforcement agencies. The imposition of criminality does not necessarily mean that any additional moral taint is attached to the acts proscribed; criminality is a consequence of the form of enforcement rather than the {157} nature of the acts. When the Industrial Commission of Wisconsin was established during Period II, a number of "crimes" were suddenly wiped off the books.[63] The conduct which had constituted a "crime" was still forbidden, but crude enforcement by that jack-of-all-duties, the district attorney, gave way to more sophisticated and flexible administration by a specialized agency (though administrative statutes usually contained criminal provisions, just as criminal statutes retained the self-executing devices which had been designed primarily to aid civil enforcement). The movement from criminal enforcement to administrative enforcement was also hastened by impatience with the slow processes of criminal law and the severe burden of proof which the state bore; these aspects of criminal law were fitting in cases of crimes of deep moral content (murder, rape) with severe penalties for guilt; they seemed inappropriate to the issues posed in charges against a man whose lemon extract contained less than the right amount of lemon oil.

The proliferation of criminal statutes (and the rise of the administrative agency) in Period II was a formal sign of the abandonment, in wide areas of public concern, of the free-contract system (or of the free-contract system somewhat dented by the passage of acts giving rise to policy defenses to be used in civil suits). Remedies were socialized for transactions whose importance in the aggregate was large, but in the particular small, or where the efficacy of free contract and civil process was thought to be nullified by inequality of economic power. The body of new law relating to the "trusts," as well as insurance and labor legislation, bore the stamp of the notion of inequality of economic power. The other type of transaction regulated bore witness to still another dominant notion of the day: the increasing sense of human interdependence.

By any measure, an extraordinary proliferation of health laws and laws relating to the quality of commodities took place in Period II. To judge by the statutes, the state had acquired a radically new awareness of disease. Government had always concerned itself with public health. But the teeming new cities magnified health and sanitation problems, and at the same time, technological and scientific discoveries provided information on the causes of disease. Each advance in technology and in the economic order made people more dependent on each other, and also made them acutely aware of the social impact of "private" contractual dealings. On the frontier, people were poor but comparatively {158} self-sufficient. Now control of disease and epidemics and protection of the biological integrity of the population required close and rigorous control over the making and selling of things which affected people's bodies—food in particular. In theory, a self-regulating free market would perhaps solve the problem of adulterated food, and bad goods in general, through the pricing mechanism. Bad goods should bring a lower price in the long run than sound goods. But for health reasons, people were not willing to wait for the long run. An action for damages was a poor substitute for a life lost through poisoned pork. Chemistry, biology, and other sciences made rapid progress in the nineteenth century; the way was open to understand the causes of illness and food poisoning and to control them. Yet those who were not chemists and biologists could not, unaided, maximize safety and health in buying food and other commodities.

The food and health problem was of national scope. A federal food and drug law was passed in 1906, but the states had been passing their own versions for some years.[64] In Wisconsin, in the 1905 session alone, the legislative hand was laid upon renovated butter, canned goods, maple syrup, lemon and vanilla extract, honey, condensed milk, vinegar, and game fish.[65] Other statutes dealt, not with particular commodities, but with commodities in general, or with general abuses like misbranding; thus it was declared a misdemeanor to sell "any canned fruits, vegetables, meats, fish or shell-fish" with "any artificial coloring, or any bleaching compound."[66] In the interests of safety, the laws of Period II also touched upon cigarettes, corn-shredders, oils and turpentine, firecrackers, insecticides, mattresses, and matches.[67] Health and safety acts ranged from the ridiculous to the sublimely important. In 1911 the superintendent of public buildings was ordered by statute to make a room in the capitol available "for thoroughly cleaning and disinfecting cuspidors"; but there was nothing trivial about forbidding a "water-closet, earth-closet, privy or ash pit" which could "communicate directly with the bake room or any other room used in the manufacture of bread."[68]

Benefits and Burdens. Of course, many laws which flew the banner of "health" legislation had dollars-and-cents motivations as well. It was sometimes more politic to appeal to the public's concern with health than to admit to lesser motives. Perhaps some protective legislation could not have been passed (or might have been greatly delayed in {159} passage) unless some strong interest group derived an economic benefit from the new law. The record suggests a good many examples of such likely double motives. Manufacturers of "pure" products clearly were benefited by laws which forced goods of less quality to confess their character. Wisconsin passed quite a few laws against "imitations"—concerning, e.g., renovated butter, artificially bleached flour, and gold and silver articles.[69] Such statutes obviously benefited those whose products were imitated. The long and bitter struggle of dairymen against oleomargarine was another instance.[70] Statutes directed against unethical marketing practices were similarly ambivalent. Laws against fraud could help the consumer or the producer, or both. Much law was passed, however, not to benefit consumers but to benefit occupational groups, producers, farmers, and businessmen.[71] Yet it was customary to appeal to the needs and interests of the public as a whole. Obviously, what benefited the public often directly or indirectly benefited some small group of the public also. Keeping out "disreputable" and marginal operators helped keep prices up or output down; at the same time the public gained protection against fraudulent operators. A child labor law protected children; it also protected adult workers from the competition of underpaid children. A pure food law safeguarded health and the food trades.

In Period II, the frontier as a symbol of autonomy and self-sufficiency had vanished. People were newly conscious of interdependence. Society was seen as a complex whole. Awareness of pressures of the social situation tended to generate belief that each class or group had to struggle for its share of a fixed universe of goods. This general point of view, in slightly different form, had always characterized public opinion at bottom points of the business cycle. In the late nineteenth and early twentieth centuries, the attitude seemed to become independent of the business cycle and to become rather a fixed feature of the American outlook. Optimistic faith in productivity had not been abandoned. Yet tension arose as it became increasingly clear that productivity was the result of large-scale economic organization in which most people had no meaningful determining role to play, in contrast to earlier generations when large numbers of people could feel confident that their personal fortunes were part of the surge of productivity.

In the new society, the primary interest of the artisan, small businessman, and professional man was to protect his share of the existing market. Since he thought that supply was flexible and demand stationary, {160} he attached enormous importance to price stability and restriction of entry into his field. His group, he felt, had a right to make rules to these ends. Reputable producers should control output or at least quality (control of which posed fewer legal hazards). In service trades, these objectives were obtained through setting "professional standards" enforced by licensing. Standardization was a valuable business end in itself; it cut down risks and helped rationalize prices. Business wished to standardize for itself; but if necessary, the benign use of state compulsion was welcome. Health measures could serve these ends as well as could other types of regulation. Louis Kuhn, a Wisconsin delegate to the National Confectioners' Association convention of 1907, praised Wisconsin's bakery and confectionery laws; they would "surely help in checking such manufacturers as have no regard for public opinion, public wish or consequences."[72] The statement implied that without legislation reputable confectioners would suffer a competitive disadvantage. It follows that business regulation was not necessarily anti-business. Standardization through law was a result favored by businessmen, or at least by those who subscribed to the credos of better business practices. Regulation, however, varied from field to field in respect to its underlying attitude toward the regulated. The Standard Fire Insurance Policy of 1895,[73] the high-water mark of forced conformity of contract, although not entirely a measure unfriendly to insurers (business pressure and economic reality saw to that), was basically aimed at protection of the public. The standard policy was a reaction against form contracts drawn up by the companies and the "inequality of bargaining power," which made one-sided draftsmanship oppressive. Forced standardization to redress inequality was also a feature of protective labor legislation. When the legislature abolished the defenses of assumption of risk and the fellow-servant rule, it was careful to specify that no "contract, rule, or regulation" might exempt the employer from the law's requirements.[74] Standardization was also a feature of weights-and-measures laws; this type of legislation attracted the attention of the legislature almost as much as in Period I. New laws were passed for cheese, milk bottles, and coal.[75] Weights-and-measures laws affected interests of broad cumulative concern, which were too trivial for private enforcement in particular instances. In short, standardization was both a technique of regulation and a recognition of the aspirations of certain economic or business groups; the two factors imperceptibly merged. {161}

Understanding the aims of post-Civil War law and society calls for analysis of subtle conflicting programs of interest groups, big and small. The tumult over government by injunction, the oil trust, the railroad barons, the Haymarket riots and the anarchists, obscure the many little nagging crises and disputes between sub-groups and sub-sub-groups, the aspirations and conflicts of cheesemakers, brokers, plumbers, druggists, and other minor groups and occupations. What these groups wanted was certainly not the pure free market. Everybody had an axe to grind, but no two axes were precisely the same. Any state's legal system was full of inconsistency; and nothing could be more natural, since the state was run not by philosopher-kings (nor by economists) but by politicians responsive to a middle class of diverse and often complex aims. The railroads had to be curbed by regulation (that is, government control). The trusts had to be curbed by breaking them up (that is, returning their components to the free market). These aims were inconsistent (if they were) only from some theoretical economic standpoint.

The struggle against the "trusts" was therefore primarily a power struggle. Anti-trust law did not rest (either in its late-nineteenth-century beginnings or in its later forms) on any well articulated economic theory, but on a complex of ill-defined political, economic, and social attitudes. A Wisconsin act of 1905 threatened with loss of its charter any corporation which entered into a "combination, conspiracy, trust, pool, agreement or contract intended to restrain or prevent competition," or to control prices or output.[76] In 1911 a joint resolution of the Wisconsin legislature demanded an investigation of the collusive activities of Madison ice and coal dealers; another demanded an investigation of the "school book trust." But a third joint resolution memorialized Congress to exempt labor unions and farm organizations from the Sherman Act.[77] Another piece of evidence of the want of an integrated anti-trust philosophy appeared in laws against discriminatory trade practices. Discrimination has an evil sound, like "monopoly" or "trust." But anti-discrimination laws, if they forced the equal treatment of unequals, were not consistent with the free market. These laws were vehicles for the attack of small men against large corporations. They came into prominence first as part of the general agrarian assault on railroads and grain elevators. In 1913, a broadly phrased statute outlawed discrimination between sections of the state or cities by manufacturers and sellers of "any commodity in general use" through {162} price-cutting, if done "intentionally, for the purpose of destroying the competition of any regular, established dealer" or to prevent competition.[78] The phrase "established dealer" was at the heart of the statute. First shots had been fired here in the battle with the chain stores and other dragons of merchandising. The free market, abstractly and concretely, did not guarantee the preservation of each corner grocery or drug store. The corner grocer and friendly druggist tolerated the pure free market (in his occupation) only as long as he felt benefited by its operation. The law came to show great concern for the status quo; each "small business" was treated as a tiny fiefdom in a shopkeepers' feudalism. Just as pure food laws subordinated the long-run operation of the market to other considerations (including health), so the long-run gains of lower prices and efficiency in marketing were to be sacrificed for the supposed virtues of a system based on small retailers, and the avoidance of the supposed social evils of dislocation and distress as the small man was driven out of business. The same type of argument through the 1950's was used to defend the "family farm."

Occupational Licensing. An outstanding characteristic of the legislation of Period II was the proliferation of occupational licensing laws—laws which limited entry into an occupation, and which prevented unlicensed practitioners from making valid service contracts with members of the public. Occupational licensing was almost invariably committed to an administrative agency. Before the turn of the century, Wisconsin already licensed attorneys, teachers, peddlers, public showmen, pharmacists, dentists, and doctors. Licensing of some forms of business—life insurance companies, telephone exchange companies—was another, similar technique of legal control.[79]

Licensing was not a single-purpose device. Licensing could be used as a quality control measure, over jobs of importance to the public (teachers, lawyers, doctors). Licensing could be part of the regulatory machinery by which the state controlled the practical power of critical industries (insurance, foreign corporations, banks). Licensing was sometimes used simply as a revenue device, a means of making a tax self-executing. Some licensing was enacted to curb trades which some influential opinion regarded as offensive, through laws thinly disguised as revenue or regulatory measures. Peddlers' laws were an example of this.

The licensing of doctors through a State Board of Medical Examiners {163} was the first in a series of licensing laws which added a new dimension to licensing. Significantly, this state law handed licensing control over to a group composed of members of the profession. The Board of Medical Examiners was appointed by the governor; but the governor was required to choose his men from a list of names furnished by the medical societies.[80] Statutes before and during Period II extended licensing in similar forms to druggists, dentists, osteopaths, midwives, and nurses,[81] in a movement not confined to Wisconsin, but occurring in most states (though somewhat unevenly in time). Occupational licensing thus advanced along the lines of the "police power," in the name of traditionally respectable objectives of legal regulation, apart from market values—legitimized, in other words, by appeals to the public interest in health and safety. In 1905, the Wisconsin state board of health was given power "to determine the qualifications necessary to enable any person to properly embalm human bodies and disinfect the premises." No person was entitled to a license "who has not practiced embalming dead human bodies for at least six months," or had "six months practical instruction in embalming and disinfecting under a licensed embalmer."[82] The connection of licensing with public health was somewhat more tenuous when barbers and plumbers came to be licensed. The statutes were careful to show concern for the public's health. No barber deserved a license without "sufficient knowledge concerning the common diseases of the face and skin to avoid the aggravations and spreading thereof in the practice of said trade."[83] The barbers' board had power to adopt "reasonable rules" for the "sanitary regulation of barbershops, subject to the approval of the state board of health." The license laws were expected to cut down the excessive number of barber schools, and to regulate entry into the trade. The Wisconsin statute required two years of carefully controlled apprenticeship. As an excited Indiana barber exclaimed in 1901, "it takes legislation to protect us from scab prices, pestilence and disease."[84] There is no reason to doubt the genuineness of the sentiment which put in one breath scab prices and diseases.

The plumbers' law had even less obvious connection with public health, and was apparently the brain child of the plumbers' union. The first licensing act in Wisconsin (1897) was declared unconstitutional; but the court made it clear that "the business of plumbing may be regulated by reasonable laws," since in modern society "the dangers to the health of the entire public, arising from defective plumbing, are so {164} great, and at the same time so insidious," that state power over plumbing was necessary "to protect the public life and health."[85]

No Wisconsin licensing act of the period was quite so bold as the Illinois statute of 1908 which created a "Miner's Examining Board" composed of miners, and prohibited mining without a certificate from the Board. This act, modeled after the licensing statutes for the health professions, was called a "safety" act; it required prospective miners to pass an "examination" in mining arts.[86] Less daring was the Wisconsin act of 1913, which placed the Certified Public Accountant on a firm and professional basis.[87] This act could be justified by pointing to the precedent of the licensing of lawyers. Even in this statute, the Wisconsin State Board of Accountancy was given the rhetorical "general duty" of bringing about a "better understanding of the relationship of the science of accounting to the problems of public welfare." Basically, however, the statute meant to safeguard the accountants' professional standing, to separate reputable accountants from others who might bring discredit on the profession. This form of self-regulation, under the umbrella of the state, was later copied by the real estate brokers to rid themselves of the onus of the "land shark" and the competition of the part-time broker.[88] And small-loan legislation was welcomed by the better class of money-lenders to get rid of the "usurer" and "loan shark."

The brokers wanted friendly state control because they found it too hard to rationalize by their own efforts a business plagued with marginal and part-time practitioners. The occupations benevolently licensed usually had in common the fact that their customers, clients, or employers were consumers or small merchants, not highly organized and powerful economic blocs or great corporations. The occupation was willing to give up a little internal and external autonomy in exchange for sound organization and standardized methods, enforced by the state, and an increase in occupational prestige through legislation. The development of occupational licensing was not exactly government "intervention" into business or the decline of freedom of contract. It was part of a general phenomenon, the increasing organization and group patterning of American economic life. A relatively free market in certain services was displaced by a relatively organized one. The shift from freedom to organization (a relative shift) proceeded in many areas of the old realm of "contract," in some smoothly, in others violently. The organization of barbers moved quickly, fairly easily, and {165} with minimal opposition once it began. Coal miners, sharecroppers, and railway workers generally had no such luck. The organization of industrial unions met with powerful opposition; blood was shed and bones broken in the process. In the courtrooms, the unions faced injunctions and statutes favorable to unions faced unconstitutionality—the forensic equivalents of blood and bones. The courts, by and large, acted differently toward a barber's law than toward a minimum wage law. The courts were middle class; they feared the masses below and the trusts above. Their sensitivity to "unreasonable" legislation seemed considerably duller when faced with the legislation advanced to further middle-class economic aims, than when they faced oligarchic aspects of restraint of trade (the "trusts" for example) and "socialistic" (pro-union) legislation. And the same legal profession which was often accused of being a tool of the trusts bitterly fought the corporate practice of law and the competition of title and trust companies.

Hostile occupational and business licensing was a somewhat different phenomenon. Historically, utility regulation began in hostile and passionate reaction against abuses of private power. But bureaucracies do not easily sustain passion; business learned to live with its commissions, and the commissions with business, on much friendlier terms. Still, the structure of hostile boards showed one important difference from the structure of friendly boards. The barbers' board was composed of barbers; in contrast, the Superior Grain and Warehouse Commission law (1905) insisted that no one interested in elevators, warehouses, the transport of grain, nor any employee of any of these operators or of a railroad might serve on the commission.[89] The licensing of employment agencies and of dealers in stocks and bonds was handed over to the Railroad Commission—a Commission hardly staffed by stock brokers and heads of employment agencies.[90] But even regulation which arose out of hostility tended to confer offsetting benefits on the regulated, particularly guaranties against unrestricted competition. This was true of public utility regulation; no new competition might enter the field without license. Even the employment agency law allowed the commission to refuse a license to an applicant if existing agencies were "sufficient to supply the needs of employers and employees."

Particularly restrictive of the regulated group were the various acts licensing hawkers, peddlers, transient merchants, and fire sale merchants. The license "fees" under some of these laws seemed almost {166} confiscatory. Anti-peddler laws were passed as early as Period I. A comprehensive new law, passed in 1905, showed no improvement in the public image of the peddler.[91] The 1905 statute generated almost no case-law, but its local importance was reflected in an unusual number of Attorney General opinions. In 1906, the Attorney General remarked that the present act "as I personally know" was passed "with the intent that its provisions should be liberally construed in respect to vendors of merchandise having a place of business, regular trade, or contracts which they are required to fill." Thus milk dealers who had "contracts with customers" were not under the act. The same "personal knowledge" that the legislature wanted to exempt "local merchants having a fixed place of business" told the Attorney General that butchers could not be transients.[92] But a merchant with a fixed place of business somewhere, who moved into a community to dump a load of goods for quick sale, was a "transient merchant."[93] Peddlers were solitary, unorganized individual entrepreneurs, without political leverage. They threatened the competitive position of local merchants. The small town merchants faced many problems; mail order houses were doing to them on a larger scale what peddlers and transient merchants did on a small scale; chain stores were just over the horizon, and the automobile was destined to carry customers over state-supported highways to distant shopping centers. The local merchants' sense of insecurity took the form of lobbying for severe anti-peddler laws and (once the laws were passed) frequent complaints to local law enforcement agencies for vigorous administration of these laws. A man who made and sold candy and ice cream cones, which he had the gall to sell "not only on the resident streets, but even upon business streets,"[94] threatened the local merchants (in their eyes) as much as the distant, powerful, and insidious trusts, and remedies were sought through the medium of legislative-executive action with the same disregard of the free contract ideology of the market.

The Labor Contract. Hardly any problem so agitated the mind of the late nineteenth and early twentieth centuries as the relation between capital and labor. The two concepts had changed in meaning, or at least in emotional tone, since Period I. "Labor" now meant the industrial worker, "capital" primarily the awesome industrial corporation. The semantic changes corresponded to the change in emphasis from {167} development of the economy to inequities in a developed economy.

Abstract theory demanded that labor be treated as a commodity, the same as any item of trade. When constitutional lawyers spoke of "freedom of contract," they included the freedom of workers and employers to contract, free of unreasonable state interference. The symbol of liberty of contract was rarely invoked with success as a weapon against middle-class aspirations expressed in law. Now, at the outset of the new century, conservatives were obsessed with fear: particularly fear of the landless foreigners who flooded into the cities, joined unions, engaged in strikes and boycotts, and showed little respect for "American ideals." In Wisconsin, the state labor movement was, comparatively speaking, quite radical. But the aims of labor were "radical" only because so defined by the rest of the population. In the 1850's, too, many foreigners emigrated to Wisconsin; and some of these men were radical for their day or in European terms. These Germans and Scandinavians settled in small towns and farms; their influence united with that of the native-born settlers in inducing the legislature to pass laws—like the homestead act—which could hardly be reconciled with the principle of laissez faire. By 1900 much of this legislation was as well accepted as workmen's compensation and social security were in the 1950's. On the other hand, the urban worker's program to improve his situation by law generated powerful opposition, and to some seemed to threaten great danger to the established order of society. Some laws favorable to urban workers were passed in Period II, though nothing remotely resembling the total program of the Social Democrats. The Wisconsin court was more conservative than the legislature, but less so than other courts (Illinois, for example),[95] which specialized in using liberty of contract as a blunt weapon against labor law. By 1905, labor law was a "special" field with a large polemic and expository literature.

The movement to abolish child labor was at least a generation old by 1905. Wisconsin's first child-labor law was passed as early as 1867.[96] Other states in the industrial East had passed child-labor laws even earlier, though typically these laws were quite ineffective. Child-labor laws had a strong emotional appeal. The constitutional problem was small. Even such a laissez faire apologist as Cooley conceded that legal regulation might take into account "distinctions that exist in the nature of things"; employment of children "in mines and manufactories is commonly, and ought always to be regulated."[97] The common law itself {168} treated the contracts of minors as voidable; thus child-labor legislation did not abolish an existing "freedom," but simply expanded a recognized area of legal concern.

Like occupational licensing law, labor law developed cautiously along the lines permitted by constitutional doctrine and by the alignment of interests. Regulation of the labor of women, which followed child-labor legislation, shared the advantage that it operated in an area not fully governed by the abstraction of classical contract law; like children, women had imperfect contractual capacity at common law. It took a combination of sentiment and calculation to get the statutes on the books. The unions were sure that women belonged in the home, not in the factory where they worked for less than men demanded in wages. This reasoning appealed also to those who had no such axe to grind, but who believed in the sanctity of women, the chivalry of men, and who saw traditional American family life endangered by working mothers.[98]

Beyond regulation of the labor of women and children lay a real constitutional frontier. Only cautious steps were taken. As a contracting party, the state had the right of contractors in general to bargain for terms in its contracts; consequently, there was no constitutional barrier to making the eight-hour day a condition of public works contracts.[99] In addition, the state might impose conditions on hours of work in private employment, if regulation had a reasonable relationship to public health or safety. For example, an exhausted or immature railroad worker could endanger the public; therefore, laws banned railroad telegraphers under the age of eighteen, and no railroad could "require or permit any operator to remain on duty for more than one period of eight consecutive hours," or to go back on duty without "at least sixteen consecutive hours off duty in any twenty-four hours."[100] The same theory could be used as a prop for statutes requiring the companies to use full crews, e.g., for "any passenger train with three cars or less," "one engineer, one fireman, one conductor and one brakeman; for more than three cars, two brakemen"; even freight trains by law had to carry "a full train crew consisting of five persons."[101] In 1913 the railroads were forbidden to "establish, enforce, or permit unreasonable conditions" in the employment of switching crews, or to use less than a "reasonable" number of employees necessary "to protect life, health and safety of employees or public."[102] That these statutes benefited railroad labor and its unions is self-evident. Significantly, these laws {169} affected the railroad industry, which had long been a center of controversy and for which substantial public opinion supported close public regulation. Efforts to press labor regulation into broader areas of conduct were generally unsuccessful. A bill was introduced in 1905 to limit to eight hours the work day in brass, steel, or iron foundries, and in tobacco or cigar factories. It failed.[103] The 1913 switching-crew law had spoken of the safety of employees and the public; it was a difficult political-legal jump to drop justification in terms of broad public concern and enact laws whose immediate impact was confined only to employees.[104] Thus labor legislation, in general, shared two characteristics with occupational licensing laws: close attention to constitutional limits, and dependence for success on the convergence of economic and humanitarian factors. The same point might be made about a new flowering in Period II of Sunday laws. The churches approved of these laws on moral and religious grounds; the trades and unions found Sunday laws a socially and legally acceptable way to restrict "unfair" labor practices. A business which operated on Sunday had a competitive advantage over those which did not: if one barbershop in town "cheated," it hurt all the rest.[105]

The use of state force (legislative and administrative) to achieve competitive goals bears comparison with the active intervention of the state in the economy in Period I through the vehicle of franchise and grant. The analogy is particularly close in the case of occupational licensing, where in effect the state franchises pursuit of occupations through grants of licensing power to the affected occupation, formally through an executive agency, practically through the occupation itself. In both cases, legal development implies a rejection of the abstraction of contract and the market as optimal methods of organizing economic life. It is true that in Period II the state no longer acted as a wasting-asset corporation. There was more conscious effort to keep public assets under public control. Continued grant of franchises and tolerance of public utility business in the private sector was tempered by close public control in the interests of the commonwealth. As a symbol of the new role of government, the conservation movement is particularly apt. In Wisconsin, 155 statutes on fish, game, and conservation of resources were passed between 1905 and 1915, 35 in the 1911 session alone.[106] The conservation movement grew out of the needs of an expanding population; but it owed much to the idea that the frontier was gone, and that national resources were finite and diminishing. This {170} was the same attitude which underlay the jockeying for competitive position that in turn underlay so much of Period II legislation. The net effect of all this legislation was to define and limit the area of abstraction, hence to curtail the area within which the law of contract, as classically defined, could operate even in theory.

Period III: Old Themes Revisited. Like its immediate predecessor, Period III generated much statute law. On the surface, many old themes had either disappeared or lapsed into relative insignificance. Other than a short act which provided that "boys 12 or over [but under 14] may be employed as caddies on golf courses if they use caddy carts,"[107] the two sessions here studied in detail (1955, 1957) were almost barren of labor law. Insurance statutes and statutes dealing with quality standards of commodities had fallen off in number. Yet the state had not by any means lost its interest in insurance, labor law, or food products. The influence of government is cumulative. The old programs continued; new ones were added. In substantial areas of public policy, the agencies of government were busy administering statutes passed in prior years; only occasionally and usually in peripheral matters did they need infusions of new law. By a mingling of inertia and experience, regulatory statutes, particularly those which set up administrative bodies, became the basis of firmly rooted institutions. Old programs needed (and sometimes got) new rationalizations as times changed; the rational onlooker might suggest outright repeal of outworn programs, but habit was itself a strong administrative force. The discussion of Period III's legislation must therefore be understood against this rich but silent background. Not only the work of Period II, but of the intervening years—in particular, depression legislation—had become a permanent part of government. The statute books retained in full force the various geological strata of homestead laws, lien laws, tax exemption laws, and matters of contract remedy.[108] Modern law preserves and adapts the frozen crises of the past.

Between Periods II and III the stream of legislation creating and amending occupational licensing laws did not subside. However, a graph of the development of occupational licensing would not describe a straight upward line. A peak was reached in the depression year 1933; more such laws were passed in that year than in any year before or any year through the end of Period III.[109] The 1955 and 1957 legislative sessions were, however, quite active in this area. Occupations {171} newly licensed or whose laws were radically changed made a sizeable list: operators of refrigerated food locker plants, business opportunity brokers, aircraft dealers, grease trap servicers, land surveyors, investment advisors, motor vehicle salvagers and wreckers, cemetery salesmen, hunting and fishing guides, motor vehicle auctioneers, operators of commercial driving schools, "sanitarians," weighers and samplers of milk.[110] These laws did not add any sizeable number of persons to the list of those who had to be licensed. But the licensing laws, too, were cumulative. Dentists, doctors, and druggists were, for example, still licensed. And these new laws brought government control to a group of workers who were not subject to other forms of regulation. Labor law and the unions governed masses of wage-earners; the farmers were smothered in federal and state agricultural law; a ton of regulations circumscribed the businessman's dealings. The list of new licensees brought to heel a group of marginal occupations.

Aside from new laws, there was a great deal of tinkering with the old ones—at least nineteen amendments, major or minor, to old licensing laws in the two sessions. Some of the changes in the laws relating to old-line professions materially strengthened the organization or "ethics" of the profession. For example, during this period the lawyers achieved an "integrated bar."[111] Only rarely did amendments relax licensing requirements, and only if trained practitioners were scarce. The law had declared that "No person shall practice ... as a trained practical nurse ... without a license." This limitation was relaxed in 1955: "No license is required for practical nursing, but no person without a license shall ... hold herself out as a trained practical nurse." There was a notorious shortage of nurses of all sorts. The new statute let unlicensed practical nurses perform "simple acts" in caring for sick people, but nothing which required "any substantial nursing skill, knowledge, or training," or the "application of nursing principles based on biological, physical or social sciences, or the understanding of cause and effect in such acts." But since the unlicensed practical nurse might not "hold herself out" as a nurse, the regulation tended to prevent competition between the two classes of practical nurse.[112]

Some license laws were almost devoid of substantive content. Anybody with $25 to spare might become a licensed wholesale fish dealer. Still, the licensing requirements gave the conservation department access to useful information; and gave them a sanction (revocation of {172} the license) to use against dealers who possessed "illegal fish."[113] An application form, $25 a year, and some bothersome paper work might be enough to restrict the business to people with some minimum commitment to it, thus tending to eliminate amateurs and casuals.

More typically, the licensing statutes went into some detail to specify the characteristics and qualifications of applicants. Despite the detail, there was a growing tendency to vest extremely flexible and vague powers in the licensing board, and the statutes often expressed a mandate to the board to enforce a vague moral standard. Thus the real estate brokers' licensing board was empowered to grant licenses only to persons who were "trustworthy and competent" to transact brokerage business "in such manner as to safeguard the interests of the public." "Competency" was defined in more or less specific terms, e.g., a "fair understanding" of the meaning and effect of "deeds, mortgages, land contracts of sale, and leases"; but "trustworthy" was left undefined. The list of grounds for revocation of a broker's license included, along with instances of specific infractions of duty, "untrustworthiness" and "any other conduct" which might be "improper."[114] These provisions were found in the original statute (1919).[115] They were characteristic of what we might call the second wave of licensing laws. The first occupations to be licensed were the traditional "professions" (e.g., law and medicine). Occupations less clearly "professional," but which required some training, skill, or technical knowledge followed next. After all, a good command of English, some idea of land law, some concept of the rules of brokerage, were necessary or at least desirable requirements for brokers. Many of the second-wave licensing laws called for an oral or written examination or at least implied that one would be held. The examination could be manipulated to restrict entry into the field, as well as to test competence. The boards made up the test, decided what raw score constituted a passing grade, and marked the examinations. But in any event, an examination system at least aspired to formal objectivity.[116]

The third wave of license laws applied to occupations which were not professions (at least in any traditional sense of the word). The less truly professional the occupation, the more the statute was likely to vest broad, undefined control in the licensing board. Objective measurements of competence simply did not exist. Statutes for those occupations for which the use of precise standards was possible did use such standards (along with more imprecise ones); as to the others, if there was to be licensing at all, vagueness of standard was {173} necessary. An act of 1955 made it unlawful to "practice land surveying" in Wisconsin without a license. To get a license an applicant needed a two-year "course in land surveying," or a long period of practical experience, or apprenticeship, or registration in another state as a land surveyor. Even here, "gross negligence, incompetence or misconduct" were grounds for revocation.[117] But precision could hardly be expected in licensing "motor vehicle salvage dealers," who were handed over to the scrutiny of the motor vehicle department in the same year. The department, on the basis of a $25 fee, an application form, and "when satisfied that the applicant [was] of good character" and was not violating the salvage laws, would issue a one-year license. No one might conduct "the business of wrecking or dismantling any motor vehicle" without the license.[118] Thus only people of "good character" (at least in theory) were allowed to make junk out of cars and sell their parts. Under a law of 1957 the commissioner of motor vehicles had the "duty" to give a "first-time applicant" for a car salesman's license "a personal written examination as to his competency." If the application and examination showed that the applicant intended "in good faith" to act as a salesman, was "of good reputation," had "experience or training" in or was "otherwise qualified for selling motor vehicles," was "reasonably familiar" with motor vehicle sales laws and contracts, and was "worthy of a license," he was entitled to get one.[119] Motor vehicle auction dealers, too, had to be "of good character" to earn a license.[120] Operators of driving schools had to submit to the motor vehicle department "satisfactory evidence of good character, reputation and fitness."[121] A driving instructor, too, might be denied a license if he could not "furnish satisfactory evidence" of the "facts required of him" and was not of "good moral character."[122] It took "good moral character" to qualify as a licensed milk weigher and sampler, along with "proof of ability to engage in such weighing and sampling to the satisfaction of the department [of agriculture] by satisfactorily passing a written examination pertaining to such activities."[123] Security dealers, agents, and investment advisers were licensed by the Department of Securities; the department issued licenses if it found, "from the information submitted and from any investigation by the department, that it is appropriate in the public interest that such license be issued."[124] The grounds for revocation of the license included (along with more specific justifications) "untrustworthiness" and lack of "good business repute." Even so, the "enumeration of the foregoing grounds" was not "exclusive," and the department {174} could revoke a license for any reason in the public interest. Again, nurserymen must "have proper facilities" to get a license; the license could be "denied, suspended or revoked if the applicant or holder thereof is not fit or qualified to engage as a nurseryman."[125]

Whatever their practical meaning, these statutory standards, on their face at least, placed heavy emphasis on morality and fair practice. The power of the state, in theory, might be used to force tradesmen to deal honestly and fairly with the public, in accordance with the community's ideas of what was fair and honest. This does not mean that the statutes originated solely as fair marketing statutes. Licensing was imposed upon the auto salvager, for example, to restrain traffic in stolen cars and parts of cars.[126] Familiar economic motives probably continued to operate: control of competition, restriction of entry into the field and (lest one seem too cynical), some real regard for the public welfare.

As in Period II, a marked number of licensed occupations were highly competitive and unusually vulnerable to incursions of fresh practitioners. The various auto trades are good examples. The typical unit of business was small, the attrition rate high. Objective barriers to entry into the business were flimsy or nonexistent. It did not take much skill, training, capital, or background to be a car salesman, or a hunting and fishing guide (all one needed was experience), or a bait dealer. The occupations were service occupations or small business; never big business.[127] Yet what prevented the grocers, candy store operators, dry cleaners from asking for and getting licensing laws? Apparently a trade needed either a strong association or, failing that, some conveniently available department of government to administer its law. The auto trades with the motor vehicle department as their governmental center, guides and bait dealers who were closely involved with the conservation department, and the various businesses connected with health and agriculture could achieve licensing laws without the help of strong unions or trade associations. For this reason, the rule-of-thumb distinction (useful in Period II) between friendly and hostile licensing, based on whether the licensing board was composed of "insiders" or men appointed through the political process, breaks down here. The economic price to be paid for licensing laws increased as the likelihood of self-regulation through a captive board decreased. Departments of government were not puppets of their licensees. The license was available at the price of somewhat more {175} stringent or unfriendly regulation than a captive board would give; the agency of the state would look out for the public interest, as it saw it. Therefore, even if the urge to license came from the trade group itself, the resulting law was apt to bear few obvious traces of its origin.

Success and failure depended on other factors, too. Problems internal to the group, the legislative climate of opinion, the types of opposing economic interests affected the course of legislative action. In the 1940's the legislature was decidedly hostile to licensing. Some laws on the books were even repealed. Some occupations consistently failed to achieve licensing: the electricians tried without success fourteen times between 1907 and 1951; and in 1955 they failed again.[128] Not all businesses felt the need for licensing. The grocers were no laissez faire theorists; they fought the chain stores bitterly through other appeals to law, but not through licensing laws. The candy store men in the small towns went after itinerant ice cream peddlers with tooth, claw, and anti-transient laws. The dry cleaners roused themselves from their legal torpor to demand in some places that the "coin-ops" either shut down at night, or take on superfluous employees, to protect the public from hypothetical rapists who specialized in all-night laundry customers.[129] In any event, new and old licensing laws extended to more and more occupations the idea that business ought not be conducted by just anybody; that the state had a legitimate administrative interest in more and more private service contracts. The process was a gradual one. In 1900 few demanded that only men of good character should sell bicycles. By the 1950's, the six volumes of the Wisconsin administrative code—which itself was only the visible part of an iceberg of control—repeated, on its own level, the characteristics of legislation, in a curious mixture of concern for public welfare and a narrow, anti-competitive mentality. The codes themselves varied from verbose to gnomic, and contained an amazing miscellany of material. The Board of Accountancy rules stood at one extreme. Accountants were told to maintain "high ideals of professional honor"; this turned out to mean, among other things, that an employee might not "undertake professional work on his separate account, either during or after hours" without written permission of his employer; that an accountant might not criticize another accountant "before the laity" for violating statutes, rules and regulations (these matters must be kept within the family); an accountant might not "minimize the value of professional accounting service" by quoting unreasonably low fees; and might not steal away {176} employees from other accountants.[130] At the other end of the scale, the careful safety rules of the Industrial Commission, though restrictive and tight-fitting, clearly reflected efforts to protect public safety, untainted by grosser motives. It is a point worth making that the law of Period III allowed both sets of rules to exist. The one agency (the court) with possible power to discriminate between them did not often do so and probably never would take an active, continuous role in policing agency rules.

Form and Content. The mass of statutes already passed, and the flow of new statutes in Period III, meant much more than that the state "regulated" many areas of economic life in many ways. The growth of statute law meant that the fundamental ideas which underlay the classical law of contract were badly damaged, perhaps destroyed. Hardly any fundamental contract notions were untouched. For example, an auto dealer's license might be revoked for willful "failure to perform any written agreement with any retail buyer."[131] Holmes said, in 1897, that "The duty to keep a contract at common law means a prediction that you must pay damages if you do not keep it—and nothing else."[132] But the legislature did not read Holmes. A transient auctioneer had to post bond, conditioned on "compliance with all laws" and with "all material oral or written statements and representations made" about the merchandise he sold.[133] In these instances, the legislature penalized breach of contract, or adjudged that some breach of contract had social consequences such as to justify state intervention. Law and morality tended to merge in Period III, but hardly in the way the ethical philosophers had dreamt of. Obviously, statutory contract forms, occupational licensing, administrative regulation of the contents of contract, taken together, tended to socialize contract remedies (that is, shift remedial action from private to public initiative), to break down the distinction between economic and non-economic damages, and to add concern for the cumulative social effect of small units of economic damages (such as arise out of particular sales of defective goods) and the threat to the integrity of the market caused by marginal dishonest operators. This is the general meaning of the legislation of Period III, and in this sense much legislation was merely a heightened form of the legislation of Period II. The proliferation of bodies which exercised control over contractual activities accounts in part for the increasing resort to standards which could not be expressed {177} in market or measurable terms; the moral rhetoric of the statutes was in part a function of the fact that such statutes were passed as part of the political process, and had to appeal to public opinion rather than or in addition to considerations based on economic law or the impersonal market. In other words, problems whose resolution had once been sought through economic processes were converted into problems to be resolved politically. In high nineteenth-century theory, quite the reverse process was looked upon as normal. Questions which might be called political were supposed to be solved by natural economic processes. Many people claimed, for example, that the battle of labor and management was best resolved by letting the labor market work its lonely magic. Political resolution was deemed futile and dangerous.

Legislation of Period III was therefore much concerned with "unfair" business practice. Many practices were regulated because they were supposed to be "unfair" to the general public; others were unfair, if at all, only to a small group of people. The economic motives of the insiders were often clear enough; but passage of these laws meant that the general (political) public was convinced that the conduct outlawed was really unfair, that it should be controlled; or that the public was neutral or indifferent. Commodity regulation in Period III was much concerned with unfairness in marketing. As compared with Period II, less emphasis was placed on the physical or biological character of products in relation to public health and safety. There were still some examples of this type of regulation, e.g., an act of 1955, outlawing the sale "for the purpose of feeding livestock, [of] any utensil painted with a substance having a toxic effect upon livestock when taken orally."[134] But the new commodity statutes were not interested in preventing physical harm as much as in preventing fraud and deceit. Public health and safety were taken as axiomatic values; many health and safety laws were already on the books, and existing agencies of government, with wide rule-making powers, actively enforced them.[135] New marketing statutes emphasized fairness in advertising and distributing goods. No person might advertise "the sale of any butter at a stated price, unless the grade of the butter is set forth in such advertisement in not less than 10 point type." An imitation ice cream product might be manufactured and sold only "in such manner as will advise the consumer of its real character and contents." Endless chain schemes used to sell cars were called "lotteries," and forbidden.[136] Undoubtedly many auto dealers disliked endless chain schemes, but were afraid that they might {178} suffer competitively unless they joined in; a better solution was to have the legislature outlaw the practice. In 1957 the legislature made it "unlawful for any owner or operator of ... a motel, motor court, tourist cabin or like accommodation to post ... on any outdoor ... advertising sign ... any rates for accommodation in such establishment unless the sign shall have posted thereon both the minimum and maximum room, or other rental unit rates." In general, motel owners might not post rate signs "which have thereon any untrue, misleading, false or fraudulent representations."[137] Another statute outlawed "bushing" (the "practice of increasing the selling price of a car above that originally quoted the purchaser after [he] ... has made an initial payment ... and signed a purchase order or contract which is subject to subsequent acceptance"), and false or misleading statements with "regard to the sale or financing of motor vehicles."[138]

Some of the major statutes of Period III showed a familiar mixture of attention both to public and to private welfare. The statute licensing driving schools required that "All driver training cars shall be equipped with approved dual controls so that the instructor can stop the car promptly." This was a perfectly rational safety device. Less warranted was the statute's enumeration of another "prohibited practice": "No licensee shall agree to give unlimited driver's lessons, nor represent or agree, orally or in writing ... to give instructions until a driver's license is obtained."[139] This "practice" perhaps was an invitation to fraud; but more likely it was nothing worse than a form of price-cutting. The continuing vendetta against the transient merchant mixed a small bit of public welfare with a large portion of private interest. In 1955 those who conducted "liquidation sales" were added to the list of the damned. The same law stipulated that "No license shall be granted for any such sale if it appears that the applicant ... has within the period of two years prior to the application, conducted a similar sale either in the same place of business or at any other place in the county." But peddlers' licenses were issued without fee to disabled veterans, the blind, and "any person disabled to the extent of the loss of one arm or one leg or more."[140]

Many of the major marketing statutes were supposed to rationalize trade practice and to eliminate undesirable competition. An elaborate "unfair sales act" was already on the books, prohibiting sales below cost and the use of loss leaders.[141] An important statute outlawed a list of "unfair" practices in dairy marketing. Wholesalers were forbidden {179} to give discounts or rebates "on selected dairy products sold to retailers"; restrictions were placed on giving advertising material to retailers, and on the financing and servicing of dairy equipment, display materials, and storage equipment. In general, wholesalers were not to "Give any other gift of money, merchandise, services or materials of any value to any retailer to assist him in the conduct of his business." Contracts in violation of the act were declared "void."[142] Indeed, the general thesis that business should be conducted "fairly" appeared in the Wisconsin statutes in black and white, in a sweeping statement going back to 1921: "Methods of competition in business and trade practices in business shall be fair. Unfair methods of competition in business and unfair trade practices in business are hereby prohibited."[143] The idea was not one which gained general adherence overnight. The old concept of unfairness, stressing imbalance of "bargaining power," was never abandoned. But something new was gradually added: a zest for regulation in the interests of more economic security for businessmen and the outlawing of "cutthroat" competition. The appeal was to substitute a more gentlemanly code for the so-called jungle ethics of the nineteenth century. In practice, this effort was most likely to add up to legal limitation of price competition.

The complicated agricultural marketing act of 1957[144] was another case in point. The act began by announcing a state policy "to promote orderly and efficient marketing of agricultural commodities and to prevent economic waste." These worthy ends were contrasted with the evils of "Unfair methods of competition" and "disorderly marketing." (Compare "disorderly conduct.") Producers were not getting a "fair return" as things stood.

> Such conditions jeopardize the continued production of an adequate food supply ... and may result in unemployment with its attendant burdens on the citizens of this state. The production, processing and marketing of agricultural commodities within this state is hereby declared to be affected with a public interest and the provisions of this section are enacted for the purpose of protecting the health, peace, safety and general welfare of the people of this state.

For a piece of blatant farmers' price-support legislation, this preamble was farfetched to say the least. It was a rhetorical set-piece, cramming in one paragraph the echoes of ancient constitutional conflict, appeals to the public for support, and an argument aimed at the cities ("food supply ... unemployment"). When the statute settled down to the {180} business of regulating, however, it did so in a characteristic Period III form. The heart of the act dealt with "marketing orders," to be issued only after approval by a referendum of "affected producers or handlers"; to become effective a marketing order needed the votes of "two-thirds of those voting, representing 51 per cent or more of the volume of the affected commodity produced or handled by those voting." Such resort to referenda went back at least as far as the National Recovery Act of 1933, which tried to attain fair competition (meaning curbs on price-cutting) by reaching a consensus within particular trade groups, and then by making law out of the consensus.[145] In the 1950's, federal agricultural law, too, made use of referenda; for example, federal marketing orders covering "grapefruit for canning or freezing" required the approval of those "engaged in canning or freezing for market more than 50 per centum of the total volume of such commodity,"[146] so that the grapefruit processors become a kind of *ad hoc* legislature. In the Wisconsin act, the "affected producers and handlers" even held a kind of taxing power.[147] This striking example of transfer from economic to political processes of the shaping of transactions was a logical extension of the occupational licensing idea. A medical or barbers' board, composed of nominees of the doctors' and barbers' associations, was selected by a process just as political as the manner in which other boards were appointed by the governor without consulting the affected group; members in good standing chose those who ran the organization of doctors or barbers. The analogous phenomenon in Period I—the cession of state power to squatter groups, bank associations, and amateur policemen— was quite different. There the political weakness of the state, not its power, led to delegation of authority.

The agricultural marketing act did not simply hand over legislative power to producers. The statute set out general categories of subjects with which the marketing orders might concern themselves; thus the orders were to be enacted by a body with limited powers. Some of the powers were relatively close to those exercised by older forms of public regulation. Marketing orders, for example, might establish grading and quality standards, or uniform brand names and devices,[148] with the added safeguard, from the industry's point of view, that the administrators must consult with the administered. The statute made specific reference to the interests of consumers; and the powers granted under the act were to be "exercised only to the extent necessary to attain such [statutory] objectives."[149] But after due allowances are made for the safeguards embodied in the act, it must be conceded that the act {181} authorized considerable regulatory powers to control output and prices. Marketing orders could prohibit "unfair trade practices" (over and above "unfair trade practices now prohibited by law")—practices which, in the light of the act's declared purposes, were "unfair and detrimental."[150] Certainly the statutory procedures could in fact be used to restrain competition and control output. The producers had the power to displace the free market system with a system of imposed contracts, legitimized not by the market but by an essentially political process.

The NRA was a product of the great depression; New Deal depression legislation experimented with control of prices and output for the benefit of farmers. But the phenomenon here discussed seems quite independent of the business cycle; measures first adopted in the depression, particularly the farm program, lessened not at all in the course of the greatest boom period in American history. The idea of political control of economic process became more and more pervasive. In the words of Adolph A. Berle:[151]

> Our individual may no longer be able to determine affairs by his action or decision in respect of a farm or a forge or a small factory. But he can decide what he will consume, what he will do with his leisure, and what political issues interest him. He can control property locally by demanding zoning laws. He can require a maximum of veracity by outlawing false advertising. He can insist on a respectable measure of economic planning.... In time he may even come to demand a civilization which is beautiful as well as productive....

Berle's "economic republic" is the Utopia of nineteenth-century liberal economists, turned upside down. Now it was not automatic economic process, but automatic political process in a democratic society, which would ultimately bring miracles to the twentieth-century United States.

Given the extent to which political controls were substituted for market controls in the legislation of Period III, anti-trust law struck an anomalous note. In Period III, "unfair" practices often meant competition pressed farther than trade could comfortably live with; yet the antitrust laws continued to declare that competition was of high social value. Anti-trust law was, as it had been since Period II, not the outward manifestation of a rigorous economic theory, but in practical effect was built upon an inductive series of judgments on particular cases and particular classes of industry. The legislature of Wisconsin went on strengthening the anti-trust laws with one hand and limiting {182} areas of competition with the other. Public utilities were forbidden to extend electric service to the "premise of any person already receiving electric service directly or indirectly from another public utility" without "consent" by the other utility or the state.[152] The agricultural marketing statute specifically made compliance with the statute or a marketing order "a complete defense" to any anti-trust suit; this provision was surely a necessary precaution.[153] Yet the anti-trust laws were strengthened in 1957 when, for the first time, treble damages in civil suits were authorized.[154] In the same year those who financed "the purchase of real or personal property," were forbidden to require use of any particular insurance agent "as a condition precedent" to the loan. The lender had the "duty" to tell the borrower he was "free to choose" his own.[155] In the 1957 session, the Wisconsin legislature memorialized Congress (a) to restrict imports of plywood, because plywood plants, "the backbone of the economy of many communities," were shutting down, and because "American industry cannot compete with [cheap] imported hardwood plywood"; (b) to "reject ... any ... proposed amendment to the Natural Gas Act ... which will create a gap in the price regulatory chain, or otherwise weaken the protection accorded consumers"; and (c) to enact higher price supports for dairy products, since the "reduction in farm income" caused "great hardship," forced young farmers and veterans to abandon "programs of expansion and modernization or to default on their debts," and hurt state revenues.[156] Clearly, anti-trust law was a set of rules which, in its appropriate sphere, determined that certain kinds of economic behavior were "unfair" because they hurt competition, just as laws on "unfair practices" proscribed conduct which was felt harmful because it engendered "excessive" competition. The mind of the mid-twentieth century was no more concerned than the mind of earlier periods with economic theory as theory; price-fixing was evil only when and because (like sales below cost and misleading advertisements) it was "unfair." The basic anti-trust laws (those which proclaimed grand principles of competition) were like the law of contract itself: generalities to be ruthlessly displaced in fields which were felt not to demand the application of such generalities. Public utilities were special because they were natural monopolies, agriculture because of the values (real or sentimental) attributed to the family farm, the practice of law and medicine because the public must rely on professional standards to insure essential services in these professions—the list could be indefinitely {183} extended. In short, the key characteristics of legislation were diversity and complexity: a multiplicity of responses to a multiplicity of stimuli. In place of the abstraction of contract theory—which posited one basic mechanism and vested its administration in private hands, with ultimate recourse to one simple agency—legislation substituted a variety of bodies and a variety of controls, on the formal side, and on the substantive side, a series of manifold and variegated precepts.

In brief, the legislative story, as it unfolded, revealed not only an absolute growth in legislation, but a qualitative change in the character of legislation. The statutes of Periods II and III represented a direct use of public power in many areas of concern, in contrast to the legislation of Period I, which was characterized by large-scale delegation of matters of public concern to private individuals and groups. Expansion of regulatory legislation was not so much a novel intrusion into the economy as a change in emphasis and scale. This change corresponded closely to change in the main currents of social life. A society of widely dispersed power (whose concerns over concentration of power occurred mostly when that power was seen as a kind of external threat, for example, eastern finance), was replaced by a society of complex and interdependent relations. The great attention paid to debtor-creditor relations in Period I contrasts with the great attention paid to rationalization of economic organization and protection of consumers in later periods. The extension of occupational licensing laws and the development of concepts of "fair" competition can be analyzed as reactions to the fear of "small" men against the competitive power of bigger institutions. Occupational licensing resembled, superficially, the delegation-legislation of Period I; but the social causes were radically different. These causes are to be sought, not in the desire to mobilize productive energy, but in the search for state aid to stabilize group aspirations in the complex world of Periods II and III. Legislation was massive in these periods; as a result, for large areas of economic life the structural framework within which contractual behavior took place was created by legislation and legislatively created agencies. By way of contrast, the basic principles of contract behavior were (relatively speaking) more a matter of judicial formulation in Period I than at any time subsequent. The court, in contract matters, dealt with residual, marginal details in the later Periods, and with questions of performance and breach, within a framework of behavior basically established by other institutions of government. {page 184 follows}

V
CONTRACT LAW IN THE COURTS: WHAT THE STUDY SHOWS

DETAILED analysis of the case-materials and statutes, as described in the foregoing chapters, will be summarized here from a double aspect. In the first place, we will attempt to draw together what the materials show of the functions and goals of the body of contract law itself. In the second place, since the body of contract law has been examined from the standpoint of materials which emanated from particular legal institutions—the Wisconsin Supreme Court and the Wisconsin legislature—we will have to examine the meaning of our findings for the light they shed on the utility and role of those institutions in shaping those aspects of law here under discussion.

Contract Law and the Market. The core of concern of the law of contract was with the market, that is, with the network of private, unregulated transactions which formed the basis of the economic system of the United States in general, and of the state of Wisconsin in particular. As was demonstrated, the body of rules of contract law was characterized by emphasis on abstraction, a concept which fit the economic presuppositions of a market economy. Legal institutions were so framed as to give support to the market. The very fact that the law did not seek to define and regulate the limits of permissible transactional activity was itself an important source of support for the market. Within the law of contract itself, support was given to the market by virtue of the fact that the law enforced market transactions, and enforced them in accordance with rules which generalized and abstracted economic behavior. In theory, parties were free to frame their own transactions, which could then be carried out without legal impediment; in the event that a bargain fell through, or if one party balked or {185} proved unable to perform, the law of contract made freely available the regular judicial processes of the court system, in which economic damages would be awarded to the party aggrieved. Legislation played an important role in supporting the market system, even at this level; legislation created agencies (principally the courts) which enforced market transactions, removed procedural clogs to rapid enforcement of contracts, and provided a general system of law and order without which the market could not readily operate.

From the very outset of Wisconsin's legal history, the classic ideals of the law of contract were not allowed full, untrammeled play. Much legislation and case-law derogated from abstraction. Some of this can be explained (or at least rationalized) in market terms. Perhaps in theory pure freedom of contract would let a man sell his own labor for life; but it can at least be plausibly argued that this kind of unrestricted freedom ultimately leads to a breakdown of the free market. Legislation and case-law even in Period I were sensitive to the requirements of the social system which people believed to be necessary if the market was to function at all. Just as free enterprise needs courts to enforce contracts, so arguably it may need restrictions on debt collection and on the wealth which any one man or entity can accumulate. The free market requires a broad base of many free, independent persons or firms without too great extremes of poverty or wealth. Thus, apart from any considerations of politics, the homestead exemption, the various lien laws, and the constitutional restrictions on feudal tenures can be defended as preconditions of a working market system.

In later periods, the same arguments could be used to defend antitrust laws. Slightly more tenuous, but still cogent, are arguments that laws favoring the farmer, the worker, the insurance policy consumer, and the small businessman serve a function favoring the market, though on the surface they derogate from abstraction. Particularly is this true if we agree that the aims which the law sought must not be explained ideologically, that free enterprise and the market were not looked upon as ends in themselves, but as means to advance the common good. There have always been theorists ready to argue for the free market in terms which bear the stamp of almost religious fervor. On the other hand, doctrinaire Marxists have denounced capitalism with equal religiosity. But even the theorists appeal to considerations above and beyond theory. And the mass of the people have never had a taste for rigorous theory. {186}

In Period I, economic theory was valued as a statement of appropriate means to ends grounded in general notions of the common good. The end which enlisted widest loyalty in nineteenth-century Wisconsin was economic growth. People felt that this end would be best served by legal arrangements which legitimized and encouraged the maximum exercise of private will. But economic growth was the end, rather than some abstract ideal of freedom of private enterprise from public interference. Positive use of law in the economy—land grants to subsidize the building of canals and railroads are a good example—was widely approved where this use of law seemed likely to promote economic development. Abstraction, then, had to give way whenever it interfered with a greater goal.

In general, however, Period I was the age of abstraction. Abstraction was not simply a tool of the law; it also reflected the actual state of the economy. It was fact, not theory, that land was often bought and sold as a colorless commodity. It was fact, not theory, that the residents of Wisconsin were mobile men, not rooted to a particular community or to ancient customs which fixed persons from birth with a given social status. It was fact, not theory, that the economy was in a state of rapid growth. Opportunities were not limited by all the built-in and conservative values which inhere in a locality of age-old settlement, whose cultural shape has been decisively molded by existing social patterns.

As the economy matured, these factual underpinnings of abstraction weakened; and the weakness of abstraction as a theory was reflected in the work of both the court and the legislature. The decay of the abstract rules of the law of contract has as one of its sources the decay of those conditions which lent strong support to abstraction in pioneer Wisconsin. But the weakening of abstraction cannot be attributed only to the differences within the state between its first age of growth and a more economically mature generation. Nor can the argument be pressed too far that the many derogations from contract abstraction (particularly the legislative derogations) were necessary to maintain the social system presupposed by abstraction. In Period II, the revolt against the full sweep of the competitive system was strong enough to indicate that it must have had broad roots in contemporary ideas and attitudes. It affected all classes of society. The urban workers expressed their opinions through unions, strikes, and boycotts. Big businesses formed "trusts." The farmers joined co-operative movements and raised {187} hell along with corn. The middle-class tradesmen, the retailers, and the wholesalers spawned great numbers of national, state, and local "associations" of one form or another, responding to the same hunger for unity and standardized strength. Because of occasional bombs, strikes, anarchists, riots, and the gray shadow of the "class struggle," organized labor in its fight against organized management justifiably attracted a major share of the attention of historians. The radical agrarian movements and the trusts also made headlines in their day and claimed space in later textbooks. But what the middle classes and the small tradesmen were doing also reflected current attitudes in an important way; and the organization of society was not untouched by these middling movements. We hear of price maintenance schemes and "unwritten" laws in associations of druggists, confectioners, and retail lumber dealers. The employing printers of New York joined in a "Ben Franklin Club"; this club bore the name of a patriarch of American individualism, but the members agreed to share price lists and avoid competitive bidding for contracts. In Wisconsin, we hear of an abortive attempt to control the output of bricks by Milwaukee brickmakers and a plan to fix rates by ice dealers in La Crosse.[1] Fred Brockhausen, the Socialist secretary-treasurer of the Wisconsin State Federation of Labor, spoke an unpleasant truth when he accused the "middle class" of hypocrisy: they "cry out the loudest against trusts and combinations," he said, yet they harbor in their bosoms "small combinations galore, fostering monopoly in restraint of trade."[2]

Thus men in the early twentieth century often took as economic goals the achievement of price-fixing, standardization of costs, risks, and markets, control over entry into an occupation or trade. But the vigor of the existing free market system destroyed the hopes of many businesses to attain these ends. When self-help failed, trades and occupations resorted to law. If legislatures would enact "friendly" regulation—nominally controlled by the government, actually controlled by the trade—the path to reduction of competitive rigors would be so much smoother. Barbers, plumbers, doctors, lawyers, miners, architects, and brokers, among others, succeeded in turning the police power to their purposes; other "professions" (such as the electricians) tried to secure similar benefits in Wisconsin but failed. We have seen how pressure for occupational licensing for certain trades became irresistible in the 1890's and 1900's. The statute books began to display a {188} new kind of administrative board, selected by the governor, but dominated by the existing members of the affected trade, empowered more or less broadly to control entry and regularize practice.

Anti-trust acts sprang into prominence at precisely that point in history when reliance on competition showed its greatest weakness. The Sherman Act did not represent a scholarly economic philosophy; it was passed, not because the public accepted completely the theories of free trade, but because popular feeling demanded a weapon against big business, the trusts, and the rich.[3] The trusts themselves were not simply the devil in modern dress. Technology, transport, and communication were the true villains; science and engineering made it possible to combine forces and pool information easily and on a grand scale. The telephone, telegraph, and railroad served the trusts by making the country one technological unit, by facilitating control of men and money in far places. Technology posed grave dangers for small- as well as for medium-sized business. It exposed small-town retailers to the competition of mail-order houses, national advertising, and mass marketing. But nineteenth-century technology allowed the small merchant to be mobile, too; now the retail druggists, newspapermen, and grocers could hold meetings, form state and local groups, pool information, decide on common tactics and goals. Loose federalism was as tricky for groceries as for states; a "chain" of independent merchants might be only as strong as its weakest link. For the merchants, as for the professionals, compulsion was the next step—borrowing the force and prestige of the state. Invariably, trade associations set up "legislative committees" to screen proposed laws, lobby, draft their own bills, and push for state action if self-help failed. But the priority of action was important: self-help first, then legislation; the courts played a role only as watchdogs of the constitution; typically, once the test case was decided, the courts bowed out of the picture.

The inner history of the Progressive Era might be written in terms of which groups succeeded in what ways in achieving legal or extra-legal support for their competitive position and why. The organization of the middle class through law and despite law met with almost none of the shrillness, the prophecies of doom, the blood and bitterness of the contest between labor and management. The courts did not often declare an occupational licensing law unconstitutional; in any case, the ideal of freedom of contract, which to some people seemed jeopardized by unions and by labor legislation, was rarely spoken of in the court {189} decisions on occupational licensing. Economic theory alone cannot explain the different legal and popular attitudes toward middle-class organization and toward the unions. If all lawyers in the country went on strike for higher fees, the strike might affect everybody slightly—which is practically the same as affecting nobody. When a union struck a plant, it affected that plant immediately and strongly. While the industrial workers and the bosses struggled over their respective shares of economic control and of national wealth, the middle groups stealthily stole some of the prize.

The economic struggle, so far as it was viewed by the unsophisticated, now centered not over position in the race to develop the economy, but over the status quo—a struggle to exact a greater share in existing product, existing wealth. If conservatives decided that freedom of contract and laissez faire were God-given rights, it was in order to stave off the urban poor who would storm the citadels of prosperity. The worker and the farmer tended to deny the truth of the free market altogether; it did not give them the fair share they deserved. We have already noted the less flamboyant attacks on the free market led by the middle groups. In this kind of society, the ideal, abstract law of contract had little to say. It did not fit the way business felt business had to work; the new world of industry, of organized mass markets, of cities full of poor foreign-born workers, could not afford the luxury of contract theory. All classes tended to unite on one goal: holding the line. This meant, however, different things to different people: breaking up the trusts; or keeping out the Chinese; or crushing unions; or getting rid of part-time brokers; or countless other ends which, if necessary, would have to be forced on society by law.

"Freedom of contract" then, as a constitutional proposition, was not a theory so much as a weapon. The concept gave business a device, a slogan, to use in protecting group interests against the forces of industrial society. Against the middle classes, this criterion of the proper scope for governmental action was hardly used at all. The effect of these grand movements of public opinion and of the critical facts of economic life—the interdependence of human relationships, the growth of technology, the increasing industrial cast of economic life—was deeply felt by the law of contract. On the legislative side, the ambit within which the law of contract was allowed to operate was increasingly narrowed. Occupational licensing was only one symptom. Commodity legislation, for example, reflected technological advance, {190} judgments concerning inequality of bargaining power (between producer and consumer), humanitarian impulses toward state action of a kind which presupposed an economically mature community, and not least of all, the attempt of "reputable" producers forcefully to insure a rationalized and standardized market through invocation of the power of the state.

Changes in the substantive law of contract, as applied by the court, were more subtle, but analysis of the case-law reveals them clearly. The cases showed litigants who sought to achieve ends typical of the time. In *Pratt v. Darling*,[4] for example, our vignette case, the small-town merchant reacted out of a sense of outrage at the salesman's misrepresentation; to him, an exclusive line of toilet goods was important, and competition was not the life of trade. The number of cases which arose out of personal, non-business situations rather than in pure market transactions also illustrated the increasing use of contract law, not for purposes of policing an abstract system, but for solving disputes of unique particularity. The docket affected deeply the court's mode of handling its cases. The heavy use of such malleable concepts as waiver and estoppel shows how the court, faced with inherited rules, but with facts which looked the other way, was inclined to use these formulae of escape from the rigors of abstraction. Concepts such as fraud and mistake, the doctrine of specific performance, the permutation of the rule of *Hadley v. Baxendale*[5]—all these illustrate the court's retreat from abstraction, its growing interest in the precise and particular facts of the immediate case.

The court's interest in the unique situation before it was only heightened in Period III. In *Kelley v. Ellis*,[6] the case of the house in Baraboo, the court dismissed a somewhat attenuated argument by Mrs. Ellis' counsel, remarking that Mrs. Ellis had really "repudiated the contract ... on other grounds" than those advanced by her lawyer as the basis of her right to repudiate. In other words, the legal arguments were an afterthought, an excuse; and the court implied that judges might legitimately feel free to disregard legal arguments based only on afterthoughts. This frame of mind appeared in a significant number of cases in Period III. The court's perception of the motivation of the parties, of the "real reasons" underlying lawsuits, were important influences on decisions in Period III.

Carried to an extreme, the search for motivation would destroy the law of contracts. For example, the use of the Statute of Frauds as a {191} defense to a contract action is always an afterthought; parties do not breach a contract merely because the contract is not in full written form. Many of the formal, technical doctrines of contract law, similarly, are brought into use as "afterthoughts," matters of offense and defense in litigation which do not reflect the real cause of a breakdown in bargaining or performance. Contract doctrine developed historically into "rules" usable primarily as judicial techniques rather than as expressions of norms of behavior; an arsenal of "afterthoughts" became available to litigants. But any increase in judicial attention to motivation, to the extent this attention influenced decision, contributed to the further decay of technical legal doctrines; and at mid-twentieth century the law markedly exhibited such decay, not only in contract law, but in all the common law fields. The judges showed more and more willingness to examine common law doctrines in the light of "justice" or "common sense" or "public policy." Precedent and legal reasoning were not always enough.

The court's changing role in the legal system was a major factor in this movement toward legal "realism." The kind of contract cases coming before the Supreme Court in Period III helps explain why the court could freely indulge its urge to reach the "fair" result as often as possible, ignoring a good deal of prior law, and often looking at the motivations of the parties. But interest in the equities of the particular situation and the emphasis on "fairness" had their parallel in the work of the legislature, which also made increasing use of verbal formulae of "fairness" and moral precepts, for example, in occupational licensing. The high estate of the concept of "fairness" related to attitudes of broader reach. In Period II, the decline of the competitive ideal seemed connected with the concept that the country had arrived at a more finite economic order with the consequent felt necessity to stake out and enforce claims to a proper share of the economic whole. This kind of outlook never died; but "fairness" in Period III was both more and less than the Progressive idea of "fairness," which had much to do with "inequality of bargaining power," and which pitted rich against middle against poor, class against class. Mid-twentieth-century society, taken in general, was middle-of-the-road. It believed in the sanctity of majority rule and majority opinion; it did not really believe that men held irreconcilable economic goals, but believed rather in the possibilities and values of teamwork and compromise; it believed that nobody gained if the farmer suffered, that strong unions and clean employee {192} cafeterias were good for business, and that it would be morally wrong for labor to lack a voice in running an industry. It was fashionable in 1955 to see (and decry) "conformity" in American society; certainly developments in mass communications and transport made cultural and moral homogeneity possible. The use of "fairness" as a criterion for settling contract disputes meant the replacement of inherited legal concepts with current concepts of what was right. Particular disputes were to be judged in terms of current ethical standards. It meant forswearing the use of general principles applied absolutely; it meant that courts were dispute-settlers, not agencies creating general norms at the impulse of particular occasions. Though the source of the sense of "fairness" in any given case arose out of current conceptions of "fairness," their use by courts implied the abandonment of the role of the courts as creators of fundamental principles whose ethical rightness lay in their general, rather than their particular, applicability.

Government never was larger, never did more than in Period III. All of the old forms of business and social regulation were used and strengthened. Programs begun in Period II, or in the midst of the depression, were continued with a subtle twist that converted them into instruments of the new jurisprudence. Marketing statutes demanded that business be conducted "fairly"; this was largely a rhetorical disguise for standardization and the elimination of "cut-throat" competition. Nonetheless, to call a "fair-trade act" fair implied that the public either believed or could be persuaded that price-cutting was "unfair," not nice, not the way people ought to behave. Of course, the economy retained many vigorously competitive segments. The words of a statute, even of a statute with "teeth," do not so easily change the workings of an economy; besides, the competitive ideal remained strong, particularly when the ideological enemy of capitalism became its political enemy as well and led men to reaffirm their economic loyalties.

Even in years of high judicial activism the judges, in their day-to-day labors, followed (or partook of) public opinion. Period III was not likely to be different; and, in fact, the times invited the judges ever more to keep in step. Nineteenth-century law was later often criticized as too moralistic, for example, because it based liability for personal injury on "fault." In tort, for example, mid-twentieth-century theorists preferred solutions to legal problems—loss-splitting, risk-spreading, insurance—which divided all-or-nothing incidence of tort losses and {193} which gave the appearance of compromise. Perhaps this means that in the new view, older law was wrong, not in stressing fault, but in its ideas of where fault lay. Contract law, as the case-law of Period III demonstrates, became quite concerned with "fault" in the moral sense—hence the search for motivation. Perhaps nineteenth-century law cared less about fault (in the moral sense) than at first appears; on reexamination, its concept of "fault" turns out to be less a moral than an economic concept.[7] Loss-splitting is a judgment that neither party is morally at fault even more than it is an economic measure. Modern contract law, where it finds no one at "fault," follows a path of loss-splitting, and thus contributes to the rationalizing of business relationships insofar as they come within its sphere. The doctrine of substantial performance, the various restitutionary remedies, and a whole host of big and small rules and attitudes were so framed as to modernize the search for fault, or, if nobody could really be blamed (as the twentieth century measured blame), to split the loss. The search for particularity, the emphasis on fairness, implied the creation of agencies of legal control with wide discretion—hence the increasing use of administrative agencies of all sorts. These agencies typically had rule-making power as well. Their rules were sometimes so detailed as almost to refute the proposition that flexible and discretionary administration was a characteristic of twentieth-century law. But a tissue of extremely detailed rules flows from a grant of power to make such rules; and the grant of power to make detailed rules is a denial that the subject to be regulated is susceptible of governance by grand and generalized propositions.[8] In part, the activism of government in Period III was a judgment that the market was a failure; in another sense, it was a judgment that the economy consisted not of a market, but of many markets, each with its appropriate modality of control. In such a context, the law of contract remained alive, not, however, as the organic law of the state's economic system—a kind of constitution for business transactions—but as one among many. It was the system of rules applicable to marginal, novel, as yet unregulated, residual, and peripheral business, and quasi-business transactions, transactions which might, in exceptional cases, call for problem-solving and dispute-settling. "Contract" stepped in where no other body of law and no agency of law other than the court was appropriate or available.

If one had to characterize these residual cases in broad terms, one might call them cases which dealt with problems of adjustment in {194} contract relationships. They do not concern the broad framework laid down by law to prescribe the conditions under which contract relations may be initiated. Rules of initiation were largely stripped from the court by successive waves of legislation, leaving the court with matters of adjustment—performance questions, fact-analysis, damage and remedy questions, construction of statutes. There is no question but that the court's role here is useful and necessary; but the losses of function make a powerful impact on the manner in which the court does its work. Freed of the necessity to pay great attention to matters of initiation (principle), the court is the more apt to turn to the particular situation before it, and to seek an adjustment which accords with current notions of fairness in the particular situation, untroubled by considerations of grand generality.

The Role of Legal Institutions in Framing the Law of Contract. By way of contrast, in Period I, the age of abstraction, the Wisconsin Supreme Court, as an institution of law-making power, possessed a degree of creativity and initiative which in most senses it has not since enjoyed. Its power in some degree was more apparent than real, but was nonetheless considerable. For one thing, the notion of abstraction vested in the court the primary function of framing the rules which were to govern the essentials of business transactions: the rules of initiation as well as adjustment, Contract law was abstract, general; the legislature was concerned with particular derogations from abstraction—in a sense, with adjustment.

Another cause of the court's apparent power was the lack of legal authority binding on the court. Except for a small group of statutes, limited in range and borrowed chiefly from other jurisdictions, in one sense a body of Wisconsin law did not exist at all in the early years of the period. The judges were apparently free to invent such legal rules as they deemed most just and suitable to fit the cases and classes of cases which came before them. For example, in *Sanderson v. Olmstead* (1849),[9] the plaintiff sought to collect on a promissory note executed by Sanderson in New York in 1817. Since 1835 Sanderson had been living in Wisconsin. At common law, after 20 years a note is presumed to have been paid, in the absence of contrary evidence; and since the note in question was more than 20 years old, it was presumptively uncollectible. In some jurisdictions, however, the courts insisted that the 20 years must be spent in the place where the action was brought. {195} Sanderson had lived in Wisconsin only some 14 years. Chief Justice Stow, deciding the case, had this to say of the problem:

> It has been decided differently by different tribunals, and differently by the same tribunal at different times. The weight of precedent (for binding authority there is none) would seem to require the entire period to have been passed within [this] ... jurisdiction.... But here the question is an open one, and one which we are at liberty to settle as we deem most expedient for the purposes of justice.

Experience and justice, Stow felt, required application of the presumption and dismissal of the plaintiff's suit:

> Once let it be known that the stale and outlawed demands of other states and countries were *prima facie* enforceable against our citizens until after a residence here for twenty years, all would be exposed to vexations and harassing suits, and many to ruin; while our courts would soon be flooded with prosecutions of musty claims which none of the tribunals of our sister states or of Europe

would entertain.

Sanderson v. Olmstead illustrates well the court's mode of operation in Period I. In particular, it illustrates the extent of the court's autonomy during the period. There was no binding precedent; the court was free to choose its own rule. But its choice was limited to existing common law options. The judges had neither the wish nor the power to break radically with the common law tradition. Whatever training they had was in that tradition. The tradition assigned a high place to precedent, and denied complete autonomy to the judges. Thus Stow's freedom was limited by his sense of role and his intellectual equipment.

Yet the legal tradition did give Stow real choices. The way Stow claimed to resolve the conflict of authorities is significant. He looked neither for the best legal logic, nor for the genius of the common law, but for the most "expedient" course for "purposes of justice." Law, for Stow, was an instrument of social and economic policy; his choices were weighed in the policy balance. For his ultimate decision he assigned two reasons: protecting residents against "vexatious and harassing suits"; and protecting the courts from a flood of "musty claims." One reason was, in other words, concerned with social policy, broadly considered; the second, with the institutional requirements of the judicial system. It is always difficult to know how much in a judicial opinion is conscious, how much that curious combination of the subconscious, the habitual, and the conventional which characterizes the {196} writing of judicial opinions. But Stow must honestly have felt the pull of social and institutional forces; and clearly, he took as his mandate the task of deciding cases from the social viewpoint—of course, within the legal tradition which set the limits of his discretion.

In *Sanderson v. Olmstead*, the court framed policy restrained mainly by institutional and traditional factors. Even in Period I, the court enjoyed less autonomy in many kinds of cases. The practical power of the court can be measured better by taking two further examples: the acrimonious dialogue between court and legislature arising out of the farm-mortgage crisis of the 1850's, and the experience of the court under the usury laws of Period I.

In the farm-mortgage crisis, the legislature, sensitive to the votes of irate farmers, passed law after law to prevent the collection of farm-mortgage debts. The court cast down almost all of these laws on constitutional grounds. Ultimately the court forced the legislature to adopt less radical solutions. Underlying the words of the judges and legislators was a basic dispute about means (but not ends): was the prosperity of the state best served by rescuing the small landholder from financial disaster; or was it best served by strictly upholding the rights of good faith purchasers for value in the market? Both values, arguably, were essentials for prosperity and economic growth. In this particular situation it was hard to realize both values at once.

The same dialogue was repeated in the state's experience with usury laws. Hardly a legislature sat between statehood and 1861 which did not tinker with the usury laws. The air rang with high minded debate about free trade in money, on the one hand, and the sad lot of the debtor class on the other. In the end, decisions were made on a more expedient economic basis: did the population, or some significant segment of it, need ready cash at any price? When the answer was yes, as in 1849, because of impending sales of public lands, the usury laws were discarded. Two years later, after a different twist of the economic wheel, the usury law was reinstated in a form more stringent than ever. Unlike the farm-mortgage crisis, the court sat out this quarrel on the sidelines. The velocity of statutory changes was such that by the time a case came up for decision, the governing statute had been repealed or amended. The court had no significant practical power over the basic aims of the usury laws; at most, it had limited powers of adjustment, exercised over particular transactions arising under the statutes.[10]

Both the practical impotence of the court vis-à-vis the usury law and {197} the flinty attitude of the court toward legislative solutions of the farm-mortgage crisis illustrate in a general way the division of labor between these two agencies of law. By and large, the court promoted economic growth by persisting in its approach to abstraction and by minor tinkering with peripheral legal rules. Moreover the court, freer of popular pressure than the legislature, could sometimes adopt an unpopular course it considered wiser in the long run. The legislature bore the burden of promoting economic growth by positive programs; and, more and more, it responded to political pressures by removing particular relations or types or aspects of transactions from the realm of abstract contract in response to particular instances and specific demands. With their relatively long term and secure tenure of office, the judges sometimes found it possible to veto legislative solutions to crisis problems, and force new solutions more in keeping with long-range values, if possible. The very concept of judicial review implied an acceptance of some division of function between the two agencies in making law; and further implied that society in general gained through the work of a safety-valve institution insulated from the grossest pressures of the moment. Under the usury laws, the court could not perform any significant work in forcing a redirection of policy. Thus *Sanderson v. Olmstead*, the farm-mortgage cases, and the usury law cases illustrate three functions of the court: (a) to create, within the existing legal system, broad expressions of policy; (b) to act as a brake on excessive and impulsive change; and (c) to work out details and iron out inconsistencies arising under expressions of policy originated elsewhere. Each of these three was extremely important in Period I, but the first perhaps most of all. Yet even in Period I, it must be remembered that the broadest expressions of policy—those relating to schools, transport, the public domain, business association, and the frame of government—were not within the scope of judicial power. Even in Period I, the court created policy mainly in matters of adjustment. *Sanderson* itself is an example. And the farm-mortgage statutes, too, were matters of adjustment. The court's chief example of initiating policy in Period I was nothing more than its vigorous general assertion of the abstraction of contract—a policy to which the legislature generally acquiesced, at least in the sense that the legislature did nothing to force an abandonment of the policy in the usual run of cases. In Periods II and III, the court lost (with respect to contract law particularly) whatever power of initiation it had once had; the safety-valve {198} function, however, was notoriously important in the late nineteenth and early twentieth centuries, the heyday of judicial (constitutional) activism. The third function, always important, is the primary judicial function today, not only in respect to contract actions. It is basically a function of adjustment; and even here, the court must share its task with the administrative agencies and other legal institutions (including the legislature) which have taken over adjustment functions in large classes of dispute situations. We must now proceed to examine the causes of the decline in the court's role as a creative force in instituting legal policy—even policy of adjustment.

The Decline of the Court: Institutional Factors. The role of the court was fixed for it by law, by custom, and by the way the judges perceived their role in the legal and social system. Both by law and by custom, however, the court lacked any authority to initiate action. It had no authority to stretch out its hand and gather in questions that urgently needed deciding. The court had to sit passively waiting for the cases to come. Thus the power of the court to create broad principles depended on a flow of work and the character of the docket—features over which the court had little control.

The law of contract deals, fundamentally, with business disputes. The framing of appropriate principles and the effective application of those principles depended and depends on the flow of appropriate business cases—on the willingness and ability of parties in market disputes to bring these disputes to court for their solution. The decline of the court's influence paralleled a decline in the percentage of cases in its contract docket which arose out of market transactions.

Businessmen will bring disputes to court if they feel that resolution in court will provide a superior solution to resolution through other formal or informal agencies. Confidence in the court system depends in part on whether the court displays insight into business matters. For business cases, the degree of insight is influenced by what we might call social distance—the relationship between the court's personal experience and the social and business life of the community. Social distance is difficult to measure. But obviously as society grows more complex, the number of potential litigants and potential issues grows accordingly, and social distance between the court and the business world grows greater. A justice of the Wisconsin Supreme Court in the 1950's probably could bring little special business insight to bear on many issues {199} which came before him. In Wisconsin of the 1850's the social distance between the experience of court and litigant was substantially less. The litigants were often prominent persons, drawn from the small class of the politically and economically ambitious. The range of economic problems was narrower than a century later. The forms of business enterprise were more restricted. The judges of the 1850's understood the usual ways of making and losing money. The bench was recruited from the bar, and the bar represented a definite, ubiquitous class of investors, claim-adjusters, general land agents and financial factotums. Counsel had a right to expect that the judges would understand the mechanics of land transfer, investment, and the general state of the economy.

By Period II, two million people lived in Wisconsin, earning their livings and doing business in a thousand and one ways; in addition, the nineteenth century had made striking advances in science and technology. A judge's grasp of the economic and social problems of the state was bound to be weaker than before. There was more to business and its economy than any panel of judges could possibly know. The judges were not ignorant of affairs; affairs had simply grown too great for mastery. Before he became a judge, Roujet D. Marshall (1847-1922), was a skillful and successful corporation lawyer who worked closely with the Weyerhaeuser lumber interests. From the late 1870's on, he was embroiled in the rough and tumble of a fabulous industry at its most fabulous stage. Robert G. Siebecker (1854-1922) was Robert M. La Follette's brother-in-law and was once his law partner; what Marshall knew about business, Siebecker must have known about politics. John Barnes (1859-1919), who served on the court from 1908 to 1916, had been a member of the state Railroad Commission; when he resigned from the court, Northwestern Life Insurance Company made him its general counsel.[11] Such men were as well exposed to the facts of business, government, and law as any group of judges could be. But the practice of law had become more widely specialized and more closely professional. A man became judge of the Supreme Court after a career as a lawyer or lower court judge. What business experience he brought with him, sharp and direct as it may have been, now lay in the past; inevitably it was partial and vague, and became more so with the passage of time. The judge of Period I, on the other hand, was a recent settler, a lawyer experienced in land claims, debt collection, and town-site booming, probably a part-time farmer or merchant, too. This kind {200} of personal history went a long way toward giving a man a total grasp of local business practice. By 1905 business was too complicated for one lifetime. Marshall no doubt knew the lumber business inside out; but what did he know about steel manufacture, breweries, department stores, stock brokerage, shoe manufacturing, construction, railroading, and lake shipping? About the fur trade, rag jobbing, or retail druggists (all represented by at least one case in the tabulation in Period II), he probably knew no more than the average educated citizen. He could bring to bear on these cases only a lawyer's experience and some general business sense, but nothing more. In Period III the distance between court and business life had, if anything, widened.

Another factor which influences the flow of business into the court is the cost of litigation. A small claim is not likely to go to court, and is even less likely to be appealed. This factor became more and more important over the years. The maturing of the economy operated to reduce the Wisconsin Supreme Court's share of economic litigation. Small claims were excluded from the court by necessity. Contract actions were handled, to be sure, in volume in the lower courts—collections, garnishments, repossessions, actions for small claims in general. But the courts here acted largely as recording and enforcement agencies. These cases almost never made the long, costly journey up the judicial ladder to the Supreme Court, where they could become the occasion for the pronouncement of principle and the framing of a precept for the ordering of all cases of their class.

Cost is only one factor limiting the court's share of contract work. There are other cogent reasons why parties avoid litigation (and appeal) not only for small, but also for large claims. A court fight is likely to be inconsistent with continuing business relationships; it makes better economic sense to compromise than to battle through the courts if the good will or potential profitability of a relationship are worth more than a possibly Pyrrhic victory in a lawsuit.[12] This is still another reason for the frequency of land cases in Period I, and to a certain extent, in later periods. In land transactions, buyer does not usually face seller more than once. As the years went on, institutional business was more and more characterized by the kind of continuous, interconnected relationships that would naturally avoid litigating. A maturing economy stores up great stocks of values-in-depth: "good will," customer and public relations, convenient business practices, standard ways and habits of operation. Businesses will litigate most where these values-in-depth are least. The house-builder or the real estate broker changes customers for each transaction; he may sue a customer more readily than a supplier of goods would sue a customer of long standing. Relationships can be disrupted by death, bankruptcy, or collapse of the market; but large corporations are less affected by such ruptures than small businesses. True, in some tabulated cases, {201} values-in-depth were the occasion for litigation, when court action was necessary for their protection. The covenant not to compete, found in contracts to sell a small business, provided one example of a device to protect going-concern values. In Period II there were at least four cases brought to enforce the covenant.[13]

The court was therefore increasingly left with a group of very personal cases, or selected business problems of men like Walter Pratt and E. L. Darling, or of the part-time brokers—problems which arose out of and because of the marginality of the litigants. In Period III, the court faced a number of cases characterized by fluidity and ambiguity in business relations—the franchised dealers, commissioned salesmen, and brokers of the tabulation in that Period. One might speak of the court as the forum of mobility, particularly in Period III. So long as social change remained possible, so long as new kinds of business, new products, new techniques kept emerging, the court retained a small but vital role. Between the time when new business practices evolve and the time when the kinks have been smoothed out of forms and documents relating to the emerging practice, some agency of law must be ready to solve unforeseen problems. When continuing relations break down, or in cases of novel business problems or fluid business hierarchical arrangements, the court performed this role.

But in the cases of business fluidity in Period III, the court did not and could not invoke the standards of a regularized, abstract market; nor could the court bring to bear on the problems before it any specific legal experience; by the nature of the relationships, specific precedent or doctrine was not available. This was not really a new problem for the court. But the dynamic fluidity of the nineteenth-century market economy was tamed through abstraction; as much as possible particularity was pruned away. In Period III, on the other hand, fluidity was not taken as a reason to be abstract, but as an excuse for discarding abstraction in favor of the "equitable" solution, the "fair" result under the (specific) circumstances.

Insofar as the court abandoned abstraction, the non-recurrence of type-situations became a more important limitation on the creativity of the court's role. Analysis of the Wisconsin's court's contract work amply demonstrates the fact of non-recurrence. The investment land cases of Period I did not recur as such. The support contract, stallion, and part-time brokerage cases of Period II did not recur as such. The testamentary claims cases and the commissioned salesmen cases were rare before Period III. Two generations was longer than most contract type-problems survived. Either social change "solved" the problem, or a business cured its sicknesses itself, without need for litigation. The docket of the Wisconsin Supreme Court contained only the new and the anomalous. This point, which is essential to an understanding of the functioning law of contracts, is lost in conventional legal literature and thought. By emphasizing doctrine and chopping chronology into bits, case-books and treatises confine most of their analysis to extinct situations and moribund problems. If the precise legal issues are examined in relation to the facts of the underlying cases (which alone give meaning to doctrine), we usually discover that the matters debated in text or class have been covered since by statute or drafted into oblivion by the legal profession. Within a system of genuine abstraction, in which the courts lay down general principles of sweeping reach to govern vast categories of type-situations, the non-recurrence of particular type-situations would not be important. In the light of what actually happened (the court's commitment to the particular), the non-recurrence of {202} type-situations added to the decline of the court's creativity. With the loss of real power to effect general principles, the court was left with tasks primarily of adjustment in going relationships; consequently, the cost of litigation and the factor of social distance were telling blows to the utility of the court. The court for the reasons outlined was simply not an efficient working agency of business adjustment.

The Court and Its Rivals. An abstract contract system heavily favors the workings of an impersonal market. In such a system, some legal agency must enunciate general principles to uphold the functioning of the market.

In some systems of law, legislation (e.g., a "Civil Code") has the task of enunciating such principles. In common law jurisdictions, this task classically has been assigned to the courts. During Period I, theory and practice coincided more closely than at later times. For the law of contract, at any rate, grand principle was most likely to be enunciated by the court, while the legislature passed laws {203} which derogated from abstraction for particular instances to solve particular problems and to handle special, favored classes of citizens. Naturally, even in Period I, the legislature, not the court, provided the framework for the working of the legal system—by creating the judicial system and regulating its procedure. The legislature, moreover, concerned itself with legislation of far-reaching importance of a sort which courts were institutionally powerless to create, e.g., quantitative statutes (such as the homestead exemption laws). But legislatures were concerned with particularity in a very tangible sense. The huge body of pre-Civil War private and local laws (far outnumbering the "general" laws) testifies to this fact. One of the private and local laws of 1857 served to legalize "the tax roll of the town of Beloit, in the county of Rock, for the year 1856."[14] In 1861 an act "to quiet title to certain lands in Rock county" clarified the title of Delos H. Palmer. An act of the same year gave Leopold Kottman "the exclusive right to pre-empt the N 1/2 of NW 1/4 and the SW 1/4 of NE 1/4 of sec. 27 in township 17 north of range 7 west of the fourth principal meridian, in La Crosse county." Another act gave the creditors of the estate of James G. Besley additional time to file claims against the estate.[15] As is well known, legislatures before the Civil War granted divorces, changed people's names, altered heirships, and in many other respects dispensed justice or perhaps equity, but strictly on an *ad hoc* basis. The legislature's host of "special" (private and local) laws were so many examples of the state's attempt to influence the economy by using one of the state's few real assets: its power to bind and to loose. On the state level, private (if not local) laws disappeared in the course of time. Constitutional change eliminated them, wholly or partially.[16] But their impact would have lessened in any event. The economy overwhelmed them; it proved impossible to handle such matters in bulk and at the same time give them the attention they deserved to assure proper generalization of policy and proper objectivity in particular dispositions. Yet the system of private laws, while it lasted, may have affected the relative firmness of the judicial attitude toward certain rules and doctrines. A tough judicial and legislative attitude toward technical flaws in local governmental procedures was perhaps supportable as long as the legislature had the power to pass an act curing defects. Even in the 1950's Congress still had the power to pass private laws; it is possible that Congressional willingness to pass a hard and hide-bound immigration law is influenced by knowledge that an occasional tubercular orphan, {204} an occasional Korean professor, can still slip through by means of a private bill. But all in all—and particularly on the state level—twentieth-century law reversed the role of the two lawmaking agencies. It was now the court which dispensed sympathetic and particularized help; the legislature laid down general rules.

This point must not be exaggerated, since legislatures in Periods II and III did not confine themselves to expressions of broad social policy. It remained as true in later periods as in Period I that the legislature, a politically sensitive institution, responded to particular pressures. The statute books were always shot through, in addition, with acts of considerable pettiness, for example, the 1911 act instituting a cleansing room for cuspidors in the Capitol.[17] Overwhelmed by the complexities of society, unsure of the techniques of control, buffeted by conflicting pressures, the legislature often saw no clear generalizations of policy and took refuge in detailed regulation, in statutes which forged meticulous, many linked chains. Although the statutes of Period III, for example, were animated by a deep concern with "unfair marketing," the range of regulation was surprisingly petty and random. What explains the legislature's interest in tourist cabins, "bushing" cars, imitation ice cream, and products represented as "blind-made,"[18] as opposed to interest in the marketing of other products? The statutes passed did not add up to a comprehensive and ordered scheme of regulation, or even to a body of laws concerning the main currents of trade. Rather, it seems that complaints against specific "abuses" reached the sympathy of a legislator, group of legislators, or department of government. A good analogy can be drawn, then, between these limited statutes and the law made by the accretion of judicial decisions. Statutes directed against specific "abuses" resembled the old private laws more than they resembled a major tax law or a law of great scope, such as the workmen's compensation act. Occupational licensing laws—handing over self-regulation to tight occupational in-groups—were the spiritual descendants of the old franchises and grants of private corporate power. But after allowing for all instances of small-scale legislation, it remains true as a grand generalization that the legislature constantly grew in power and activity as the creator of fresh law and fresh principle in the legal system, either by itself or through setting up administrative agencies. As legislative-executive agencies took over more of the business of controlling the economy, the court's potential power diminished. {205}

The administrative agency existed in embryo much earlier than 1887, the date the Interstate Commerce Commission was established. By then the states (including Wisconsin) had had a considerable history of creating, abolishing, and recreating executive or independent agencies to deal with banking, insurance, land marketing, education, warehousing, and transportation. From about 1890 on, the boards, commissions, agencies, and departments multiplied rapidly. New policy created not only new work for old institutions, but also new institutions. The business of the new bureaucracy largely (and in some cases entirely) ignored the courts. In truth, administrative adjudication was grinding finer than the slow mills of the court could grind; in 1913, for example, Wisconsin created an Athletic Commission;[19] an inspector appointed by the Commission had to attend every boxing match and enforce the rules (e.g., that "Contestants shall break clean, and must not hold and hit"). The most passionate critic of "administrative law" would not have wanted the court to decide whether a boxer broke clean. The most power-hungry court would not have regretted losing this business. But questions of boxing propriety were questions of adjustment, and the use of a non-judicial agency to handle these matters was a judgment on the propriety of courts handling even that kind of particularized dispute with which the courts were themselves more and more concerned. The Standard Fire Insurance Policy of 1895[20] showed another kind of subtraction of potential influence for the court; here, however, what the court lost was its ability to prescribe the fundamental bases for the formation and the fundamental terms of an important type of contract. Not often was an entire contract, prepackaged and complete, made mandatory by legislation. More restricted examples, however, were common. For example, by statute no public warehouseman might insert in a warehouse receipt certain limitations of liability; by the same statute, all receipts had to be consecutively numbered.[21] The statute thus (a) prohibited certain possible contract terms, and (b) specifically prescribed one aspect of the form of warehouse receipts. In general, and in varying degree, the whole vast statutory body of social, labor, welfare, marketing, and insurance law limited the applicability of the abstraction of the law of contract. To the same degree, such legislation derogated from the possible discretion of the court, both in matters of initiation and adjustment. Of course, the court construed statutes, fleshing out ambiguities, filling gaps (sometimes creating new gaps and ambiguities); and the court {206} did have some power of judicial review over the actions of state officials and administrators. But usually only a major issue or a test case brought a constitutional question or a question of serious statutory policy to the court; traditions of judicial behavior as well as the patterns of the statute book limited the court's policy-making role through statutory interpretation. Again, Period III merely intensified this process.

Increasingly, it was also true that disputes which avoided the courts were handled through private dispute-settling procedures. On one level, no "rivalry" with the court is implied if parties prefer to iron out their own difficulties out of court. If all disagreements had to be litigated, the court system would have to be greatly expanded, and it is hard to see how everyday business could get done. Where private dispute-settling (adjustment) takes institutional forms, however, it tends to merge with private rule-making (initiation); and the position of the private and official institutions toward each other tends to become much more complicated.

The law of contracts is (like the law of wills) an area of allowed private law-making. By law, individuals have wide autonomy to fix the terms at which they buy and sell goods and labor. The law recognizes many other substitutes for itself as the source of accepted rules of behavior. Parents, teachers, corporations, churches, unions—all have rule-making power. Arbitration laws give people permission to bypass the courts. "Judgment notes" allow parties to agree even on how legal process is to be used. In addition, when commercial law recognizes the binding nature of "custom and usage" and "business practice," it makes possible the free evolution of lay patterns of behavior into law. Lawyers who draft documents and invent new forms of doing business create law in a real and important way.

There is and was no single legal attitude toward private rule-makers and private decision-makers. Legal attitudes range from out-and-out hostility (toward crime rings and gangs) to permissiveness (toward private contractual bargaining). Any increase in social distance between the courts and the life of the community works toward proliferation of private law-making. So does the existence of gaps between what is legally and what is socially approved. In Period I, unable by their situation to make full use of legitimate legal organs, squatters on the public lands often formed "claims associations" to dominate the formal procedures of public auction of lands.[22] They adopted among themselves {207} rules and procedures for recording and judging their own land claims, and thus invented in effect their own system of land transfer and acquisition. The attitude of Wisconsin's court and legislature to these clubs was complicated and somewhat ambivalent. In part, the ambivalence is explainable in terms of the dual function of the claim clubs. Insofar as the clubs worked to negate public land law, they intruded upon the generalizing function of the legitimate legal agencies; insofar as they provided private procedures for settling disputes within their membership, they could successfully invoke symbols of respectability, since they were working for the same ends of adjustment as the regular judicial processes. But generally speaking, the legal attitude toward the clubs was consistent with and influenced by the law's dominant approach toward the economy: the political power of the settlers (even when the settler was a "squatter") and the preference for "labor" over "capital" made it just as difficult to repress the claim clubs as it would have been to impose set governmental patterns upon private bargains of other kinds. And the wide use of statute law to ratify the assertion of rule-making power by private groups in Period I was both a sign of weakness on the part of the legitimate organs of law and a desire to accommodate the law to actual alignments of power and interest in the social order.

Yet the diffusion of rule-making and decision-making power among private groups could not be said to rival the court's contract work in Period I. Each agency, public and private, had its own sphere of influence and power. In Period II, the growth of private codes of law went further and deeper. Some social groups avoided the courts because they were afraid of lawsuits. Labor unions and their friends tended to shy away from the courts, which were part of the "system." To the left wing of the labor movement, particularly, lawyers were tools of the capitalists, and the courts themselves were "capitalistic annexes."[23] The businessman, too, looked on courts with "instinctive distrust and dislike"; law was "complicated, indirect, dilatory, wasteful,"[24] too apt to misunderstand the facts. Technical reforms, however, would not have changed the businessman's mind about the courts. Commercial arbitration, widely used in the period, was not "a friendly method of settlement of disputes," but a "substitute for the courts." Its advantage lay in the fact that business arbitrators, as one authority put it, "approach cases from an individual and not from a social viewpoint."[25] Probably the business arbitrator, too, approached cases from a "social {208} viewpoint"; but his "society" was the microcosm of his particular business. From the businessman's viewpoint, the courts lacked the feel needed to unravel the facts and understand what was really going on. Only an insider could have this feel, this insight. When men in business quarreled over the meaning of particular technical terms of the business, an unbiased colleague might possibly sense and solve in a minute what "your selection" meant in the fur trade; or what "blues" were to a rag dealer.[26] The judge could do his best to weigh evidence; but evidence, in a court of law, was always slanted by the parties and hamstrung in scope by the rules of evidence. On the appellate level, evidence was even more remote from the businessman's view of reality. The judge might be impartial, but he was also foreign. This fact of social distance was, in the nature of things, irremedial.

Furthermore, whatever the general bias of a judge, he did, after all, in a real sense usually express the "social viewpoint." In labor disputes, most judges were moderates. They found for employees sometimes and employers other times. A court cannot avoid taking sides in any given case—for a depositor and against the bank, or vice versa; for the insurance companies and against the policy holder, or vice versa; for or against the state. The courts are not arbitrators called in by mutual agreement; one side or the other is usually dragged into court against its will. Where economic controversy is shrill and desperate, the losing side is not likely to shrug its shoulders and say, the law has spoken. On issues that draw blood and break bones, the courts are no substitute for comprehensive social solutions. The Wisconsin Supreme Court in Period II was sincere and hard working. It was a middle-of-the-road, middle-class court. Aside from a certain flair for discovering new "natural" rights,[27] the court avoided blatant subjectivity in formulating policy; it was fairly loyal to the best craft traditions of judicial self-restraint. But it could not help making decisions; that was its job. Nor could it help applying the law. It could push and pull in marginal areas of policy not yet fully defined, but only so far. Where law was hostile or insensitive to particular forms of business, business had to learn how to keep its disputes "within the family." The futures market, for example, was forced to sidestep regular legal process because of adverse legal rulings. The Milwaukee Board of Trade set up "rules"—really a private code of contract and procedural law—which, despite some points of contact, was not exactly the procedure and the contract law that the courts would have applied.[28] This code was accepted by the trade in {209} self-defense and for convenience. Similarly, business codes of ethics and "gentlemen's agreements" often verged on violation of the antitrust laws—or tended toward dubious border areas of legality. Business attempts to regularize and standardize their trade practices, a marked characteristic of the times, had to proceed, as much as possible, through internal organization; there were many reasons why the process avoided the courts, but the uncertainties of the legal response may well have been one factor.

The combination of institutional pressures—legislative, executive, private—narrowed the court's role in contract litigation to a small corner of the dispute-settling and law-making business within society; paradoxically, this process also created a new role for the court. Twentieth-century organized society, with its big government and its private power groups big and small, needed some agency to protect the rights of the individual against power aggregates. This role was, in some cases, filled by the court. The court is equipped in structure and procedure to handle this role; and the court is also relatively independent of politics, and relatively impartial among contending non-political interests. Litigation is expensive—but not as expensive as the costs of drafting and lobbying a bill through the legislature, even when the bill stands a good chance of success. Thus the court's boldest role in Period III was that of protector of "civil liberties"; its boldest role in Period II, by way of contrast, was to protect the economic order by using the due process clause to strike down "class" legislation; in Period I, the court protected the processes of economic growth, partly through the use of the contracts clause, partly through creative lawmaking in support of market processes. In fulfilling its role as protector of the individual, the court sometimes made use of contract law. But it used it as a weapon, not as a body of doctrine; contract principles that fit could be pulled out of the court's armory when they were needed to achieve what the court thought was a good result. In *Pattenge v. Wagner Iron Works* (1957),[29] a group of employees sued the company for vacation pay which they felt was wrongfully denied them. Wagner was a unionized plant; Pattenge and his co-plaintiffs were all members of Local No. 471, International Association of Bridge, Structural and Ornamental Iron Workers (AFL). The collective bargaining agreement between the local and the company contained a no-strike clause. Pattenge and the other claimants became CIO sympathizers and struck as part of the rival union's attempt to organize the plant. The company fired them. {210} The AFL naturally enough had no particular sympathy for the Pattenge group and gave them no help in their claim. The company had two major defenses: first, and probably most important, that the strike was a breach of contract; second, that the plaintiffs should have exhausted normal grievance procedures before suing. The first defense was eliminated by an NLRB finding that the company was guilty of unfair labor practices. The court rejected the second defense by calling Pattenge and the other employees "third party beneficiaries" of the collective bargaining contract with the personal rights of such beneficiaries to enforce the main contract. Furthermore the law did not require an individual employee to use grievance procedures "where it is reasonably apparent that the union is hostile to him and will not give him adequate representation. To do so would place the employee's accrued rights against his employer more or less at the mercy of an unfriendly union."

In *Pattenge*, the contract point (a subsidiary one) wriggled through technical gaps in the applicable "special" field (federal and state labor law). The result achieved was (in the court's view) eminently desirable; but "contract law" here was not a symbol of the market, or even a set of interstitial principles to be applied residually, where legislation was silent. It was a weapon of due process.

The Decline of the Court: Style and Technique. All of the various factors which determined the court's effective role in the legal system and toward the economic order influenced its style of deciding cases and drafting opinions. In Period I, for example, opinions were written with businesslike vigor and with a fairly frank discussion of policy issues as the court saw them. A certain amount of candor was necessary because the judges sensed the significance of what they were doing. They were, fairly often, deciding on a new rule to govern a considerable class of transactions. Once decided upon, the rule was announced in broad terms. Cases tended not to bristle with citations (although the form of printed reports and certain simple technical facts explain in part the relative infrequency of citations of cases and other authority). The court did not often discuss facts in detail, because the court was much concerned with laying down general principles to cover broad classes of fact-situations. In short, style and technique were appropriate to a court committed to abstraction as a general principle, and operating in a new jurisdiction with little native authority. {211}

Period II was, in a sense, the golden age of contract. Both primary senses of the word contract—the legal and the social—seemed then to shine with a golden ardor. "Freedom of contract" was one of the slogans under which the courts of the country, in some key cases, struck down as unconstitutional social legislation,[30] letting down on their own heads a storm of criticism and abuse from large segments of society. It is easy to exaggerate, as we have seen, the extent to which the courts really protected liberty of contract. Great cases distort the mine-run of small ones. But it is significant to note that the courts assumed a great power which they exercised in a highly controversial manner, even if sparingly.

In the same years, the lawyer's law of contract reached full maturity of doctrine and influence. Great expository treatises were written. C. C. Langdell, the reformer of legal education, had earlier awarded to contracts the honor of the first case-book (1871). From then on, students were led into the world of legal reasoning through the door of the law of contracts. The law of contracts was treated as a fundamental, archetypical branch of "legal science," as one of the pillars on which the temple of common law was said to rest. The abstract, negative, and impersonal character of classical contract law made it relatively simple to freeze contract law into what Professor Page, writing in 1905, called a "rational and harmonious system."[31] The treatise-writers wove contract law into a set of "scientific" principles, logically interrelated and stated in an orderly manner. C. O. Ashley hoped his short treatise (1911) would aid "efforts being made to place the law on a more philosophic and satisfactory basis."³² On paper at least, the treatises transformed the living law of contract into a fabric of black-letter rules—a kind of unwritten and sluggishly evolutionary civil code.

Roujet D. Marshall, the most interesting judge sitting on the Wisconsin court in Period II, went even further. To Marshall, the case-method of teaching law was wrong, not because it was too abstract, but because it was not abstract enough: the great "mass of our law," he wrote, "is grounded on principles found in the unwritten law. Those principles are the embodiment of the experience of the ages and so are older than precedents and more reliable."³³ Marshall's hunger for "principles" was so great that he took the trouble to write his own headnotes in important cases.³⁴ These headnotes were as bloodless as possible; as far as possible, every living fact was ruthlessly expunged. For Marshall, "the keynote of an adjudication is the ruling principle. {212} The details showing the particular facts ... are helpful; but in the end, it is the principle, not the detail circumstances ... which is the important feature."³⁵ The abstraction achieved by Marshall's headnotes was not the willful abstraction of classical contract law—the abstraction of the market—but a dry, dreary logic, unrelated to the economic order, or indeed, to anything much else. Luckily, neither Marshall nor any other judge decided cases in the same way they wrote headnotes. But the works of leading scholars of contract law in Marshall's day have the same barren quality. Facts, situations, and policies were not mentioned except in the most general way. Contract law was judged by its logical symmetry. Langdell himself was a master of this approach:

> Lord Mansfield appears to have entertained the opinion that a mere promise to do what the promisor was already under a moral obligation to do was binding. Whether his theory was that the antecedent moral obligation furnished a sufficient consideration for the promise ... may not be clear; but [this] ... theory is the one that has commonly been attributed to him, and hence the obligation which was supposed to make the promise binding has acquired the name of moral consideration.... The theory of moral obligation was liable to the [great] ... objection, at least in a scientific point of view, that it could only succeed at the expense of involving a fundamental legal doctrine in infinite confusion.³⁶

The liberty of contract cases and the tendency to turn contract law (indeed, all branches of law) into a "science" were not unrelated to each other. In constitutional cases, the court invoked "higher law" to explain what it was doing; in ordinary contract cases, it hid its work under a screen of "principle." One may well contrast Marshall's technique in a case which engaged his deepest sympathies with his technique in writing headnotes. In *Leonard v. Prudential Insurance Company* (1907),³⁷ the terms of Leonard's insurance policy allowed him to cure any lapse in premiums by paying overdue premiums with interest and by proving he was still in good enough health to be insured. Leonard's policy lapsed; thereafter he offered to pay what was due on the policy. The company asked for a medical examination; Leonard took it and was told informally that he was insurable. The company delayed a while; then the home office decided to reject Leonard's request for reinstatement of his policy, acting on the basis of a "secret inquiry" which hinted that Leonard was a drunkard. After some delay, notice of the rejection reached the company's local agency; delivery of the rejection notice was delayed still more, and Leonard died thinking {213} he was insured. Marshall began the court's opinion by solemnly stating that the case must be "tested by the plain obligations of the insurance contract, and a few ... familiar principles of law." But after this bow to theory, Marshall proceeded to "construe" the contract in a most highhanded manner, discoursed at length on the necessity of insurance "to security of the family" and on the social obligations of insurance companies, paused along the way to invoke an "implied obligation ... to act with reasonable promptness," and ended with a tirade against the company's "fraud," "stealth," and outrageous behavior. The "array of authorities pressed upon our attention" by the insurance company, he concluded, "are doubtless right as regards the facts with which they deal, but they are entirely unsuitable as guides in reaching a proper decision in this case."

Events had conspired to rob the court of some of the most vital parts of its contract docket. The same events colored the judges' own viewpoints; responsive to their times, they were abandoning abstraction as a working principle. The legislature, too, was discarding abstraction in many highly important regards; legislation was determining what areas should be left to private initiative, what areas to be governed by imposed ground rules of contractual behavior. The court was left with its functions of adjustment; but here, too, the judges were abandoning their habit of abstraction, slowly, subtly, and in forms dictated by the legal tradition and their own habits. The character of their cases gave them liberty to particularize. The scope of their cases was narrow. They decided small personal disputes—like the support contract cases—and cases arising out of marginal business transactions. The problems did not go to the heart of social disorder. The judges were free to tinker and patch, to chip away at the "rules," and to do justice in particular cases. By and large, the court did its work in a fashion not overly technical, not untrue to reality, particularly if we look at action, not talk, at results, not opinions. After all, insofar as the cases were trivial, far removed from great questions of economics and politics, insofar as they were personal, sentimental, and peripheral, the judges bore no crushing responsibility to serve values of wide scope, and could safely pay heed to the particular merits of situations before them. So the boundaries of contract eroded. The net effect was ironic. As a working body of law, the law of contract was weakened and warped by the court's attention to the particulars of its cases. The theory was precisely the reverse: pure contract theory should have ruthlessly ignored {214} the personal, the special, the temporary, sweeping all these away in favor of the bold but cleansing abstraction of the market. By the time of Period II, the malleable exceptions were threatening to swallow up the rules.

We cannot directly prove the state of mind of these judges. What happened in another area of law, however, offers some indirect confirmation of the proposition that the judges sensed, if they were not fully aware, that their opportunity for influencing the economy had narrowed, leaving them, however, with considerable freedom to tinker with what remained. During the last years of the fellow-servant doctrine in Wisconsin, the court sometimes applied common law tort doctrines with great rigor, carefully pointing out how obnoxious were the results, and begging the legislature for help. In *Monte v. Wausau Paper Mills Co.* (1907),[38] a worker was killed in a paper mill accident. "It would be a hard heart," said Winslow, J., "which could contemplate the facts ... without feeling ... sympathy." The deceased was a "good citizen" who labored with "manful courage" and was faithfully devoted to his "modest home," his wife and children. His life was snuffed out as "one would snuff a candle." But the law "deals not with sentiment.... Justice is blindfolded"; if the court disobeyed its "certain ... fixed abstract rules" "absolute chaos," "favoritism," and "injustice" would result. In *Michalski v. Cudahy Bros. Co.* (1913),[39] plaintiff, not quite 18 years old, lost parts of both hands in a machine. Winslow saw this as "one of the many cases which vividly illustrate the absolute necessity for workmen's compensation laws." Under common law tort rules, however, Michalski could not recover; and it was so held by the court.

In these cases, the judges confessed their impotence openly. Thorough reform was beyond their power. Thorough reform meant a state program, tax supported if necessary, administered by civil servants whom no court could select or manage. In dealing with the massive and intricate social problems of industrial accidents, a case-by-case approach, wearing out the common law system with estoppels and similar devices, might have done more harm than good. The court's deliberate behavior in the industrial accident cases contrasts vividly with the way marginal, personal, trivial contract cases were handled; the contrast speaks volumes about the court's perception of its role in the legal system.

Thus, style and technique were functions of movements of the time. The high formalism of the court in Period II was a phenomenon of {215} significance (even though it was more apparent than real): the competition of other law-making agencies had worn down the power of the judges; except in the constitutional area, the court had small say over the economy. In constitutional cases, the court used formalism in defense of its role; and in mine-run civil cases, the court used high doctrine to structure its increasingly marginal role in the legal system, to shore up its prestige; with doctrine the court appealed to a tradition of past honor, skill, and creativity. Behind the curtain of formal rules, the law of contract steadily decayed, due to the triviality of the court's work and the cumulative effect of the use of such concepts as estoppel. The industrial accident cases show still another, much rarer use of principle—as a method of forcing the hand of the legislature.

By Period III, the court felt the influence of more than a generation of legal "realism." Legal scholarship had largely given up its search for science and rational order in formal doctrine. The realists pointed out contradictions in existing law; they derided formal logic; they showed the legal world the gap between what courts said and what they did. When old legal theories had been taken apart brick by brick, there was nothing to stop the court from doing directly what it used to do by indirection. Old techniques remained alive; but the writing of headnotes was not usually regarded as a task important enough to engage a judge's time.

Indeed, if anything the court's place in the legal system was more modest than before. No longer a creative force, no longer an arbiter of the business transactions of the community (if the court had really ever had this role), the court paid ever more attention to the particularities of the situations before it—thus more attention to "fairness," less heed to general principles. Its techniques were appropriate to its role, primarily as an agency of marginal adjustments. It handled problems growing out of economic dealings of small consequence in themselves, or problems which had not yet been solved through other means. In Period III, the court spent much of its time on cases arising out of auto accidents; it would be safe to predict that in two generations or less some non-judicial method of administration will handle legal consequences of death and destruction on the highway. By then, some problem as yet unborn will engross the major attention of the courts. Whether it will engross the attention of legal scholars is not so certain. In American law, creeping theory has yet to catch up with the race of actual events.

Reference Matter

APPENDIX

TABLE III. Wisconsin Contract Cases by Fact-Category

	Period I: No.	Period II: No.	Period III: No.	Total
1. Land	54	46	22	122
2. Labor	31	61	34	126
3. Sales	30	32	12	74
4. Merchandise	12	15	4	31
5. Insurance	8	15	9	32
6. Business ventures	11	16	10	37
7. Credit	31	14	8	53
8. Government	15	12	6	33
9. Public utilities	4	5	1	10
10. Arbitration	8	5	3	16
11. Miscellaneous	2	6	3	11
12. Testamentary	—	—	8	8
	206	227	120	553

TABLE IV. Wisconsin Contract Cases by Categories of Doctrine

	Period I: No.	Period II: No.	Period III: No.	Total
1. Capacity	9	13	3	25
2. Offer, acceptance	4	10	4	18
3. Consideration	7	14	9	30
4. Mutuality	4	7	10	21
5. Statute of Frauds	21	17	12	50
6. Parol evidence	6	16	9	31
7. Fraud, etc. (warranty)	31	37	14	82
8. Construction	14	21	16	51
9. Illegality	36	33	14	83
10. Performance, breach	22	34	19	75
11. Waiver	12	21	12	45
12. Damages	11	17	6	34
13. Assignment	14	11	6	31
14. Implied contract	7	9	4	20
15. Enforcement, procedure, miscellaneous	25	9	7	41
16. Constitutional questions	6	4	1	11
	229	273	146	648

General Comments. A contracts opinion frequently mentions more than one legal issue or doctrine. Furthermore, the line between issues and doctrines is often indistinct. Only those issues and doctrines considered controlling or important have been counted; sometimes more than one for a particular case. But the process is necessarily so subjective that the figures can be taken only as rough indications of the attention paid by the court to specific legal aspects of these cases.

Category 7 (fraud, etc.) also includes those "warranty" and "representation" cases which were tabulated.

Category 8 (construction) includes cases on fact-analysis and the construction of documents which were not classified elsewhere, or which discussed some specific doctrine of contract construction. Obviously, all contract cases contain some elements of construction and fact-analysis.

Category 10 (performance and breach) was impossible to distinguish sharply, in many instances, from category 8 (construction), since the fact-analysis involved in many cases is whether or not performance measured up to the terms of the contract or not. Reference to this or that category depended on whether the court placed emphasis on one or the other feature.

Category 15 (enforcement, procedure, miscellaneous) includes cases on points of procedure only if the point is peculiar to the law of contracts, and generally only if the case could not be subsumed under some other definite heading. The category also includes cases on the availability of specific performance; and a few cases which could not be readily classified elsewhere.

Category 16 (constitutional law) includes only some of the constitutional law cases discussed in the text; in particular, those which (under the contracts clause) concerned themselves with the question, what is a contract? and a few others which for one reason or another found it necessary to discuss problems of substantive contract law in the context of constitutional adjudication.

NOTES

Introduction

[1] 2 Wis. 261 (1853); for further information on this case see Mrs. Peck's account in *Collections of the State Historical Society of Wisconsin*, VI (1872), 360-2. A WPA typescript biography of Mrs. Peck is on file in the archives of the State Historical Society in Madison, Wisconsin. Benjamin H. Hibbard, *History of Agriculture in Dane County, Wisconsin* (Madison, 1905), p. 97, is aware of the incident but apparently unaware of the judicial decision.

[2] 125 Wis. 93, 103 N.W. 229 (1905). Additional facts were gathered from *Cases and Briefs,* "Record," and from 1903-1904 Polk's *Wisconsin State Gazetteer and Business Directory* [cited hereafter as *PWG*], pp. 595-6.

[3] 272 Wis. 333, 75 N.W.2d 569, 76 N.W.2d 540 (1956); additional facts from *Cases and Briefs,* "Record."

[4] Basic historical and statistical information on Wisconsin has been drawn from the 1962 *Wisconsin Blue Book* and from William F. Raney, *Wisconsin: A Story of Progress* (New York, 1940).

Chapter I

[1] "A contract is a promise or a set of promises for the breach of which the law gives a remedy, or the performance of which the law in some way recognizes as a duty." Restatement, Contracts, § 1 (1932); Samuel Williston, *The Law of Contracts*, 5 vols. (New York, 1920-1922), I, § 1, 1.

[2] E.g., *In re Duncan's Estates*, 40 Wash.2d 850, 246 P. 2d 445 (1952). Admittedly, this is not the usual state of the law; statute governs [e.g., *So. Car. Code of Laws* § 19-5 (1962)] and in the absence of statute judicial ingenuity can find ways to keep the murderer from reaping benefits. *In re Wilkins' Estate*, 192 Wis. 111, 211 N.W. 652 (1927).

[3] 2 Bl. Comm. *442-70 (including much commercial law); 3 Bl. Comm. *154-66; Charles Viner, *A General Abridgment of Law and Equity* (2nd ed., London, 1792), V, 504-51.

[4] J. Willard Hurst, *Law and the Conditions of Freedom in the Nineteenth-Century United States* (Madison, 1956), p. 10, speaks of the "overwhelming predominance of the law of contract in all its ramifications in the legal growth of the first seventy-five years of the nineteenth century."

[5] Christopher C. Langdell, *A Selection of Cases on the Law of Contracts* (Boston, 1871).

[6] Notably in *Ancient Law,* first published in 1861.

[7] Nathan Isaacs, "John Marshall on Contracts. A Study in Early American Juristic Theory," 7 *Virginia L. Rev.* 413, 427-8 (1921). For a helpful analysis and classification of modern limitations on freedom of contract see Harold C. Havighurst, *The Nature of Private Contract* (Evanston, 1961), pp. 103-28.

[8] Langdell's concern was with law as "science" to be imparted by the teacher, in the manner of mathematics or physics: "Law, considered as a science, consists of certain principles or doctrines.... Each of these doctrines has arrived at its present state by slow degrees.... This growth is to be traced in the main through a series of cases.... Moreover, the number of

fundamental legal doctrines is much less than is commonly supposed." Langdell, *Cases on Contracts*, p. vi. Chief Justice Stow, in *Matter of the County Seat of LaFayette County*, 2 Pin. 523, 530, 2 Chand. 212 (1850), in deciding that Shullsburg was the county seat, even though the legislature had passed a law declaring otherwise, denied the power of the legislature "to pass such a declaratory law. The judiciary alone is to determine what the law is.... And when the legislature ... undertakes to declare ... the existing law, it ... goes beyond its constitutional sphere, and usurps powers which do not belong to it." There is a connection, of course, between Langdell's "scientific" preference for the judiciary, and Stow's; but the difference is far more important. For Stow, the respective roles of court and legislature were politically determined by the scheme of American government; case-law was not necessarily higher and purer, but operated on a different plane from legislation.

Chapter II

[1] In "Contracts in a Prosperity Year," 6 *Stan. L. Rev.* 208 (1954), Prof. Harold Shepherd undertook to tabulate and analyze 500 of the reported contract cases of a single year (1951). Unfortunately, his article does not make explicit exactly how he determined what a "contract" case was. Nonetheless, his factual breakdown agrees, in a very general way, with that of this study for Period III. His major headings are:

Real property	27.6%
Services	18.7%
Personal property (contract of sale)	14.9%
Real estate brokers' contracts	9.9%
Construction	5.4%
Business agreements	4.0%
Contracts to bequeath	3.4%

Insurance cases were excluded by Shepherd. The correspondences with this study—e.g., the heavy number of broker cases—are more striking than the disagreements.

There is no easy way to analyze the work of the lower courts. Francis W. Laurent, *The Business of a Trial Court* (Madison, 1959) [cited hereafter as Laurent], studied the work of the trial courts of Chippewa County, Wisconsin, from 1855 through 1954. Laurent's categories, however, cannot be correlated with the classification adopted here. But it is worth noting that for the decade 1855-1864, 178 out of 291 civil cases in the Circuit Court were "contract" cases, chiefly promises to pay money. (Laurent, Tables 84, 87, pp. 161, 165.) Laurent uses the term "contract" in the strict legal sense, and classifies on the basis of the pleadings. "Contract" problems in our sense may be hidden in some of the 26 mortgage cases (Table 88, p. 166) and some of the 14 "wrongful refusals to surrender" personal property (Table 89, p. 167). Lower court cases are most conveniently categorized according to the pleadings; appellate cases can be classified in terms of the underlying dispute. Thus an appealed mortgage foreclosure may call for a decision on the validity of the underlying debt; this case might be here treated as contractual, but Laurent would classify it as a "real property" action. Another difficulty is that almost all appeal cases are dispute cases, while trial courts serve other functions as well. See Lawrence M. Friedman, "Book Review" [Laurent], 5 *St. Louis U.L.J.* 454, 465 (1959). Nonetheless, Laurent's figures show that the proportion of "contract" actions brought in the lower courts declined over the century relative to the number of tort actions brought (Table 84, p. 161). For the decade 1865-1874, less than 2 per cent of the civil actions brought in the circuit court of Chippewa County sounded in tort; for the decade 1945-1954, more than 40 per cent. For contracts, the percentage in the decade 1865-1874 was about 45 per cent; for 1905-1914, about 20 per cent; for 1945-1954, about 25 per cent.

For the work of a Wisconsin small claims court, see Ira J. Rapson, Jr., "The Dane County Small Claims Court" (unpub. Ph.D. thesis, U. Wis., 1961), p. 36, showing the types of claims now enforced in this court. Very striking is the high percentage of unsecured debts (book accounts, 22.9 per cent; charge accounts, 13.1 per cent; medical, dental and hospital, 14.6 per cent) compared to consumer installment debt (presumably secured), 3.2 per cent, and other secured debts. The court is used by relatively small business and professional men who do not or cannot make use of court-avoiding business practices.

It is not likely that the decline in major commercial cases in the Wisconsin Supreme Court is due to the use of federal courts. A spot check for Period III failed to disclose more than a handful of contract cases of *any* sort decided by federal courts sitting in Wisconsin. The only two of interest were *Colamatteo v. Schenkenberger*, 163 F. Supp. 693 (D.C.E.D. Wis. 1958) (Statute of Frauds); and *Paper Makers Importing Co., Inc. v. City of Milwaukee*, 165 F. Supp. 491 (D.C.E.D. Wis. 1958), an action for damages against the city for breach of contract to unload cargo destined for the strike-bound Kohler Company. Note that these were both federal *trial* court decisions.

In Period I, the court did not publish all its opinions; some were simply withheld (or lost). Wis. Laws 1861, ch. 198, § 1, authorized selective publication of "important" decisions and opinions; less explicitly, Rev. Stats. Wis. 1849, c. 22, § 1, directed publication of those Supreme Court cases which were "decided by said court to be published."

See *Porter v. Vandercook*, 11 Wis. 70, 71 (1860), referring to the unreported case of *Lawrence v. Brown*, decided in 1859; in *Dean v. City of Madison*, 9 Wis. 402, 408-9 (1859), the court cited *Walker v. Carpenter*, decided in 1856, with an "opinion ... prepared by Justice Smith.... This opinion it seems has been unfortunately lost." Letter of J. T. Mills to George W. Lakin, Jan. 14, 1848, George W. Lakin Papers, State Historical Society of Wisconsin, refers to a point in *Fowler v. Cotton*, Burnett 175 (1843) and states: "I wish to examine your manuscript decisions to see if there be any more cases on this subject."

[2] Jackson, J., in *Woodward v. McReynolds*, 2 Pin. 268, 273, 1 Chand. 244 (1849).

[3] *Wis. Const.* Art. I, § 14.

[4] *N.Y. Const.* Art. I, § 13 (1846); Edward P. Cheyney, "The Anti-rent Movement and the Constitution of 1846," *History of the State of New York*, Vol. VI, *The Age of Reform* (New York, 1934), 281.

[5] 12 Wis. 243, 254-5 (1860).

[6] *Hurd v. Hall*, 12 Wis. 112, 135 (1860). For the rule in personal property, see *Lane v. Romer*, 2 Pin. 404, 2 Chand. 61 (1850).

[7] Kenneth W. Duckett, *Frontiersman of Fortune: Moses M. Strong of Mineral Point* (State Histl. Soc. of Wis.: Madison, 1955), p. 22; Larry Gara, *Westernized Yankee: the Story of Cyrus Woodman* (Madison, 1956), pp. 20ff. See, e.g., the description of the work of Marshall Strong in *Strong v. Catton*, 1 Wis. 471 (1853).

[8] Quoted in Bayrd Still, "The Growth of Milwaukee as Recorded by Contemporaries," *Wisconsin Magazine of History* [cited hereafter as *WMH*], XXI (1938), 262, 270 n33.

[9] Merle Curti, *The Making of an American Community* (Stanford, 1959), p. 23. For a description of an Easterner who came in person to finance land acquisitions, see *Rogan v. Walker*, 2 Pin. 463, 2 Chand. 133 (1850).

[10] Joseph G. Baldwin, "Simon Suggs, Jr., Esq.: A Legal Biography," in *Flush Times of Alabama and Mississippi* (Amer. Cent. Series: N.Y., 1957), pp. 83-103. The tabulation has examples of very poor or amateur draftsmanship, e.g., *Stevens v. Coon*, 1 Pin. 356 (1843), and of somewhat more sophistication, e.g., *Waterman v. Dutton*, 6 Wis. 265 (1857), where the documentation was devised by Marshall Strong. John Keating Williams, a young

lawyer who settled in Shullsburg in 1846, owned a book called the "Illinois Conveyancer," along with a few other treatises and practice books, "John Keating Williams, Diary" (1846-1853) (Typescript, State Historical Society of Wisconsin), p. 20, entry of Jan. 22, 1847. In the early 1840's Cyrus Woodman sold land in Illinois and Wisconsin on deed forms sent to him by Boston lawyers. Gara, *Westernized Yankee*, p. 28.

[11] *Crocker v. Bellangee*, 6 Wis. 645, 646 (1858). For other examples, see, e.g., *Bowman v. Page*, 11 Wis. 301 (1860).

[12] *Pratt v. Ayer*, 3 Pin. 236, 256, 3 Chand. 265 (1851). On the squatter problem in general, see Lawrence M. Friedman, "The Usury Laws of Wisconsin: A Study of Legal and Social History," 1963 *Wis. L. Rev.* 515.

[13] *Wis. Const.* Art. 1, § 17.

[14] *Smith v. Clarke*, 7 Wis. 551 (1858); *Whitney v. The State Bank*, 7 Wis. 620 (1858). See Paul W. Gates, *The Wisconsin Pine Lands of Cornell University* (Ithaca, 1943), pp. 26-41; *Nichols v. Nichols*, 3 Pin. 174, 3 Chand. 189 (1851).

[15] *Mowry v. Wood*, 12 Wis. 413 (1860).

[16] *Keogh v. Daniell*, 12 Wis. 163, 170 (1860).

[17] The Janesville case is *Hutson v. Field*, 6 Wis. 407, 408 (1857); the brass band figures in *Higgins v. Riddell*, 12 Wis. 587 (1860). For the general, dynamic American attitude toward fixtures see, e.g., *VanNess v. Pacard*, 2 Pet. (27 U.S.) 137, 7 L. Ed. 374 (1829).

[18] E.g., *Darlington v. J. L. Gates Land Co.*, 151 Wis. 461, 138 N.W. 72 (1913).

[19] "Agricultural Opportunities in Wisconsin," address delivered Nov. 18, 1911 (Pamphlet, Legislative Reference Library, Madison).

[20] The size of the holdings of the Gates company is given in a brochure, dated November, 1911, of the Wisconsin Advancement Association (Legislative Reference Library, Madison). The Gates company figured in several land cases in the tabulation. There were other large-scale dealings, e.g., *Woodman v. Blue Grass Land Co.*, 125 Wis. 489, 103 N.W. 236 (1905) (arising in Oneida County out of a contract for the sale of 9,000 acres of timberland).

[21] See *Zwietusch v. Becker*, 153 Wis. 213, 140 N.W. 1056 (1913), in which amusement park property was leased, with a covenant that no soda fountain be installed "except such as may be manufactured by Otto Zwietusch Company." *Cases and Briefs*, "Case," 18.

[22] E.g., *Wanner v. Wanner*, 134 Wis. 71, 113 N.W. 1096 (1907).

[23] Eliot O. Waples, "Farm Ownership Processes in a Low Tenancy Area" (unpub. Ph.D. thesis, U. Wis., 1946), p. 222, found that use of "bonds of maintenance" or "bonds of support" in Manitowoc County reached a peak in the decade 1900-1909. Carl F. Wehrwein, in "Bonds of Maintenance as Aids in Acquiring Farm Ownership," *J. Land & Pub. Util. Econ.*, VIII (1932), 396, 402, studying the town of Newton in the same county, showed the crest period as 1880-1889; but the number of such bonds was still substantial until about 1910. For the *padrone* labor system see John R. Commons and John B. Andrews, *Principles of Labor Legislation* (Rev. ed., New York, 1927), pp. 45-6.

[24] "Many of the parents retire to the city now." James D. Tarver, "Wisconsin Century Farm Families: A Study of Farm Succession Processes" (unpub. Ph.D. thesis, U. Wis., 1950), p. 90.

[25] The cases cited are, in order, *Gall v. Gall*, 126 Wis. 390, 105 N.W. 953 (1905); *Mash v. Bloom*, 130 Wis. 366, 110 N.W. 203, 110 N.W. 268 (1907); *Maxham v. Stewart*, 133 Wis. 525, 526, 113 N.W. 972 (1907); and *Wanner v. Wanner*, 134 Wis. 71, 113 N.W. 1096 (1907). On the legal aspects of the support contract see August G. Eckhardt, "The Support Contract," 1951 *Wis. L. Rev.* 581.

26 126 Wis. 390, 105 N.W. 953 (1905); *Cases and Briefs*, "Record," 95-6, 100.

27 126 Wis. 385, 105 N.W. 831 (1905); *Cases and Briefs*, "Record," 17.

28 However, some non-tabulated cases arose out of support contracts, but turned on other issues—ranging from *Maxham v. Stewart*, 133 Wis. 525, 113 N.W. 972 (1907), where the issue on appeal was whether ejectment or unlawful detainer was a proper remedy, to *Schwantes v. State*, 127 Wis. 160, 106 N.W. 237 (1906), in which Schwantes was accused of murdering an elderly couple who had conveyed their property to him in exchange for an agreement to support them. The underlying contract in *Schwantes* is unusual in that Schwantes was not a relative, but a neighbor and friend of the grantors.

29 The cases are, respectively, *Rosenheimer v. Krenn*, 126 Wis. 617, 106 N.W. 20 (1906); *Gross v. Arians*, 153 Wis. 435, 141 N.W. 224 (1913); *Krueger v. Buel*, 153 Wis. 583, 142 N.W. 264 (1913).

30 Some more regularized real estate transactions were also represented in the cases, as well as such sophisticated techniques as escrow agreements, e.g., *James v. Knox*, 155 Wis. 118, 143 N.W. 1071 (1913). There were many lease cases, too, residential [*Auer v. Hoffman*, 132 Wis. 620, 112 N.W. 1090 (1907)] and commercial [*Cawker v. Trimmel*, 155 Wis. 108, 143 N.W. 1046 (1913)].

31 E.g., annexation and platting: *Alan Realty Co. v. Fair Deal Investment Co.*, 271 Wis. 336, 73 N.W.2d 517 (1955); extension of municipal sewer system: *Long Investment Co. v. O'Donnell*, 3 Wis.2d 291, 88 N.W.2d 674 (1958); zoning change: *Sweeney v. Stenjem*, 271 Wis. 497, 74 N.W.2d 174 (1956) (offer to buy lots "conditioned upon zoning ... being changed to Commercial B"); see also *Russell Dairy Stores v. Chippewa Falls*, 272 Wis. 138, 74 N.W.2d 759 (1956) (curb and driveway restrictions).

32 *Long Investment Co. v. O'Donnell*, 3 Wis.2d 291, 88 N.W.2d 674 (1958).

33 *Stadele v. Resnick*, 274 Wis. 346, 80 N.W.2d 272 (1957); *Morris v. Resnick*, 268 Wis. 410, 67 N.W.2d 848 (1955), factually connected with *Stadele*; *Georgiades v. Glickman*, 272 Wis. 257, 75 N.W.2d 573 (1956).

34 *Beiler v. Krnak*, 273 Wis. 85, 76 N.W.2d 545 (1956); *Cases and Briefs*, "Appellant's Brief," 112, 113, "Respondent's Brief," 3. Another resort case was *Wiegman v. Alexander*, 4 Wis.2d 118, 90 N.W.2d 273, 91 N.W.2d 335 (1958); the total purchase price was $22,000. Sale of resort property also figured in *Niske v. Nackman*, 273 Wis. 69, 76 N.W.2d 591 (1956), a real estate brokerage case. The original offering price ($35,000) included "3 cottages and 3 overnights; 1 tavern building, and 1 gas station building, and 1 central shower building."

35 See Introduction, pp. 7-9.

36 See *Kovarik v. Vesely*, 3 Wis.2d 573, 89 N.W.2d 279 (1958); Walter Raushenbush, "Problems and Practices with Financing Conditions in Real Estate Purchase Contracts," 1963 *Wis. L. Rev.* 566.

37 In *Roelvink v. City of Milwaukee*, 273 Wis. 605, 79 N.W.2d 106 (1956), the emotional ties of two women to their home, taken by the city of Milwaukee for school purposes, led them to the extreme measure of protracted litigation, even though presumably the price paid them was fair.

The form of a land transaction may influence the rate of litigation. Other things being equal, land description by metes and bounds should be open to error more often than legal description, e.g., *Lange v. Andrus*, 1 Wis.2d 13, 83 N.W.2d 140 (1957). Whether this is true on the trial court level cannot be certainly demonstrated.

38 E.g., agricultural labor, *Martin v. Martin*, 3 Pin. 272, 275, 3 Chand. 303 (1851); construction, *Learmonth v. Veeder*, 11 Wis. 138 (1860); brokerage, *Power v. Kane*, 5 Wis. 265 (1856); claims of attorneys, *Bryan v. Reynolds*, 5 Wis. 200 (1856).

39 *Martin v. Martin*, 3 Pin. 272, 275, 3 Chand. 303 (1851).

40 *Gordon v. Brewster*, 7 Wis. 355 (1858). See Laurent, Table 87, p. 165: of 178 contract actions in Chippewa County 1855-1864, only one was based on a promise "to perform services."

41 See below, C. 4, pp. 144-5, for a discussion of these various acts. Mechanics' lien actions and similar proceedings such as log lien actions were also frequent at the trial court level; see Laurent, Tables 88 and 89, pp. 166, 167.

42 The cases are, respectively, *DuBay v. Uline*, 6 Wis. 588 (1858); *Bailey v. Hull*, 11 Wis. 289 (1860). But in *Dewey v. Fifield*, 2 Wis. 73 (1853) the claim was for $4.05 worth of lumber furnished. On the origin and early history of mechanics' lien laws, see Henry W. Farnam, *Chapters in the History of American Social Legislation* (Washington, 1938), pp. 152-6.

43 Alexander C. Guth, "Early Day Architects in Wisconsin," WMH, XVIII (1934), 141; see *Baasen v. Baehr*, 7 Wis. 516 (1859) (brick building to be erected "according to certain plans and specifications furnished by John Dillenburg, the architect, for the sum of $4,350"). Of course, the line between classes in early Wisconsin was not hard and fast. Joseph Schafer, "Epic of a Plain Yankee Family II: The Milwaukee County Howards," WMH, IX (1926), 284, 291, describes a prosperous farmer who hired carpenters, masons, and bricklayers, and who lent out surplus money at interest.

44 The cases are, respectively, *Maynard v. Tidball*, 2 Wis. 34, 36 (1853); *Taylor v. Williams*, 6 Wis. 363 (1858); *Rogers v. Brightman*, 10 Wis. 55 (1859); *Bradley v. Levy*, 5 Wis. 400 (1856).

45 Water wheels: *Cole v. Clark*, 3 Pin. 303, 4 Chand. 29 (1851); *Butler v. Titus*, 13 Wis. 429 (1861); lumber slide: *Warren v. Bean*, 6 Wis. 120 (1856); fulling-mill irons: *Turton v. Burke*, 4 Wis. 119 (1855); threshing machines: *Stone v. Talbot*, 4 Wis. 442 (1855); boat boilers and engine: *Fisk v. Tank*, 12 Wis. 276 (1860).

46 The doctor: *Reynolds v. Graves*, 3 Wis. 416 (1854); farrier: *Kuehn v. Wilson*, 13 Wis. 104 (1860); land agent: *Power v. Kane*, 5 Wis. 265 (1856), and other cases.

47 On Paine, see the advertisement in the *Independent American* (Platteville), March 31, 1854; in the same issue Isaac S. Clark, attorney at law, held himself out as "notary public and general insurance and land agent." On Cary, *Racine Argus*, August 15, 1838; materials on Cary can also be found in the Jacob A. Barker Papers, State Historical Society of Wisconsin.

Commercial specialists and brokers, even in Period I, began to appear, ultimately driving out the factotums. Futures trading began in Milwaukee as early as 1855. Harry C. Emery, *Speculation on the Stock and Produce Exchanges of the United States* ("Columbia University Studies in History, Economics and Public Law," Vol. VII, No. 2 [New York, 1896]), 41; *Hall v. Storrs*, 7 Wis. 253 (1858). Hoel H. Camp began as a wholesale grocer, then shifted to banking, H.C. Campbell, ed., *Wisconsin in Three Centuries, 1634-1905*, 5 vols. (New York, 1906), V, 279-83. For a good description of the work of a financial factotum, see *Chappell v. Cady*, 10 Wis. 111 (1859).

48 *Chase v. Hinkley*, 126 Wis. 75, 105 N.W. 230 (1905); *Cass v. Haskins*, 154 Wis. 472, 143 N.W. 162 (1913).

49 This is suggested by Laurent's figures for Chippewa County, at least as far as suits against laborers are concerned. See Laurent, Tables 87, 94, pp. 165, 172.

50 Arthur J. Altmeyer, *The Industrial Commission of Wisconsin* (Madison, 1932) pp. 12, 240, 246-68.

51 E.g., *Marx v. Marx*, 132 Wis. 113, 111 N.W. 1103 (1907). In Period I, *Fisher v. Fisher*, 5 Wis. 472 (1856).

52 On J. L. Gates and the Tomahawk Land Company, see Arlan C. Helgeson, "Promotion of Agricultural Settlement in Northern Wisconsin 1880-1925" (unpub. Ph.D. thesis, U. Wis., 1951), pp. 138-46, 162ff.

53 Willis figured in *Bowe v. Gage*, 127 Wis. 245, 106 N.W. 1074 (1906), *Cases and Briefs*, "Record," 67. A lawyer land-dealer was Salmon W. Dalberg, in *Dalberg v. Jung Brewing Co.*, 155 Wis. 185, 144 N.W. 198 (1913), *Cases and Briefs*, "Record," 22, 45-6. Real estate and insurance: Rowland T. Burdon, in *Burdon v. Briquelet*, 125 Wis. 341, 104 N.W. 83 (1905); Wright's *Directory of Green Bay, with DePere and Brown County* (1901), p. 86.

54 *Zitske v. Grohn*, 128 Wis. 159, 107 N.W. 20 (1906), *Cases and Briefs*, "Record," 19-20.

55 E.g., flat sum as commission: *Schultz v. Eberle*, 124 Wis. 594, 102 N.W. 1055 (1905), *Cases and Briefs*, "Record," 26 ($100 for sale of a farm); 2 per cent: *Tasse v. Kindt*, 125 Wis. 631, 104 N.W. 703 (1905); 2.5 per cent: *Hoskins v. O'Brien*, 132 Wis. 453, 112 N.W. 466 (1907); 3 per cent: *Hensel v. Witt*, 134 Wis. 55, 113 N.W. 1093 (1907); 5 per cent on the first $1,000, 2.5 per cent on the next: *Hoffman v. Steele*, 152 Wis. 84, 139 N.W. 733 (1913), *Cases and Briefs*, "Record," 20; 5 per cent: *Burdon v. Briquelet*, 125 Wis. 341, 104 N.W. 83 (1905), *Cases and Briefs*, "Record," 111, 123-4, 126; minimum sale price, broker to take one-half of anything received in addition, Helgeson, "Promotion of Agricultural Settlement," p. 31, or all additional, *McCune v. Badger*, 126 Wis. 186, 105 N.W. 667 (1905).

56 Testimony of J. A. Cusick, in *Burdon v. Briquelet*, 125 Wis. 341, 104 N.W. 83 (1905), *Cases and Briefs*, "Record," 124.

57 Brokers "do not wish longer to be called land sharks," John A. McCormick, broker, quoted in *Milwaukee Journal*, Feb. 16, 1917, p. 18. The desire to become "professional" was one factor which lay behind the licensing movement, on which see below, C. 4, pp. 162-6; George Howe, *Memoirs of a Westchester Realtor* (New York, 1959), p. 29; A. D. Theobald, "Real Estate License Laws in Theory and Practice," *J. Land & Pub. Util. Econ.*, VII (1931), 13.

Exclusive agency agreements (or variants) were frequent in brokerage contracts in Period II, e.g., *Hoskins v. O'Brien*, 132 Wis. 453, 112 N.W. 466 (1907) ("Exclusive Sale Contract" for six months).

58 Many agents represented more than one company, see *Costello v. Grant County Mutual Fire & Lightning Ins. Co.*, 133 Wis. 361, 113 N.W. 639 (1907). For side-line sales of insurance, see *Korrer v. Madden*, 152 Wis. 646, 140 N.W. 325 (1913), *Cases and Briefs*, "Record," 51-2 (insurance agent peddled corporate stock to a widowed hotel owner); in *Whitman v. Milwaukee Fire Ins. Co.*, 128 Wis. 124, 107 N.W. 291 (1906), *Cases and Briefs*, "Record," 72, a banker placed insurance. The cases occasionally touch on the internal business hierarchy of insurance organizations, e.g., *Security Trust & Life Ins. Co. v. Ellsworth*, 129 Wis. 349, 109 N.W. 125 (1906).

59 See Introduction, pp. 5-7.

60 *Manthey v. Stock*, 133 Wis. 107, 113 N.W. 443 (1907); *Manthey v. Manger*, 155 Wis. 51, 143 N.W. 1036 (1913).

61 The "builder" in *Lindenmann v. Kopczynski*, 155 Wis. 164, 144 N.W. 196 (1913), *Cases and Briefs*, "Record," 28. In *Sherry v. Madler*, 123 Wis. 621, 101 N.W. 1095 (1905), plaintiff James Sherry, an Appleton "carpenter" in 1905 (1905-1906 *PWG*, 158) was listed as a "contractor" in 1911 (1911-1912 *PWG*, 154).

62 The impression of marginality is confirmed by other occupations represented by cases in Period II's tabulation, e.g., the printer of letterheads for a hopeful senatorial candidate, *Vader v. Ballou*, 151 Wis. 577, 139 N.W. 413 (1913); an organizer for a radical farmers' movement, *Crawley v. American Society of Equity*, 153 Wis. 13, 139 N.W. 734 (1913). For an interesting interplay between "personal" and "business" elements in contract, see *Klug v. Sheriffs*, 129 Wis. 468, 109 N.W. 656 (1906) (arising out of a contract by a commercial

184 | CONTRACT LAW IN AMERICA

portraitist to execute a portrait from a photograph of plaintiff's deceased wife).

[63] *Estate of Kandall*, 270 Wis. 349, 71 N.W.2d 283 (1955); other estate cases are *Estate of Gerke*, 271 Wis. 297, 73 N.W.2d 506 (1955); *Estate of Rule*, 3 Wis.2d 301, 88 N.W.2d 734 (1958).

[64] *Karl M. Elbinger Co. v. Geo. J. Meyer Mfg. Co.*, 3 Wis.2d 202, 87 N.W.2d 807 (1958)

[65] The brokers' Statute of Frauds (Wis. Laws 1917, ch. 221) was introduced into the Assembly by V. V. Miller, Republican of Rusk and Sawyer counties (1917 Wis. *Assembly Journal*, 221) who also introduced at the same session a bill (No. 377A) to license brokers (1917 Wis. *Assembly Journal*, 290). The unmistakable inference is that the same interests were behind both bills. The established brokers strongly favored licensing. See "Licensing of Brokers," *National Real Estate Journal*, XVI (1917), 226.

The first case arising under the Wisconsin law was *Gifford v. Straub*, 172 Wis. 396, 179 N.W. 600 (1920). A contract stating "I agree to give [Gifford] ... all he gets for my place over $11,500. Sept. 20-1919 exclusive sale [sic]" violated the Statute and gave rise to no action for commission. Gifford, of Pierce County, was a man about 60 years old. He testified: "I have tried to sell a little real estate. I never went to school very much.... I have no permanent office." *Cases and Briefs*, "Record," 17. This was precisely the kind of operator the Statute was meant to help drive out of business.

[66] See, e.g., *Gilbert v. Ludtke*, 1 Wis.2d 228, 83 N.W.2d 669 (1957).

[67] E.g., *Garvey v. Wenzel*, 272 Wis. 606, 76 N.W.2d 291 (1956).

[68] 270 Wis. 133, 70 N.W.2d 585 (1955); same case, 274 Wis. 478, 80 N.W.2d 461 (1957).

[69] 272 Wis. 257, 75 N.W.2d 573 (1956).

[70] 4 Wis.2d 36, 90 N.W.2d 123 (1958).

[71] E.g., *Sewell v. Eaton*, 6 Wis. 490 (1857); *Murphy v. Sagola Lumber Co.*, 125 Wis. 363, 103 N.W. 1113 (1905). On the historical relationship between sales law and contract law, see Lawrence M. Friedman, "Formative Elements of the Law of Sales: The Eighteenth Century," 44 *Minn. L. Rev.* 411 (1960).

[72] *Walton v. Cody*, 1 Wis. 420 (1853).

[73] On chattel mortgages, see Rev. Stats. Wis. 1849, ch. 38, § 3; *ibid.*, ch. 76, § 9. Crop mortgage: *Comstock v. Scales*, 7 Wis. 159 (1860); mortgage on a stock of goods: *Chynoweth v. Tenney*, 10 Wis. 397 (1860). See *Hunter v. Warner*, 1 Wis. 141 (1853), for an evolutionary ancestor of the modern conditional sale: a horse was sold, for $40, $25 to be paid in two weeks, the balance later, with reservation of title.

[74] On the marketing of agricultural machines, see *Brayton v. Chase*, 3 Wis. 456 (1854) ("New York" reaper); *Pitts v. Owen*, 9 Wis. 152 (1859) (threshing machine); Reynold M. Wik, "J. I. Case: Some Experiences of an Early Wisconsin Industrialist," *WMH*, XXXV (1951), 3, 64. The McCormick Papers, State Historical Society of Wisconsin, are a rich source of information, preserving many form contracts; of particular importance is a typescript compiled in 1934, "Copies of Printed and Manuscript Material Showing the Credit Policy of the Various McCormick Companies, 1839-1902."

[75] *Bird v. Mayer*, 8 Wis. 362 (1859) (varnish); *Getty v. Rountree*, 2 Pin. 379, 2 Chand. 28 (1850) (pump); *Mann v. Stowell*, 3 Pin. 220, 3 Chand. 243 (1851) (wagon). See also *Malbon v. Birney*, 11 Wis. 107 (1860) (lumber for building a house).

[76] Horses: e.g., *Hunter v. Warner*, 1 Wis. 141 (1853); sheep: *Williams v. Slaughter*, 3 Wis. 347 (1854), see L. G. Connor, "A Brief History of the Sheep Industry in the United States," in *Annual Report, American Historical Association* (1918), I, 93, 116; oxen: *Hall v. Wood*, 3 Pin. 308, 4 Chand. 36 (1851); wheat, e.g., *Hardell v. McClure*, 2 Pin. 289, 1 Chand. 271 (1849), John G. Thompson, *The Rise and Decline of the Wheat Growing Industry in Wis-*

consin (Madison, 1909); barley: *Hodson v. Carter*, 3 Pin. 212, 3 Chand. 234 (1851); lumber and logs: e.g., *Catterill v. Stevens*, 10 Wis. 422 (1860).

77 Wis. Laws 1911, ch. 549.

78 *Dunham v. Salmon*, 130 Wis. 164, 167-8, 109 N.W. 959 (1906).

79 *Twentieth Century Co. v. Quilling*, 130 Wis. 318, 324, 110 N.W. 174 (1907), *Cases and Briefs*, "Record," 11, 102, 104, 105; see *Kipp v. Gates*, 126 Wis. 566, 105 N.W. 947 (1906), *Cases and Briefs*, "Record," 28-9. Similar rackets occurred elsewhere, see *Couch v. Hutchinson*, 2 Ala. App. 444, 57 So. 75 (1911).

For legislative reaction, see Wis. Laws 1901, ch. 268 (patent rights); declared unconstitutional in *J. H. Clark Co. v. Rice*, 127 Wis. 451, 106 N.W. 231 (1906). The problem was not new: *Hollida & Ball v. Hunt*, 70 Ill. 109 (1873). Interestingly enough, the U.S. Supreme Court ultimately upheld these statutes, *Ozan Lumber Co. v. Union County National Bank of Liberty*, 207 U.S. 251, 28 S. Ct. 89, 52 L. Ed. 195 (1907); *Allen v. Riley*, 203 U.S. 347, 27 S. Ct. 95, 51 L. Ed. 216 (1906). Laws Wis. 1903, ch. 438 (stallions), was upheld in *Quiggle v. Herman*, 131 Wis. 379, 111 N.W. 479 (1907); as to the sale of lightning rods, in *Arnd v. Sjoblom*, 131 Wis. 642, 111 N.W. 666 (1907). For another scheme of dubious legality, involving the sale of cherry trees and stock in a nursery company, see 5 Rpts. Att'y Gen. Wis. 787 (June 15, 1909).

80 See *Estey Organ Co. v. Lehman*, 132 Wis. 144, 111 N.W. 1097 (1907) (organ); *Chickering-Chase Bros. Co. v. White*, 127 Wis. 83, 106 N.W. 797 (1906) (piano sold by chattel mortgage).

81 Farm machinery: *Fox v. Wilkinson*, 133 Wis. 337, 113 N.W. 669 (1907); the horse market: *Davis v. Schmidt*, 126 Wis. 461, 106 N.W. 119 (1906); *Gunsten v. Green*, 153 Wis. 413, 141 N.W. 239 (1913).

82 For example, S. F. Bowser & Co., a foreign corporation, appealed two cases in 1913, to collect the price of clothes-cleaning equipment sold to retail cleaning firms. *S. F. Bowser & Co. v. Schwartz*, 152 Wis. 408, 140 N.W. 51 (1913); *S. F. Bowser & Co. v. Savidusky*, 154 Wis. 76, 142 N.W. 182 (1913). (Savidusky Bros., dyers and cleaners, was a small chain with branches in Eau Claire, Chippewa Falls, and Menominee. See advertisement in 1909-1910 *PWG*, 269).

Sales of raw materials or industrial products to processors or manufacturers: *Forster, Waterbury Co. v. F. MacKinnon Mfg. Co.*, 130 Wis. 281, 110 N.W. 226 (1907); *Listman Mill Co. v. Miller*, 131 Wis. 393, 111 N.W. 496 (1907) (sale of screenings by flouring mill); *No. Baltimore Bottle Glass Co. v. Altpeter*, 133 Wis. 112, 113 N.W. 435 (1907)

83 *Korrer v. Madden*, 152 Wis. 646, 140 N.W. 325 (1913).

84 129 Wis. 524, 109 N.W. 576 (1906).

85 *Catlin & Powell Co. v. Schuppert*, 130 Wis. 642, 110 N.W. 818 (1907), *Cases and Briefs*, "Record," 28, quoting a letter of Schuppert's: "I had ... bought for another party.... This party has ... refused to accept the stock." William L. Schuppert was probably the person of that name listed in 1905-1906 *PWG*, 178, as county superintendent of schools of Ashland County.

86 E.g., *Anderson v. Tri-State Home Improvement Co.*, 268 Wis. 455, 67 N.W.2d 853 (1955) (siding); *Milwaukee Cold Storage Co. v. York Corp.*, 3 Wis.2d 13, 87 N.W.2d 505 (1958) (air-conditioning equipment).

87 *Automobiles: Scherg v. Puetz*, 269 Wis. 561, 69 N.W.2d 490 (1955); home improvements: *Anderson v. Tri-State Home Improvement Co.*, 268 Wis. 455, 67 N.W.2d 853 (1955); refrigerator: *Padgham v. Wilson Music Co.*, 3 Wis.2d 363, 88 N.W.2d 679 (1958); pleasure boat: *Leiske v. Baudhuin Yacht Harbor Inc.*, 4 Wis.2d 188, 89 N.W.2d 794 (1958).

88 E.g., *Milwaukee Cold Storage Co. v. York Corp.*, 3 Wis.2d 13, 87 N.W.2d 505 (1958);

Anderson v. Tri-State Home Improvement Co., 268 Wis. 455, 67 N.W.2d 853 (1955): "The company prohibits the making of any promise, or representations, unless ... inserted in writing in this agreement before signing." In formal sales contracts, particularly for consumer sales, such a clause was standard. An exculpatory clause was litigated in *Metz v. Medford Fur Foods Inc.*, 4 Wis.2d 96, 90 N.W.2d 106 (1958).

[89] 274 Wis. 290, 79 N.W.2d 649 (1956); on the statutory prohibition of sale without a "report of complete negative Brucellosis test," see Wis. Stats. § 95.49 (1961).

[90] *Metz v. Medford Fur Foods, Inc.*, 4 Wis.2d 96, 90 N.W.2d 106 (1958); *Genrich v. Medford Fur Foods Inc.*, 4 Wis.2d 103, 90 N.W.2d 109 (1958). The statute, Wis. Stats. § 94.72 (14) (b) (1961) prohibited the sale of any "feeds mixed or adulterated with any substance or substances injurious to the health of livestock." Medford learned of the application of this statute to his business in *Arndt Bros. Minkery v. Medford Fur Foods, Inc.*, 274 Wis. 627, 80 N.W.2d 776 (1957), which undoubtedly occasioned the drafting of the exculpatory clause at issue in the *Metz* case.

[91] *Chapman v. Zakzaska*, 273 Wis. 64, 76 N.W.2d 537 (1955), arising under Wis. Stats. § 218.01 (7a) (a) (1961).

[92] *Milwaukee Cold Storage Co. v. York Corp.*, 3 Wis.2d 13, 87 N.W.2d 505 (1958). Even in this case, one party was small business (a coldstorage warehouse).

[93] *Scherg v. Puetz*, 269 Wis. 561, 69 N.W.2d 490 (1955), *Cases and Briefs*, "Appellant's Brief," Appendix, 136.

[94] *Fay v. Oatley*, 6 Wis. 42, 54 (1857); see *Reid v. Hibbard*, 6 Wis. 175 (1858). Letters of credit: *McNaughton v. Conklings*, 9 Wis. 316 (1859). See, in general, Henry Stern, "Life Story of a Milwaukee Merchant," *WMH*, IX (1925), 63. A fine treatment of Wisconsin's early commerce is Frederick Merk, *Economic History of Wisconsin During the Civil War Decade* (Madison, 1916), pp. 220-37, 344-91.

[95] The case of the ill-fated salt is *Ranney v. Higby*, 4 Wis. 154 (1855); 5 Wis. 62 (1856); 6 Wis. 28 (1857); 12 Wis. 61 (1860). On Higby, see [Frank A. Flower?], *History of Milwaukee* (Chicago, 1881), p. 360; he later served as president of the Milwaukee Chamber of Commerce, Elmer E. Barton, *Industrial History of Milwaukee* (Milwaukee, 1886), p. 47; on the peddlers, see Henry Stern, "Life Story of a Milwaukee Merchant," 63, 69-70; for the legislation, see below, C. 4, pp. 165-6.

[96] *Bradley v. Denton*, 3 Wis. 557 (1854).

[97] *Allen v. Newberry*, 21 How. 244 (U.S. 1858). See also *Brooks v. The Peytona*, Fed. Cas. No. 1,959 (D.C. Wis. 1858) (steamboat of the Milwaukee & Horicon Railroad, used on Lake Winnebago and the Fox and Wolf Rivers).

[98] 12 How. 443 (U.S. 1851); see Charles Warren, *The Supreme Court in United States History*, 3 vols. (Boston, 1922), II, 512-5. On the tendency to treat lake commerce "contractually," see *Medbery v. Sweet*, 3 Pin. 210, 3 Chand. 231 (1851). The *Genessee Chief* held that federal admiralty power extended to the Great Lakes, although some prior decisions had held that (as in England) the limits of admiralty jurisdiction were the "ebb and flow of the tides."

[99] *Milwaukee Boston Store v. Katz*, 153 Wis. 492, 140 N.W. 1038 (1913).

[100] *American Lumberman*, Mar. 10, 1906, p. 38. A written code of ethics had foundered.

[101] E.g., *Main v. Procknow*, 131 Wis. 279, 111 N.W. 508 (1907); *Standard Manufacturing Co. v. Stallmann*, 128 Wis. 375, 107 N.W. 662 (1906). "Beware of the Sole Agency Bait," warned D. Charles O'Connor, author of a *Treatise on Commercial Pharmacy* (3rd ed., Philadelphia, 1925), p. 191.

[102] E.g., *LaCrosse Plow Co. v. Helgeson*, 127 Wis. 622, 106 N.W. 1094 (1906) (sale of cream

separators; breach of performance warranty); *Engeldinger v. Stevens*, 132 Wis. 423, 112 N.W. 507 (1907) (dealings in wood; buyer complained of "short measurement").

[103] *Abrohams v. Revillon Freres*, 129 Wis. 235, 107 N.W. 656 (1906) (fur trade); *Burstein v. Phillips*, 154 Wis. 591, 143 N.W. 679 (1913) (rag trade).

[104] 133 Wis. 85, 113 N.W. 393 (1907).

[105] The clause was held ineffective in *First Nat. Bank of El Paso v. Miller*, 235 Ill. 135, 85 N.W. 312 (1908).

[106] *Woodward v. Vegetable Packing House*, 4 Wis.2d 310, 90 N.W.2d 586 (1958).

[107] 5 Wis. 62 (1856). On marine insurance, see Spencer L. Kimball, "The Role of the Court in the Development of Insurance Law," 1957 *Wis. L. Rev.* 520, 523-4 n7.

[108] Flower, *History of Milwaukee*, p. 360.

[109] See *Kelly v. Troy Fire Insurance Co.*, 3 Wis. 254 (1854).

[110] *Clark v. Durand*, 12 Wis. 223 (1860). The advertisement quoted in the text appeared in the *Fond du Lac Union* (Nov. 20, 1856). An 1858 pamphlet of the Northwestern Mutual Life Insurance Company of Milwaukee, quoted in *Semi-Centennial History of the Northwestern Mutual Life Insurance Company of Milwaukee* (Milwaukee, 1908), p. 79, complained of the contrast between the "almost universal" use of fire insurance and the "comparatively few policies" of life insurance.

[111] *Prieger v. Exchange Mutual Insurance Co.*, 6 Wis. 89, 104 (1858).

[112] Robert S. Maxwell, *La Follette and the Rise of the Progressives in Wisconsin* (State Histl. Soc. of Wis.: Madison, 1956), p. 115.

[113] Clarence Morris, "Waiver and Estoppel in Insurance Policy Litigation," 105 *U. Pa. L. Rev.* 925-6 (1957).

[114] *Wausau Telephone Co. v. United Firemen's Insurance Co.*, 123 Wis. 535, 101 N.W. 1100 (1905); but see 4 *Biennial Rep. Wis. Att'y Gen.* 439 (Aug. 6, 1906). On the development of insurance regulation in Wisconsin see Spencer L. Kimball, *Insurance and Public Policy* (Madison, 1960); on insurance regulation in general, see Edwin W. Patterson, *The Insurance Commissioner in the United States* (Cambridge, 1927).

[115] Marshall, J., in *Whitman v. Milwaukee Fire Ins. Co.*, 128 Wis. 124, 131, 107 N.W. 291 (1906).

[116] *Roloff v. Farmers' Home Mutual Insurance Co. of Ellington*, 130 Wis. 402, 403, 110 N.W. 261 (1907). See also *Schultz v. Frankfort Marine Accident & Plate Glass Ins. Co.*, 151 Wis. 537, 139 N.W. 386 (1913), an action brought against a company, its firm of private detectives, and a particular detective for shadowing and harassing a claimant.

[117] E.g., *Metcalf v. Mutual Fire Insurance Co. of Albany*, 132 Wis. 67, 112 N.W. 22 (1907).

[118] E.g., *Rief v. Continental Casualty Co.*, 131 Wis. 368, 111 N.W. 502 (1907).

[119] E.g., *Perlick v. Country Mutual Casualty Co.*, 274 Wis. 558, 80 N.W.2d 921 (1957).

[120] *Albert v. Home Fire and Marine Ins. Co. of California*, 275 Wis. 280, 81 N.W.2d 549 (1957) ("monthly reporting insurance"). The insured had understated the value of his stock-in-trade. This was precisely the kind of risk an insurance company would resist; see also *Haas v. Integrity Mutual Ins. Co.*, 4 Wis.2d 198, 90 N.W.2d 146 (1958) (concealment of fact that prior policy had been revoked). Business uses of life insurance: *Boek v. Wagner*, 1 Wis.2d 337, 83 N.W.2d 916 (1957), *Albrent v. Spencer*, 275 Wis. 127, 81 N.W.2d 555 (1957); group insurance: *Kaiser v. Prudential Ins. Co. of America*, 272 Wis. 527, 76 N.W.2d 311 (1956).

[121] See Shaw Livermore, *Early American Land Companies: Their Influence on Corporate*

188 | CONTRACT LAW IN AMERICA

Development (New York, 1939). The period of the special charter in Wisconsin is dealt with in George J. Kuehnl, *The Wisconsin Business Corporation* (Madison, 1959). John W. Cadman, *The Corporation in New Jersey, 1791-1875* (Cambridge, 1949), is the best of the few studies of other states.

122 *Bulger v. Woods*, 3 Pin. 460 (1852).

123 *Rockwell v. Daniels*, 4 Wis. 432 (1856).

124 11 Wis. 307, 321, 327 (1860); on the farm-mortgage episode, see Robert S. Hunt, *Law and Locomotives* (Madison, 1958), pp. 44-65.

125 *Downie v. Hoover*, 12 Wis. 174 (1860); *Downie v. White*, 12 Wis. 176 (1860); *Racine County Bank v. Ayers*, 12 Wis. 512 (1860).

126 132 Wis. 177, 111 N.W. 1123 (1907).

127 *Cottington v. Swan*, 128 Wis. 321, 107 N.W. 336 (1906) (livery); *My Laundry Co. v. Schmeling*, 129 Wis. 597, 109 N.W. 540 (1906), *Cases and Briefs*, "Record," 157, 231 (laundry); *Kradwell v. Thiesen*, 131 Wis. 97, 111 N.W. 233 (1907), *Cases and Briefs*, "Record," 8-9 (drug store).

128 The teller: *Schwab v. Esbenshade*, 151 Wis. 513, 139 N.W. 420 (1913); the doctor: *Hurley v. Walter*, 129 Wis. 508, 109 N.W. 558 (1906); the banker and farmer: *Kellogg v. Malick*, 125 Wis. 239, 103 N.W. 1116 (1905).

129 *Rust v. Fitzhugh*, 132 Wis. 549, 112 N.W. 508 (1907), *Cases and Briefs*, "Record," 32-78.

130 *Baker v. Becker*, 153 Wis. 369, 141 N.W. 304 (1913), *Cases and Briefs*, "Record," 157-8.

131 But see, for a partial exception, *Milwaukee Boston Store v. Katz*, 153 Wis. 492, 140 N.W. 1038 (1913), arising out of a leased department arrangement in a leading urban department store. Another department store case was *Ott v. Boring*, 131 Wis. 472, 110 N.W. 824 (1907). Here, however, the problem arose out of an employment contract dating from the days before the store made its transition from a small retail establishment in Ashland to a department store.

Two cases dealt with agricultural co-operatives: *Briere v. Taylor*, 126 Wis. 347, 105 N.W. 817 (1905) (cranberries); *Golden v. Meier*, 129 Wis. 14, 107 N.W. 27 (1906) (creamery).

132 *Culligan, Inc. v. Rheaume*, 269 Wis. 242, 68 N.W.2d 810 (1955); for an earlier phase of this case, see 268 Wis. 298, 67 N.W.2d 279 (1954); *Touchett v. E Z Paintr Corporation*, 268 Wis. 635, 68 N.W.2d 442 (1955); *Johann v. Milwaukee Electric Tool Corp.*, 270 Wis. 573, 72 N.W.2d 401 (1955).

133 The cases cited are, respectively, *Larson v. Superior Auto Parts, Inc.*, 270 Wis. 613, 72 N.W.2d 316 (1955); same case, 275 Wis. 261, 81 N.W.2d 505 (1957); *Sponholz v. Meyer*, 270 Wis. 288, 70 N.W.2d 619 (1955); *Cram v. Bach*, 1 Wis.2d 378, 83 N.W.2d 877, 85 N.W.2d 673 (1957).

134 270 Wis. 488, 71 N.W.2d 420 (1955), discussed in Robert H. Skilton, "Cars for Sale: Some Comments on the Wholesale Financing of Automobiles," 1957 *Wis. L. Rev.* 352, 366-7, n28. The case arose under a Wisconsin law regulating dealerships, first passed in 1935, Wis. Laws 1935, ch. 474; a cancellation-of-franchise provision appeared in Wis. Laws 1937, ch. 378; see also Wis. Laws 1945, ch. 171, at 283. The present text is Wis. Stats. § 218.01 (3) (a) 17. State and federal law are discussed in Walston S. Brown and Allan F. Conwill, "Automobile Manufacturer-Dealer Legislation," 57 *Columbia L. Rev.* 218 (1957). The authors of this article assume that the state statutes have little or no effect, basing their assumption on the absence of appellate litigation. An unpublished empirical study by Professor Stewart Macaulay, of the University of Wisconsin Law School, on the administrative process within the Wisconsin Department of Motor Vehicles shows this assumption to be unfounded in Wisconsin. The Department uses in the main techniques of con-

ciliation rather than adjudication.

135 *Johnson v. Shell Oil Co.*, 274 Wis. 375, 80 N.W.2d 426 (1957).

136 Respectively, *Mallory v. Lyman*, 3 Pin. 443, 4 Chand. 143 (1852); *Rector v. Drury*, 3 Pin. 298, 4 Chand. 24 (1851); *Taylor v. Pratt*, 3 Wis. 674 (1854); *Garrison v. Owens*, 1 Pin. 471 (1844). Of course, chattel notes were not negotiable, strictly speaking, and were thus not "promissory notes" at all, see Rev. Stats. Wis. 1849, ch. 44, § 1, which speaks of "notes... signed by any person, whereby he shall promise to pay ... any sum of money."

137 *Fond du Lac Union* (December 12, 1856); Letter of Thomas J. Walker & Co., Agents, October 14, 1857, in "Copies of Printed and Manuscript Material Showing the Credit Policy of the Various McCormick Companies 1839-1902," McCormick Papers.

138 E.g., *Tobey v. McAllister*, 9 Wis. 463 (1859).

139 E.g., demand: *Drury v. Mann*, 4 Wis. 202 (1855); "Nine months after date": *Cowles v. McVickar*, 3 Wis. 725 (1854); bearer paper: *Gorsuth v. Butterfield*, 2 Wis. 237 (1853).

140 Bills of exchange: *Thomas v. Thomas*, 7 Wis. 476 (1859), in sets, see *Walsh v. Blatchley*, 6 Wis. 422 (1853); certificates of deposit: *O'Neill v. Bradford*, 1 Pin. 390 (1844), see *State Bank of Illinois v. Corwith*, 6 Wis. 551 (1858). In *Rock River Bank v. Sherwood*, 10 Wis. 230 (1860), a promissory note was given to a bank to cover overdrafts. Domiciled paper: see *Carruth v. Walker*, 8 Wis. 252 (1858) (note executed in Philadelphia, payable "at the Bank of Pennsylvania"); warrant of attorney: *Vliet v. Camp*, 13 Wis. 199 (1860).

141 Exceptions were rare; *Cowles v. McVickar*, 3 Wis. 725 (1854) (chattel mortgage, lease, and "two policies of insurance").

142 On the usury laws, see Lawrence M. Friedman, "The Usury Laws of Wisconsin: A Study in Legal and Social History," 1963 *Wis. L. Rev.* 515.

143 Lumber loans: *Durkee v. City Bank of Kenosha*, 13 Wis. 216 (1860); wheat: *Racine County Bank v. Lathrop*, 12 Wis. 466 (1860); railroad board of directors: *Richard v. Globe Bank*, 12 Wis. 692 (1860). See *Racine County Bank v. Keep*, 13 Wis. 209 (1860) (discounting of commercial paper). On the banks of Wisconsin, see Frederick Merk, *Economic History of Wisconsin*, pp. 187-219; Leonard B. Krueger, *History of Commercial Banking in Wisconsin* (Madison, 1933); Theodore A. Andersen, *A Century of Banking in Wisconsin* (Madison, 1954); William Ward Wight, "Early Legislation Concerning Wisconsin Banks," in *Proceedings of the State Historical Society of Wisconsin, 1895* (Madison, 1896), p. 145; Richard H. Marshall, "Samuel Marshall, Pioneer Banker," *WMH*, XXXII (1948), 26.

144 Helene Dyer's case: *Estate of Dyer*, 3 Wis.2d 305, 88 N.W.2d 737 (1958). Examples of private suretyship included (in Period II) *Klee v. Stephenson*, 130 Wis. 505, 110 N.W. 479 (1907), where a merchant tailor's debt to a New York merchant was rashly guaranteed by a neighbor storekeeper, a coal dealer, and an insurance and real estate man, *Cases and Briefs*, "Case," 13; 1905-1906 *PWG*, 1187 (entry under "Stephenson & Co."). In Period III, see *Turck v. Seefeldt*, 268 Wis. 559, 68 N.W.2d 534 (1955) (a farmer "who had money to lend" financed a building contractor, with a lawyer acting as intermediary).

145 *Knuth v. Fidelity & Cas. Co. of New York*, 275 Wis. 603, 83 N.W.2d 126 (1957); a companion case is *Hribar v. Johnson*, 275 Wis. 610, 83 N.W.2d 130 (1957). Fidelity insurance began in the United States about the time of the Civil War, James G. Smith, *The Development of Trust Companies in the United States* (New York, 1928), pp. 309-11; on corporate suretyship in Wisconsin see Spencer L. Kimball, *Insurance and Public Policy* (Madison, 1960), p. 13.

146 Internal improvements: *Gee v. Swain*, 12 Wis. 450 (1860), *Hasbrouck v. City of Milwaukee*, 13 Wis. 36 (1860) (harbor); licensing: *Lessey v. Green Bay*, 1 Pin. 486 (1845) (grocery license). See also *Pulling v. Board of Supervisors of Columbia County*, 3 Wis. 337 (1854) (public prosecutor); *Baxter v. State*, 9 Wis. 38 (1859) (building of state capitol).

147 The struggle over the printing contract in 1849 is richly documented in the Charles M. Baker Papers, State Historical Society of Wisconsin; see *Sholes v. State*, 2 Pin. 499, 2 Chand. 182 (1850). See Kenneth W. Duckett, *Frontiersman of Fortune: Moses M. Strong of Mineral Point* (State Histl. Soc. of Wis.: Madison, 1955), pp. 80 ff., on the struggle over the appointment of a territorial printer in 1846. At least two cases arose out of newspaper contracts to print lists of forfeited or delinquent public lands: *State ex rel. Harney v. Hastings*, 12 Wis. 596 (1860); *Beal v. Supervisors of St. Croix County*, 13 Wis. 500 (1861).

148 Larrabee, J., in *Sholes v. State*, 2 Pin. 499, 510, 2 Chand. 182 (1850).

149 E.g., *Town of Rochester v. Alfred Bank*, 13 Wis. 432 (1861) (action to restrain collection of a tax levied to pay allegedly void bonds); *State ex rel. Damman v. Commissioners of School and University Lands*, 4 Wis. 414 (1855).

150 E.g., Rev. Stats. Wis. 1849, ch. 21, § 2.

151 See for example, Louis Hartz, *Economic Policy and Democratic Thought; Pennsylvania, 1776-1860* (Cambridge, 1948), on the involvement of the Commonwealth of Pennsylvania with the Pennsylvania Railroad.

152 See *Allen v. City of Milwaukee*, 128 Wis. 678, 106 N.W. 1099 (1906); *Cawker v. City of Milwaukee*, 133 Wis. 35, 113 N.W. 417 (1907); Laws Wis. 1909, ch. 417, p. 509.

153 E.g., *Connor v. Marshfield*, 128 Wis. 280, 107 N.W. 639 (1906) (municipal acquisition of a waterworks).

154 *Trustees of Dartmouth College v. Woodward*, 4 Wheat. (U.S.) 518, 4 L. Ed. 629 (1819); see C. 3, pp. 133-4.

155 *Smith v. City of Wisconsin Rapids*, 273 Wis. 58, 76 N.W.2d 595 (1956).

156 *Millar v. Jt. School District*, 2 Wis.2d 303, 86 N.W.2d 455 (1957); see *Russell Dairy Stores v. Chippewa Falls*, 272 Wis. 138, 74 N.W.2d 759 (1956) (validity of ordinance revoking a permit to perform highway curb work).

157 *Denning v. City of Green Bay*, 271 Wis. 230, 72 N.W.2d 730 (1955); *Ellerbe & Co. v. City of Hudson*, 1 Wis.2d 148, 83 N.W.2d 700, 85 N.W.2d 663 (1957).

158 *Marshall v. American Express Co.*, 7 Wis. 1 (1858); see *Doty v. Strong*, 1 Pin. 313 (1843).

159 6 Wis. 539 (1858); 11 Wis. 234 (1860).

160 *Wenzel v. Great Northern Railway Co.*, 152 Wis. 418, 140 N.W. 81 (1913); for a variation on the same theme—contract principles versus utility law—in Period III, see *Wisconsin Power & Light Co. v. Berlin Tanning & Manufacturing Co.*, 275 Wis. 554, 83 N.W.2d 147 (1957).

161 9 Exch. 341 (1854).

162 1 Pin. 520 (1845).

163 *Gear v. Bracken*, 1 Pin. 249 (1842).

164 E.g., *Blakesley v. Johnson*, 13 Wis. 530 (1861).

165 See *Clason v. Shepherd*, 10 Wis. 356, 358 (1860). In *La Crosse & Milwaukee Railroad Co. v. Seeger*, 4 Wis. 268 (1855), the court said (with reference to an agreement to arbitrate the amount to be paid by the railroad for taking certain lands) that "when the amount was ascertained, the contract was complete; to be enforced like all other contracts of the kind."

166 Rev. Stats. Wis. 1858, ch. 131, an elaborate statute with twenty-five sections. Note § 2: "No such submission [to arbitration] shall be made respecting the claim of any person to any estate, in fee or for life, to real estate."

167 But see *Schneider v. Reed*, 123 Wis. 488, 101 N.W. 682 (1905) (discussion of an agreement to arbitrate). Chief Justice Winslow, in 1914, remarked that: "We have a complete scheme of arbitration upon our statute books which has been there since the state came into existence, but which is rarely used." John B. Winslow, "Tribunals of Conciliation," *Proceedings, State Bar Association of Wisconsin*, X (1914), 206, 227-8.

168 Julius H. Cohen, *Commercial Arbitration and the Law* (New York, 1928), Appendix H, p. 303; the Milwaukee Chamber of Commerce provided for Boards of Arbitration and set up in essence a private code of procedure, e.g., *Charter and Rules of the Chamber of Commerce of the City of Milwaukee* (bound with the annual report of the Milwaukee Chamber of Commerce, for 1906-1907), Rule VII, § 2, at p. 20, calling for a complaint "in plain language" giving the "substance and particulars" of the demand, and further providing for notice, answer, and appeal (§ 3).

169 In *Bessey v. Minneapolis St. Paul & S.S. R.R. Co.*, 154 Wis. 334, 141 N.W. 244 (1913), young Millard Bessey, seriously injured, signed away for $117 all his rights against the company, after the third visit to the hospital by the claims agent. In *Gustafson v. Whitney Bros. Co.*, 154 Wis. 8, 141 N.W. 1008 (1913), Gustafson was 20 years old; he was injured while driving piles for the company. He had no counsel. He released his claims for $150 after a doctor told him his injuries would not be permanent. His mother could read no English; his father was an employee of the company, afraid of losing his job. The doctor was also an employee.

170 E.g., *Estate of Ansell*, 273 Wis. 189, 77 N.W.2d 422 (1956).

171 E.g., *Estate of Pearce*, 273 Wis. 140, 77 N.W.2d 420 (1956), where a mother went to live at her daughter's home, supposedly promising to make payment for board in her will. In *Estate of Wallace*, 270 Wis. 636, 72 N.W.2d 383 (1955), a sister claimed the fair rental value of the home she and her brother owned as cotenants, but in which he alone resided.

172 *Schwartz v. Schwartz*, 273 Wis. 404, 78 N.W.2d 912 (1956); see, on this point, Wis. Laws 1957, ch. 211.

173 Twelve cases—two in Period I, six in Period II, four in Period III—were classified as miscellaneous. These were cases which further showed how the field of "contract" served to impose superficial order upon what were in fact scattered phenomena. Thus (in Period I) *Murdock v. Kilbourn*, 6 Wis. 468 (1857), arose out of a bet; Murdock bet Shoyer $50 on the result of a gubernatorial election, "Murdock that Barstow is elected, and Shoyer that Bashford is elected." Unfortunately, this was Wisconsin's famous disputed election, so that the winner of the bet was not easy to name. In Period II, we had such oddities as an alleged contract to reconcile an estranged husband and wife, *Kiepert v. Nugent*, 153 Wis. 127, 140 N.W. 1123 (1913). A few other cases in this category arose out of business situations not classifiable elsewhere, e.g., *Brown v. Search*, 131 Wis. 109, 111 N.W. 210 (1907) (a contract to take a course in the "Cream City Business College"); in *Schubert v. Midwest Broadcasting Co.*, 1 Wis.2d 497, 85 N.W.2d 449 (1957), the producer of a show called the "Movie Quick Quiz" licensed the show to a local television broadcaster for a minimum fee of $100 a week.

Chapter III

1 Prof. Harold Shepherd's article, "Contracts in a Prosperity Year," 6 *Stan. L. Rev.* 208 (1954), analyzed doctrine as well as the facts of 500 reported contract cases of 1951. Comparison with the results of this study is less satisfactory than was the case with fact-analysis; the judicial style makes classification of doctrine necessarily more subjective than classification of fact-situations. There are also some unanswered questions in Shepherd's article. Statutes, we are told "appear to be the turning point of decision in 79 or 13.8 per

cent of the cases. Of these, statutes requiring writings head the list with 20 cases" (p. 218). Yet he lists 42 cases arising under the Statute of Frauds alone (p. 223) and most of his 39 "illegality" cases (p. 225) are clearly statutory.

2 *Taylor v. Pratt*, 3 Wis. 674, 692 (1854).

3 See Joseph Chitty, *A Practical Treatise on the Law of Contracts* (5th American ed., Springfield, 1842), p. 9.

4 Theophilus Parsons, *The Law of Contracts*, 2 vols. (4th ed., Boston, 1860), I, 242. For Wisconsin, see, e.g., *Ripley v. Babcock*, 13 Wis. 425 (1861) (lunatic); *International Textbook Co. v. McKone*, 133 Wis. 200, 113 N.W. 438 (1907) (minor).

 A minor's contract, of course, was "voidable" but not "void"; he could ratify it on majority. *Stokes v. Brown*, 3 Pin. 311, 4 Chand. 39 (1851). Another complication was the concept of "necessaries," see *Berg v. U.S. Leather Co.*, 125 Wis. 262, 104 N.W. 60 (1905).

5 Joseph Chitty, *Treatise on the Law of Contracts*, p. 141. "The lenity of the law toward them [minors] is intended for their exclusive benefit in protecting them from the frauds and deceptions which, owing to their weakness and inexperience, others of riper years might be enabled to practice upon them," Dixon, C. J., in *Davies v. Turton*, 13 Wis. 185, 186 (1860).

6 *Wis. Const.* Art. 1, § 15. For the common law rule and its American fate, see James Kent, *Commentaries on American Law*, 4 vols. (2nd ed., New York, II, 1832), 53-70. In some states (not Wisconsin), there were disabilities on the right of Indians to own land, see 1 Rev. Stats. N.Y. 1827-8, Part II, Title I, Art. II, § 12, p. 719.

7 Jt. Res. No. 3, 1860, Wis. Laws 1860, at 422.

8 Married women's rights were an issue quite early in Wisconsin, see Ray A. Brown, "The Making of the Wisconsin Constitution," 1949 *Wis. L. Rev.* 648, 682-4; *Norval v. Rice*, 2 Wis. 22, 31 (1853); Rev. Stats. Wis. 1858, ch. 95, "Of the Rights of Married Women."

 Slavery was forbidden by the Wisconsin Constitution, Art. I, § 2. The slave codes are treated in detail in Henry W. Farnam, *Chapters in the History of Social Legislation in the United States to 1860* (Washington, 1938), pp. 167-210. On the legal status of the free Negro see, for example, John Hope Franklin, *The Free Negro in North Carolina 1790-1860* (Chapel Hill, 1943), pp. 55-120.

9 153 Wis. 583, 587-8, 142 N.W. 264 (1913).

10 The farm-mortgage system was upheld against the charge of *ultra vires* in *Clark v. Farrington*, 11 Wis. 306 (1860); in *Blunt v. Walker*, 11 Wis. 334 (1860), against the charge that the system was a "dealing in real estate"; and see *Rockwell v. Elkhorn Bank*, 13 Wis. 653 (1861), allowing a bank to issue negotiable promissory notes, despite a prohibition against the floating of paper money.

11 Marshall, J., in *Eastman v. Parkinson*, 133 Wis. 375, 381, 113 N.W. 649 (1907); see 6 Bien. Rep. Wis. Att'y Gen. 47 (May 15, 1912) (guarantee of payroll checks by bank is *ultra vires* and void).

12 For example, in *Denning v. Green Bay*, 271 Wis. 230, 72 N.W.2d 730 (1955), concerning a bond issue for water supply purposes, the Supreme Court puzzled through six distinct statutory enactments, overlapping and interrelated, in the course of a six-page opinion.

13 Theophilus Parsons, *Law of Contracts*, p. 399.

14 "Preliminary negotiations": see *J. L. Gates Land Co. v. Ostrander*, 124 Wis. 287, 102 N.W. 558 (1905); *Abrohams v. Revillon Freres*, 129 Wis. 235, 107 N.W. 656 (1906). "Counter-offer" as opposed to "acceptance": *Cram v. Long*, 154 Wis. 13, 142 N.W. 267 (1913).

15 "[T]he words and acts of the parties are themselves the basis of contractual liability, and not merely evidence of a mental attitude required by the law.... [An] expression of mutual

assent, and not the assent itself, is the essential element of contractual liability." Samuel Williston, "Mutual Assent in the Formation of Contracts," 14 *Ill. L. Rev.* 85, 87 (1919); on the "objective theory" see further Arthur L. Corbin, *Contracts* (1 vol. ed., St. Paul, 1952), pp. 154-7, 509-12; Frank, J., concurring in *Ricketts v. Pennsylvania R.R. Co.*, 153 Fed.2d 757 (C.C.A.2d, 1946).

[16] E.g., *Manufacturers & Merchants Inspection Bureau v. Everwear Hosiery Co.*, 152 Wis. 73, 138 N.W. 624 (1913). A letter referred to a "verbal agreement"; evidence of the nature of this agreement could have been excluded both because of the parol evidence rule and because of "acceptance" of the written formulation in the letter.

[17] Good examples are *Phillips Petroleum Co. v. Taggart*, 271 Wis. 261, 73 N.W.2d 482 (1955), and *Nelsen v. Farmers Mutual Auto Insurance Co.*, 4 Wis.2d 36, 90 N.W.2d 123 (1958).

[18] 127 Wis. 382, 105 N.W. 1067 (1906) (one party made no specific promise; thus contract allegedly one-sided); see also *Whitman v. Milwaukee Fire Ins. Co.*, 128 Wis. 124, 107 N.W. 291 (1906) (oral insurance contract; no agreement as to when the insurance should begin to take effect); *Burstein v. Phillips*, 154 Wis. 591, 143 N.W. 679 (1913) (price uncertainty in mercantile contract).

[19] 131 Wis. 216, 109 N.W. 983 (1907).

[20] The doctrine was successfully invoked in *Batavian National Bank of La Crosse v. S. & H. Inc.*, 3 Wis.2d 565, 89 N.W.2d 309 (1958). A partial success was *Larson v. Superior Auto Parts, Inc.*, 270 Wis. 613, 72 N.W.2d 316 (1955). A corporate buy-sell agreement in a small corporation could not be enforced against one party by virtue of a statute voiding such restrictions unless appearing on the face of the certificate. This made the promise one-sided. But the court granted relief on other grounds. In addition, there are cases in which one party or another made much of "mutuality," only to be totally ignored by the court. See *Scherg v. Puetz*, 269 Wis. 561, 69 N.W.2d 490 (1955), *Cases and Briefs*, "Appellant's Brief," Appendix, 113.

The court found fatal "indefiniteness" in *Wagner v. Falbe & Company*, 272 Wis. 25, 74 N.W.2d 742 (1956), an action based on an agent's supposed promise to procure fire insurance.

[21] E.g., *Nelsen v. Farmers Mutual Automobile Ins. Co.*, 4 Wis.2d 36, 90 N.W.2d 123 (1958).

[22] But Wisconsin was rather less likely, perhaps, than most jurisdictions to enforce a requirements contract. See *Hoffmann v. Pfingsten*, 260 Wis. 160, 50 N.W.2d 369 (1951). The business in this case was new, however; no established standard provided by experience could give content to the concept of "requirements." Cf. *Schlegel Manufacturing Co. v. Cooper's Glue Factory*, 231 N.Y. 459, 132 N.E. 148 (1921). See Uniform Commercial Code, § 2-306.

The "open price" contract, too, has now generally been recognized, *A. M. Webb & Co. v. Robert P. Miller Co.*, 157 F.2d 865 (C.A. 3, 1946); Uniform Sales Act, § 9, § 10; Uniform Commercial Code, § 2-305. See, in general, William L. Prosser, "Open Price in Contracts for the Sale of Goods," 16 *Minn. Law Rev.* 733 (1932).

[23] On the essential nature of consideration, see Theophilus Parsons, *Law of Contracts*, p. 415; Joseph Chitty, *Treatise on the Law of Contracts*, pp. 26-27; Theodore F. T. Plucknett, *A Concise History of the Common Law* (5th ed., Boston, 1956), pp. 649-51; *Messenger v. Miller*, 2 Pin. 60 (1847); *Eycleshimer v. Van Antwerp*, 13 Wis. 546 (1861).

[24] J. Willard Hurst, *Law and the Conditions of Freedom in the Nineteenth-Century United States* (Madison, 1956), p. 11.

[25] *Sir Anthony Sturlyn v. Albany*, Cro. Eliz. 67 (K.B. 1587).

[26] *Messenger v. Miller*, 2 Pin. 60, 64 (1847); see *Bowen v. Burnett*, 1 Pin. 658 (1846)

(unentered though improved claim is not an asset in the hands of an executor).

[27] 132 Wis. 549, 112 N.W. 508 (1907).

[28] The three cases are, respectively, *Rosenheimer v. Krenn*, 126 Wis. 617, 106 N.W. 20 (1906); *Quinn v. Quinn*, 130 Wis. 548, 110 N.W. 488 (1907); *Moore v. Michaelson*, 152 Wis. 352, 140 N.W. 28 (1913).

Two other technical uses of the doctrine of consideration in Period II are worth mentioning: first, the convenient technique of holding that an "unauthorized" act (e.g., by an agent) was not supported by the requisite consideration, e.g., *Pelton v. Spider Lake Sawmill & Lumber Company*, 132 Wis. 219, 112 N.W. 29 (1907); and the ingenious distinction between "modification" of a contract, without consideration, and "rescission" followed by a fresh contract, *Sherry v. Madler*, 123 Wis. 621, 101 N.W. 1095 (1905); *Aebi v. Bank of Evansville*, 124 Wis. 73, 102 N.W. 329 (1905).

In Period III, *Estate of Kandall*, 270 Wis. 349, 71 N.W.2d 283 (1955); *Estate of Gerke*, 271 Wis. 297, 73 N.W.2d 506 (1955), noted 40 *Marq. L. Rev.* 345 (1957), raised the issue of "moral consideration." Wisconsin has been somewhat more permissive toward this than most jurisdictions. *Park Falls State Bank v. Fordyce*, 206 Wis. 628, 238 N.W. 516 (1932), began a line of cases which certainly looks in that direction, though never conclusively. See William H. Page, "Consideration: Genuine and Synthetic," 1947 *Wis. L. Rev.* 483, 498-9.

The use of the doctrine of consideration as technical make-weight continued in Period III. See *Perry v. Riske*, 2 Wis.2d 377, 86 N.W.2d 429 (1957). *State v. Laven*, 270 Wis. 524, 71 N.W.2d 287 (1955), voided, as contrary to *Wis. Const.* Art. IV, § 24 (forbidding lotteries), a statute which provided that no radio or television show would be considered a lottery unless participants provided "consideration," consisting either of "the payment of money" or "an expenditure of substantial effort or time." "Mere technical contract consideration shall not be sufficient. Listening to a radio, or listening to and watching a television show shall not be deemed consideration given or received." Laws Wis. 1951, ch. 463. The *Laven* case was cited in 44 *Ops. Wis. Att'y Gen.* 268 (Oct. 7, 1955), ruling that a local radio show, "Let's Quiz the Mrs.," was a lottery.

[29] *Williams v. Starr*, 5 Wis. 534, 549 (1856); Rev. Stats. Wis. 1849, ch. 55, § 4; see *Woolsey v. Henke*, 125 Wis. 134, 103 N.W. 267 (1905).

[30] Wisconsin passed such an act very early, Wis. Terr. Laws 1839-40, No. 8, "An Act to provide for recording contracts relating to lands, and for other purposes." On the antiquity of American recording acts, see Mark DeWolfe Howe, "The Recording of Deeds in the Colony of Massachusetts Bay," 28 *Boston U.L. Rev.* 1 (1948); George L. Haskins, "The Beginnings of the Recording System in Massachusetts," 21 *Boston U.L. Rev.* 281 (1941).

[31] The original statute was 29 Charles II, c. 3, § 4, § 17 (1677); it has been repealed in England, but only within this century. For the Statute of Frauds as it existed in Period I, see Rev. Stats. Wis. 1858, ch. 106, § 6, § 8, ch. 107, § 2, § 3. The modern version is found in Wis. Stats. § 240.06, § 240.08, § 241.02 (1961). The "sale of goods" provision is Wis. Stats. § 121.04 (1961) (part of the Uniform Sales Act). The special brokers' provision is Wis. Stats. § 240.10 (1961). For the history of this provision, see C. 2, p. 50.

[32] *Day v. Elmore*, 4 Wis. 190, 193 (1855).

[33] Hubbell, J., in *Hardell v. McClure*, 2 Pin. 289, 293, 1 Chand. 271 (1849); see Dixon's remarks in *Fairchild v. Rasdall*, 9 Wis. 379, 380 (1859).

[34] *Korrer v. Madden*, 152 Wis. 646, 653, 140 N.W. 325 (1913); see the remarks of Marshall, J., in *Rowell v. Smith*, 123 Wis. 510, 526, 102 N.W.1 (1905); and of Dodge, J., in *McCord v. Edw. Hines Lumber Co.*, 124 Wis. 509, 512, 102 N.W. 334 (1905).

[35] The application of the Statute was refused in *Wiger v. Carr*, 131 Wis. 584, 111 N.W. 657 (1907); see also *Knauf & Tesch Co. v. Elkhart Lake Sand & Gravel Co.*, 153 Wis. 306, 141 N.W. 701 (1913); *McCord v. Edward Hines Lumber Co.*, 124 Wis. 509, 102 N.W. 334

(1905).

[36] To a limited degree, the stringent text of the Wisconsin Statute (borrowed from the New York version) tended to facilitate rigorous application. Wisconsin required, for example, that the "consideration" be expressed in writing in contracts "not to be performed within one year" and promises "to answer for the debt, default, or miscarriage of another person," Rev. Stats. Wis. 1858, ch. 107, § 2; the original Statute did not. In *Taylor v. Pratt*, 3 Wis. 674 (1854), this enabled the court to hold a *written* guaranty of a promissory note to be within the Statute. See, however, *Day v. Elmore*, 4 Wis. 190 (1855), which held that the words "for value received" were enough to satisfy the Statute.

The Period I cases were unevenly distributed throughout the period: 7 of the 19 cases appeared in the 3 volumes of *Pinney's Reports* Possibly this was because the Statute had not "received a judicial construction in the Supreme Court of Wisconsin," its questions being therefore "open" and subject to "careful scrutiny." Hubbell, J., in *Hardell v. McClure*, 2 Pin. 289, 292, 1 Chand. 271 (1849).

In Period II, there were only five clear cases arising under the "debt, default, or miscarriage" provision; in Period III, only one or two. Some cases invoked more than one section and make it difficult to attain an accurate count.

For a good example of the use of the Statute in cases of imperfect business rationalization see, e.g., *Scheuer v. Cochem*, 126 Wis. 209, 105 N.W. 573 (1905).

[37] *Cooper v. Tappan*, 4 Wis. 362, 369 (1855); see the remarks of Cole, J., in *Heath v. Van Cott*, 9 Wis. 516, 522 (1859), and of Chief Justice Whiton in *Reed v. Jones*, 8 Wis. 392, 413 (1855); Chitty, *Treatise on the Law of Contracts*, p. 99.

[38] Arthur L. Corbin, "The Parol Evidence Rule," 53 *Yale L. J.* 603, 609 (1944). On the relationship between the parol evidence rule and the "objective theory" of contracts, see Samuel Williston, *The Law of Contracts* (New York, 1920), I, 20-1; Frank, J., in *Zell v. American Seating Company*, 138 F.2d 641 (C.C.A.2d 1943).

[39] E.g., *Root v. Pinney*, 11 Wis. 84 (1860); see *Wood v. Lake*, 13 Wis. 84 (1860).

[40] 12 Wis. 176 (1860).

[41] See Introduction, pp. 5-7.

[42] Fairly clear uses of the rule included *Kruse v. Koelzer*, 124 Wis. 536, 102 N.W. 1072 (1905) (land contract); *Mohlzahn v. Christensen*, 152 Wis. 520, 139 N.W. 429 (1913) (construction contract; evidence of "preliminary negotiations" excluded).

[43] *Pratt v. Darling*, 125 Wis. 93, 103 N.W. 229 (1905). The rule concerning conditions precedent: *Golden v. Meier*, 129 Wis. 14, 107 N.W. 27 (1906); but see *Foster v. Lowe*, 131 Wis. 54, 110 N.W. 829 (1907). The "instrument never had vitality as a contract": *Hodge v. Smith*, 130 Wis. 326, 110 N.W. 192 (1907) (one of the stallion cases); parol evidence admissible to show an illegal scheme: *Twentieth Century Co. v. Quilling*, 130 Wis. 318, 110 N.W. 174 (1907); *Manufacturers & Merchants Inspection Bureau v. Everwear Hosiery Co.*, 152 Wis. 73, 138 N.W. 624 (1913); parol evidence admissible to avoid injustice or fraud: *Jost v. Wolf*, 130 Wis. 37, 110 N.W. 232 (1906); documents treated as "cumulative": *Security Trust & Life Ins. Co. v. Ellsworth*, 129 Wis. 349, 109 N.W. 125 (1906); "modification" of an agreement: see *Wisconsin Sulphite Fibre Co. v. D. K. Jeffris Lumber Co.*, 132 Wis. 1, 111 N.W. 237 (1907); *Morehouse v. Voight*, 151 Wis. 580, 139 N.W. 423 (1913).

The manifold exceptions to the parol evidence rule were in use in Period III, e.g., such evidence was admissible to show fraud in the inducement: *Anderson v. Tri-State Home Improvement Co.*, 268 Wis. 455, 67 N.W.2d 853 (1955). Parol evidence does not bar unmasking underlying contract of questionable legality: *Albrent v. Spencer*, 275 Wis. 127, 81 N.W.2d 555 (1957); and, with a slightly different twist, the sequel to this case, 3 Wis.2d 273, 88 N.W.2d 333 (1958).

[44] *Berger v. Alan Realty Co.*, 273 Wis. 427, 78 N.W.2d 747 (1956). *Cernohorsky v. North-*

ern Liquid Gas Co., 268 Wis. 586, 68 N.W.2d 429 (1955), was another example of the "plain meaning" rule. The counter-rule allowed parol evidence if necessary to cure "ambiguity." *Georgiades v. Glickman*, 272 Wis. 257, 75 N.W.2d 573 (1956).

45 Cole, J., in *Heath v. Van Cott*, 9 Wis. 516, 522 (1859); Dixon, C. J., in *Clason v. Shepherd*, 10 Wis. 356, 358 (1860).

46 The maxim was quoted in *Chynoweth v. Tenney*, 10 Wis. 397 (1860), in connection with an attempted mortgage of after-acquired property.

47 11 Wis. 146 (1860); see also *Kilbourn v. Pacific Bank*, 11 Wis. 230 (1860).

48 3 Pin. 220, 3 Chand. 243 (1851). See also *Miner v. Medbury*, 6 Wis. 295 (1858); *Bowman v. Page*, 11 Wis. 301 (1860).

49 131 Wis. 109, 111 N.W. 210 (1907).

50 See *Krueger v. Buel*, 153 Wis. 583, 142 N.W. 264 (1913), and *Leonard v. Prudential Insurance Co. of America*, 128 Wis. 348, 107 N.W. 646 (1906).

51 123 Wis. 627, 101 N.W. 1092 (1905).

52 124 Wis. 536, 102 N.W. 1072 (1905).

53 128 Wis. 375, 107 N.W. 662 (1906).

54 130 Wis. 485, 110 N.W. 401 (1907).

55 133 Wis. 485, 113 N.W. 977 (1907). See also *Knauf & Tesch Co. v. Elkhart Lake Sand & Gravel Co.*, 153 Wis. 306, 141 N.W. 701 (1913).
   The court accepted, as a verbal formula at least, the standard view that documents could be reformed for mutual mistake of fact, *Scheuer v. Chloupek*, 130 Wis. 72, 109 N.W. 1035 (1906), but not of law, *Rowell v. Smith*, 123 Wis. 510, 102 N.W. 1 (1905).

56 See *W. H. Hobbs Supply Co. v. Ernst*, 270 Wis. 166, 70 N.W.2d 615 (1955) and *Sweeney v. Stenjem*, 271 Wis. 497, 74 N.W.2d 174 (1956). Compare *Estate of Draheim*, 273 Wis. 189, 77 N.W.2d 422 (1956), in which the court "inferred" a "fraud upon the court"; *Polley v. Boehck Equipment Co.*, 273 Wis. 432, 78 N.W.2d 737 (1956).
   On reformation for mistake in Period III, contrast *Center Street Fuel Co. v. Hanover Fire Ins. Co.*, 272 Wis. 370, 75 N.W.2d 462 (1956) with *Estate of Seefeldt*, 275 Wis.2d 509, 85 N.W.2d 500 (1957), where even unilateral mistake was grounds for relief of a fiduciary. Again, *Stadele v. Resnick*, 274 Wis. 346, 80 N.W.2d 272 (1957), excusing a simple farmer from failure to read, contrasts with *Institute of Commercial Art v. Maurice*, 272 Wis. 499, 76 N.W.2d 332 (1956), where the court found "ample opportunity" to read the contract and refused to excuse failure to do so.
   Duress was a rare defense. Only two cases were of any significance, *Brown v. Peck*, 2 Wis. 261 (1853), discussed in the Introduction, pp. 3-5, and *Roelvink v. City of Milwaukee*, 273 Wis. 605, 79 N.W.2d 106 (1956).

57 Chitty, *Treatise on the Law of Contracts*, p. 450; see *Getty v. Rountree*, 2 Pin. 379, 2 Chand. 28 (1850) (manufactured goods); *Bird v. Mayer*, 8 Wis. 362 (1859) (varnish for carriages).

58 *Kuehn v. Wilson*, 13 Wis. 104 (1860); see *Fisk v. Tank*, 12 Wis. 276 (1860) (installation of boiler); *Butler v. Titus*, 13 Wis. 429 (1860) (installation of water-wheel); *Reynolds v. Graves*, 3 Wis. 416 (1854) (doctor's undertaking to cure a patient).

59 *Lane v. Romer*, 2 Pin. 404 (1850); see *Hurd v. Hall*, 12 Wis. 112 (1860).

60 1850 *Calif. Senate Journal*, Appendix "O," at 468 (report of Committee of Judiciary on whether the common or the civil law system should be adopted in California); see 1 *Western Journal* 199, 201 (St. Louis, 1848), expressing a similar idea.

61 13 Wis. 600, 602 (1861); compare the well-known English case of *Jones v. Bright*, 5

Bing. 533 (Exch. 1829).

⁶² *McFarland v. Newman*, 9 Watts 55 (Pa. 1839).

⁶³ 9 Exch. 341 (1859).

⁶⁴ 152 Wis. 570, 140 N.W. 292 (1913); *Hasbrouck v. Armour*, 139 Wis. 357, 121 N.W. 157 (1909), a negligence case (in which a bar of soap was sold with a needle imbedded in it), prepared the way. See *Ketterer v. Armour & Co.*, 200 Fed. 322, 323 (D.C. N.Y. 1912): "The remedies of injured consumers ought not to be made to depend upon the intricacies of the law of sales. The obligation of the manufacturer should not be based alone upon privity of contract. It should rest ... upon 'the demands of social justice.' "; Lindsey R. Jeanblanc, "Manufacturers' Liability to Persons Other Than Their Immediate Vendees," 24 *Va. L. Rev.* 134 (1937); notice the partial relaxation of the privity doctrine in Uniform Commercial Code, § 2-318.

⁶⁵ Theophilus Parsons, *Law of Contracts*, II, 7.

⁶⁶ Spencer L. Kimball, *Insurance and Public Policy* (Madison, 1960), p. 211.

⁶⁷ *Edwards v. Wisconsin Investment Co.*, 124 Wis. 315, 102 N.W. 575 (1905); *Rief v. Continental Casualty Co.*, 131 Wis. 368, 111 N.W. 502 (1907).

⁶⁸ E.g., "a modifying clause is ordinarily to be confined to the last antecedent," quoted (and not followed) in *Georgiades v. Glickman*, 272 Wis. 257, 75 N.W.2d 573 (1956). See *Johnson v. Green Bay Packers, Inc.*, 272 Wis. 149, 74 N.W.2d 784 (1956) (written provisions prevail over printed provision).

⁶⁹ On the rule requiring strict construction of insurance policies against the insurer, see *Kaiser v. Prudential Insurance Co. of America*, 272 Wis. 527, 76 N.W.2d 311 (1956); *Matteson v. Johnson*, 275 Wis. 615, 82 N.W.2d 881 (1957). See also *Jeske v. General Accident Fire & Life Assurance Corp.*, 1 Wis.2d 70, 78-9, 83 N.W.2d 167 (1957): "to justify reformation the evidence must be clear and convincing ... [but] a distinction is made between ordinary contracts and contracts of insurance, and less is required in cases dealing with the latter." As applied to corporate suretyship companies, see *Knuth v. Fidelity & Cas. Co. of N.Y.*, 275 Wis. 603, 607, 83 N.W.2d 126 (1957).

A particular kind of fact-analysis concerns legal doctrines of custom and usage, and these doctrines had an especial impact in Period I. Actually, "custom" was a double concept, referring either to usages "ancient and universal, and perfectly established," Theophilus Parsons, *Law of Contracts*, II, 53, *Lee v. Merrick*, 8 Wis. 229, 234 (1859); or to nothing more than current business practice: of land-agents and brokers, *Pfeil v. Kemper*, 3 Wis. 315 (1854); *Power v. Kane*, 5 Wis. 265 (1856); banks, *Stacy v. Dane County Bank*, 12 Wis. 629 (1860); dock procedure in Milwaukee, *Steamboat Sultana v. Chapman*, 5 Wis. 454 (1856); and the like. In this sense, custom was simply another way of allocating contractual risks in terms of reasonable market expectations. But when the court says that proof of usage "must be clear and explicit," and "so well established, uniform, and so notorious that the parties must be presumed to know it, and to have contracted in reference to it," *Power v. Kane*, 5 Wis. 265, 268-9 (1856); see *Whitney v. Tibbitts*, 17 Wis. 359 (1863), the court is employing a muffled policy rule disguised as a rule of evidence; and the muffled policy rule in question is related to the concept of assent, so central to the work of the court in Period I.

⁷⁰ 5 Wis. 125 (1856).

⁷¹ The cases are, respectively, *Kingston v. Preston*, 2 Doug. 684 (K.B. 1772); *Powers v. Ware*, 2 Pick. (19 Mass.) 451 (1824); *Barruso v. Madan*, 2 John. Rep. 148 (1813); *Cunningham v. Morrell*, 10 John. Rep. 203 (1813). I have been unable to discover any trace of "*Smith v. Woodhouse*, 2 Penn. R. 240," the fifth case cited.

⁷² *Collins v. Schmidt*, 126 Wis. 227, 105 N.W. 671 (1905); cf. *James v. Knox*, 155 Wis. 118,

143 N.W. 1071 (1913); *Foster v. Lowe*, 131 Wis. 54, 110 N.W. 829 (1907). See also *Auer v. Vahl*, 129 Wis. 635, 109 N.W. 529 (1906), another case of "independent covenants."

[73] 132 Wis. 1, 111 N.W. 237 (1907).

[74] *Halsey v. Waukesha Springs Sanitarium Co.*, 125 Wis. 311, 104 N.W. 94 (1905).

On the use of American Institute of Architects standard contract forms in the field of private construction, see Harold C. Havighurst, *The Nature of Private Contract* (Evanston, 1961), p. 97; on Builders' Risk Insurance Policies, see Stewart Macaulay, *Supplement to Kessler and Sharp "Contracts Cases and Materials"* (Mimeo., 1963), pp. 109-10.

[75] *Manthey v. Stock*, 133 Wis. 107, 113 N.W. 443 (1907); *Manning v. School District No. 6 of Fort Atkinson*, 124 Wis. 84, 102 N.W. 356 (1905). On substantial performance, see the opinion of Cardozo, J., in the famous case of *Jacob & Youngs v. Kent*, 230 N.Y. 239, 129 N.E. 889 (1921).

In some cases, of course, performance was clearly substantial or, conversely, clearly not. See *Whalen v. Eagle Lime Products Co.*, 155 Wis. 26, 143 N.W. 689 (1913).

[76] See *Lindenmann v. Kopczynski*, 155 Wis. 164, 144 N.W. 196 (1913); *Cawker v. Trimmel*, 155 Wis. 108, 143 N.W. 1046 (1913).

[77] Period III more explicitly made "motivation" for breach a factor to consider. *Restatement, Contracts*, § 275 (e) lists "wilful, negligent or innocent behavior of the party failing to perform" as an "influential" circumstance in determining the materiality of a failure to perform. See also *Wm. G. Tannhaeuser Co. v. Holiday House, Inc.*, 1 Wis.2d 370, 83 N.W.2d 880 (1957); *George v. Oswald*, 273 Wis. 380, 78 N.W.2d 763 (1956).

Over the last century, the concept of impossibility as a defense to breach of contract has been extensively developed. In classic common law theory, impossibility of performance was no defense. This rule weakened in the nineteenth century, if it did not altogether disappear. The development may be related to the rise of the doctrine of substantial performance. Technological advance and increasing complexity of contractual arrangements often multiplied the hazards to performance. The increasing judicial concern with "fairness," and the increasing response to assertion of "personal" equities, also led away from the strict view of impossibility. This development found little reflection in the Wisconsin cases of the three periods. The tabulation shows few cases of impossibility; in the few examples found, the concept was used chiefly metaphorically, e.g., *Estate of Zellmer*, 1 Wis.2d 46, 82 N.W.2d 891 (1957), noted 41 *Marq. L. Rev.* 314 (1957). See further *Restatement, Contracts*, §§ 454-7; Arthur L. Corbin, "Recent Developments in the Law of Contracts," 50 *Harv. L. Rev.* 449, 464-6 (1937).

[78] Samuel Williston, *Cases on the Law of Contracts*, ed., William Laube (6th ed., Boston, 1954), pp. 449-87; Christopher C. Langdell, *A Summary of the Law of Contracts* (2nd ed., Boston, 1880), p. 101. Further evidence, if any is needed, comes from the fact that student treatises and abridgments of larger works on contracts omit entirely or virtually entirely any material on illegality. See Samuel Williston and George J. Thompson, *Selections from Williston's Treatise on the Law of Contracts* (Rev. ed., New York, 1938), p. 15. Practically speaking, the only real treatment of this vast subject is found on this one page of this work "Printed especially for the use of Law Students."

[79] On the importance of the usury laws, Lawrence M. Friedman, "The Usury Laws of Wisconsin: a Study in Legal and Social History," 1963 *Wis. L. Rev.* 515. There was one case of the foreign corporation defense in Period I, *Aetna Insurance Co. v. Harvey*, 11 Wis. 412 (1860).

[80] Statutory cases in Period I (aside from the usury cases) included cases arising under the Sunday laws, e.g., *Hill v. Sherwood*, 3 Wis. 343 (1854), and under a territorial law forbidding the credit sale of liquor, e.g., *Bird v. Fake*, 1 Pin. 290 (1843). Judge-made policy: e.g., *Fay v. Oatley*, 6 Wis. 42 (1857) (perversion of legal process); *Murdock v. Kilbourn*, 6 Wis. 468 (1857) (wagering contract); *Bryan v. Reynolds*, 5 Wis. 200 (1856) (lobbying contract).

81 *Carson v. Milwaukee Produce Co.*, 133 Wis. 85, 113 N.W. 393 (1907). A more conventional "gambling" case was *Clark v. Slaughter*, 129 Wis. 642, 109 N.W. 556 (1906). See, in Period III, *Albrent v. Spencer*, 275 Wis. 127, 81 N.W.2d 555 (1957) (speculative transfer of life insurance policies).

82 *Twentieth Century Co. v. Quilling*, 130 Wis. 318, 110 N.W. 174 (1907).

83 3 Pin. 123 (1851).

84 *McKinley Telephone Co. v. Cumberland Telephone Co.*, 152 Wis. 359, 140 N.W. 38 (1913). The other cases: *Cottington v. Swan*, 128 Wis. 321, 107 N.W. 336 (1906); *My Laundry Co. v. Schmeling*, 129 Wis. 597, 109 N.W. 540 (1906); *Kradwell v. Thiesen*, 131 Wis. 97, 111 N.W. 233 (1907); *Ruhland v. King*, 154 Wis. 545, 143 N.W. 681 (1913). *Ruhland* was the only case which found the covenant to be unreasonable; the covenant, in a deed for tavern property, provided that only one brand of beer could be sold on the premises.

85 270 Wis. 133, 135-6, 70 N.W.2d 585 (1955); same case, 274 Wis. 478, 80 N.W.2d 461 (1957). None of the cases cited in *Fullerton* held squarely that ten years was too long for a covenant of the type in issue. The court *could* have held that ten years was not too long, under the circumstances of the case, and given Fullerton relief without upsetting either the dissenting judges or accepted Wisconsin doctrine.

Torborg claimed he understood ten years to be an illegally long period; in the light of this claim, the record in *Maslow Cooperage Corp. v. Weeks Pickle Co.*, 270 Wis. 179, 70 N.W.2d 577 (1955), is interesting. This was a warranty case, which had nothing to do with covenants. Incidentally, however, the record shows that Weeks had, in 1950, sold his pickle company, executing a ten-year covenant not to compete. He breached the covenant in 1953; was enjoined; and thenceforth ran the business through members of his family, *Cases and Briefs*, "Plaintiff's Brief," 6-7. This leads one to wonder how frequent was the ten-year covenant, how often was it enforced, and how effective was the enforcement? Laws Wis. 1957, ch. 444, overturned the result of *Fullerton*.

86 *Fullerton Lumber Co. v. Torborg*, 270 Wis. 133, 148, 70 N.W.2d 585 (1955).

87 See *S. F. Bowser & Co. v. Schwartz*, 152 Wis. 408, 140 N.W. 51 (1913) (interstate commerce); *Greek-American Sponge Co. v. Richardson Drug Co.*, 124 Wis. 469, 102 N.W. 888 (1905) (original package doctrine); *Presbyterian Ministers' Fund v. Thomas*, 126 Wis. 281, 105 N.W. 801 (1905) (discussing and refusing to apply the doctrine of "comity.").

88 270 Wis. 157, 70 N.W.2d 652 (1955).

89 E.g., Harlan F. Stone, "The Common Law in the United States," 50 *Harv. L. Rev.* 4, 13-16 (1936); Roscoe Pound, "Common Law and Legislation," 21 *Harv. L. Rev.* 383, 385 (1908).

90 270 Wis. 488, 71 N.W.2d 420 (1955). The statute construed is Wis. Stats. § 218.01(3) (a) 17 (1961).

The brief statement in the text hardly does justice to the difficulties of the case. The assumption that the statute was not meant to say all that was to be said on the subject may be incorrect. Compare, for example, the much more explicit provision [Wis. Stats. § 218.01 (2) (h) (1961)] on the licensing of auto dealers, authorizing the bonding of certain dealers "as indemnity for any loss sustained by any person by reason of any acts of the licensee constituting grounds for suspension.... The bonds shall be executed in the name of the state for the benefit of any aggrieved parties." The court was both willing and able to construe this statute broadly, see *State ex rel. MacNaughton v. New Amsterdam Cas. Co.*, 1 Wis.2d 494, 85 N.W.2d 337 (1957).

91 273 Wis. 64, 76 N.W.2d 537 (1956). See *Alan Realty Co. v. Fair Deal Investment Co.*, 271 Wis. 336, 73 N.W.2d 517 (1955). The contract called for the purchase of 200 lots in a subdivision. Defendant agreed to have the tract annexed to Milwaukee, and to secure final approval and recording of the plat. Plaintiff backed out, declared the contract void, and asked for return of down payments, relying on a statute forbidding sale of subdivision land

until final recording of a plat. But the contract, said the court, was "in harmony with the legislative purpose of orderly urban development," and "expressly avoided just what the statute was designed to prevent."

In *Metz v. Medford Fur Foods*, 4 Wis.2d 96, 90 N.W.2d 106 (1958), *Kuhl* rather than *Chapman* was followed, in a case arising under Wis. Stats. § 94.72 (14) (b) (1961), on adulterated livestock feed. See also *Ebenreiter v. Freeman*, 274 Wis. 290, 79 N.W.2d 649 (1956).

[92] "[T]hough the law does not admit an assignment of a chose in action, this court does." Lord Chancellor Hardwicke in *Row v. Dawson*, 1 Ves. Sr. 331 (1749).

[93] See *Parkinson v. McKim*, 1 Pin. 214 (1842).

[94] Wisconsin's adoption took place in 1856, Laws Wis. 1856, ch. 120. For a brief summary of the early progress of the Field Code, see Robert W. Millar, *Civil Procedure of the Trial Court in Historical Perspective* (New York, 1952), pp. 52-5.

[95] *Downie v. Hoover*, 12 Wis. 174, 175 (1860); see also *Rockwell v. Daniels*, 4 Wis. 432 (1855) (assignment of subscription for building a flour mill). On assignments to attorneys, see *Strong v. Catton*, 1 Wis. 471, 492 (1853); *Minert v. Emerick*, 6 Wis. 355 (1858).

[96] 1 Pin. 563 (1845); on military bounty lands, see *Nichols v. Nichols*, 3 Pin. 174, 3 Chand. 189 (1851). Material on the system can be found in standard histories of the public domain, such as Benjamin H. Hibbard, A *History of the Public Land Policies* (New York, 1924).

[97] 7 Wis. 582, 594 (1859); Seymour D. Thompson, A *Treatise on Homestead and Exemption Laws* (San Francisco, 1886), pp. 384ff.

The legislature passed an act in 1859, allowing multiple lien claimants to assign their claims to one of their number for purposes of suit, Laws Wis. 1859, ch. 113, § 2. The court in *Caldwell v. Lawrence*, 10 Wis. 331, 332 (1860), referred to this statute, but held that it showed "that a special provision was considered necessary to enable any assignee to have such benefit, and implies that no other assignee is entitled to it now."

[98] Note the comments of Marshall, J., dissenting in *Canterbury v. Northwestern Mutual Life Insurance Company*, 124 Wis. 169, 196, 102 N.W. 1096 (1905); *Boehmer v. Kalk*, 155 Wis. 156, 144 N.W. 182 (1913); Rev. Stats. Wis. 1858, ch. 95, § 5.

[99] On the spendthrift trust, see Lawrence M. Friedman, "The Dynastic Trust," 73 Yale L. J. 547 (1964); *Broadway National Bank v. Adams*, 133 Mass. 170 (1882); in general, Erwin N. Griswold, *Spendthrift Trusts* (2d. ed., New York, 1947).

The restrictive covenant, historical precursor of the zoning laws, attempted to protect land values from damages brought about by environmental change—change inevitable in a system where land interests were freely assignable. The English case of *Tulk v. Moxhay*, 2 Phil. 774 (Ch. 1848), opened the door to enforcement of restrictive covenants by interested neighbors; the influence of the case soon spanned the Atlantic.

[100] See, for example, Laws Wis. 1861, ch. 88, § 5, providing that a defense of fraud in farm-mortgage cases raised a presumption that the plaintiff had "full notice" of "all equities."

[101] On the school land certificates: Rev. Stats. Wis. 1849, ch. 24, § 22; *Smith v. Clarke*, 7 Wis. 551 (1858); *Whitney v. State Bank*, 7 Wis. 620 (1858); *Mowry v. Wood*, 12 Wis. 413 (1860); *Dodge v. Silverthorn*, 12 Wis. 644 (1860); Joseph Schafer, "Wisconsin's Farm Loan Law, 1849-1863," in *Proceedings of the State Historical Society of Wisconsin, 1920* (Madison, 1921), p. 156.

[102] *Lawrence v. Fox*, 20 N.Y. 268 (1859). Dictum in *Hodson v. Carter*, 3 Pin. 212, 3 Chand. 234 (1851), seemed to foreshadow this case, but went unnoticed; see William H. Page, "Beneficiary Contracts in Wisconsin," 1 *Wis. L. Rev.* 216, 217ff. (1921).

[103] 127 Wis. 135, 106 N.W. 391 (1906); see also *Connor v. City of Marshfield*, 128 Wis. 280, 107 N.W. 639 (1906). For a less attenuated use of the doctrine, see, e.g., *Smith v. Pfluger*,

126 Wis. 253, 105 N.W. 476 (1905).

104 The union case: *Pattenge v. Wagner Iron Works*, 275 Wis. 295, 82 N.W.2d 172 (1957); compare *Wonder-Rest Corp. v. Galina*, 275 Wis. 273, 81 N.W.2d 512 (1957); the sub-contractor case: *Knuth v. Fidelity & Cas. Co. of N.Y.*, 275 Wis. 603, 83 N.W.2d 126 (1957); *Hribar v. Johnson*, 275 Wis. 610, 83 N.W.2d 130 (1957); the joint savings account: *Kelberger v. First Federal Savings & Loan Association*, 270 Wis. 434, 71 N.W.2d 257 (1955); see also *Schwartz v. Schwartz*, 273 Wis. 404, 78 N.W.2d 912 (1956) (beneficiaries of joint will as third-party beneficiaries).

105 Many other legal problems were related to questions of the identity of the parties. For example, it was sometimes a defense to argue that the proper defendant had not been chosen in an action. Thus (taking Period II cases as examples), in *Vader v. Ballou*, 151 Wis. 577, 139 N.W. 413 (1913), the problem was whether one member of an electoral campaign committee could be sued for the committee's debt. In *Crawley v. American Society of Equity*, 153 Wis. 13, 139 N.W. 734 (1913), the problem was, should a national farmers' union bear the debt of one of its locals? In *Cointe v. Congregation of St. John the Baptist*, 154 Wis. 405, 143 N.W. 180 (1913), the dilemma was minister or congregation? These cases remind one of the many questions of agency and authority in Period II, inevitable as business hierarchies become more complex. Yet, only a special type of "business" was concerned in each of these cases. The difficulty came not so much from the complexity of the business hierarchy, but, on the contrary, from the marginal, ill-defined nature of the business and the difficulty of ascertaining the precise line of authority.

106 *Mueller v. Cook*, 126 Wis. 504, 105 N.W. 1054 (1906) (complex large-scale lumbering contract); *Milwaukee Boston Store v. Katz*, 153 Wis. 492, 140 N.W. 1038 (1913) (department-store lease); contrariwise, *Eastern Railway Company of Minnesota v. Tuteur*, 127 Wis. 382, 105 N.W. 1067 (1906), where the court found that plaintiff had not waived its rights under a complicated contract, for the same underlying reasons that the court *did* find waiver (of breaches) in the last two cases cited.

107 *Raube v. Christenson*, 270 Wis. 297, 308, 70 N.W.2d 639 (1955) (auto liability insurance issued to a county); see *Ellerbe & Co. v. City of Hudson*, 1 Wis.2d 148, 83 N.W.2d 700, 85 N.W.2d 663 (1957) (refusing to find "ratification" of a void contract); and *State v. Josefsberg*, 275 Wis. 142, 81 N.W.2d 735 (1957), holding the doctrine of laches inapplicable to an action "brought by the state in its sovereign capacity" (revocation of a doctor's license).

108 *Russell Dairy Stores v. Chippewa Falls*, 272 Wis. 138, 74 N.W.2d 759 (1956).

109 See *Sherry v. Madler*, 123 Wis. 621, 101 N.W. 1095 (1905).

110 274 Wis. 290, 79 N.W.2d 649 (1956); contractual waivers appeared in other cases, e.g., *Hyland v. GCA Tractor & Equipment Co.*, 274 Wis. 586, 80 N.W.2d 771 (1957).

111 Campbell, *Industrial Accidents and Their Compensation* (Boston & New York, 1911), p. 57; Laws Wis. 1907, ch. 254, at 496.

112 *Gainsford v. Carroll*, 2 B. & C. 624 (K.B. 1828); see *Ganson v. Madigan*, 13 Wis. 67 (1860); Uniform Sales Act § 67(3). For an excellent short account of the development of the law of damages, see Friedrich Kessler and Malcolm P. Sharp, *Contracts Cases and Materials* (New York, 1953), pp. 552-4.

113 *Hoy v. Grenoble*, 34 Pa. St. 9 (1859); Theodore Sedgwick, *A Treatise on the Measure of Damages* (New York, 1847), pp. 205-13; see *Shepard v. Milwaukee Gas Light Co.*, 15 Wis. 318 (1862).

114 9 Ex. 341 (1854); see Edwin W. Patterson, "The Apportionment of Business Risks through Legal Devices," 24 *Columbia L. Rev.* 335, 342 (1924).

115 3 Wis. 456 (1854); see also *Hinckley v. Beckwith*, 13 Wis. 31 (1860); and for early limita-

tions on the rule, *Shepard v. Milwaukee Gas Light Co.*, 15 Wis. 318 (1862).

[116] 155 Wis. 146, 144 N.W. 294 (1913); see *Cook v. Minneapolis, St. Paul & S.S.M. R.R. Co.*, 125 Wis. 528, 103 N.W. 1097 (1905).

[117] The dairy case: *Kellogg v. Malick*, 125 Wis. 239, 103 N.W. 1116 (1905); the soda water bottle case: *No. Baltimore Bottle Glass Co. v. Altpeter*, 133 Wis. 112, 113 N.W. 435 (1907).

[118] *Spafford v. McNally*, 130 Wis. 537, 110 N.W. 387 (1907). Conversely, if the contractor's performance was not perfect, the landowner's damages were usually limited to deducting from the agreed price only enough to make good the imperfections. Compare *Manning v. School District No. 6 of Ft. Atkinson*, 124 Wis. 84, 102 N.W. 356 (1905) with *Lindenmann v. Kopczynski*, 155 Wis. 164, 144 N.W. 196 (1913). In general, see Edwin W. Patterson, "Builder's Measure of Recovery for Breach of Contract," 31 *Columbia L. Rev.* 1286 (1931).

[119] 152 Wis. 193, 139 N.W. 740 (1913).

[120] 3 Wis.2d 13, 87 N.W.2d 505 (1958), *Cases and Briefs*, "Plaintiff's Exhibit 3," p. 10. The clause is in standard use and conforms to business expectations; manufacturers at least do not think of or expect consequential damages for breach of contract. (Information supplied by Professor Stewart Macaulay, University of Wisconsin Law School, who has studied business practices relating to contracts, interviewed businessmen, and collected a large number of contract forms used by manufacturers.)

[121] *Clark v. Marsiglia*, 1 Denio 317 (N.Y. 1845), is a leading American case on the duty to mitigate. See *Medbery v. Sweet*, 3 Pin. 210, 3 Chand. 231 (1851); *Waite v. Anderson*, 152 Wis. 206, 139 N.W. 738 (1913).

[122] *Nelsen v. Farmers Mutual Auto Ins. Co.*, 4 Wis.2d 36, 90 N.W.2d 123 (1958).

[123] 273 Wis. 432, 78 N.W.2d 737 (1956). The "benefit of bargain" theory was adopted in *Anderson v. Tri-State Home Improvement Company*, 268 Wis. 455, 67 N.W.2d 853 (1955); the same measure of damages was used in *Chapman v. Zakzaska*, 273 Wis. 64, 76 N.W.2d 537 (1956). Compare the measure of damages for breach of warranty set out in the Uniform Sales Act, Wis. Stats. § 121.69(7) (1961), *Ross v. Faber*, 2 Wis.2d 296, 86 N.W.2d 409 (1957).

[124] 14 Wis. 5, 8 (1861).

[125] E.g., *Taylor v. Thieman*, 132 Wis. 38, 111 N.W. 229 (1907); *Voss v. Voss*, 134 Wis. 52, 113 N.W. 1097 (1907). See Harold C. Havighurst, "Services in the Home—A Study of Contract Concepts in Domestic Relations," 41 *Yale L.J.* 386 (1932).

[126] See, for example, *Manning v. School District No. 6 of Ft. Atkinson*, 124 Wis. 84, 102 N.W. 356 (1905). "Reasonableness" was also an appropriate measure of the quantum of recovery in the estate claim cases of Period III, e.g., *Estate of Pearce*, 273 Wis. 140, 77 N.W.2d 420 (1956).

[127] 42 N.C. 190, 192 (1851).

[128] *Crittenden v. Drury*, 4 Wis. 205 (1854). In *Bull v. Bell*, 4 Wis. 54 (1855), the buyer went into possession, exercising dominion by "building some picket-fence and removing some manure from the barn." In *District No. 3 v. Macloon*, 4 Wis. 79 (1855), the school district had built a schoolhouse on the land.

[129] U.S. Const. Art. I, § 10; Wis. Const. Art I, § 12; Benjamin F. Wright, Jr., *The Contract Clause of the Constitution* (Cambridge, 1938).

[130] 6 Cranch 87 (U.S. 1810).

[131] *Dartmouth College v. Woodward*, 4 Wheat. 518 (U.S. 1819).

[132] 12 Wheat. 213 (U.S. 1827).

133 1 How. 311 (U.S. 1843).

134 *Piqua Branch of State Bank of Ohio v. Knoop*, 16 How. 369 (U.S. 1853).

135 *Wis. Const.* Art. XI, § 1: "All general laws or special acts enacted under the provisions of this section [relating to corporations] may be altered or repealed by the legislature at any time after their passage." *Pratt v. Brown*, 3 Wis. 603, 611-2 (1854). Prior to the enactment of the Wisconsin Constitution, it was common to insert in charters a reservation of the right to alter or repeal, see for example, Wis. Terr. Laws 1847, at 17 (§ 6 of an act to "authorize the construction of a dam across Rock river"); compare Wis. Terr. Laws 1847, at 43 (§ 9 of an act "to incorporate the Mississippi and Lake Erie Navigation Company"), which gave the legislature the right to "resume all and singular, the rights and privileges hereby granted to said company" in the event of "misuse or abuse" of such privileges.

136 11 Pet. 420, 553 (U.S. 1837).

137 *Sturges v. Crowninshield*, 4 Wheat. 122, 201 (U.S. 1819); see *Mason v. Haile*, 12 Wheat. 370, 378 (U.S. 1827); *Beers v. Haughton*, 9 Pet. 329, 359 (U.S. 1835). The Wisconsin Constitution specifically forbade imprisonment for debt. *Wis. Const.* Art. I, § 16: "No person shall be imprisoned for debt arising out of or founded on a contract, expressed implied."

Similar factors, mixing abstraction, mercantile ideals, and humanitarianism, had helped to soften the punitive nature of English bankruptcy law, see Lawrence M. Friedman and Thadeus F. Niemira, "The Concept of the 'Trader' in Early Bankruptcy Law," 5 *St. Louis U.L.J.* 223 (1958).

138 3 Pin. 203, 206-7, 3 Chand. 222 (1851). The constitutionality of the milldam act was upheld in *Newcomb v. Smith*, 2 Pin. 131, 1 Chand. 71 (1849).

139 3 Wis. 603 (1854).

140 In *State ex rel. Mariner v. Gray*, 4 Wis. 380 (1855), it was argued that the school land laws (together with petitioner's application to purchase lands) constituted a contract which the legislature could not impair by changing the law. The court disagreed, but on the narrow ground that "an application to purchase is not a purchase nor is an attempt to acquire a right to be adjudged a right vested."

141 13 Wis. 233, 242 (1860).

142 153 Wis. 592, 142 N.W. 491 (1913). In the critical case of *State v. Railway Co.'s*, 128 Wis. 449, 505, 108 N.W. 594 (1906), the contracts clause was discussed but had no direct bearing on the decision.

143 For example, in *Servonitz v. State*, 133 Wis. 231, 113 N.W. 277 (1907), the peddlers' law was attacked as embodying a classification invalid under the Wisconsin constitution.

144 269 Wis. 252, 68 N.W.2d 714 (1955); Wis. Stats. § 105.13 (1961), first enacted as Laws Wis. 1913, ch. 663, at 885-6.

145 See also *State v. Kerndt*, 274 Wis. 113, 79 N.W.2d 113 (1956), arising under Wis. Stats. § 97.61(2) (1961), prohibiting the sale of canned fruit "containing any artificial coloring." Kerndt claimed his artificial coloring was harmless and not deceptive. The court said, "we are not experts on food coloring or food quality," and deferred to the legislature.

The court was less deferential toward municipalities. The court let Milwaukee fluoridate its water supply, *Froncek v. City of Milwaukee*, 269 Wis. 276, 69 N.W.2d 242 (1955), and upheld the city's authority to stop moonlighting among firemen, *Huhnke v. Wischer*, 271 Wis. 66, 72 N.W.2d 915 (1955); but in *Katt v. Village of Sturtevant*, 269 Wis. 638, 70 N.W.2d 188 (1955), the court voided an ordinance which banned new fur ranches while allowing old ones to stay in business; the court said no again in *Town of Hobart v. Collier*, 3 Wis.2d 182, 87 N.W.2d 868 (1958), where the town (mostly a farming area) tried to get rid of an automobile salvage yard by zoning itself exclusively residential.

146 Miscellaneous doctrines came up for discussion in many of the tabulated cases—nota-

bly incidental problems of contract procedure, jurisdiction, and half-procedural, half-substantive questions (such as issues of the conflict of laws or under the statute of limitations).

The range of procedural issues intimately tied to contract problems was particularly large in Period I prior to the reform of civil procedure, e.g., the distinction between the common counts and special contract, see *Baxter v. Payne*, 1 Pin. 501 (1845).

Close reading of the "miscellaneous" cases shows that social, economic, and political factors influenced these cases, just as was true for cases utilizing concepts from the central body of contract doctrine. Space does not permit demonstration of this fact. One example may be worth illustrative mention. In *Pritchard v. Howell*, 1 Wis. 131 (1853) the statute of limitations was strictly applied to a contract problem, despite a split in common law precedents, in a decision resting explicitly on a policy base appropriate to the period: "The residence here of a large majority of the population has been of short duration. Nearly all have removed ... from distant homes.... It is hardly to be presumed, that they have been able to preserve and transport with them the evidences of their former transactions.... Sound policy ... requires that this law [the statute of limitations] should be so administered, as to ... be, 'a statute of repose.'"

In Period III, the court in *Estate of Fredericksen*, 273 Wis. 479, 78 N.W.2d 878 (1956), manipulated sections of the statute in order to reach a characteristic compromise result, cutting off part (but not all) of a claim for services against an estate. In *Davies v. J. D. Wilson Co.*, 1 Wis.2d 443, 85 N.W.2d 459 (1957), a salesman's claim to commissions was not barred by the two-year statute of limitations because the court was conveniently able to call the contract "entire," and find that the cause of action accrued late enough so that the statute had not run its fatal course.

Chapter IV

1 Arvo Van Alstyne, *The California Civil Code* (St. Paul, 1954). The California Civil Code stemmed from the code drafted by David Dudley Field, a New Yorker whose codes won many adoptions in the new states of the West. A good sample of the provisions of the Code is Cal. Civil Code § 1605, on consideration: "Any benefit conferred, or agreed to be conferred, upon the promisor, by any other person, to which the promisor is not lawfully entitled, or any prejudice suffered, or agreed to be suffered, by such person, other than such as he is at the time of consent lawfully bound to suffer, as an inducement to the promisor, is a good consideration for a promise."

2 See the discussion, C. 3, pp. 93-95.

3 Rev. Stats. Wis. 1849, ch. 127, § 14(1), p. 643 (statute of limitations for unsealed contracts); § 14(4); § 20, p. 644 (other contract actions). Fraudulent conveyances: Rev. Stats. Wis. 1849, ch. 76, § 5, p. 389.

4 Stats. Terr. Wis. 1839, § 5, p. 156. Gambling contracts: Gen'l Laws Wis. 1858, ch. 117, §§ 6, 7, 14; Acts Terr. Wis. 1837-8, No. 65, p. 372.

5 Acts Terr. Wis. 1837-8, No. 47, p. 226. A later version was passed in 1857, Laws Wis. 1857, ch. 97, p. 126. See George J. Kuehnl, *The Wisconsin Business Corporation* (Madison, 1959), pp. 36-7, 138-40; 1 Rev. Stats. N.Y. 1827-8, Part II, ch. 4, p. 763.

6 E.g., Rev. Stats. Wis. 1849, ch. 44, § 1, making promissory notes "negotiable in like manner, as inland bills of exchange"; 1 Rev. Stats. N.Y. 1829, p. 768, § 1, resting ultimately on 3 & 4 Anne ch. 9, § 1 (1704). See Frederick Beutel, "The Development of State Statutes on Negotiable Paper Prior to the Negotiable Instruments Law," 40 *Columbia L. Rev.* 836, 846-9 (1940).

7 The earliest of the uniform acts to be adopted in Wisconsin was the Negotiable Instruments Law, Laws Wis. 1899, ch. 356, p. 681. Wisconsin has recently adopted the Uniform

Commercial Code, which supersedes the N.I.L. and most of the other uniform commercial acts.

8 Between 1848 and 1871, 1,130 business corporations were chartered by special act; the peak year in Period I was 1853, when 94 special-act charters were granted; in 1858, on the other hand, there were only 2 such acts. George J. Kuehnl, *Wisconsin Business Corporation*, pp. 143, 144.

9 *Wis. Const.* Art. I, § 16; Acts Terr. Wis. 1837-8, No. 37, p. 213; Laws Terr. Wis. 1842, p. 58.

10 "An Act concerning judgments and executions," Stats. Terr. Wis. 1838-9, § 42, p. 231.

11 *Wis. Const.* Art. I, § 17.

12 Laws Wis. 1848, p. 40, § 1.

13 Henry Farnam, *Chapters in the History of Social Legislation in the United States to 1860* (Washington, 1938), pp. 149-52.

14 Laws Wis. 1848, p. 101.

15 1848 Wisconsin *Senate Journal*, Appendix 13, 72-81; on the ideological meanings of the homestead exemption, see Lena London, "Homestead Exemption in the Wisconsin Constitution," *WMH*, XXXII (1948), 176.

16 E.g., Laws Wis. 1850, ch. 198, § 1, p. 159 ("any infant child" of a deceased land-holder); Laws Wis. 1857, ch. 28 (debtors' libraries, but not "circulating libraries"); Laws Wis. 1858, ch. 148 ("earnings of all persons for sixty days next preceding the issuance of any process" declared exempt); Laws Wis. 1860, ch. 192 (family sewing machines).

17 Rev. Stats. Wis. 1849, ch. 102, § 52.

18 Acts Terr. Wis. 1837-8, No. 50, p. 232.

19 Henry Farnam, *History of Social Legislation*, pp. 152-6.

20 Stats. Terr. Wis. 1838-9, p. 141.

21 See Rev. Stats. Wis. 1849, ch. 120, § 1. The lien resembled the homestead exemption in that it applied to the "dwelling house ... and to the land upon which the same shall be situated, not exceeding forty acres, or if erected within the limits of any city, town, or village plot, the lot on which such ... house ... shall be situated, not exceeding ... one acre...."

22 Gen'l Laws Wis. 1858, ch. 59; see Gen'l Laws Wis. 1861, ch. 215 (work done on bridges).

23 Rev. Stats. Wis. 1849, ch. 102, § 52.
In 1860, the legislature created an analogous device by "providing for a lien for labor and service upon logs and lumber," in favor of those who performed service in "cutting, falling, hauling, driving, running, rafting, booming, cribbing or towing any logs or timber in the counties of Shawano, Waupaca, Outagamie, Winnebago, Fond du Lac, or upon the waters of Lake Winnebago." Gen'l Laws Wis. 1860, ch. 215. Thus the log lien (like the mechanics' lien) was at first a geographically limited device. Gen'l Laws Wis. 1861, ch. 186 extended the act to Chippewa County. A lien for the benefit of any "mechanic or artizan who shall make, alter or repair any article of personal property" was also provided, Rev. Stats. Wis. 1849, ch. 120, § 14.

24 Gen'l Laws Wis. 1858, ch. 113.

25 Gen'l Laws Wis. 1858, ch. 49.

26 Gen'l Laws Wis. 1861, ch. 88, at 99, 101. *Cornell v. Hichens*, 11 Wis. 353 (1860), had voided the act of 1858.

27 "Without impairing the obligation of the contract, the remedy may certainly be modified as the wisdom of the nation shall direct." Marshall, C. J., in *Sturges v. Crowninshield*, 4 Wheat. 122, 200 (U.S. 1819).

28 See Rev. Stats. Wis. 1849, ch. 16, § 33, at 172.

29 See Gen'l Laws Wis. 1858, ch. 117; for the criminal law, see Rev. Stats. Wis. 1849, ch. 138.

30 Acts Wis. 1850, ch. 139, § 5, at 109; on the contemporary temperance movement, see Wm. F. Raney, *Wisconsin: A Story of Progress* (New York, 1940), pp. 143-4; Joseph Schafer, "Prohibition in Early Wisconsin," *WMH*, VIII (1925), 281.

31 Gen'l Laws Wis. 1853, ch. 28.

32 Gen'l Laws Wis. 1854, ch. 34; see also Gen'l Laws Wis. 1861, ch. 242. George J. Kuehnl, *Wisconsin Business Corporation*, p. 43; for the prior law, see Rev. Stats. Wis. 1849, ch. 39; Stats. Terr. Wis. 1838-9, p. 145.

33 The statutes mentioned are: railroad financing, Gen'l Acts. Wis. 1856, ch. 121; school financing, Gen'l Acts Wis. 1857, ch. 15; wolf bounties, see Rev. Stats. Wis. 1849, ch. 10, § 28(6), at 96; livestock protection, Gen'l Laws Wis. 1861, ch. 222; note redemption, Gen'l Laws Wis. 1861, ch. 242; see Frederick Merk, *Economic History of Wisconsin during the Civil War Decade* (Madison, 1916), pp. 190-202.

34 George J. Keuhnl, *Wisconsin Business Corporation*, is a detailed study of the era of the special charter in Wisconsin.

35 Acts Wis. 1854, ch. 99, § 2.

36 Rev. Stats. Wis. 1849, ch. 17, § 10, at 185. The same requirement was sometimes inserted in special charters of ferries and bridges, e.g., Laws Terr. Wis. 1842, at 53, § 8 of the act incorporating the Beloit and Rock River Bridge Company.

37 Gen'l Laws Wis. 1861, ch. 83, §§ 2-6. The act authorized the governor to appoint "surveyors general" for river districts, who, at the request of log owners, would measure and record data, giving a copy of the document to the owner. On log marks, see Elizabeth M. Bachmann, "Minnesota Log Marks," *Minnesota History*, XXVI (1945), 126.

38 Rev. Stats. Wis. 1849, ch. 38, §§ 1, 2. *The Laws and Liberties of Massachusetts* (Cambridge, 1929), p. 7 (act of 1646, requiring "everie towne" to "give some distinct Brandmark appointed by this court ... upon the horn, or left buttock or shoulder of all their cattle which feed in open common without constant keepers").

39 See Laws Terr. Wis. 1848, p. 67 (log measurement); Laws Wis. 1848, p. 51 ("weighing of Lead Ore, Copper Ore, and other mineral substances"); Gen'l Acts Wis. 1854, ch. 45 ("weight and measure of Flax seed, Timothy Seed and Potatoes").

40 Stats. Terr. Wis. 1838-9, p. 55, § 5.

41 *Charter and Ordinances of the City of Milwaukee* (Milwaukee, 1853), p. 73 (ordinance of Feb. 8, 1847); *ibid.*, p. 112 (ordinance of Apr. 29, 1852) (market for hay and wood in the first ward).

42 Fish inspectors: Priv. & Local Laws Wis. 1859, ch. 119, § 11, at 168; *ibid.*, ch. 173 (Milwaukee). Fence viewers: Rev. Stats. Wis. 1849, ch. 14, § 22, at 137; surveyors: Rev. Stats. Wis. 1849, ch. 10, § 131, at 112; sealer of weights: Rev. Stats. Wis. 1849, ch. 42, § 7, at 261. See Acts Wis. 1851, ch. 177, § 1, requiring fire insurance agents in Kenosha to pay 20 per cent of their gross premiums to the city for the benefit of the city fire department, an example of the fee principle carried to an extreme—and a confession of municipal poverty.

43 Rate of toll: Rev. Stats. Wis. 1858, ch. 60, §1; see Laws Terr. Wis. 1840-1, No. 10, p. 35; Stats. Terr. Wis. 1838-9, p. 131. Such regulation was of ancient standing [*The Laws and Liberties of Massachusetts*, p. 43 ("no miller shall take above the sixteenth part of the corn he grinds"); Henry Farnam, *History of Social Legislation*, pp. 94-100], but retained its importance. In 1849 certain Wisconsin farmers petitioned for rate reductions, 1849 WLB Box No. 23 (petitions) (State Historical Society of Wisconsin).

44 Laws Terr. Wis. 1842, § 7, p. 54.

45 Acts Wis. 1852, ch. 178, § 2; on the ferry charters see Joseph Schafer, "Ferries and Ferryboats," *WMH*, XXI (1938), 432, 443-50.

46 Rev. Stats. Wis. 1849, ch. 50, §§ 27-9, at 280.

47 See, e.g., the 1850 charter of the Shullsburg Branch Railroad Company, providing that all "persons paying ... toll ... may use ... said road," Acts Wis. 1850, ch. 147, § 10, at 117.

48 Priv. & Local Laws Wis. 1859, ch. 85, § 2.

49 Laws Wis. 1848, p. 254.

50 Priv. & Local Laws Wis. 1859, ch. 161, § 10, at 280.

51 See Beverley W. Bond, *The Civilization of the Old Northwest* (New York, 1934), p. 393.

52 Stats. Terr. Wis. 1838-9, p. 126.

53 Gen'l Acts. Wis. 1856, ch. 88.

54 Rev. Stats. Wis. 1858, ch. 58, § 12, at 407.

55 Rev. Stats. Wis. 1858, ch. 36.

56 *Proceedings, Illinois State Bar Association, 32nd Annual Meeting* (Springfield, 1908), Part I, pp. 177-88.

57 See Spencer L. Kimball, *Insurance and Public Policy* (Madison, 1960), pp. 171-2 (withdrawal of insurance companies from Wisconsin—and their return).

58 Isaiah L. Sharfman, *The Interstate Commerce Commission*, 5 vols. (New York, 1931), I, 15-19; see Laws Wis. 1907, ch. 205 (reliance on U.S.D.A. standards in local food laws).

59 Yet the actual number of statutes passed was not materially greater, if at all, than in Period I, with its mass of special charters. The legislature in Period II met biennially, not annually (Art. IV, § 11 of the Constitution). In 1909, 549 "chapters" (acts) in the statute books compare with 247 private and local laws and 223 general laws for 1859, fifty years before.

60 Insurance: Laws Wis. 1911, ch. 84; lemon extract: Laws Wis. 1905, ch. 228; catfish: Laws Wis. 1913, ch. 415, § 3(a), at 455; usury: Laws Wis. 1905, ch. 278 (amendment).

61 E.g., Laws Wis. 1905, ch. 187 (labeling of packages of buckwheat flour).

62 Laws Wis. 1913, ch. 92.

63 E.g., Wis. Rev. Stats. 1898, § 1021*i* ("forfeits" for failure to fill out forms of the Bureau of Labor and Industrial Statistics); repealed by § 2 of Laws Wis. 1911, ch. 485. See Laws Wis. 1913, ch. 154, dealing with insurance companies whose licenses had expired or been revoked. The statute empowered the Commissioner of Insurance to bring a kind of class action on behalf of contract- or policy-holders for any dereliction of contract duty on the part of the insurance company. Expenses of suit were to be borne by the state. The statute was probably designed to control withdrawn insurance companies; see Spencer L. Kimball, *Insurance and Public Policy*, p. 284.

64 On the background of the federal law, see Harry A. Toulmin, Jr., *A Treatise on the Law of Foods, Drugs and Cosmetics*, 4 vols. (2nd ed., Cincinnati, 1963), I, 3-5; C. C. Regier, "The Struggle for Federal Food and Drugs Legislation," 1 *Law and Contemporary Problems* 3 (1933); Oscar E. Anderson, *The Health of a Nation* (Chicago, 1958).

65 Laws Wis. 1905, ch. 34, ch. 104, ch. 151, ch. 152, ch. 187, ch. 228, ch. 229, ch. 247, ch. 297, ch. 489.

66 Laws Wis. 1911, ch. 46; see also Laws Wis. 1905, ch. 33 (chemical preservatives); Laws Wis. 1907, ch. 173 (misbranded articles of food).

67 See Laws Wis. 1905, ch. 82 (cigarettes); Laws Wis. 1909, ch. 373 (corn-shredders not to be sold without safety devices); *ibid.*, ch. 532 (oils and turpentines); Laws Wis. 1911, ch. 313 (firecrackers); *ibid.*, ch. 325 (insecticides); Laws Wis. 1913, ch. 297 (mattresses); *ibid.*, ch. 317 (matches).

68 The cuspidor act, Laws Wis. 1911, ch. 438; bakeshops, Laws Wis. 1903, ch. 230, § 2.

69 E.g., Laws Wis. 1905, ch. 34; Laws Wis. 1909, ch. 399; Laws Wis. 1911, ch. 316.

70 Shirley S. Abrahamson, "Law and the Wisconsin Dairy Industry; Quality Control of Dairy Products, 1838-1929" (unpub. J.S.D. thesis, U. Wis. Law School, 1962), pp. 182-90; Laws Wis. 1895, ch. 30, § 2 forbade the sale of yellow margarine.

71 E.g., Laws Wis. 1907, ch. 529 (inspection of nursery stock).

72 *Proceedings, 24th Annual Convention National Confectioners Association* (Cincinnati, 1907), p. 196; see Thomas C. Cochran, *The Pabst Brewing Company* (New York, 1948), pp. 204-5, on the favorable attitude of Pabst toward pure food laws, for business reasons.

73 Rev. Stats. Wis. 1898, § 1941-42. For other examples of standard clauses, see Laws Wis. 1911, ch. 84 (accident and health insurance); Laws Wis. 1905, ch. 19, § 13, at 42 (Superior warehouse receipts).

74 Laws Wis. 1911, ch. 50; Laws Wis. 1915, ch. 114, requiring semimonthly or more frequent wage-payments, provided that no corporation might "by special contract with employees ... secure exemption from ... this act."

75 Laws Wis. 1911, ch. 381 (mode of weighing and paying for cheese bought in quantities of fifty pounds or more); see Laws Wis. 1915, ch. 95 (milk bottles); Laws Wis. 1911, ch. 399 (coal; amendment); Laws Wis. 1905, ch. 56. "All contracts for the sale of cranberries by the barrel or crate, unless it is otherwise specially stipulated shall be construed to mean barrels or crates of the capacity herein prescribed."

76 Laws Wis. 1905, ch. 507, § 7, at 944.

77 Jt. Res. No. 57, Laws Wis. 1911, p. 1128; No. 68, p. 1137; No. 33, p. 1111. On anti-competitive practices in the ice business (La Crosse), see 4 Rpts. Att'y Gen. Wis. 267 (July 23, 1906). Laws Wis. 1915, ch. 460 regulated the sale of school textbooks.

78 Laws Wis. 1913, ch. 165; the act also applied to analogous behavior in the buying of goods. See also Laws Wis. 1909, ch. 395 (price discrimination in the buying of milk and cream, "for the purpose of creating a monopoly or of destroying the business of a competitor"). The act was aimed at the "so-called centralized creamery," said to pay high prices to farmers until the competition was destroyed, when the prices received by the farmers would fall again. *Milwaukee Daily News*, March 31, 1911, p. 4.

79 See, in general, Robert La Follette Sucher, *Licensing of Occupations in Wisconsin* (unpub. M.LL. thesis, U. Wis. Law School, 1955), p. 3; on teachers, see Conrad E. Patzer, *Public Education in Wisconsin* (Madison, 1924), pp. 124-30; on the licensing of lawyers, Alfred Z. Reed, *Training for the Public Profession of the Law* (Carnegie Foundation for the Advancement of Teaching, Bulletin Number Fifteen, New York, 1921).

80 Wis. Stats. 1898, § 1435.

81 E.g., Laws Wis. 1907, ch. 456 (assistant pharmacists); Laws Wis. 1909, ch. 79 (veterinary medicine); Laws Wis. 1909, ch. 528 (midwifery); Laws Wis. 1911, ch. 346 (nursing).

82 Laws Wis. 1905, ch. 420, § 3, at 722.

83 Laws Wis. 1907, ch. 54 (amendment). See 3 Rpts. Att'y Gen Wis. 338, 340-1 (May 17, 1905), discussing a proposed bill creating a State Board of Examiners of Architects. If, said the Attorney General, "the business of an architect as it is now practiced endangers the life or health of the state," the bill would be constitutional.

84 *The Barbers' Journal*, XII (1901) 35, address of S. J. Errington. Errington's talk also castigated the quick courses in barbering.

85 *State ex rel. Winkler v. Benzenberg*, 101 Wis. 172, 176, 76 N.W. 345 (1898), following closely the decision in *State v. Gardner*, 58 Ohio St. 599, 51 N.E. 136 (1898).

86 Laws Ill. Adjourned Sess. 1908, p. 90.

87 Laws Wis. 1913, ch. 337.

88 On the licensing of brokers, see A. D. Theobald, "Real Estate License Laws in Theory and Practice," *J. Land & Pub. Util. Econ.*, VII (1931), 13.

89 Laws Wis. 1905, ch. 19, § 2.

90 Laws Wis. 1913, ch. 756 (dealers in stocks and bonds); Laws Wis. 1913, ch. 663 (employment agencies).

91 Laws Wis. 1905, ch. 490. The statute provided for state licensing, but preserved the right of local governments to license on their own; cities and village might require a license fee of up to $25 a day from transient merchants. As of 1948, half of all Wisconsin cities and villages included in a survey of 369 communities licensed peddlers and transient merchants; 67 licensed junk dealers; 19 licensed second hand dealers; 45 licensed auctioneers. "Municipal Licenses in Effect in Wisconsin Cities and Villages," *The Municipality*, XLIII (1948), 92, 93.

92 These opinions are 4 Rpts. Att'y Gen. Wis. 602, 605, 606 (July 25, 1906) (milk dealers); *ibid.*, 607, 608 (July 30, 1906) (butchers); see also 3 Rpts. Att'y Gen. Wis. 496 (Sept. 15, 1905).

93 5 Rpts. Att'y Gen. Wis. 551 (Dec. 18, 1909).

94 5 Rpts. Att'y Gen. Wis. 546 (Aug. 2, 1909); see also 3 Ops. Wis. Att'y Gen. 614 (July 11, 1914). See Alfred R. Schumann, *No Peddlers Allowed* (Appleton, 1948), p. 41. Dinsdale, of Crawford County, introduced a bill in 1905 to define peddlers to include sellers by sample and for future delivery, "who do not ... pay taxes in the county," but exempting "traveling salesmen doing business with retail merchants." 1905 *Wisconsin Assembly Bills*, Bill No. 41A, § 1, § 9. The Attorney General opinions are particularly revealing, since each ruling probably rested ultimately on the complaint of some local merchant. In 1 Ops. Wis. Att'y Gen. 420 (Feb. 24, 1913), the Attorney General was asked whether a baker, who sold goods from a wagon in a nearby city (where he did not operate his bakery), was a peddler. In 1 Ops. Wis. Att'y Gen. 417 (Nov. 7, 1911), a Milwaukee merchant opened a store in Watertown, on a two-month lease. He was heard to say he would discontinue the store if it did not pay. Was he a transient?

95 See Clyde E. Jacobs, *Law Writers and the Courts* (Berkeley, 1954), pp. 64-97, for an analysis of the doctrine of "liberty of contract" in the state courts.

96 Gordon M. Haferbecker, *Wisconsin Labor Laws* (Madison, 1958), p. 69; see, in general, Gertrude Schmidt, *History of Labor Legislation in Wisconsin* (unpub. Ph.D. thesis, U. Wis., 1933). Frederic J. Stimson, *Handbook to the Labor Law of the United States* (New York, 1896), pp. 58-71. New Jersey had a child labor law in 1851, which forbade child factory labor under the age of 10, and limited the maximum hours of work. The act imposed a fine of $50, to be recovered "in an action of debt, in the name of the overseer of the poor of the township in which such minor may be employed." Laws N.J. 1851, p. 322.

97 Thomas M. Cooley, A *Treatise on Constitutional Limitations* (5th ed., Boston, 1883), p. 745.

98 "[A]s healthy mothers are essential to vigorous offspring, the physical well-being of woman becomes an object of public interest and care in order to preserve the strength and vigor of the race.... [H]istory discloses the fact that woman has always been dependent

210 | CONTRACT LAW IN AMERICA

upon man.... [S]he has been looked upon in the courts as needing especial care that her rights may be preserved.... [H]er physical structure and a proper discharge of her maternal functions ... justify legislation to protect her from the greed as well as the passion of man." Brewer, J., in *Muller v. Oregon*, 208 U.S. 412, 421-2 (1907). For labor laws in Wisconsin during Period II relating to women, see Laws Wis. 1911, ch. 548; Laws Wis. 1913, ch. 466. Laws Wis. 1913, ch. 712, spoke of the right of women and minors to a "living wage."

[99] Laws Wis. 1909, ch. 391; Laws Wis. 1911, ch. 171.

[100] Laws Wis. 1907, ch. 477 (minor telegraphers); ch. 575 (consecutive hours of railroad operators); ch. 655 (consecutive hours of employees of common carriers). See also Jt. Res. No. 1, Laws Wis. 1907, p. 1268, memorializing Congress on this subject.

[101] Laws Wis. 1907, ch. 402; see 5 Rpts. Att'y Gen. Wis. 124 (June 7, 1907).

[102] Laws Wis. 1913, ch. 63.

[103] 1905 *Wisconsin Assembly Bills,* Bill No. 100A; 1905 Wis. *Assembly Journal,* p. 643 (bill indefinitely postponed).

[104] But Laws Wis. 1911, ch. 453, authorized the Bureau of Labor and Industrial Statistics to investigate labor contracts or rules which were "unjust or unfair."

[105] On Sunday barbering, see Laws Wis. 1909, ch. 300; see Report, *Proceedings of the Twelfth Convention, Journeymen Barbers' International Union* (Milwaukee, 1909), p. 3. The Sunday Closing Committee of the barber's union of Philadelphia had 239 barbers arrested in a period of approximately two years beginning December, 1898. *The Barbers' Journal,* XII (1902), 28. For new Sunday legislation in Period II, see, e.g., Laws Wis. 1911, ch. 393.

[106] See Laws Wis. 1915, ch. 594, an omnibus revision and consolidation act, which repealed the 155 statutes mentioned in the text.

[107] Laws Wis. 1955, ch. 315.

[108] E.g., Laws Wis. 1955, ch. 72 (voluntary amortization of debts by wage-earners); Laws Wis. 1957, ch. 301 (minor amendment to homestead law); Laws Wis. 1957, ch. 407 (addition of "one television set" and "one radio" to list of exempt property).

[109] See the valuable survey, *Licensing by the State of Wisconsin* (Research Bulletin 108, Wisconsin Legislative Reference Library, December, 1952), p. 43. Thirty-five licensing laws were enacted in 1933; in 1951, 17. The figures given in this survey include such licenses as automobile drivers' licenses, which are not considered in the text discussion of occupational licensing. But the general trend holds for all kinds of licensing laws.

[110] Laws Wis. 1955, ch. 293 (food locker plants); Laws Wis. 1955, ch. 359 (business opportunity broker); Laws Wis. 1955, ch. 444 (aircraft dealers); Laws Wis. 1955, ch. 551 (investment advisers); Laws Wis., 1955, ch. 583 (motor vehicle salvage dealers); Laws Wis. 1957, ch. 159 (cemetery salesmen); Laws Wis. 1957, ch. 165 (guides); Laws Wis. 1957, ch. 354 (wholesale automobile auctioneers); Laws Wis. 1957, ch. 396 (commercial driving schools); Laws Wis. 1957, ch. 530 ("sanitarians"); Laws Wis. 1957, ch. 548 (weighers and samplers of milk).

[111] The basic statute was Wis. Stats. § 256.31, which provided that "There shall be an association to be known as the 'State Bar of Wisconsin,' " membership in which "shall be a condition precedent to the right to practice law in Wisconsin"; but "appropriate orders" for its "organization and government" were in the hands of the Supreme Court. The court ordered integration, *In re Integration of the Bar,* 273 Wis. 281, 77 N.W.2d 602 (1956); 273 Wis. vii (1956). The forced contribution of dues, coupled with the possibility that the dues might be spent for supporting or opposing legislation, posed a serious constitutional problem, which the Supreme Court, in *Lathrop v. Donohue,* 367 U.S. 820 (1961), resolved in favor of the organized bar. See Comment, "The Compelled Contribution in the Integrated

Bar and the All Union Shop," 1962 *Wis. L. Rev.* 138.

[112] Laws Wis. 1955, ch. 333, at 396, 397; Wis. Stats. §§ 149.09(4) (c), 149.10(2) (1961). Prior law: Wis. Stats. § 149.065(3) (1953). See also Laws Wis. 1955, ch. 581 (temporary medical licenses in case of "an emergency need for medical personnel"); Wis. Stats. § 147.15 (2) (1961).

[113] Wis. Stats. § 29.135 (1961) (wholesale fish dealers); see also the guide license statute, Wis. Stats. § 29.165 (1961), Laws Wis. 1957, ch. 165. The statute licensing bait dealers, Wis. Stats. § 29.137(3) (1953), had exempted "persons whose sales of bait to persons do not exceed $500 annually." In 1957, this was amended so that only "resident children under 16 years of age, without license ... may barter or sell bait to consumers ... but no such resident child shall make bait sales totaling more than $500 annually." Laws Wis. 1957, ch. 384.

[114] Membership in the board: see Laws Wis. 1955, ch. 7; Wis. Stats. §136.03 (1961). Standards quoted are now Wis. Stats. §136.05(1) (e) (1961); revocation, Wis. Stats. § 136.08(2) (b), (i), (k) (1961).

[115] Laws. Wis. 1919, ch. 656.

[116] For a revealing discussion of the brokers' examination, see *Wall v. Wisconsin R.E. Brokers' Board*, 4 Wis.2d 426, 90 N.W.2d 589 (1958). In 1951, the board granted 347 licenses and rejected 178 applications; one license was revoked. *Licensing by the State of Wisconsin*, p. 55.

[117] Laws Wis. 1955, ch. 547.

[118] Laws Wis. 1955, ch. 583. Licensing and regulation of "dealers in secondhand motor vehicles, wreckers of motor vehicles, or the conduct of motor vehicle junking" was also a power of the county, Laws Wis. 1955, ch. 651; Wis. Stats. § 59.07(38) (1961). The ostensible reason for regulation was the prevention of theft and fraud, see Laws Wis. 1957, ch. 260, replacing the 1955 law cited above.

[119] Laws Wis. 1957, ch. 307; Wis. Stats. § 218.01(2) (k) (1961). See also, on the "business of servicing septic tanks, seepage pits, grease traps or privies," Laws Wis. 1957, ch. 86; Wis. Stats. § 146.20(3) (1961); revocation for incompetency, Wis. Stats. § 146.20(5) (c) (1961).

[120] Laws Wis. 1957, ch. 354; Wis. Stats. § 218.32 (1961). Insurance agents, under Wis. Stats. § 209.04(3) (b) (1961) must be "trust-worthy" and "worthy of a license."

[121] Laws Wis. 1957, ch. 396; Wis. Stats. § 343.64(4) (1961).

[122] Laws Wis. 1957, ch. 396; Wis. Stats. § 343.65(2) (1961).

[123] Laws Wis. 1957, ch. 548; Wis. Stats. § 98.146(2) (1961).

[124] Wis. Stats. §189.04(1) (a) (1961); Laws Wis. 1955, ch. 551. Grounds of revocation: Wis. Stats. § 189.04(2) (e), § 189.04(3) (1961).

[125] Laws Wis. 1955, ch. 168; Wis. Stats. § 94.60(3) (1961).

[126] Laws Wis. 1955, ch. 583.

[127] The "licensing" of automobile manufacturers, see Wis. Stats. § 218.01(2) (am) (1961), is an apparent exception, and must be understood in the context of the elaborate statute attempting to rationalize the retail automobile business, internally and externally. Still, the "licensing" of these manufacturers is more like nineteenth-century railroad regulation than it is like a twentieth-century dentist's licensing act.

[128] *Licensing by the State of Wisconsin*, p. 41; 1955 Wisconsin *Senate Bills*, Bill No. 424S. In the 1930's the legislature was decidedly favorable to licensing, in the forties relatively hostile, and several licensing laws were even repealed between 1939 and 1943. *Licensing by the State of Wisconsin*, p. 43.

129 See *Schacht v. City of N.Y.*, 30 Misc.2d 77, 219 N.Y.S.2d 53 (1961).

130 Wisconsin Administrative Code, Rules of Accountancy Board, § 1.01(1) (a); § 1.01(2) (h), (j), (k), and (l). The statute gives the Board power to prescribe "reasonable standards of professional conduct and reasonable rules defining unethical practice." Wis. Stats. § 135.01(4) (1961). Violation of any "duly promulgated standard or rule" may be grounds for revocation of a certificate. Wis. Stats. §135.12(1) (1961).

131 Wis. Stats. § 218.01(3) (a) 6 (1961).

132 Oliver Wendell Holmes, Jr., "The Path of the Law," 10 *Harvard L. Rev.* 457, 462 (1897).

133 Wis. Stats. § 130.065(4) (1961); amended in Laws Wis. 1955, ch. 247. See also Laws Wis. 1955, ch. 355, requiring food processors to satisfy the department of agriculture of ability to pay in full the price due to the producer, or post bond, before making such purchase. The change in the law extended it to purchases through a subsidiary or affiliate. See Wis. Stats. § 100.03(1) (b) (1961).

134 Laws Wis. 1955, ch. 81; Wis. Stats. § 97.685 (1961).

135 Wis. Stats. § 97.022 (1961): "Whenever in the judgment of the department [of Agriculture] such action will promote honesty and fair dealing in the interest of consumers it shall ascertain and by regulation fix for foods ... reasonable definitions and standards of identity, reasonable standards of quality, and reasonable standards of fill of container...." Note in this statute the blend of health and fair marketing.

136 Sale of butter: Laws Wis. 1955, ch. 38; Wis. Stats. 1961, § 97.43(7) (1961); imitation ice cream: Laws Wis. 1955, ch. 123 (amendment); Wis. Stats. § 97.025(3) (1961); endless chain schemes in the sale of automobiles: Laws Wis. 1957, ch. 231; Wis. Stats. § 945.12 (1961).

137 Laws Wis. 1957, ch. 216; Wis. Stats. § 160.37 (1961).

138 Laws Wis. 1957, ch. 477; Wis. Stats. § 218.01(3) (a) 18, 19 (1961).

139 Laws Wis. 1957, ch. 396; Wis. Stats. § 343.72(12) (1961) (dual control cars); Wis. Stats. § 343.72(2) (1961) (unlimited driver's lessons).

140 Laws Wis. 1955, ch. 247, on liquidation sales and the two-year proviso; see Wis. Stats. § 130.065(6)-(12) (1961). The exemption for disabled veterans and the blind was extended to those without an arm or leg by Laws Wis. 1957, ch. 189; Laws Wis. 1957, ch. 630; Wis. Stats. § 129.02(2) (1961).

141 Wis. Stats. § 100.30 (1961). See Laws Wis. 1957, ch. 371, for a minor amendment of § 100.30. In December, 1955, the Attorney General solemnly informed the District Attorney of Sheboygan County that merchants who advertised "Free Tonight ... Cello Package of Finest California Carrots. Nothing to buy—just present this coupon..." were not violating the statute. 44 Ops. Att'y Gen. Wis. 352 (Dec. 22, 1955).

142 Laws Wis. 1955, ch. 597, at 775; Wis. Stats. §§ 100.201, .202 (1961); see Laws Wis. 1957, ch. 516 at 675 (merchants may give stamps and tokens "redeemable only for parking privileges" or "fares on urban passenger transit facilities"); Wis. Stats. § 100.15(3) (1961).

143 Wis. Stats. § 100.20(1) (1961); originally, Laws Wis. 1921, ch. 571, at 957.

144 Laws Wis. 1957, ch. 511, at 657.

145 73rd Cong. Sess. I. Ch. 90, 48 Stat. 1953 (1933). On the background in the twenties, see Murray R. Benedict, *Farm Policies of the United States 1790-1950* (New York, 1953), pp. 207-38.

146 7 U.S.C.A. § 608(c) (2); § 608(c) (19) deals with the necessary referendum.

147 To raise "funds to defray the necessary expenses" of formulating, issuing, administer-

ing and enforcing marketing orders, each such order "shall provide for the levying and collection of assessments in sufficient amounts to defray such expenses," levied on "each producer and handler directly affected by such marketing order." Laws Wis. 1957, ch 511, at 661.

[148] Laws Wis. 1957, ch. 511, at 657, 658.

[149] Laws Wis. 1957, ch. 511, at 659.

[150] Laws Wis. 1957, ch. 511, at 663. Market orders could be proposed by the director himself, or upon petition signed by 5 per cent or 100 of the affected producers or handlers, "whichever is less." Laws Wis. 1957, ch. 511, at 658.

[151] Adolf A. Berle, Jr., *Power Without Property* (New York, 1959), p. 138.

[152] Laws Wis. 1955, ch. 432, at 518; Wis. Stats. § 196.495(1) (1961).

[153] Laws Wis. 1957, ch. 511, at 663-4. On the other hand, the act specifically disclaimed any intent to authorize "price-fixing."

[154] Laws Wis. 1957, ch. 397; Wis. Stats. § 133.01(1) (1961).

[155] Laws Wis. 1957, ch. 448 at 597; Wis. Stats. §§ 134.10, 134.11 (1961). Violation of these sections was made grounds for revocation of an agent's license. Wis. Stats. § 209.04(9)-(12) (1961).

[156] Jt. Res. No. 60, Laws Wis. 1957, p. 881; Jt. Res. No. 66, Laws Wis. 1957, p. 888; Jt. Res. No. 67, Laws Wis. 1957, p. 889.

Chapter V

[1] On the druggists, see Paul C. Olsen, *The Marketing of Drug Products* (New York, 1940), p. 119; confectioners: *Proceedings, 24th Annual Convention, National Confectioners' Association* (Cincinnati, 1907), p. 37; lumber dealers: *American Lumberman*, Mar. 10, 1906, p. 37; printers: Charlotte E. Morgan, *The Origin and History of the New York Employing Printers' Association* (New York, 1930), pp. 89-92; brickmakers: see *Davelaar v. City of Milwaukee*, 123 Wis. 413, 101 S.W. 361 (1905); ice dealers: 4 Rpts. Att'y Gen. Wis. 267 (July 23, 1906).

[2] *Proceedings, 13th Annual Convention, Wisconsin State Federation of Labor* (Marinette, 1905), p. 32.

[3] See William L. Letwin, "Congress and the Sherman Antitrust Law: 1887-1890," 23 *U. Chi. L. Rev.* 221 (1955).

[4] See Introduction, pp. 5-7.

[5] 9 Exch. 341 (1854); see the discussion, pp. 125-30.

[6] See Introduction, pp. 7-9.

[7] For example, the fellow-servant rule, as exemplified in the great case of *Farwell v. Boston and Worcester Railroad*, 4 Metc. 49 (Mass. 1842), where Chief Justice Shaw rested the non-liability of the employer on "implied contract"—that is, on economic considerations—and remarked that the employee "takes upon himself the natural and ordinary risks and perils incident to the performance of [his] ... services, and in legal presumption, the compensation is adjusted accordingly."

[8] Note that Llewellyn, writing about "legal realism," expresses a "belief in the worthwhileness of grouping cases and legal situations into narrower categories than has been the practice in the past," and a "distrust of verbally simple rules—which so often cover dis-

similar and non-simple fact situations." Karl N. Llewellyn, *Jurisprudence* (Chicago, 1962), pp. 56-7.

9 2 Pin. 224, 1 Chand. 190 (1849).

10 On the farm-mortgage crisis, Frederick Merk, *Economic History of Wisconsin during the Civil War Decade* (Madison, 1916), pp. 238-70; John Winslow, *Story of a Great Court* (Chicago, 1912), pp. 137-42; on the usury story, Lawrence M. Friedman, "The Usury Laws of Wisconsin: A Study in Legal and Social History," 1963 *Wis. L. Rev.* 515.

11 The major source on Marshall's life is his autobiography, *Autobiography of Roujet D. Marshall*, ed. Gilson G. Glasier, 2 vols. (Madison, 1923, 1931); on Siebecker, see *Dictionary of Wisconsin Biography*, p. 327 and *WMH*, VI (1922), 107-8; on Barnes, *Dictionary of Wisconsin Biography*, p. 27.

12 See Stewart Macaulay, "Non-Contractual Relations in Business: A Preliminary Study," *Am. Sociological Rev.*, XXVIII (1963), 55, 63.

13 See the discussion, pp. 114-5.

14 Priv. & Local Laws Wis. 1857, ch. 4.

15 Respectively, Priv. & Local Laws Wis. 1861, ch. 228, ch. 17, ch. 18.

16 E.g., in *Wisconsin Const.* Art. IV, § 31 (1871).

17 Laws Wis. 1911, ch. 438.

18 Blind-made goods: Laws Wis. 1957, ch. 400. For the other statutes, see pp. 177-9.

19 Laws Wis. 1913, ch. 632.

20 See Spencer L. Kimball, *Insurance and Public Policy* (Madison, 1960), pp. 231-2.

21 Laws Wis. 1905, ch. 19.

22 On the Wisconsin clubs, see Benjamin H. Hibbard, *History of Agriculture in Dane County* (Madison, 1905), pp. 94-104; J. Willard Hurst, *Law and the Conditions of Freedom in the Nineteenth-Century United States* (Madison, 1956), pp. 3-6. The clubs existed in many public-land states. An important recent analysis of their aims and composition is Allan Bogue, "The Iowa Claim Clubs: Symbol and Substance," *Miss. Valley Hist. Rev.*, XLV (1958), 231.

23 *Proceedings, 13th Annual Convention, Wisconsin State Federation of Labor* (Marinette, 1905), p. 39.

24 Judge William L. Ranson, quoted in Julius H. Cohen, *Commercial Arbitration and the Law* (New York, 1918), p. 2.

25 Philip G. Phillips, "A Lawyer's Approach to Commercial Arbitration," 44 *Yale L.J.* 31, 35, 36 (1934).

26 See *Abrohams v. Revillon Freres*, 129 Wis. 235, 107 N.W. 656 (1906); *Burstein v. Phillips*, 154 Wis. 591, 143 N.W. 679 (1913).

27 E.g., *Nunnemacher v. State*, 129 Wis. 190, 108 N.W. 627 (1906), which discovered a "natural right" to inherit property. But the case itself sustained a progressive inheritance tax law.

28 On the Board of Trade rules, see C. 2, *n*168.

29 275 Wis. 495, 82 N.W.2d 172 (1957).

30 E.g., the famous case of *Lochner v. N.Y.*, 198 U.S. 45 (1905), declaring unconstitutional a maximum hours law for New York bakers.

31 William Herbert Page, *The Law of Contracts* (Cincinnati, 1905), p. 19.

32 Clarence D. Ashley, *The Law of Contracts* (Boston, 1911), preface, p. vii.

33 *Autobiography of Roujet D. Marshall*, ed., Glasier, I, 224.

34 E.g., *Hodge v. Smith*, 130 Wis. 326, 110 N.W. (1906). Other members of the court occasionally tried their hand at the same practice, e.g., Kerwin, J., in *Boyden v. Roberts*, 131 Wis. 659, 111 N.W. 701 (1907).

35 Marshall, J., in *Northwestern Mutual Life Ins. Co. v. Wright*, 153 Wis. 252, 261, 140 N.W. 1078 (1913).

36 Christopher C. Langdell, *A Summary of the Law of Contracts* (Boston, 1880), p. 89.

37 128 Wis. 348, 107 N.W. 646 (1907).

38 132 Wis. 205, 111 N.W. 1114 (1907).

39 152 Wis. 268, 138 N.W. 1002 (1913). In *City of Milwaukee v. Miller*, 154 Wis. 652, 660, 144 N.W. 188 (1913), Marshall described the common law system as "characterized by incalculable waste ... unequal distribution of misfortune ... perversion of human perceptions of individual responsibility"; he praised the new compensation act in *Minneapolis, St. Paul & S.S. M. Rr. Co. v. Industrial Comm'n*, 153 Wis. 552, 555, 141 N.W. 1119 (1913). On Marshall's role in the passage of the act see *Autobiography of Roujet D. Marshall*, ed., Glasier, II, 53-83, 239-46.

INDEX

Page references are from the original edition and refer to the pagination embedded into the present text by the use of {brackets}. The previous page numbers are inserted into this edition for purposes of continuity and citation; and to allow uniform pagination in ebook editions.

Abstraction: of contract law, 20, 214; rise and fall of, 24, 186-7; and land cases, 29-30, 35; and exemption laws, 32; in insurance cases, 61; and business venture, 65-6; in government contracts, 73-5; and testamentary claim cases, 81; and contractual capacity, 83; and fairness of bargains, 98-9; and interpretation of contracts, 105; and breach of contract, 108-9; and restraint of trade, 114, 185; and assignability of contract, 118-20; and waiver and estoppel, 122-3; and implied contract, 130; and specific performance, 131-2; and constitutional doctrine, 134, 137; and regulation of labor, 167; relationship to legal and market institutions, 184-5, 194, 197, 201; effect of non-recurrence of fact situations on, 202

Acceptance. *See* Offer and acceptance

Accountants, certified public: licensed, 164

Adjustment, of disputes: as task of court, 193-4, 196, 197, 213

Administrative agencies: growth of, 205

Agricultural machines. *See* Sales

Agricultural marketing act, 179-81

Altschuler v. Atchison, Topeka & S.F., 127

American Express Company, 77

American Law Institute, 25

Anti-trust: relationship to contract and abstraction, 16-17, 185; law and policy, 115, 157, 188; Sherman

Anti-Trust Law, 161; in Wisconsin, 161-2; and concept of fairness, 181-2

Arbitration and settlement: cases on, 79-80

Architect's certificates: as mode of rationalizing construction business, 48

Ashley, C. O., 211

Assent, concept of, 83

Assignment, of contracts, 118-20

Athletic Commission, Wisconsin, 205

Attorney General, Wisconsin: on scope of government, 74; and peddlers' laws, 166

Baldwin, Joseph G., 31

Banks: in early Wisconsin, 71; in Civil War monetary crisis, 148

Barbers: licensed, 163

Barnes, John, 199

Berger v. Alan Realty Co., 98

Berle, Adolph A., 181

Bills of exchange, 70

Board of Accountancy, Wisconsin: 164; rules of, 175-6

"Boat and vessel act," 119, 144

Branding, of cattle: laws on, 150

Brayton v. Chase, 125-6

Breach of contract, 107-10

Bridges, 151-2

Brockhausen, Fred, 187

Brokers, real estate: as litigants, 46-8, 49-50; rate of commissions, 47; licensing of, 164, 172

Bronson v. Kinzie, 133

218 | CONTRACT LAW IN AMERICA

Brown v. Peck, 3-5

Brown v. Search, 101

Bull v. Conroe, 136

"Bushing," 178

Business ventures: cases on, 65-9. *See also* Corporations

Businessmen: attitudes of toward litigation and courts, 57, 198-9, 200-1, 207

California: reception of common law, 103; codification in, 140

Capacity, contractual: 19, 83-6; and freedom of contract, 19; and assent, 83; of aliens, 83-4; failure to expand concept of, 85; doctrines applied to corporations and government bodies, 86; and labor law, 167-8

Capital: meaning of concept of, 32, 166-7; shortage of, 43, 66, 69-71

Carson v. Milwaukee Produce Company, 59-60

Caveat emptor. See Warranty

Chapman v. Zakzaska, 117

Charles River Bridge v. Warren Bridge, 134

Chattel mortgages, 53

Child-labor laws, 167-8

Civil liberties: and role of court, 138, 209

Claims adjustment, 79-80

Claims associations. *See* Public lands

Clark v. Farrington, 67

"Class" legislation, 209

Commercial arbitration: as substitute for courts, 207-8. *See also* Arbitration and settlement

Commissioned employees: as contract litigants, 50

Commodity regulation, 153, 158-9, 160, 170, 177-8, 189-90

Common carriers, 77

Conditional sales contracts, 53

Conditions precedent, 107-8

Conservation: laws on, 169; department of, 174

Consideration: 89-91; defined, 21; three basic uses of, 90, 244; "peppercorn" theory of, 91

Constitution, Wisconsin: abolition of feudal tenures by, 29; debtor exemption laws of, 32, 143; and alien landholding, 84

Constitutional law: and definition of "issues," 105; and law of contracts, 132-8; and economic struggles, 188-9; court's role in, 215

Construction, 105-7

Construction contracts, 43, 48-9, 109, 128

Contract: working definition of, 15-21; and private property, 19; objective theory of, 87; breach of contract, 107-10; implied, 130-1; concept of, in constitutional cases, 133-4

Contract, law of: and social background, 10; in Blackstone's *Commentaries*, 17; in Viner's *Abridgment*, 17; expansion in the 19th century, 18; contrasted with real property law, 18; and abstraction, 20; and economic theory, 20-1; vocabulary of, 23; as judge-made, 24-5; and "inequality of bargaining power," 38, 85, 191; scope of, 39-40, 99, 193, 206; as metaphor, in testamentary cases, 81; concern with "practical interpretation," 87, 89, 98; and limitation of liability, 104; and legislation, 176; doctrines of, 191; penchant for compromise, 192-3; and concept of "fault," 193

Contract, litigation on: for nonbusiness claims, 49. *See also* Businessmen

Contract remedies: replaced by criminal sanctions, 156; socialized, 176

"Contracting out": of accident claims, 124

Contracts, interpretation of, 105-7

Contracts clause: 132-6, 138, 209; in farm-mortgage crisis, 146

Cooley, Thomas M.: and child-labor laws, 167

Corporations: sale of stock in, 56; under special charter system, 65, 148-9; transfer of stock subscriptions, 67, 119; charters of, as "contracts," 133-4; competition for incorporation of, 154-5

Courts: role of, compared to legislature, 25, 137, 196, 197-8; as reviewing board in government cases, 76-7; role in farm-mortgage crisis, 146, 196, 197; role in framing law of contract, 194-202, 213-4; and usury laws, 196-7; as forum of mobility, 201; and administrative regulation, 205-6; and economic controversy, 208-9; and civil liberties, 209; style of opinions of, 210-13; as forum of adjustment, 215

Covenants: against competition, 68, 114-6

Credit and finance: cases on, 69-73; and shortage of liquid capital, 69-70

Criminal law: civil consequences of, 117-8; and economic regulation, 155-8

Custom and usage, 206, 248-9

Dairy marketing, regulation of, 178-9

Damages, contract: relationship to economic theory, 21, 124-5; in public utility and carrier cases, 78-9; doctrines of, 124-30; mitigation of, 129-30; "benefit of bargain" theory, 129-30; "out of pocket" theory, 130

Dartmouth College v. Woodward, 75-6, 133-4

Davidor v. Bradford, 56

Debt, collection of: proposed abolition of, 143

Deeds: and contracts, 29; forms for, 91

Department of Securites: licensing activities of, 173-4

Downie v. White, 96

Driving schools: licensed and regulated, 173, 178

Due process clause, 137, 138, 209

"Duty to read": in contract cases, 101-2

Eastern Railway Co. of Minnesota v. Tuteur, 88

Ebenreiter v. Freeman, 57, 124

Economic growth: as dominant legislative theme, 142

Electricians: failure to achieve licensing, 175

Embalmers: licensed, 163

Enforcement, law: shift from private to public means of, 86; manipulated for policy purposes, 144-6. *See also* Contract remedies

Equity of redemption: defined, 33

Estoppel: defined, 22. *See also* Waiver

Exemption laws, 142-3. *See also* Homestead exemption laws

Fact-analysis, 105-7

Fact-situations: non-recurrence of, in litigation, 201-2

Fairness: and abstraction, 98-9; concept of, in work of court, 98-102, 191, 192, 201, 215; and reliance, 102; in legislation regulating business practice, 177-81

Farm-mortgage system: described, 66; legality of, 67, 86; crisis over, 120, 145-6, 196, 197

Federalism: as curb on state power, 154-5

Fee principle, 151

Fellow-servant doctrine, 214, 270

Ferries and bridges: rates regulated, 151-2

Field, David Dudley: code of procedure of, 118

Fixtures: dynamic attitude toward, in American law, 34

Fletcher v. Peck, 132, 133

Food and drug laws, 158

Formality: in law of contracts, 91-5; business function of, 92

Fraud: mistake, misrepresentation, 99-102; and security of market transactions, 99-101; in nonbusiness cases, 101

Frauds, Statute of: 50, 93-5, 140, 190-1; and real estate brokers, 50, 230; judicial attitude toward, 94-5; adoption of in Wisconsin, 140

Frear, James A.: address on "Wisconsin Day," 34

Freedom of contract: relationship to social legislation, 167, 211; in constitutional cases, 189, 211

Freeman v. Morris, 88

Fullerton Lumber Co. v. Torborg, 50, 115-6

Gale, George: land transactions of in Trempealeau County, 30-1

Gall v. Gall, 37

Gambling contracts, 141, 147

Game laws, 147-8

Gates, J. L., 46

Gates, J. L., Land Company, 35

Genessee Chief, The, 59

Georgiades v. Glickman, 50-1

Glassner v. Johnston, 102

Government: weakness of, in early Wisconsin, 73, 146-7; and freedom of contract, 74; as "regulated industry," 75; as proprietor and sovereign, 76-7

Government contracts: 73-7; and theory of abstraction, 73-5

Graebner v. Industrial Commission, 138

Graves v. Smith, 130

Grist mills: rates regulated, 151

Hadley v. Baxendale, 79, 104, 125-9, 190. *See also* Damages, contract

Haley v. Swift & Co., 104

Hess v. Zimmer, 128-9

Highway tax, 147

Holmes, Oliver Wendell, Jr., 176

Homestead act, federal: attitude of Wisconsin legislature toward, 84

Homestead exemption laws: 132; and abstraction of contract, 24-5; and debt collection, 70; and alienability, 119, 120; waiver of, 124; and contract clause, 136; passage and growth of, 143-4

Howe, Timothy O.: opinion in Kellogg v. Larkin, 113-4

Hubbell, J.: attitude toward squatters, 31-2

Illegality: and freedom of contract, 16; as defense to contract actions, 111-8; role of court and legislature in defining, 112-3

Immigration, encouraged in Wisconsin, 34, 84

Impossibility: as defense to contract actions, 250

Imprisonment for debt, abolished, 142

Indefiniteness, 87-9

Industrial Commission of Wisconsin: 157; safety rules of, 176

"Inequality of bargaining power." *See* Contract, law of

Initiation: court's role of, 194, 197

Insurance: agents, 48; cases on, 60-4; life insurance, 61; abstraction and cases on, 61, 63; legislation on, 61; claim adjustment, 62-3; judicial interpretation of policies, 106-7, 123; judicial control over, 116-7; assignability of policies, 120

Interest rates. *See* Usury and usury laws

Interpretation of contracts: cases on, 105-7

Interstate Commerce Commission, 155, 205

Judicial Review: and freedom of contract, 211. *See also* Constitutional law

Judges: grasp of business affairs of, 198-200. *See also* Courts

Judgment notes, 206

Kelley v. Ellis, 7-9, 40, 41, 190
Kellogg v. Larkin, 113-4
Kellogg v. Nelson, 107-8
Kitchen v. Herring, 131-2
Krueger v. Buel, 85
Kruse v. Koelzer, 102
Kuhl Motor Co. v. Ford Motor Co., 69, 117-8

Labor, concept of, 32, 166-7
Labor arbitration, 79-80
Labor and service contracts: 41-52; and frontier economy, 42; types of claims, 42-5; regulation of, 153, 166-9, 170
Labor movement: distrust of courts and lawyers, 207
La Follette, Robert M., 199
Land: cases concerning, 28-41; law of England, contrasted with Wisconsin, 28-9; frontier attitude toward, 29; agents, 30, 44; "cutover," 34-5, 46; marketing of, 38-9, 40; as collateral, 70; alienability of, 120; and specific performance, 131-2
Langdell, C. C.: reform of legal education, 18, 141; and legal "science," 25, 222; and illegal contracts, 111; treatise on contracts, 141; case-book on contracts, 211; on logical symmetry of contract law, 212
Lapham, Increase, 30
Law-merchant, development of, 54
Lawrence v. Fox, 121
Lawyers: and functioning of land market, 30-1; in frontier period, 31, 44; and debt collection, 71, 118-9; and competition, 165; and integrated bar, 171; as creators of law, 206

Leases, 34

Legal realism, 123, 191, 215

Legislation: 140-83, passim; and contract law, 24-5; and court, 116, 117-8; private and local, 203

Legislature: 140-83, passim; composition of, 142; and farm-mortgage crisis, 145-6, 196, 197; control of corporations by, 148-50; ratemaking by, 151-2; division of labor with court, 196-8

Leonard v. Prudential Insurance Company, 212-3

Liberty of contract. *See* Freedom of contract

Limited Liability: and contract damages, 128

Limited Partnership Act, 141

Litigation, cost of: 200; and business relations, 200-1

Local government: and concepts of waiver and estoppel, 123

Loss splitting, 193

Loyd v. Phillips, 102

McCormick reaper. *See* Sales
McFarland v. Newman, 104
Maine, Sir Henry, 18
Mann v. Stowell, 100-1
Marshall, Roujet D.: 199, 200, 211-3; wrote headnotes, 211-2
Maxwell v. Reed, 119-20
Mechanics' liens: defined, 42; use of, in early Wisconsin, 42-3; and debt collection, 70; origin and growth of, 145
Mercantile contracts: 58-60, 104; and admiralty, 58-9; divergent development, 59; relation of to law of warranty, 104
Michalski v. Cudahy Bros. Co., 214

Military bounty lands, 119

Milldam law, 135-6

Milwaukee: as wheat- and flour-milling center, 113-4; banks of, in Civil War era, 148

Milwaukee Board of Trade, 208-9

Milwaukee Cold Storage Co. v. York Corp., 129

Milwaukee Electric Railway & Light Co. v. Railroad Commission, 136-7

Miners, licensed in Illinois, 164

Misrepresentation. *See* Fraud

Mistake. *See* Fraud

Monopoly. *See* Anti-trust, Restraint of trade

Monte v. Wausau Paper Mills Co., 214

Mortgages: and homestead exemption, 144; and lien laws, 145

Motels: regulation of advertising, 178

Motivation: of parties, as theme in contract law, 125, 190-1, 193

Motor vehicle trades: licensed, 172, 174

Mowry v. Hill, 99, 100

Mutuality, 87-9

National Recovery Act of 1933, 180, 181

Negotiable instruments: in credit system, 70; and parol evidence rule, 97; in the economy, 99; law of, 141

Negotiability: of school-land certificates, 33; of chattel notes, 70; of farm-mortgage documents, 120, 145-6

Nelsen v. Farmers' Mutual Auto Insurance Co., 51

New York State: tenure problems in, 29; as source of Wisconsin Statute of Frauds, 93, 140; as source of code of procedure, 118; as source of limited partnership act, 141

Northwestern Life Insurance Company, 199

Nursing: licensed, 171

Objective theory, of contracts, 87

Occupational licensing: 162-6, 170-5, 187-8; as form of franchising, 169; and constitutional law, 188-9

Offer and acceptance: 86-7; and "assent," 86; and "preliminary negotiations," 87

Ogden v. Saunders, 133

Padrone labor system, 36

Page, William Herbert, 211

Parol evidence rule: defined, 7; cases on, 95-8; exceptions to, 96-8; in usury cases, 96

Pattenge v. Wagner Iron Works, 209-10

Peddlers: in early Wisconsin, 58; laws regulating, 165-6, 178

Performance and breach of contract, cases on, 107-10

"Plain meaning" rule, 98

Plankroads and turnpike companies: general law on, 152

Plumbers: licensed, 163-4

"Police power": as concept of constitutional law, 137; and occupational licensing, 163

Polley v. Boehck Equipment Co., 129-30

Poor relief, 147

Pratt v. Ayer, 31

Pratt v. Brown, 135

Pratt v. Darling, 5-7, 48, 59, 63, 97, 190

Precedent: lack of, in early years of court, 195-6

Price-discrimination. *See* Anti-trust

Price-fixing, 187

Principles: framing of, as judicial function, 202; as legislative function, 203

Private and local laws. *See* Legislation

Private decision- and rule-making: legal attitude toward, 206-7
Private property: and contract, 19
Privity of contract, 104-5
Progressivism, 154, 188-9
Promissory notes, 69-70, 72
Public health: concern for, 157-8; laws on, 177-8
Public lands: squatters on, 31-2, 206-7
Public market system, 150-1, 153
Public policy. *See* Illegality
Public utilities: cases on, 77-9; regulation of, 165
Public works, 168
Putnam v. Deinhamer, 116-7

Quantum meruit, 110, 130-1

Ranney v. Higby, 61
Railroad Commission, Wisconsin, 165
Railroads: financing of, 148; early charters of, 152; regulation of labor on, 168-9; full-crew laws, 168. *See also* Farm-mortgage system
Realism, legal, 123, 191, 215
Recording acts, 92-3
Resorts, 40
Restatements of the Law, 25
Restraint of trade, 60, 113-7. *See also* Antitrust
Risk-limitation: and law of damages, 126-7; and "individualism," 128
Rules of law: 82-139, passim; manner of framing, 99
Rust v. Fitzhugh, 68, 90

Sales: cases on, 52-7; law of, distinguished from contract, 52, 54; of agricultural machines, 53, 55; of farm commodities and animals, 53, 57; of breeding stallions, 54-5; of patent schemes, 55; of manufactured goods, 56; of corporate stock, 56; of goods with "service" element, 56-7; regulation of, 153
Sanderson v. Olmstead, 194-6, 197
School land certificates, 32-3, 120
Seal: use of, 91; statute on, 141
Self-executing and self-supporting laws, 147, 150
Shepard v. Milwaukee Gas and Light Company, 77, 78
Sherman Anti-Trust Law, 161
Sholes, C. Latham, 73
Siebecker, Robert G., 199
Slocum v. Damon, 79
Small-loan laws, 164
Smith v. Burns Boiler & Manufacturing Company, 67
Smith v. Justice, 103, 104
Social Democratic Party, Wisconsin, 167
"Social distance": as factor in role of court, 198-9
Specific performance, 131-2
"Speedometer" statute, 57, 117
Spendthrift trust doctrine, 120
Squatters, 31-2, 206-7
Standard Fire Insurance Policy, 63, 160, 205
Standard Manufacturing Co. v. Stallmann, 102
State Board of Medical Examiners, 162-3
Statute of Frauds. *See* Frauds, Statute of
Statutes. *See* Legislation
Steffen v. Supreme Assembly of the Defenders, 102
Stephens v. Marshall, 135
Stock, corporate. *See* Corporations
Strong, Moses, 30
Substantial performance, doctrine of,

109-10, 131

Sunday: regulation of labor on, 147, 169

Superior, Wisconsin: and grain and warehouse commission, 165

Support contracts: cases on, 36-8; and fact-analysis, 105

Suretyship: cases on, 71; institutionalized, 72-3

Taney, Roger Brooke, 134

Temperance movement, 147

Testamentary claims: 49; cases on, 80-1; and informality of contract law, 93

Texas, Republic of: and origin of homestead exemption, 143

Third-party beneficiary doctrine, 121-2

Tomahawk Land Company, 46

Torts: law of, 104, 214

Trusts: dynastic and spendthrift, 120

Turnpike companies, 152

Ultra vires, concept of: and scope of government, 74; and contractual capacity, 86

Unfair marketing laws, 204

Unfair sales act, 178-9

Uniform Sales Act: 53, 57, 141; adopted in Wisconsin, 53

Usury and usury laws: 71, 72, 140, 147, 196-7; and parol evidence rule, 97; and contract litigation, 111, 112

"Value," as concept in case law, 100-1

Waiver: defined, 22; of statutory liens, 119-20; cases on, 122-4; and abstraction, 122-3; contractual, 124; of consequential damages, 129

Ward v. Schooner *Dolphin*, 119

Warranty: in sales cases, 57; development of doctrines of, 103-5; and *caveat emptor*, 103-5

Washington, D.C.: and origin of mechanics' lien, 145

Weights and measures: regulation of, 150, 153, 160

Welch v. Sackett, 29

Whiting v. Hoglund, 121

Williston, Samuel B., 111

Wisconsin: population growth and economic development of, 13-4; and codification movement, 140-1; as "welfare state," 143-4. *See also* Constitution, Wisconsin

Wisconsin Retail Lumber Dealers' Association, 59

Wisconsin State Board of Accountancy. *See* Board of Accountancy

Wisconsin Sulphite Fibre Company v. D. K. Jeffris Lumber Company, 108-9

Wisconsin Supreme Court. *See* Courts

Women: regulation of labor of, 168

Woodman, Cyrus, 30

Workmen's compensation laws: as solution to problems of claims adjustment, 80; court's plea for, 214

About the Author

Lawrence M. Friedman is the Marion Rice Kirkwood Professor of Law at Stanford University, where he teaches legal history and law and society. An internationally renowned, prize-winning legal historian, Friedman has for a generation been the leading expositor of the history of American law to a global audience of lawyers and lay people alike — and a leading figure in the law and society movement. He is particularly well known for treating legal history as a branch of general social history. From his award-winning *History of American Law*, first published in 1973, to his *American Law in the 20th Century*, published in 2003, his canonical works have become classic textbooks in legal and undergraduate education.

Friedman is a prolific author on crime and punishment, and his numerous books have been translated into multiple languages. He is the recipient of six honorary law degrees and is a fellow in the American Academy of Arts and Sciences. Before joining the Stanford Law School faculty in 1968, he was a professor of law at the University of Wisconsin Law School and at Saint Louis University School of Law.

In addition to his position at Stanford Law School, he has an appointment (by courtesy) with the Stanford University Department of History and the Department of Political Science.

Visit us at *www.quidprobooks.com.*

www.ingramcontent.com/pod-product-compliance
Lightning Source LLC
Chambersburg PA
CBHW070732160426
43192CB00009B/1415